Everything for Math & Reading
Grades 2/3
Table of Contents

Language Arts

Reading

Math

LANGUAGE
ARTS

Phonics

Some words are more difficult to read because they have one or more silent letters. Many words you already know are like this.

Examples: wrong and **night**

Directions: Circle the silent letters in each word. The first one is done for you.

wrong	answer	autumn	whole
knife	hour	wrap	comb
sigh	straight	knee	known
lamb	taught	scent	daughter
whistle	wrote	knew	crumb

Directions: Draw a line between the rhyming words. The first one is done for you.

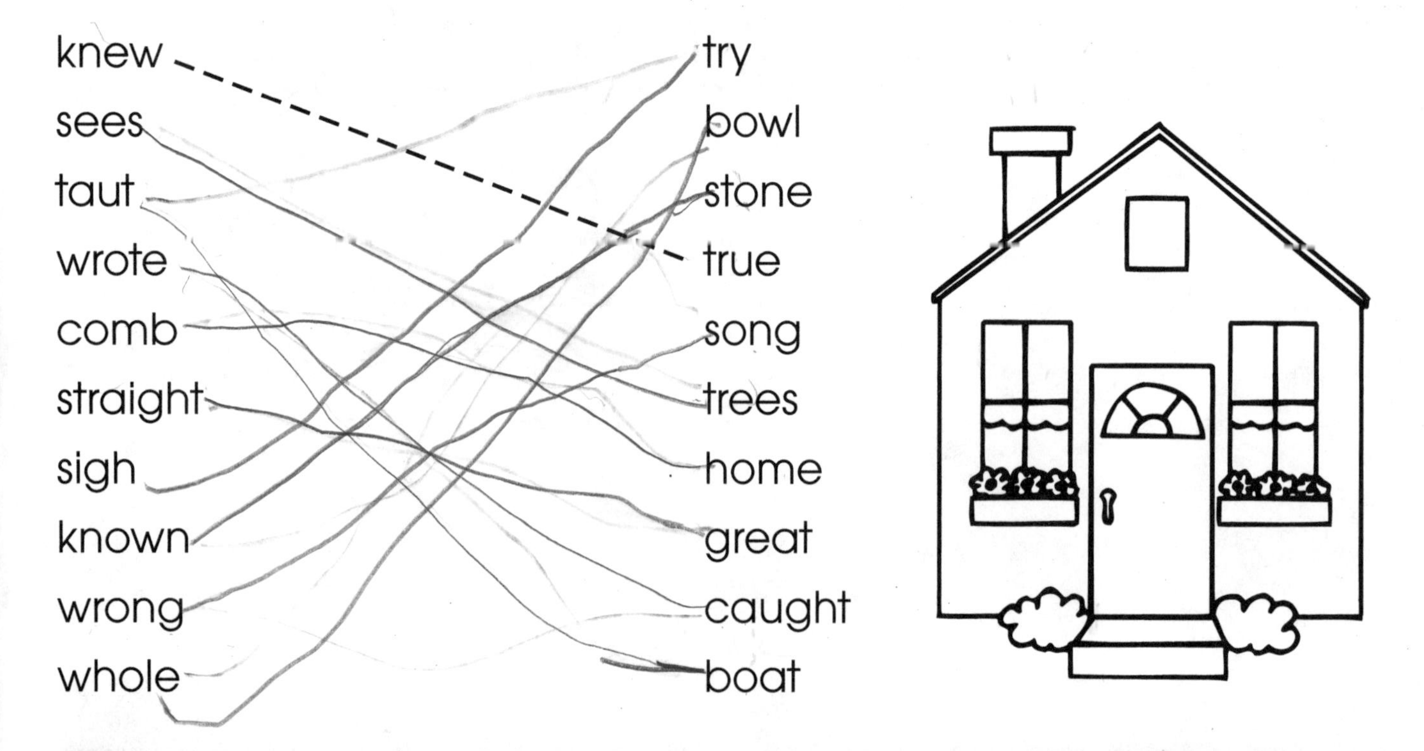

Consonant Teams

Directions: Look at the words in the word box. Write all of the words that end with the **ng** sound in the column under the picture of the **ring**. Write all of the words that end with the **nk** sound under the picture of the **sink**. Finish the sentences with words from the word box.

strong	rank	bring	bank	honk	hang	thank
long	hunk	song	stung	bunk	sang	junk

ng	nk
______	______
______	______
______	______
______	______
______	______
______	______
______	______

1. ______ your horn when you get to my house.
2. He was ______ by a bumblebee.
3. We are going to put our money in a ______.
4. I want to ______ you for the birthday present.
5. My brother and I sleep in ______ beds.

Phonics

There are several consonants that make the **k** sound: **c** when followed by **a**, **o** or **u** as in **cow** or **cup**; the letter **k** as in **milk**; the letters **ch** as in **Christmas** and **ck** as in **black**.

Directions: Read the following words. Circle the letters that make the **k** sound. The first one is done for you.

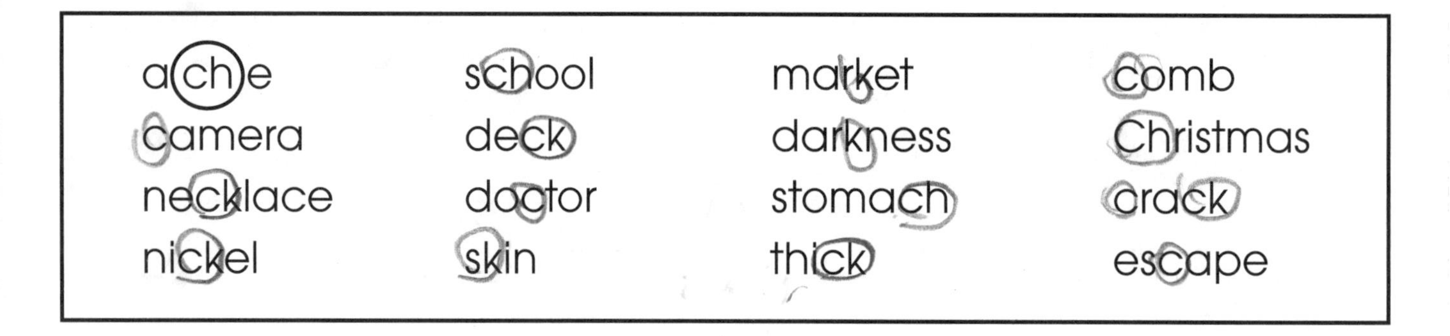

ache	school	market	comb
camera	deck	darkness	Christmas
necklace	doctor	stomach	crack
nickel	skin	thick	escape

Directions: Use your own words to finish the following sentences. Use words with the **k** sound.

1. If I had a nickel, I would ____________.

2. My doctor is very ____________.

3. We bought ripe, juicy tomatoes at the ____________.

4. If I had a camera now, I would take a picture of ____________.

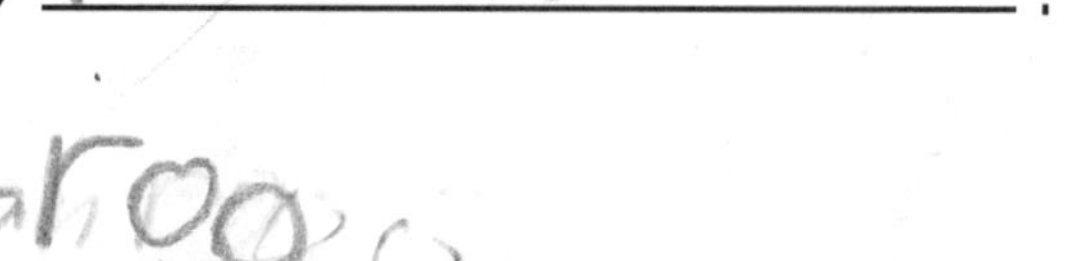

5. When my stomach aches, ____________.

Hard and Soft c

When **c** is followed by **e**, **i** or **y**, it usually has a **soft** sound. The **soft c** sounds like **s**. For example, **c**ircle and fen**c**e. When **c** is followed by **a** or **u**, it usually has a **hard** sound. The **hard c** sounds like **k**.

Examples: **c**up and **c**art

Directions: Read the words in the word box. Write the words in the correct lists. Write a word from the word box to finish each sentence.

Words with soft c	Words with hard c
pencil	popcorn
dance	lucky
cent	tractor
mice	cookie
circus	card

pencil	cookie
dance	cent
popcorn	circus
lucky	mice
tractor	card

1. Another word for a penny is a cent.
2. A cat likes to chase mice.
3. You will see animals and clowns at the circus.

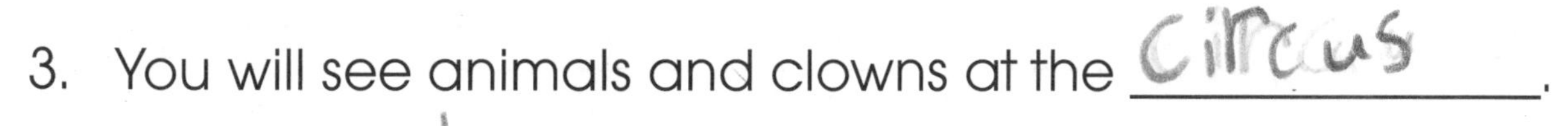

4. We like to dance to the music.
5. Will you please sharpen my pencil?

277

Hard and Soft g

When **g** is followed by **e**, **i** or **y**, it usually has a **soft** sound. The **soft g** sounds like **j**. **Example:** chan**g**e and **g**entle. The **hard g** sounds like the **g** in **g**irl or **g**ate.

Directions: Read the words in the word box. Write the words in the correct lists. Write a word from the box to finish each sentence.

engine	glove	cage	magic	frog
giant	flag	large	glass	goose

Words with soft g

engine
giant
cage
____
____

Words with hard g

glove
Flag
glass
Frog
goose

1. Our bird lives in a ____________________ .
2. Pulling a rabbit from a hat is a good ____________________ trick.
3. A car needs an ____________________ to run.
4. A ____________________ is a huge person.
5. An elephant is a very ____________________ animal.

Long Vowels

Directions: Use the word list below. Write each word on the vowel which has its sound. Say each word as you write it.

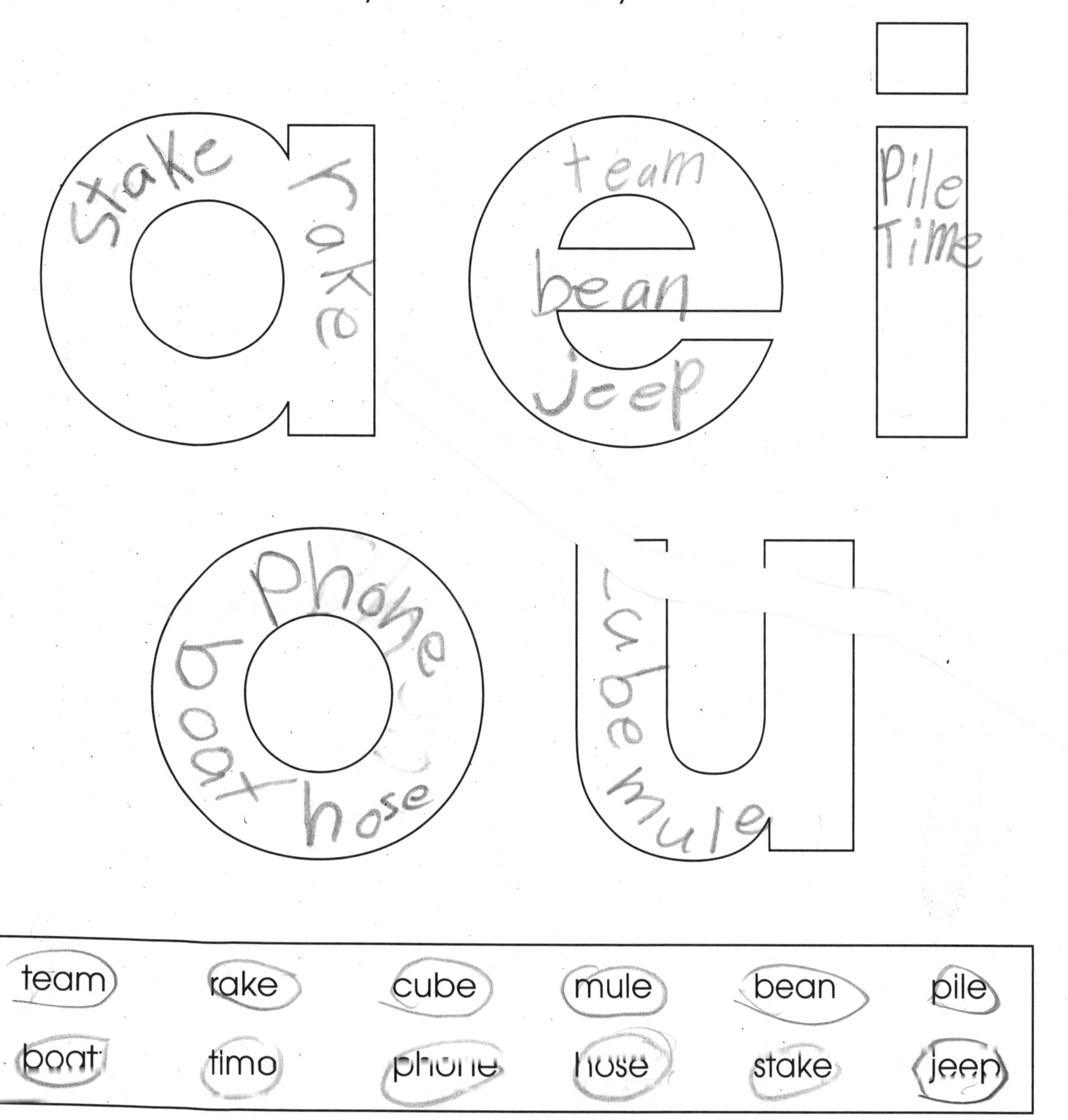

team rake cube mule bean pile
boat time phone hose stake jeep

Review

Directions: Read the words in each box. Cross out the word that does not belong.

long vowels	short vowels
cube cup rake me	man pet fix ice
long vowels	**short vowels**
soap seed read mat	cat pin rain frog

Directions: Write **short** or **long** to label the words in each box.

________ vowels	________ vowels
hose take bead cube eat see	frog hot sled lap block sit

Y as a Vowel

When **y** comes at the end of a word, it is a vowel. When **y** is the only vowel at the end of a one-syllable word, it has the sound of a long **i** (like in **my**). When **y** is the only vowel at the end of a word with more than one syllable, it has the sound of a long **e** (like in **baby**).

Directions: Look at the words in the word box. If the word has the sound of a long **i**, write it under the word **my**. If the word has the sound of a long **e**, write it under the word **baby**. Write the word from the word box that answers each riddle.

happy	penny	fry	try	sleepy	dry
bunny	why	windy	sky	party	fly

my	**baby**
______	______
______	______
______	______
______	______
______	______
______	______

1. It takes five of these to make a nickel. ______
2. This is what you call a baby rabbit. ______
3. It is often blue and you can see it if you look up. ______
4. You might have one of these on your birthday. ______
5. It is the opposite of wet. ______
6. You might use this word to ask a question. ______

Phonics

Sometimes, vowels have unusual sounds that are neither short nor long. For example, often when an **a** is followed by an **l**, instead of the short **a** sound, as in **apple**, it has the sound in **ball**. Sometimes an **o** has the sound of short **u**, as in **done**.

Directions: Read the words in the following word "families." Write another word in each group.

The **al** and **all** families:
also, always, ball, small, tall, ______________________

The **alk** family:
chalk, stalk, talk, ______________________

The **alt** family:
halt, malt, ______________________

The **o** family:
done, come, other, ______________________

Directions: Draw lines to match the rhyming words.

glove	call
pull	halt
wall	shove
salt	talk
walk	full

Vowel Teams

The vowel teams **ou** and **ow** can have the same sound. You can hear it in the words **clown** and **cloud**. The vowel teams **au** and **aw** have the same sound. You hear it in the words **because** and **law**.

Directions: Look at the pictures. Write the correct vowel team to complete the words. The first one is done for you. You may need to use a dictionary to help you with the correct spelling.

Vowel Teams

The vowel teams **oi** and **oy** have the same sound. You can hear it in the words **oil** and **boy**.

Directions: Finish each sentence by writing the correct word from the word box.

boil	point	coin
boy	toy	joy
join	enjoy	voice
soil		

1. You need a pencil with a sharp ________________.
2. A dime is a kind of ________________.

3. Leah's doll is her favorite ________________.

4. The opposite of girl is ________________.
5. To be a member of a club you must ________________.

6. Another word for dirt is ________________.
7. When you talk, we hear your ________________.

8. Ice cream is a dessert I ________________.
9. If water is very hot, it will ________________.
10. Another word for happiness is ________________.

Vowel Teams

The vowel team **oo** has two sounds. You can remember them with this sentence: Your **foot** goes in your **boot**.

Directions: Look at the pictures. Say their names. If the vowel sounds like the **oo** in **foot**, draw a line to the foot. If it sounds like the **oo** in **boot**, draw a line to the boot.

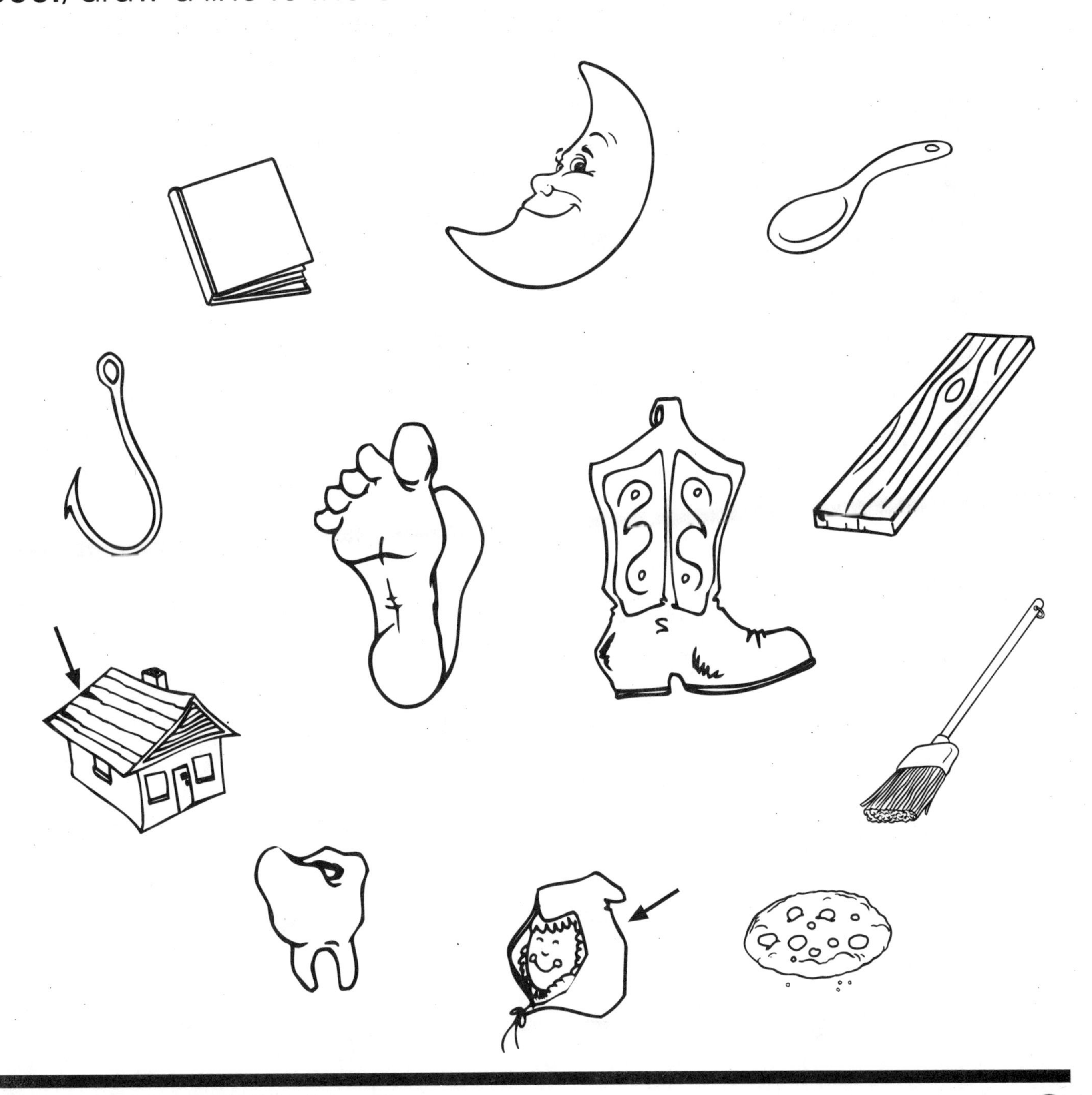

Vowel Teams

The vowel team **ea** can have a short **e** sound like in **head** or a long **e** sound like in **bead**. An **ea** followed by an **r** makes a sound like the one in **ear** or like the one in **heard**.

Directions: Read the story. Listen for the sound **ea** makes in the bold words.

Have you ever **read** a book or **heard** a story about a **bear**? You might have **learned** that bears sleep through the winter. Some bears may sleep the whole **season**. Sometimes they look almost **dead**! But they are very much alive. As the cold winter passes and the spring **weather** comes **near**, they wake up. After such a nice rest, they must be **ready** to **eat** a **really** big **meal**!

words with long **ea**	words with short **ea**	**ea** followed by **r**
____________	____________	____________
____________	____________	____________
____________	____________	____________
____________	____________	____________

R-Controlled Vowels

When a vowel is followed by the letter **r**, it has a different sound.

Example: he and **her**

Directions: Write a word from the word box to finish each sentence. Notice the sound of the vowel followed by an **r**.

park	chair	horse	bark	bird
hurt	girl	hair	store	ears

1. A dog likes to bark.
2. You buy food at a store.
3. Children like to play at the park.
4. An animal you can ride is a horse.
5. You hear with your ears.
6. A robin is a kind of bird.
7. If you fall down, you might get hurt.
8. The opposite of a boy is a girl.
9. You comb and brush your hair.
10. You sit down on a chair.

Syllables

One way to help you read a word you don't know is to divide it into parts called **syllables**. Every syllable has a vowel sound.

Directions: Say the words. Write the number of syllables. The first one is done for you.

bird	1	rabbit	______
apple	______	elephant	______
balloon	______	family	______
basketball	______	fence	______
breakfast	______	ladder	______
block	______	open	______
candy	______	puddle	______
popcorn	______	Saturday	______
yellow	______	wind	______
understand	______	butterfly	______

Syllables

When a double consonant is used in the middle of a word, the word can usually be divided between the consonants.

Directions: Look at the words in the word box. Divide each word into two syllables. Leave space between each syllable. One is done for you.

butter	puppy	kitten	yellow
dinner	chatter	ladder	happy
pillow	letter	mitten	summer

but ter ____________ ____________

____________ ____________ ____________

____________ ____________ ____________

____________ ____________ ____________

Many words are divided between two consonants that are not alike.

Directions: Look at the words in the word box. Divide each word into two syllables. One is done for you.

window	doctor	number	carpet
mister	winter	pencil	candle
barber	sister	picture	under

win dow ____________ ____________

____________ ____________ ____________

____________ ____________ ____________

____________ ____________ ____________

Suffixes

Suffixes are word parts added to the ends of words. Suffixes change the meaning of words.

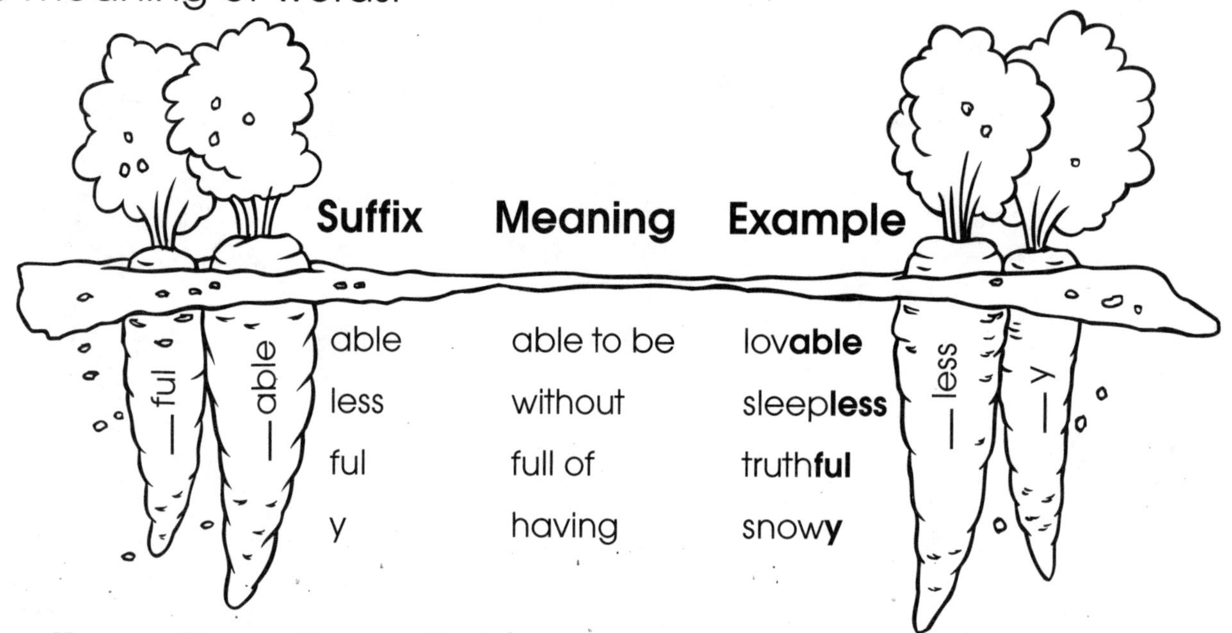

Suffix	Meaning	Example
able	able to be	lov**able**
less	without	sleep**less**
ful	full of	truth**ful**
y	having	snow**y**

Directions: Circle the suffix in each word below.

Example: fluff(y)

rainy	thoughtful	likeable
blameless	enjoyable	helpful
peaceful	careless	silky

Directions: Write a word for each meaning.

full of hope ____________ having rain ____________

without hope ____________ able to break ____________

without power ____________ full of cheer ____________

Suffixes

A **suffix** is a syllable added to the end of a word which changes its meaning, as in small, small**er**, small**est**. The word you start with is called the root word. Some root words change their spelling before adding **er** and **est**. **Example:** in the word **big**, another **g** is added to make the words big**ger** and big**gest**. In the word **pretty**, the **y** changes to an **i** to make the words prett**ier** and prett**iest**.

Directions: Use words from the word box to help you add **er** and **est** to the root words.

prettier	happier	luckiest	busiest	tinier
luckier	silliest	greener	madder	busier
prettiest	funnier	tiniest	happiest	bigger
biggest	greenest	sillier	maddest	funniest

	er	est
happy	__________	__________
busy	__________	__________
tiny	__________	__________
pretty	__________	__________
lucky	__________	__________
big	__________	__________
silly	__________	__________
green	__________	__________
mad	__________	__________
funny	__________	__________

Suffixes

Adding **ing** to a word means that it is happening now. Adding **ed** to a word means it happened in the past.

Directions: Look at the words in the word box. Underline the root word in each one. Write a word to complete each sentence.

snowing	wished	played	looking	crying
talking	walked	eating	going	doing

1. We like to play. We ______________________ yesterday.
2. Is that snow? Yes, it is ______________________.
3. Do you want to go with me? No, I am ______________________ with my friend.
4. The baby will cry if we leave. The baby is ______________.
5. We will walk home from school. We ______________ to school this morning.
6. Did you wish for a new bike? Yes, I ______________ for one.
7. Who is going to do it while we are away? I am __________ it.
8. Did you talk to your friend? Yes, we are ______________ now.
9. Will you look at my book? I am ______________ at it now.
10. I like to eat pizza. We are ______________________ it today.

Review

Directions: Read the word in bold in each sentence and circle each suffix. Write the root word on the line. Remember that some root words are changed when an ending is added.
Example: silliness → silly

1. Sue and Tim were **dancing** at the party. ____________
2. The children were **careful** not to play in the street. ____________
3. We made a mistake and put the door on **backward**. ____________
4. This is the **funniest** movie I ever saw. ____________
5. A new baby is **helpless**. ____________
6. I **asked** Mike to bring his wagon to my house. ____________
7. I'm really tired today because I had a **sleepless** night. ____________
8. My teacher is **really** nice. ____________
9. The book I am **reading** is good. ____________
10. Everyone wants to find **happiness**. ____________
11. The game isn't **likely** to end soon. ____________
12. My plant seems to grow **taller** every day. ____________
13. Don't be **careless** with your nice toys. ____________

Prefixes

Prefixes are special word parts added to the beginnings of words. Prefixes change the meaning of words.

Prefix	Meaning	Example
un	not	**un**happy
re	again	**re**do
pre	before	**pre**view
mis	wrong	**mis**understanding
dis	opposite	**dis**obey

Directions: Circle the word that begins with a prefix. Then write the prefix and the root word.

1. The dog was unhappy. ________ + ____________

2. The movie preview was interesting. ________ + ____________

3. The referee called an unfair penalty. ________ + ____________

4. Please do not misbehave. ________ + ____________

5. My parents disapprove of that show. ________ + ____________

6. I had to redo the assignment. ________ + ____________

Prefixes

Directions: Read the prefix and its meaning. Add each prefix to a root word to make a new word. Write the new word. Finish the sentences using the words you just wrote.

Prefixes	(Meaning)	Root Word	New Word
bi	(two)	cycle	______
dis	(away from)	appear	______
ex	(out of)	change	______
im	(not)	polite	______
in	(within)	side	______
mis	(wrong)	place	______
non	(not)	sense	______
pre	(before)	school	______
re	(again)	build	______
un	(not)	happy	______

1. Did you go to ______ before kindergarten?
2. The magician made the rabbit ______ .
3. Put your things where they belong so you don't ______ them.
4. Can you ride a ______ ?
5. Do you want to ______ your shirt for one that fits?

Review

Directions: Read each sentence. Look at the words in bold. Circle the prefix and write the root word on the line.

1. The **preview** of the movie was funny. ______________________
2. We always drink **nonfat** milk. ______________________
3. We will have to **reschedule** the trip. ______________________
4. Are you tired of **reruns** on television? ______________________
5. I have **outgrown** my new shoes already. ______________________
6. You must have **misplaced** the papers. ______________________
7. Police **enforce** the laws of the city. ______________________
8. I **disliked** that book. ______________________
9. The boy **distrusted** the big dog. ______________________
10. Try to **enjoy** yourself at the party. ______________________
11. Please try to keep the cat **inside** the house. ______________________
12. That song is total **nonsense**! ______________________
13. We will **replace** any parts that we lost. ______________________
14. Can you help me **unzip** this jacket? ______________________
15. Let's **rework** today's arithmetic problems. ______________________

ABC Order

Directions: Put the words in ABC order on the bags.

Alphabetical Order

Directions: Write the words in alphabetical order. Look at the first letter of each word. If the first letter of two words is the same, look at the second letter.

Example: l(a)mp Lamp comes first because
l(i)ght **a** comes before **i** in the alphabet.

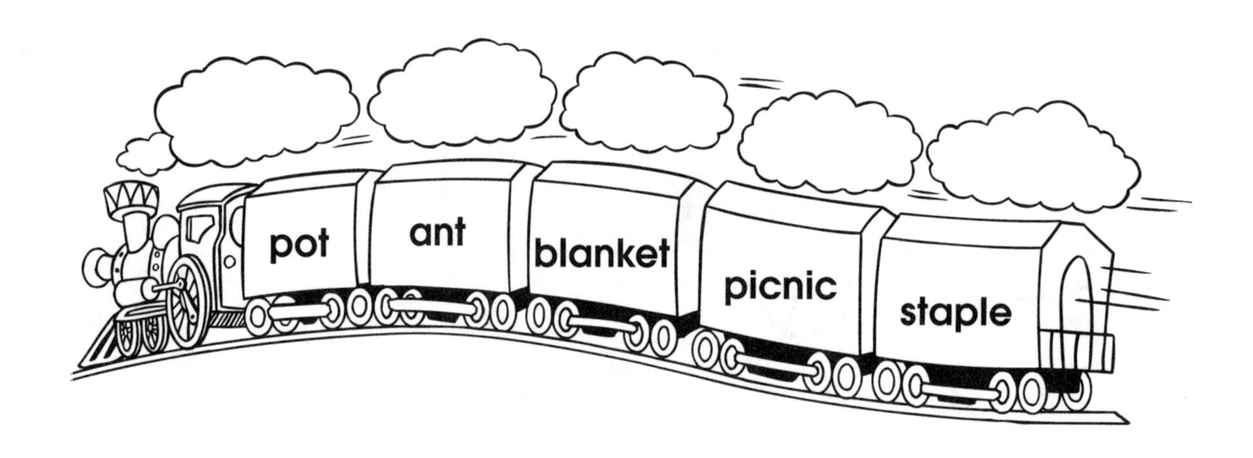

__________ __________ __________ __________ __________

__________ __________ __________ __________ __________

Sequencing: ABC Order

If the first letters of two words are the same, look at the second letters in both words. If the second letters are the same, look at the third letters.

Directions: Write 1, 2, 3 or 4 on the lines in each row to put the words in ABC order.

Example:

1. __1__ candy __2__ carrot __4__ duck __3__ dance

2. ______ cold ______ hot ______ carry ______ hit

3. ______ flash ______ fan ______ fun ______ garden

4. ______ seat ______ sun ______ saw ______ sit

5. ______ row ______ ring ______ rock ______ run

6. ______ truck ______ turn ______ twin ______ talk

7. ______ seven ______ shoe ______ soup ______ smell

Compound Words

Compound words are two words that are put together to make one new word.

Example:

nut + **shell** = **nutshell**

Directions: Choose a word from the box to make compound words in the sentences below.

board	bone	ground	prints	shake	house
brush	man	top	shell	ball	hive

Example:

The bird built its nest in the **treetop**.

1. We pitched our tent at the camp_______________.
2. You would not be able to stand up without your back___________.
3. The police officer looked for finger_______________.
4. She placed the hair_________________ in her purse.
5. It is important to have a firm hand_______________.
6. The teacher wrote on the chalk_________________.
7. The egg______________ is cracked.
8. Our whole family plays foot________________ together.
9. Be sure to put a top hat on the snow_______________.
10. Spot never sleeps in his dog_______________.
11. The beekeeper must check the bee______________ today.

Compound Words

Directions: Cut out the words below. Glue them together in the box to make compound words.

Can you think of any more compound words?

sun	air	mail	ball
box	room	water	guard
foot	living	class	flower
plane	room	melon	body

This page is blank for the cutting exercise
on the previous page.

Compound Words

Directions: Read the compound words in the word box. Then use them to answer the questions. The first one is done for you.

sailboat	blueberry	bookcase	tablecloth	beehive
dishpan	pigpen	classroom	playground	bedtime
broomstick	treetop	fireplace	newspaper	sunburn

Which compound word means . . .

1. a case for books? bookcase
2. a berry that is blue? ____________

3. a hive for bees? ____________
4. a place for fires? ____________
5. a pen for pigs? ____________
6. a room for a class? ____________

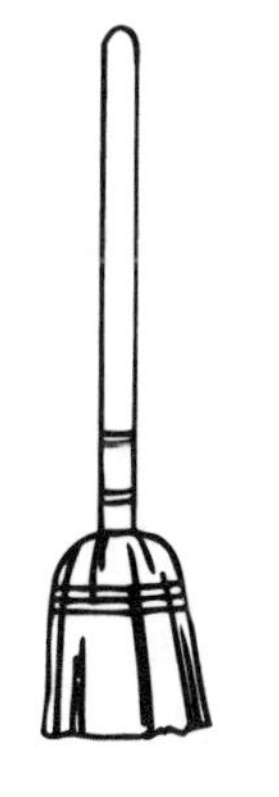

7. a pan for dishes? ____________
8. a boat to sail? ____________
9. a paper for news? ____________
10. a burn from the sun? ____________
11. the top of a tree? ____________
12. a stick for a broom? ____________

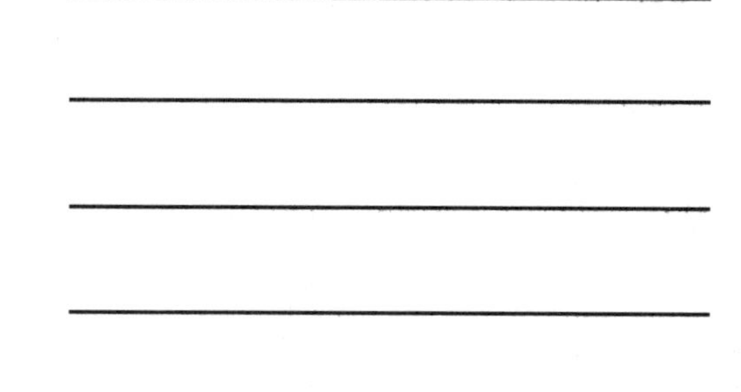

13. the time to go to bed? ____________
14. a cloth for the table? ____________
15. ground to play on? ____________

Contractions

Contractions are shortened forms of words. An apostrophe is added in place of the letters taken away.

Directions: Help the mother kangaroos find their babies. Draw a line to match the contractions with the words they stand for.

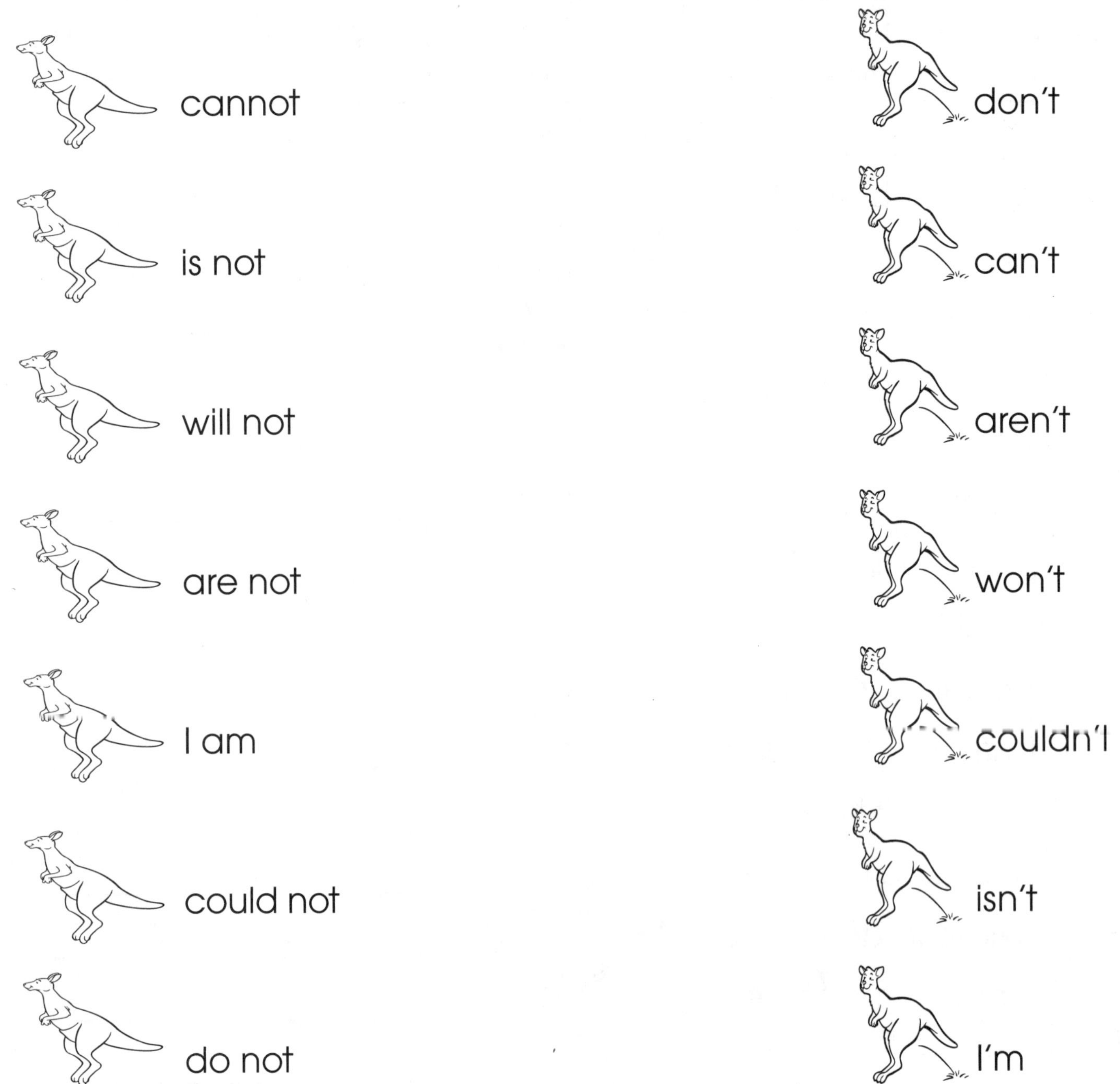

Contractions

Directions: Write your own contractions in each column below.

Contractions with not	Contractions with will	Contractions with have

Challenge: Write the two words that formed each contraction.

Synonyms

Words that mean the same or nearly the same are called **synonyms**.

Directions: Read the sentence that tells about the picture. Draw a circle around the word that means the same as the bold word.

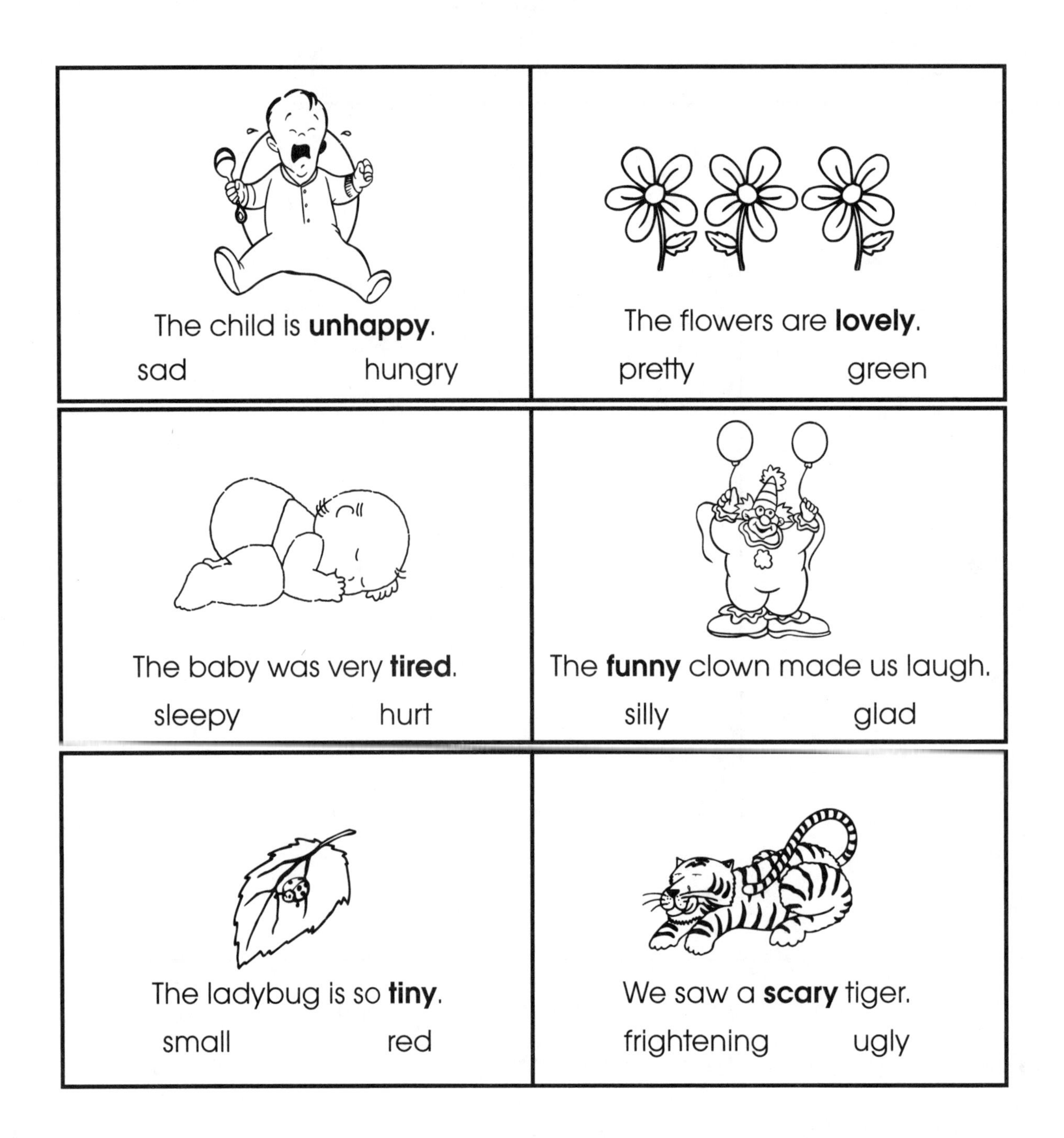
The child is **unhappy**.
sad hungry
The flowers are **lovely**.
pretty green
The baby was very **tired**.
sleepy hurt
The **funny** clown made us laugh.
silly glad
The ladybug is so **tiny**.
small red
We saw a **scary** tiger.
frightening ugly

Synonyms

Directions: Read each sentence. Fill in the blanks with the synonyms.

friend	tired	story
presents	little	

I want to go to bed because I am very sleepy. ______________

On my birthday I like to open my gifts. ______________

My pal and I like to play together. ______________

My favorite tale is *Cinderella*. ______________

The mouse was so tiny that it was hard to catch him. ______________

Synonyms

Synonyms are words with nearly the same meaning.

Directions: Draw a line to match each word on the left with its synonym on the right.

infant	hello
forest	coat
bucket	grin
hi	baby
bunny	woods
cheerful	fall
jacket	repair
alike	small
smile	same
autumn	hop
little	skinny
thin	top
jump	rabbit
shirt	pail
fix	happy

Antonyms

Directions: Write the antonym pairs from each sentence in the boxes.

Example: Many things are bought and sold at the market.

bought	sold

1. I thought I lost my dog, but someone found him.

2. The teacher will ask questions for the students to answer.

3. Airplanes arrive and depart from the airport.

4. The water in the pool was cold compared to the warm water in the whirlpool.

5. The tortoise was slow, but the hare was fast.

Homophones

Homophones are words that sound alike but have different meanings. The spellings are usually different, too.

Example: write and **right** are homophones.

Directions: Look at the pictures. Circle the word that tells what it is. The first one is done for you.

Homophones

Homophones are words that sound the same but are spelled differently and have different meanings.

Example:

So what do I do now?

sew **sow** **so**

Directions: Read the sentences and write the correct word in the blanks.

Example:

blue	**blew**	She has **blue** eyes.
		The wind **blew** the barn down.
eye	**I**	He hurt his left ____________ playing ball.
		________ like to learn new things.
see	**sea**	Can you __________ the winning runner from here?
		He goes diving for pearls under the ____________ .
eight	**ate**	The baby ____________ the banana.
		Jane was ____________ years old last year.
one	**won**	Jill ____________ first prize at the science fair.
		I am the only __________ in my family with red hair.
be	**bee**	Jenny cried when a ____________ stung her.
		I have to _______ in bed every night at eight o'clock.
two	**to too**	My father likes ____________ play tennis.
		I like to play, ____________ .
		It takes at least ____________ people to play.

Homophones

Directions: Circle the words that are not used correctly. Write the correct word above the circled word. Use the words in the box to help you. The first one is done for you.

road	see	one	be	so	I	brakes	piece	there
wait	not	some	hour	would	no	deer	you	heard

Jake and his family were getting close to Grandpa's. It had taken them

hour

nearly an (our) to get their, but Jake knew it was worth it. In his mind, he could already sea the pond and could almost feel the cool water. It had been sew hot this summer in the apartment.

"Wood ewe like a peace of my apple, Jake?" asked his big sister Clare. "Eye can't eat any more."

"Know, thank you," Jake replied. "I still have sum of my fruit left."

Suddenly, Dad slammed on the breaks. "Did you see that dear on the rode? I always hord that if you see won, there might bee more."

"Good thinking, Dad. I'm glad you are a safe driver. We're knot very far from Grandpa's now. I can't weight!"

Multiple-Meaning Words

Many words have more than one meaning. These words are called **multiple-meaning words**. Think of how the word is used in a sentence or story to determine the correct meaning.

Directions: The following baseball words have multiple meanings. Write the correct word in each baseball below.

play	bat	ball	fly	run

_______ This word means . . .

1. a flying mammal
2. a special stick used in baseball

_______ This word means . . .

1. a small insect
2. to soar through the air

_______ This word means . . .

1. a big dance
2. a round object used in sports

_______ This word means . . .

1. a performance
2. to amuse oneself

Which word is left? _______ Write sentences using two different meanings of the word.

1.____

2.____

Antonyms

Antonyms are words that are opposites.

Directions: Read the words next to the pictures. Draw a line to the antonyms.

dark	empty
hairy	dry
closed	happy
dirty	bald
sad	clean
full	light
wet	open

Antonyms

Directions: Write the antonym pairs from each sentence in the boxes.

Example: Many things are bought and sold at the market.

bought	sold

1. I thought I lost my dog, but someone found him.

2. The teacher will ask questions for the students to answer.

3. Airplanes arrive and depart from the airport.

4. The water in the pool was cold compared to the warm water in the whirlpool.

5. The tortoise was slow, but the hare was fast.

Antonyms

Antonyms are words that are opposites.

Example:

hairy

bald

Directions: Choose a word from the box to complete each sentence below.

open	right	light	full	late	below
hard	clean	slow	quiet	old	nice

Example:

My car was dirty, but now it's **clean**.

1. Sometimes my cat is naughty, and sometimes she's ________.
2. The sign said, "Closed," but the door was ________.
3. Is the glass half empty or half ________?
4. I bought new shoes, but I like my ________ ones better.
5. Skating is easy for me, but ________ for my brother.
6. The sky is dark at night and ________ during the day.
7. I like a noisy house, but my mother likes a ________ one.
8. My friend says I'm wrong, but I say I'm ________.
9. Jason is a fast runner, but Adam is a ________ runner.
10. We were supposed to be early, but we were ________.

Review

Directions: Draw a line from each word on the left to its antonym on the right.

high	down
in	you
big	low
up	little
me	out

Directions: Look at each picture. Circle the correct word.

Directions: Write the homophone for each word.

right ____________________ new ____________________

blew ____________________ dear ____________________

Common Nouns

Common nouns are nouns that name any member of a group of people, places or things, rather than specific people, places or things.

Directions: Read the sentences below and write the common noun found in each sentence.

Example: socks My socks do not match.

1. ______________ The bird could not fly.
2. ______________ Ben likes to eat jelly beans.
3. ______________ I am going to meet my mother.
4. ______________ We will go swimming in the lake tomorrow.
5. ______________ I hope the flowers will grow quickly.
6. ______________ We colored eggs together.
7. ______________ It is easy to ride a bicycle.
8. ______________ My cousin is very tall.
9. ______________ Ted and Jane went fishing in their boat.
10. ______________ They won a prize yesterday.
11. ______________ She fell down and twisted her ankle.
12. ______________ My brother was born today.
13. ______________ She went down the slide.
14. ______________ Ray went to the doctor today.

Proper Nouns

Proper nouns are the names of specific people, places and pets. Proper nouns begin with a capital letter.

Directions: Write the proper nouns on the lines below. Use capital letters at the beginning of each word.

logan, utah

____

mike smith

____

lynn cramer

____

buster

____

fluffy

____

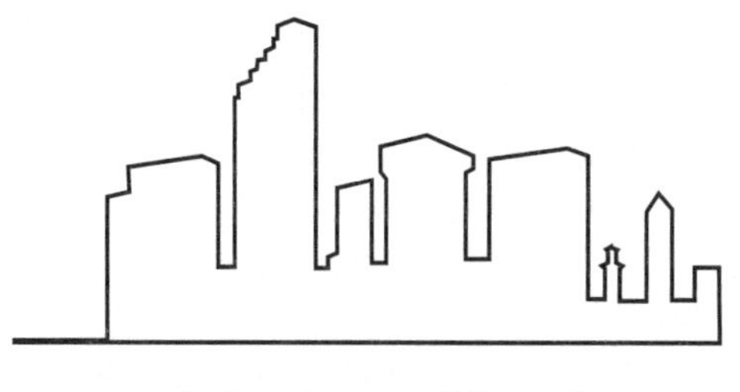

chicago, illinois

____

Proper Nouns

Directions: Read the sentences and circle the proper nouns.

How do you get to Minneapolis?
MAP

1. My mom, Carol, lives in Wisconsin.

2. Aunt Lorraine lives in Minneapolis.

3. Jack and Jill eat at Dawn's house.

4. Dr. Saxton gave Ron a sticker.

5. Movie stars live in Hollywood, California.

6. Andrea went to Hawaii on her vacation.

7. George Washington was the first president of the United States.

Proper Nouns

The days of the week and the months of the year are always capitalized.

Directions: Circle the words that are written correctly. Write the words that need capital letters on the lines below.

sunday	July	Wednesday	may	december
friday	tuesday	june	august	Monday
january	February	March	Thursday	April
September	saturday	October		

Days of the Week

1. ____________________
2. ____________________
3. ____________________
4. ____________________

Months of the Year

1. ____________________
2. ____________________
3. ____________________
4. ____________________
5. ____________________

Common and Proper Nouns

Directions: Look at the list of nouns in the box. Write the common nouns under the kite. Write the proper nouns under the balloon. Remember to capitalize the first letter of each proper noun.

lisa smith
cats
shoelace
saturday
dr. martin
whistle
teddy bears
main street
may
boy
lawn chair
mary stewart
bird
florida
school
apples
washington, d.c.
pine cone
elizabeth jones
charley reynolds

COMMON NOUNS

PROPER NOUNS

____________	____________
____________	____________
____________	____________
____________	____________
____________	____________
____________	____________
____________	____________
____________	____________
____________	____________
____________	____________

Nouns

Nouns can also name ideas. **Ideas** are things we cannot see or touch such as bravery, beauty or honesty.

Directions: Underline the "idea" nouns in each sentence.

1. Respect is something that must be earned.

2. Truth and justice are two things that are highly valued.

3. The beauty of the flower garden was breathtaking.

4. Skills must be learned in order to master new things.

5. His courage impressed everyone.

Plural Nouns

A **plural** is more than one person, place or thing. We usually add an **s** to show that a noun names more than one. If a noun ends in **x**, **ch**, **sh** or **s**, we add an **es** to the word.

Example: **pizza**  **pizzas**  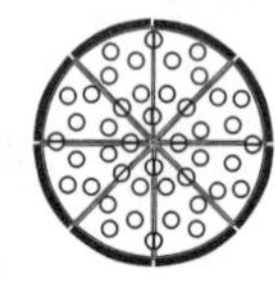 

Directions: Write the plural of the words below.

Example: dog + s = dogs

cat ____________________

boot ____________________

house ____________________

Example: peach + es = peaches

lunch ____________________

bunch ____________________

punch ____________________

Example: ax + es = axes

fox ____________________

tax ____________________

box ____________________

Example: glass + es = glasses

mess ____________________

guess ____________________

class ____________________

Example: dish + es = dishes

bush ____________________

ash ____________________

brush ____________________

walrus 

walruses  

Plural Nouns

Directions: Write the plural of each noun to complete the sentences below. Remember to change the **y** to **ie** before you add **s**!

1. I am going to two birthday ____________________ this week.
(party)

2. Sandy picked some ________________ for Mom's pie.
(cherry)

3. At the store, we saw lots of ____________________.
(bunny)

4. My change at the candy store was three ____________________.
(penny)

5. All the ____________________ baked cookies for the bake sale.
(lady)

6. Thanksgiving is a special time for ________________ to gather together.
(family)

7. Boston and New York are very large ____________________.
(city)

Plural Nouns

Some words have special plural forms.

Example: **leaf** **leaves**

Directions: Some of the words in the box are special plurals. Complete each sentence with a plural from the box. Then write the letters from the boxes in the blanks below to solve the puzzle.

tooth	teeth
child	children
foot	feet
mouse	mice
woman	women
man	men

1. I lost my two front ___ ___ ___ [___] ___!

2. My sister has two pet ___ ___ ___ [___].

3. Her favorite book is Little ___ ___ ___ [___] ___.

4. The circus clown had big ___ ___ ___ [___].

5. The teacher played a game with the ___ [___] ___ ___ ___ ___ ___ ___.

Take good care of this pearly plural!

___ ___ ___ ___ ___
1 2 3 4 5

Singular Nouns

Directions: The **singular form** of a word shows one person, place or thing. Write the singular form of each noun on the lines below.

cherries ______________________________

lunches ______________________________

countries ______________________________

leaves ______________________________

churches ______________________________

arms ______________________________

boxes ______________________________

men ______________________________

wheels ______________________________

pictures ______________________________

cities ______________________________

places ______________________________

ostriches ______________________________

glasses ______________________________

Possessive Nouns

Possessive nouns tell who or what is the owner of something. With singular nouns, we use an apostrophe **before** the **s**. With plural nouns, we use an apostrophe **after** the **s**.

Example:

singular: one elephant

The **elephant's** dance was wonderful.

plural: more than one elephant

The **elephants'** dance was wonderful.

Directions: Put the apostrophe in the correct place in each bold word. Then write the word in the blank.

1. The **lions** cage was big. ____________________
2. The **bears** costumes were purple. ____________________
3. One **boys** laughter was very loud. ____________________
4. The **trainers** dogs were dancing about. ____________________
5. The **mans** popcorn was tasty and good. ____________________
6. **Marks** cotton candy was delicious. ____________________
7. A little **girls** balloon burst in the air. ____________________
8. The big **clowns** tricks were very funny. ____________________
9. **Lauras** sister clapped for the clowns. ____________________
10. The **womans** money was lost in the crowd. ____________________
11. **Kellys** mother picked her up early. ____________________

Possessive Nouns

Directions: Circle the correct possessive noun in each sentence and write it in the blank.

Example: One ___girl's___ mother is a teacher.
girl's   girls'

1. The ____________ tail is long.
cat's   cats'

2. One ____________ baseball bat is aluminum.
boy's   boys'

3. A ____________ aprons are white.
waitresses'   waitress's

4. My ____________ apple pie is the best!
grandmother's   grandmothers'

5. My five ____________ uniforms are dirty.
brother's   brothers'

6. The ____________ doll is pretty.
child's   childs'

7. This ____________ collars are different colors.
dog's   dogs'

8. The ____________ tail is short.
cow's   cows'

Pronouns

Pronouns are words that are used in place of nouns.
Examples: he, she, it, they, him, them, her, him

Directions: Read each sentence. Write the pronoun that takes the place of each noun.

Example:
The **monkey** dropped the banana. It

1. **Dad** washed the car last night. ________
2. **Mary and David** took a walk in the park. ________
3. **Peggy** spent the night at her grandmother's house. ________
4. The **baseball players** lost their game. ________
5. **Mike Van Meter** is a great soccer player. ________
6. The **parrot** can say five different words. ________
7. **Megan** wrote a story in class today. ________
8. They gave a party for **Teresa**. ________
9. Everyone in the class was happy for **Ted**. ________
10. The children petted the **giraffe**. ________
11. Linda put the **kittens** near the warm stove. ________
12. **Gina** made a chocolate cake for my birthday. ________
13. **Pete and Matt** played baseball on the same team. ________
14. Give the books to **Herbie**. ________

Pronouns

We use the pronouns **I** and **we** when talking about the person or people doing the action.

Example: I can roller skate. **We** can roller skate.

We use **me** and **us** when talking about something that is happening to a person or people.

Example: They gave **me** the roller skates.
They gave **us** the roller skates.

Directions: Circle the correct pronoun and write it in the blank.

Example:

We are going to the picnic together. **We, Us**

1. ______ am finished with my science project. **I, Me**
2. Eric passed the football to ______ . **me, I**
3. They ate dinner with ______ last night. **we, us**
4. ______ like spinach better than ice cream. **I, Me**
5. Mom came in the room to tell ______ good night. **me, I**
6. ______ had a pizza party in our backyard. **Us, We**
7. They told ______ the good news. **us, we**
8. Tom and ______ went to the store. **me, I**
9. She is taking ______ with her to the movies. **I, me**
10. Katie and ______ are good friends. **I, me**

Possessive Pronouns

Possessive pronouns show ownership.

Examples: his hat, **her** shoes, **our** dog

We can use these pronouns before a noun:
my, our, you, his, her, its, their

Examples: That is **my** bike.

We can use these pronouns on their own:
mine, yours, ours, his, hers, theirs, its

Example: That is **mine**.

Directions: Write each sentence again, using a pronoun instead of the words in bold letters. Be sure to use capitals and periods.

Example:

My **dog's** bowl is brown. **Its** bowl is brown.

1. That is **Lisa's** book. ______________________________

2. This is **my pencil**. ______________________________

3. This hat is **your hat**. ______________________________

4. Fifi is **Kevin's** cat. ______________________________

5. That beautiful house is **our home**.

____

6. **The gerbil's** cage is too small.

____

Pronouns

Singular Pronouns	Plural Pronouns
I me my mine	we us our ours
you your yours	you your yours
he she it her	they them their theirs
hers his its him	

Directions: Underline the pronouns in each sentence.

1. Mom told us to wash our hands.

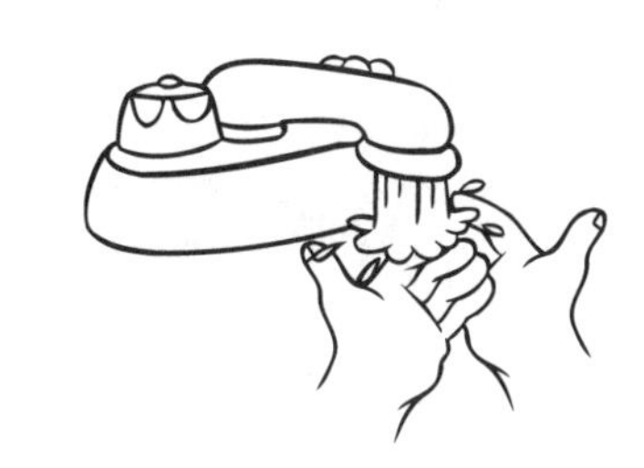

2. Did you go to the store?

3. We should buy him a present.

4. I called you about their party.

5. Our house had damage on its roof.

6. They want to give you a prize at our party.

7. My cat ate her sandwich.

8. Your coat looks like his coat.

Articles

Articles are small words that help us to better understand nouns. **A** and **an** are articles. We use **an** before a word that begins with a vowel. We use **a** before a word that begins with a consonant.

Example: We looked in **a** nest. It had **an** eagle in it.

Directions: Read the sentences. Write **a** or **an** in the blank.

1. I found _______ book.

2. It had a story about _______ ant in it.

3. In the story, _______ lion gave three wishes to _______ ant.

4. The ant's first wish was to ride _______ elephant.

5. The second wish was to ride _______ alligator.

6. The last wish was _______ wish for three more wishes.

Adjectives

Adjectives are words that tell more about a person, place or thing.

Examples: cold, fuzzy, dark

Directions: Circle the adjectives in the sentences.

1. The juicy apple is on the plate.

2. The furry dog is eating a bone.

3. It was a sunny day.

4. The kitten drinks warm milk.

5. The baby has a loud cry.

Adjectives

Directions: Think of your own adjectives. Write a story about Fluffy the cat.

1. Fluffy is a _______________________ cat.

2. The color of his fur is ___________________ .

3. He likes to chew on my_____________________ shoes.

4. He likes to eat _____________________ cat food.

5. I like Fluffy because he is so _______________________.

Verbs

Directions: Write each verb in the correct column.

rake	talked	look	hopped	skip
cooked	fished	call	clean	sewed

Yesterday	Today
__________	__________
__________	__________
__________	__________
__________	__________
__________	__________

Verbs

A **verb** is the action word in a sentence, the word that tells what something does or that something exists. **Examples: run, jump, skip**

Directions: Draw a box around the verb in each sentence below.

1. Spiders spin webs of silk.
2. A spider waits in the center of the web for its meals.
3. A spider sinks its sharp fangs into insects.
4. Spiders eat many insects.
5. Spiders make their nests with silk.
6. Female spiders wrap silk around their eggs to protect them.

Directions: Choose the correct verb from the box and write it in the sentences below.

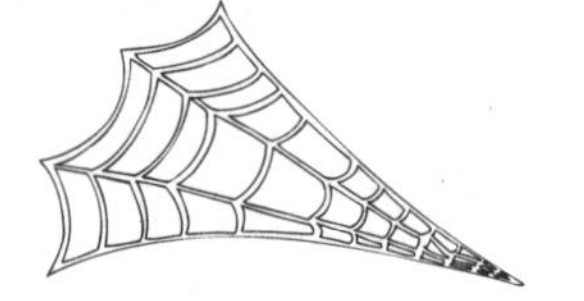

hides	swims	eats	grabs	hurt

1. A crab spider ____________ deep inside a flower where it cannot be seen.
2. The crab spider ____________ insects when they land on the flower.
3. The wolf spider is good because it ____________ wasps.
4. The water spider ____________ under water.
5. Most spiders will not ____________ people.

Verbs

When a verb tells what one person or thing is doing now, it usually ends in **s**. **Example:** She **sings**.

When a verb is used with **you**, **I** or **we**, we do not add an **s**.

Example: I **sing**.

Directions: Write the correct verb in each sentence.

Example:

I write a newspaper about our street. **writes, write**

1. My sister _____ me sometimes. **helps, help**
2. She _____ the pictures. **draw, draws**
3. We _____ them together. **delivers, deliver**
4. I _____ the news about all the people. **tell, tells**
5. Mr. Macon _____ the most beautiful flowers. **grow, grows**
6. Mrs. Jones _____ to her plants. **talks, talk**
7. Kevin Turner _____ his dog loose every day. **lets, let**
8. Little Mikey Smith _____ lost once a week. **get, gets**
9. You may _____ I live on an interesting street. **thinks, think**
10. We _____ it's the best street in town. **say, says**

Is, Are and Am

Is, **are** and **am** are special action words that tell us something is happening now.

Use **am** with **I**. **Example:** I **am**.
Use **is** to tell about one person or thing. **Example:** He **is**.
Use **are** to tell about more than one. **Example:** We **are**.
Use **are** with **you**. **Example:** You **are**.

Directions: Write **is**, **are** or **am** in the sentences below.

1. My friends ________________ helping me build a tree house.

2. It________________ in my backyard.

3. We ________________ using hammers, wood and nails.

4. It________________ a very hard job.

5. I ________________ lucky to have good friends.

Was and Were

Was and **were** tell us about something that already happened.

Use **was** to tell about one person or thing. **Example:** I **was**, he **was**. Use **were** to tell about more than one person or thing or when using the word **you**. **Example:** We **were**, you **were**.

Directions: Write **was** or **were** in each sentence.

1. Lily____________________eight years old on her birthday.

2. Tim and Steve ____________________happy to be at the party.

3. Megan ____________________ too shy to sing "Happy Birthday."

4. Ben____________________ sorry he dropped his cake.

5. All of the children____________________happy to be invited.

Go, Going and Went

We use **go** or **going** to tell about now or later. Sometimes we use **going** with the words **am** or **are**. We use **went** to tell about something that already happened.

Directions: Write **go**, **going** or **went** in the sentences below.

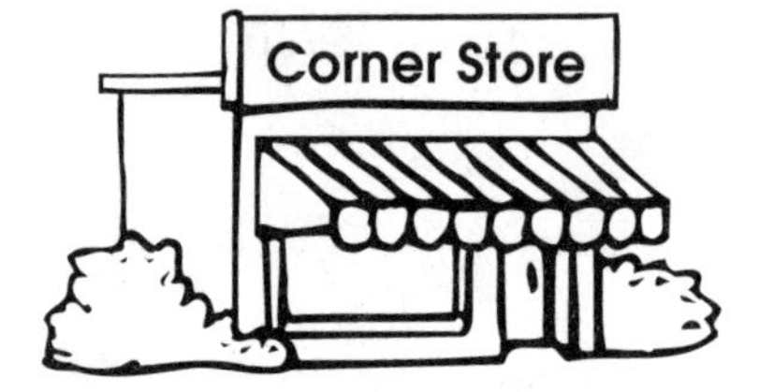

1. Today, I will ____________ to the store.

2. Yesterday, we ________________ shopping.

3. I am ____________________ to take Muffy to the vet.

4. Jan and Steve ________________ to the party.

5. They are ____________________ to have a good day.

Have, Has and Had

We use **have** and **has** to tell about now. We use **had** to tell about something that already happened.

Directions: Write **has, have** or **had** in the sentences below.

1. We ____________________ three cats at home.

2. Ginger ____________________ brown fur.

3. Bucky and Charlie ____________________ gray fur.

4. My friend Tom ____________________ one cat, but he died.

5. Tom ____________________ a new cat now.

See, Saw and Sees

We use **see** or **sees** to tell about now. We use **saw** to tell about something that already happened.

Directions: Write **see**, **sees** or **saw** in the sentences below.

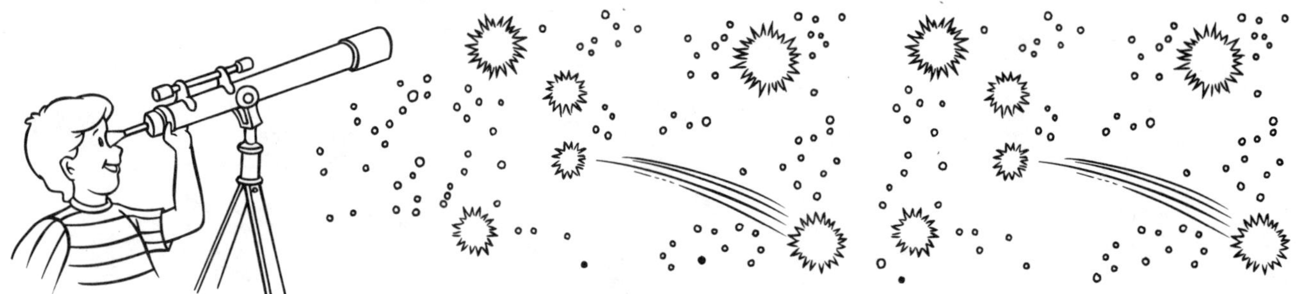

1. Last night, we ________________ the stars.

2. John can ________________ the stars from his window.

3. He ________________ them every night.

4. Last week, he ________________ the Big Dipper.

5. Can you ________________ it in the night sky, too?

6. If you ________________ it, you would remember it!

7. John ________________ it often now.

8. How often do you ________________ it?

Eat, Eats and Ate

We use **eat** or **eats** to tell about now. We use **ate** to tell about what already happened.

Directions: Write **eat**, **eats** or **ate** in the sentences below.

1. We like to ________________________ in the lunchroom.

2. Today, my teacher will ___________________ in a different room.

3. She ________________________________ with the other teachers.

4. Yesterday, we ________________________ pizza, pears and peas.

5. Today, we will _________________________ turkey and potatoes.

Leave, Leaves and Left

We use **leave** and **leaves** to tell about now. We use **left** to tell about what already happened.

Directions: Write **leave**, **leaves** or **left** in the sentences below.

1. Last winter, we _______________ seeds in the bird feeder every day.

2. My mother likes to _____________________ food out for the squirrels.

3. When it rains, she ___________________ bread for the birds.

4. Yesterday, she _____________________ popcorn for the birds.

Review

Directions: Ask someone to give you nouns, verbs and adjectives where shown. Write them in the blanks. Read the story to your friend when you finish.

The ______________ (noun) was barking in the yard. My dad ______________ (verb + ed) at the dog. The dog crawled under the ______________ (noun). He found a ______________ (noun). It made him very ______________ (adjective). The ______________ (noun) played with the dog. They ______________ (verb + ed) together until it was ______________ (adjective).

Draw a picture to go with your story.

Subjects

The **subject** of a sentence is the person, place or thing the sentence is about.

Directions: Underline the subject in each sentence.

Example: Mom read a book.
(Think: Who is the sentence about? Mom)

1. The bird flew away.

2. The kite was high in the air.

3. The children played a game.

4. The books fell down.

5. The monkey climbed a tree.

Predicates

The **predicate** is the part of the sentence that tells about the action.

Directions: Circle the predicate in each sentence.

Example: The boys ran on the playground.
(Think: The boys did what? (Ran))

1. The woman painted a picture.

2. The puppy chases his ball.

3. The students went to school.

4. Butterflies fly in the air.

5. The baby wants a drink.

Subjects and Predicates

The **subject** part of the sentence is the person, place or thing the sentence is about. The **predicate** is the part of the sentence that tells what the subject does.

Directions: Draw a line between the subject and the predicate. Underline the noun in the subject and circle the verb.

Example: The furry <u>cat</u> | (ate) food.

1. Mandi walks to school.

2. The bus drove the children.

3. The school bell rang very loudly.

4. The teacher spoke to the students.

5. The girls opened their books.

Compound Subjects

Two similar sentences can be joined into one sentence if the predicate is the same. A **compound subject** is made up of two subjects joined together by the word **and**.

Example: Jamie can sing.
Sandy can sing.

Jamie **and** Sandy can sing.

Directions: Combine the sentences. Write the new sentence on the line.

1. The cats are my pets.
   The dogs are my pets.

____

2. Chairs are in the store.
   Tables are in the store.

____

3. Tom can ride a bike.
   Jack can ride a bike.

____

Compound Predicates

A **compound predicate** is made by joining two sentences that have the same subject. The predicates are joined together by the word **and**.

Example: Tom can jump.
Tom can run.

Tom can run **and** jump.

Directions: Combine the sentences. Write the new sentence on the line.

1. The dog can roll over.
   The dog can bark.

____

2. My mom plays with me.
   My mom reads with me.

____

3. Tara is tall.
   Tara is smart.

____

Compound Subjects and Predicates

The following sentences have either a compound subject or a compound predicate.

Directions: If the sentence has a compound subject (more than one thing doing the action), **underline** the subject. If it has a compound predicate (more than one action), **circle** the predicate.

Example: Bats and owls like the night.

The fox (slinks and spies.)

1. Raccoons and mice steal food.

2. Monkeys and birds sleep in trees.

3. Elephants wash and play in the river.

4. Bears eat honey and scratch trees.

5. Owls hoot and hunt.

Compound Subjects and Predicates

Directions: Write one new sentence using a compound subject or predicate.

Example: The boy will jump. The girl will jump.

The boy and girl will jump.

1. The clowns run. The clowns play.

____

2. The dogs dance. The bears dance.

____

3. Seals bark. Seals clap.

____

4. The girls play. The girls laugh.

____

READING

Word Order

Word order is the logical order of words in sentences.

Directions: Put the words in order so that each sentence tells a complete idea.

Example: outside put cat the

Put the cat outside.

1. mouse the ate snake the

____

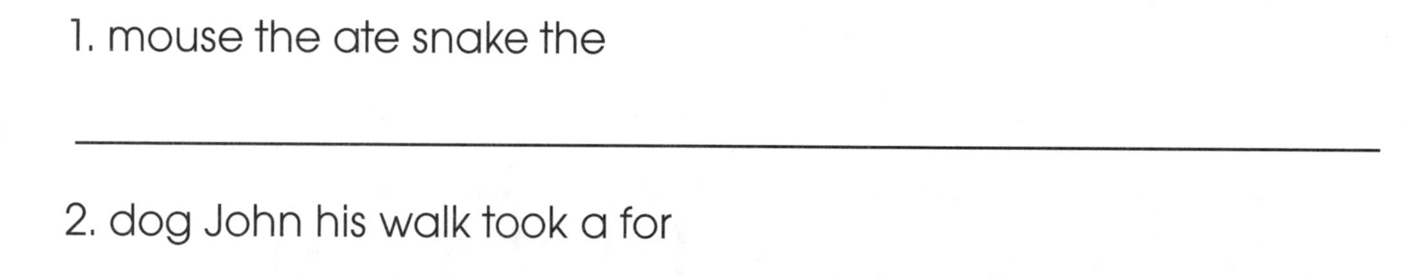

2. dog John his walk took a for

____

3. birthday Maria the present wrapped

____

4. escaped parrot the cage its from

____

5. to soup quarts water three of add the

____

6. bird the bushes into the chased cat the

____

Sentences and Non-Sentences

A **sentence** tells a complete idea. It has a noun and a verb. It begins with a capital letter and has punctuation at the end.

Directions: Circle the group of words if it is a sentence.

1. Grass is a green plant.

2. Mowing the lawn.

3. Grass grows in fields and lawns.

4. Tickle the feet.

5. Sheep, cows and horses eat grass.

6. We like to play in.

7. My sister likes to mow the lawn.

8. A picnic on the grass.

9. My dog likes to roll in the grass.

10. Plant flowers around.

Statements

Statements are sentences that tell us something. They begin with a capital letter and end with a period.

Directions: Write the sentences on the lines below. Begin each sentence with a capital letter and end it with a period.

1. we like to ride our bikes

___

2. we go down the hill very fast

___

3. we keep our bikes shiny and clean

___

4. we know how to change the tires

___

Questions

Questions are sentences that ask something. They begin with a capital letter and end with a question mark.

Directions: Write the questions on the lines below. Begin each sentence with a capital letter and end it with a question mark.

1. will you be my friend

____

2. what is your name

____

3. are you eight years old

____

4. do you like rainbows

____

Surprising Sentences

Surprising sentences tell a strong feeling and end with an exclamation point. A surprising sentence may be only one or two words showing fear, surprise or pain. **Example: Oh, no!**

Directions: Put a period at the end of the sentences that tell something. Put an exclamation point at the end of the sentences that tell a strong feeling. Put a question mark at the end of the sentences that ask a question.

1. The cheetah can run very fast
2. Wow
3. Look at that cheetah go
4. Can you run fast
5. Oh, my
6. You're faster than I am
7. Let's run together
8. We can run as fast as a cheetah
9. What fun
10. Do you think cheetahs get tired

Commands

Commands tell someone to do something. **Example: "Be careful."** It can also be written as "Be careful!" if it tells a strong feeling.

Directions: Put a period at the end of the command sentences. Use an exclamation point if the sentence tells a strong feeling. Write your own commands on the lines below.

1. Clean your room

2. Now

3. Be careful with your goldfish

4. Watch out

5. Be a little more careful

____

____

Same/Different: Venn Diagram

A **Venn diagram** is a diagram that shows how two things are the same and different.

Directions: Choose two outdoor sports. Then follow the instructions to complete the Venn diagram.

1. Write the first sport name under the first circle. Write some words that describe the sport. Write them in the first circle.
2. Write the second sport name under the second circle. Write some words that describe the sport. Write them in the circle.
3. Where the 2 circles overlap, write some words that describe both sports.

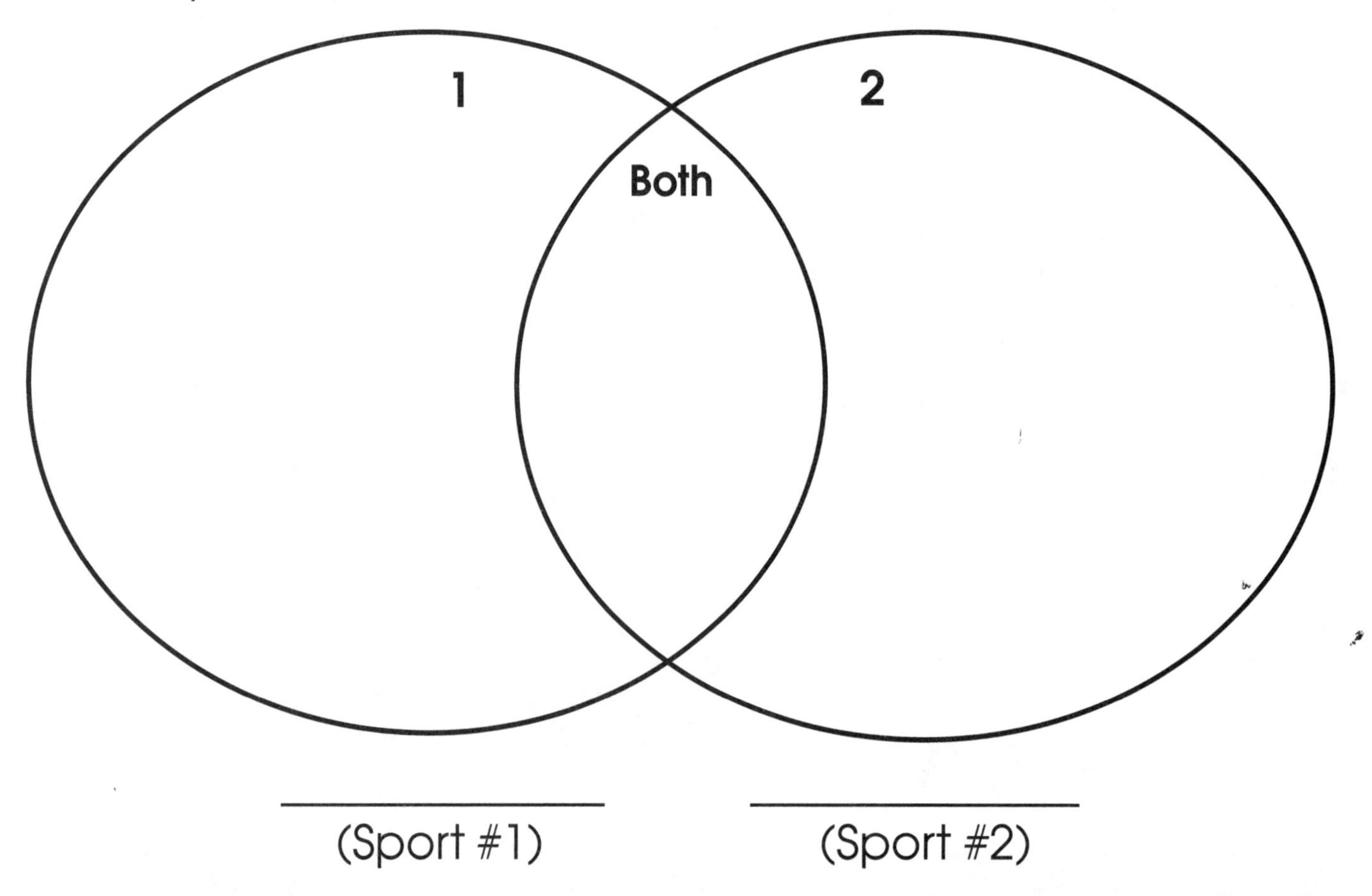

Same/Different: Cats and Tigers

Directions: Read about cats and tigers. Then complete the Venn diagram, telling how they are the same and different.

Tigers are a kind of cat. Pet cats and tigers both have fur. Pet cats are small and tame. Tigers are large and wild.

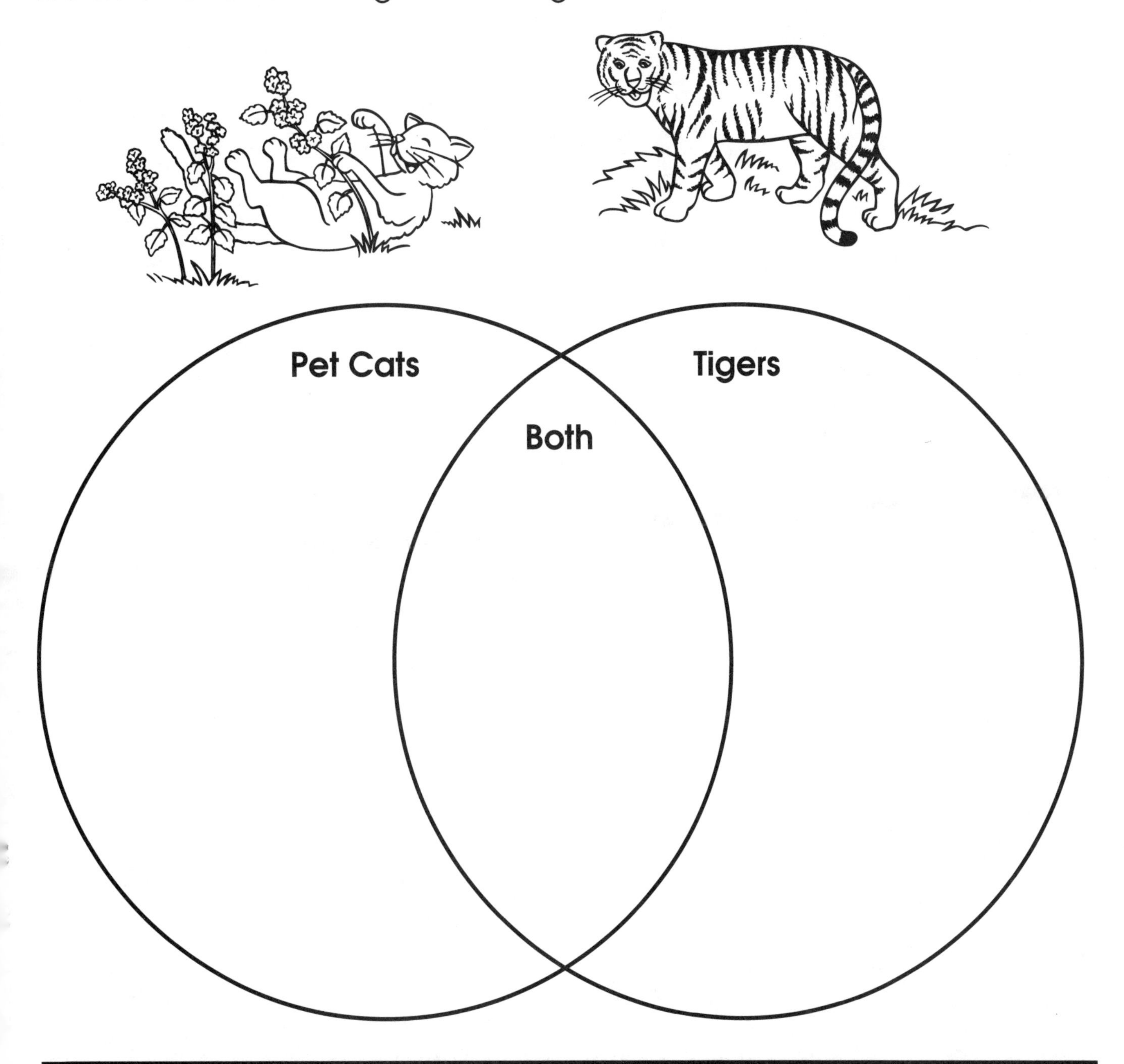

Similes

A **simile** is a figure of speech that compares two different things. The words **like** or **as** are used in similes.

Directions: Draw a line to the picture that goes with each set of words.

as hard as a

as hungry as a

as quiet as a

as soft as a

as easy as

as light as a

as tiny as an

Analogies

Analogies compare how things are related to each other.

Directions: Complete the other analogies.

Example: Finger is to **hand** as **toe** is to **foot**.

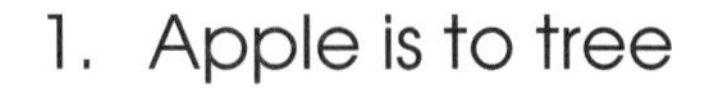

1. Apple is to tree as flower is to __________ .

2. Tire is to car as wheel is to __________ .

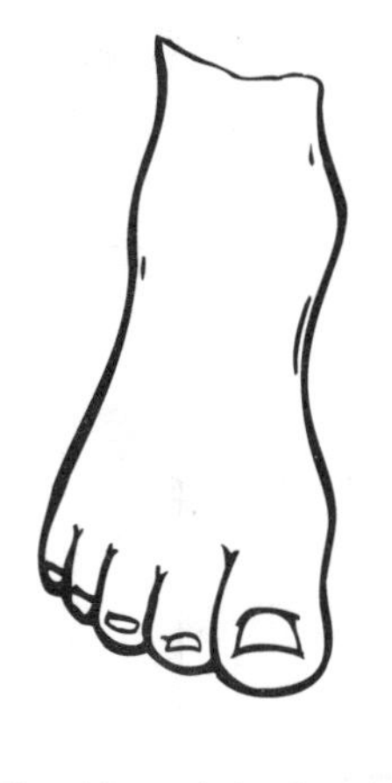

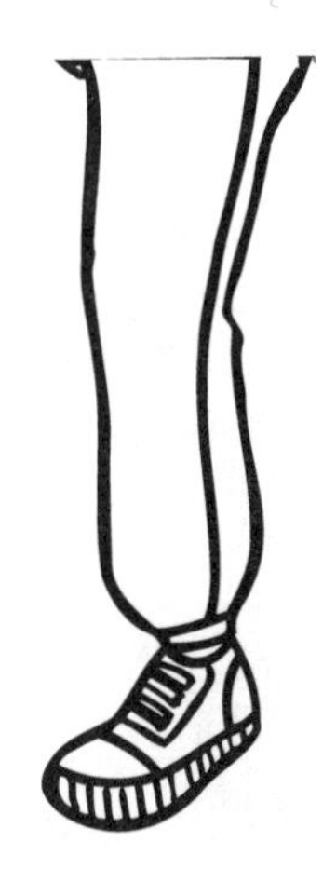

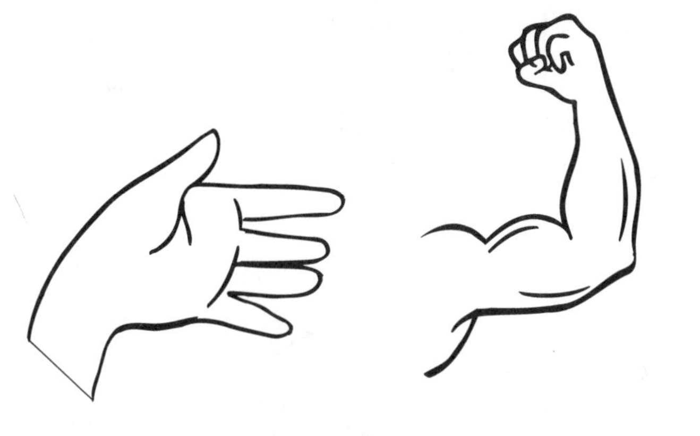

3. Foot is to leg as hand is to __________ .

Finding Analogies: Shapes

Example:

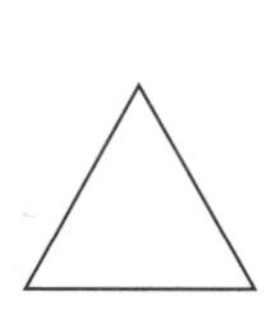
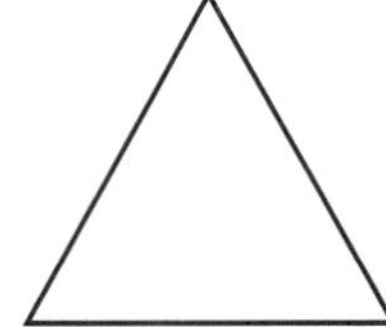
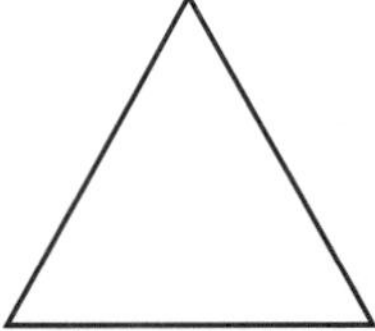
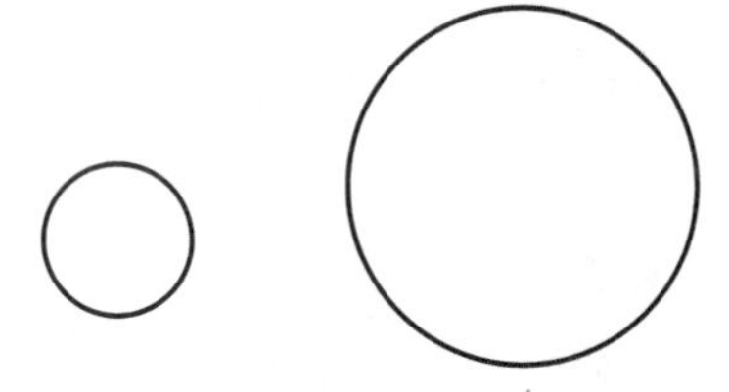

A **little triangle** is to a **big triangle** as a **little circle** is to a **big circle**

Directions: Look at each set of shapes. Draw the shape to complete the analogy.

1. 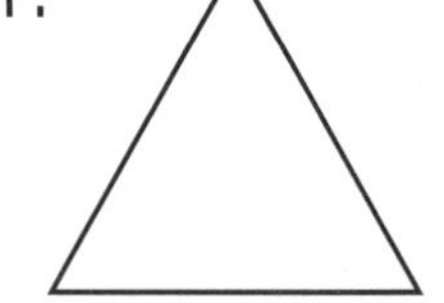 as 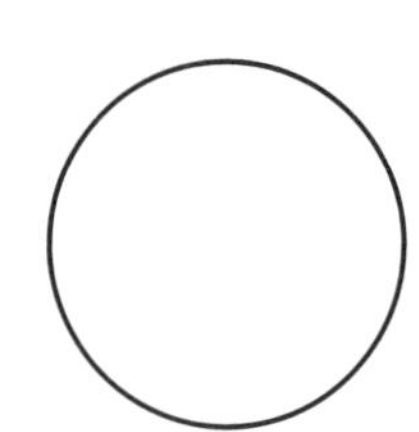

2.   as 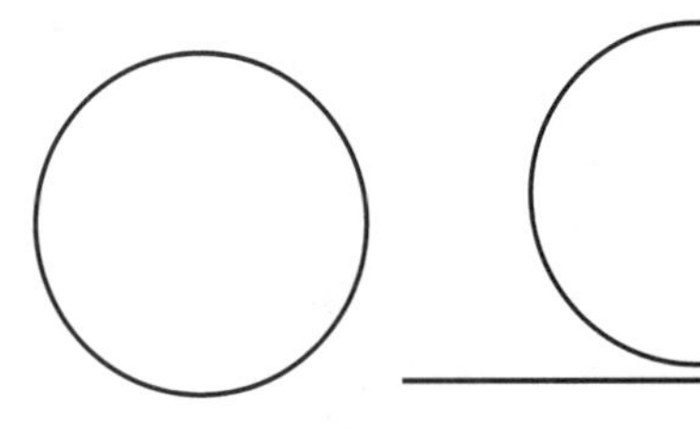

3. 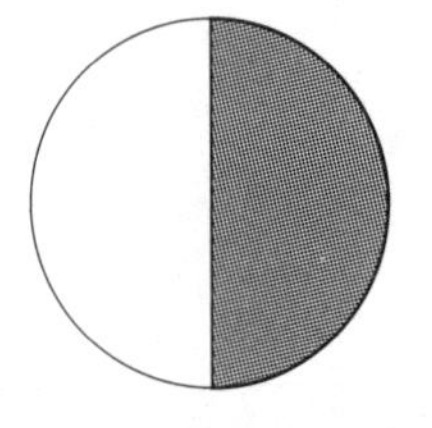  as 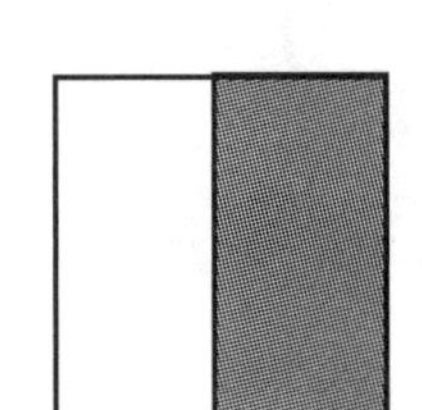 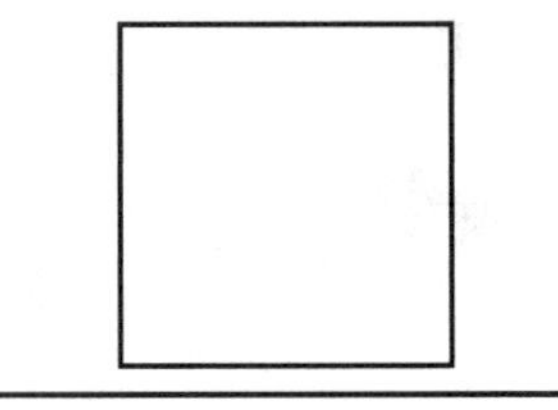

Classifying

Classifying is putting similar things into groups.

Directions: Write each word from the word box on the correct line.

baby	donkey	whale	family	fox
uncle	goose	grandfather	kangaroo	policeman

people

1. ____________________
2. ____________________
3.  ____________________   
4. ____________________
5. ____________________

animals

1. ____________________
2. ____________________
3. ____________________
4. ____________________
5. ____________________

Classifying: A Rainy Day

Directions: Read the story. Then circle the objects Jonathan needs to stay dry.

It is raining. Jonathan wants to play outdoors. What should he wear to stay dry? What should he carry to stay dry?

Classifying: Words

Dapper Dog is going camping.

Directions: Draw an **X** on the word in each row that does not belong in that group.

1.	flashlight	candle	radio	fire
2.	shirt	pants	coat	bat
3.	cow	car	bus	train
4.	beans	hot dog	ball	bread
5.	gloves	hat	book	boots
6.	fork	butter	cup	plate
7.	book	ball	bat	milk
8.	dogs	bees	flies	ants

Classifying

Directions: The words in each box form a group. Choose the word from the word box that describes each group and write it on the line.

clothes	family	noises	colors	flowers
fruits	animals	coins	toys	

rose buttercup tulip daisy __________	crash bang ring pop __________	mother father sister brother __________
puzzle wagon blocks doll __________	green purple blue red __________	grapes orange apple plum __________
shirt socks dress coat __________	dime penny nickel quarter __________	dog horse elephant moose __________

Classifying

Directions: In each box, circle the word that names the group the other words belong in. The first one is done for you.

cookies cakes (sweets) candy	shapes square circle triangle
diamond pearl ruby jewels	piano instruments drum horn
metals copper iron gold	lambs babies kittens puppies
door house floor window	pineapple coconut banana fruits
canary birds robin parrot	tiger jaguar lion cats
tree plants grass daffodil	coffee milk drinks juice
rain water steam ice	corn beans vegetables squash

Classifying

Directions: After each sentence, write three words from the word box that belong.

eagle	whistle	horn	frog
dime	wheel	throat	ball
sun	airplane	penny	marble
banana	balloon	dollar	heart
camel	grasshopper	horse	kangaroo
chipmunk	lemon	butterfly	mouth

1. These are things that can hop.

_______________ _______________ _______________

2. These things all have wings.

_______________ _______________ _______________

3. These are types of money.

_______________ _______________ _______________

4. These are four-legged animals.

_______________ _______________ _______________

5. These are parts of your body.

_______________ _______________ _______________

6. These things are yellow.

_______________ _______________ _______________

7. These things can roll.

_______________ _______________ _______________

8. These are things you can blow.

_______________ _______________ _______________

Sequencing: Packing Bags

Directions: Read about packing bags. Then number the objects in the order they should be packed.

Cans are heavy. Put them in first. Then put in boxes. Now, put in the apple. Put the bread in last.

Sequencing: 1, 2, 3, 4!

Directions: Write numbers by each sentence to show the order of the story.

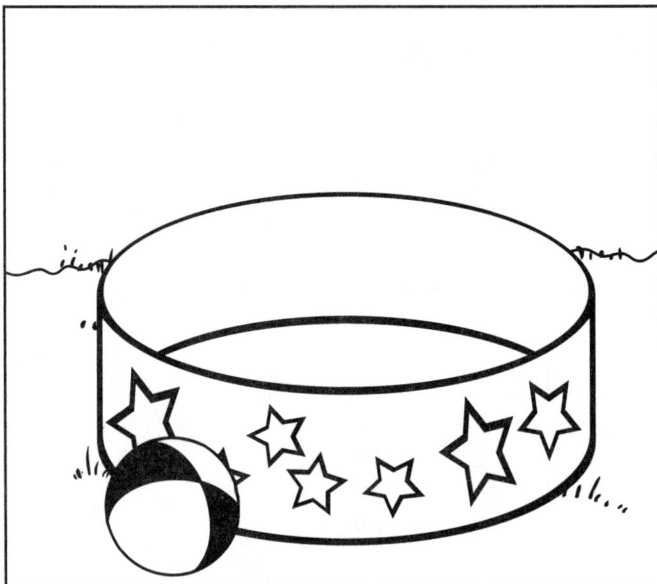

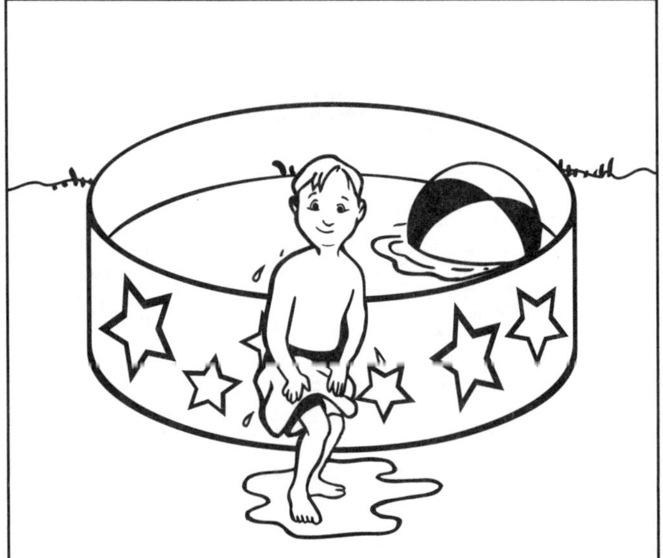

The pool is empty. __________ Ben plays in the pool. __________

Ben gets out. __________ Ben fills the pool. __________

Sequencing: Making a Snowman

Directions: Read about how to make a snowman. Then follow the instructions.

It is fun to make a snowman. First, find things for the snowman's eyes and nose. Dress warmly. Then go outdoors. Roll a big snowball. Then roll another to put on top of it. Now, roll a small snowball for the head. Put on the snowman's face.

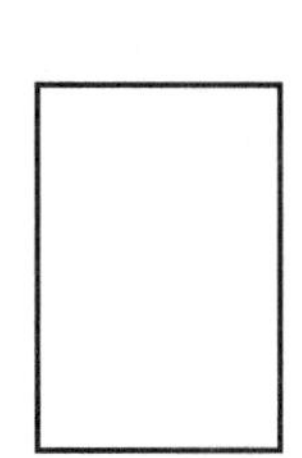

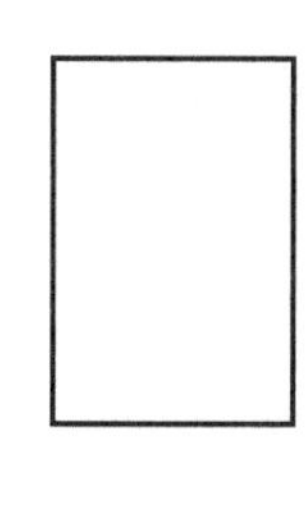

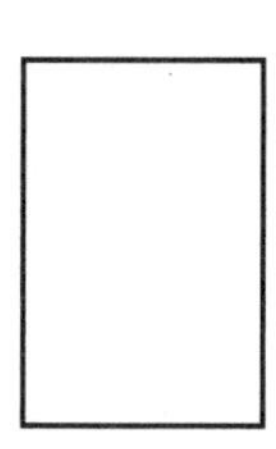

1. Number the pictures in order.

2. Write two things to do before going outdoors.

1) ______________________________

2) ______________________________

Sequencing: Why Does It Rain?

Directions: Read about rain. Then follow the instructions.

Clouds are made up of little drops of ice and water. They push and bang into each other. Then they join together to make bigger drops and begin to fall. More raindrops cling to them. They become heavy and fall quickly to the ground.

Write **first**, **second**, **third**, **fourth** and **fifth** to put the events in order.

______________ More raindrops cling to them.

______________ Clouds are made up of little drops of ice and water.

______________ They join together and make bigger drops that begin to fall.

______________ The drops of ice and water bang into each other.

______________ The drops become heavy and fall quickly to the ground.

Following Directions

Following directions carefully and doing things in the correct order are very important when you are following a recipe.

Directions: Follow the recipe to make goop. Then answer the questions.

Goop

1. Mix equal parts of cornstarch and water. Begin with 1 cup each.
2. Mix it the best you can. Watch out — it's tricky!
3. Pour the mixture onto a tray.
4. Try to squeeze it, pick it up and draw on it.
5. Have fun!

1. What does the goop look like? ____________________

2. How does the goop feel? ____________________

3. What does the goop smell like? ____________________

4. Does your goop make any noise? ____________________

Following Directions: Draw a House

Nick and Miguel like to draw pictures using shapes. You can help them draw a house.

Directions: Follow the instructions to create a geometric house in the bubble.

1. Draw a big square in the middle of the bubble.
2. On top of the square, draw a big triangle.
3. Inside the square, draw small squares on the left and right sides.
4. Between the two small squares, draw an upright rectangle.
5. On the rectangle, draw a small hexagon at the top.
6. Draw your face looking out the hexagon window.

Following Directions: How to Treat a Ladybug

Directions: Read about how to treat ladybugs. Then follow the instructions.

Ladybugs are shy. If you see a ladybug, sit very still. Hold out your arm. Maybe the ladybug will fly to you. If it does, talk softly. Do not touch it. It will fly away when it is ready.

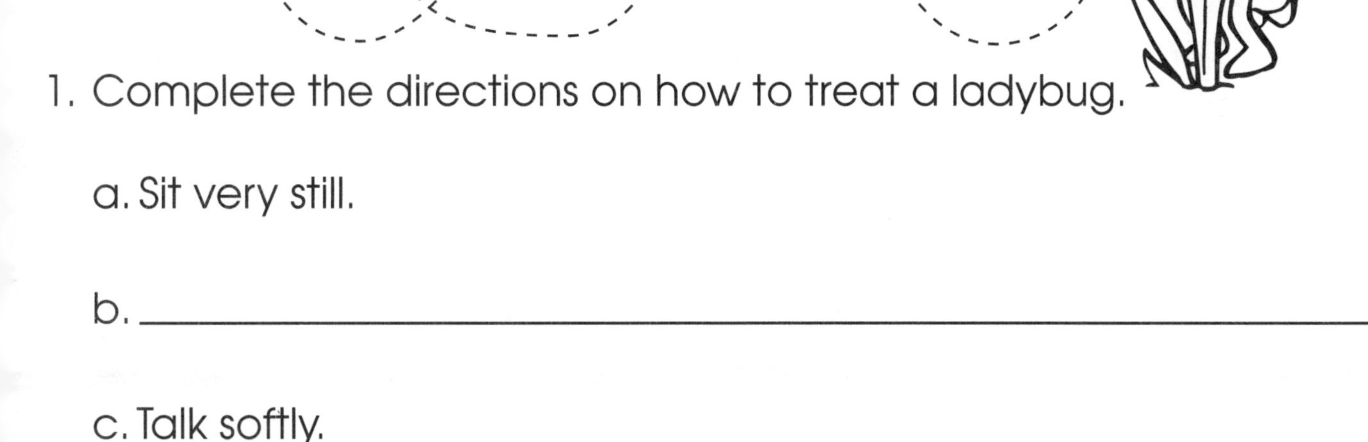

1. Complete the directions on how to treat a ladybug.

   a. Sit very still.

   b. ______________________________

   c. Talk softly.

   d. ______________________________

2. Ladybugs are red. They have black spots. Color the ladybug.

Following Directions

Directions: Read the story. Answer the questions. Try the recipe.

Cows Give Us Milk

Cows live on a farm. The farmer milks the cow to get milk. Many things are made from milk. We make ice cream, sour cream, cottage cheese and butter from milk. Butter is fun to make! You can learn to make your own butter. First, you need cream. Put the cream in a jar and shake it. Then you need to pour off the liquid. Next, you put the butter in a bowl. Add a little salt and stir! Finally, spread it on crackers and eat!

1. What animal gives us milk? ______________________________

2. What 4 things are made from milk?

   ____________ ____________ ____________ ____________

3. What did the story teach you to make? ______________________

4. Put the steps in order. Place 1, 2, 3 or 4 by the sentence.

   _____ Spread the butter on crackers and eat!

   _____ Shake cream in a jar.

   _____ Start with cream.

   _____ Add salt to the butter.

Comprehension: Types of Tops

The **main idea** is the most important point or idea in a story.

Directions: Read about tops. Then answer the questions.

Tops come in all sizes. Some tops are made of wood. Some tops are made of tin. All tops do the same thing. They spin! Do you have a top?

1. Circle the main idea:

   There are many kinds of tops.

   Some tops are made of wood.

2. What are some tops made of? ______________________

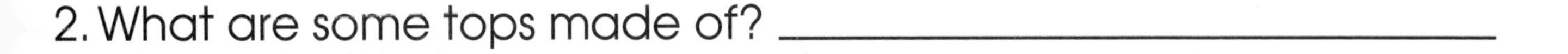

3. What do all tops do? ______________________

Comprehension: Paper-Bag Puppets

Directions: Read about paper-bag puppets. Then follow the instructions.

It is easy to make a hand puppet. You need a small paper bag. You need colored paper. You need glue. You need scissors. Are you ready?

1. Circle the main idea:

   You need scissors.

   Making a hand puppet is easy.

2. Write the four objects you need to make a paper-bag puppet.

   1) ______________________________

   2) ______________________________

   3) ______________________________

   4) ______________________________

3. Draw a face on the paper-bag puppet.

Main Idea

Directions: Read about spiders. Then answer the questions.

Many people think spiders are insects, but they are not. Spiders are the same size as insects, and they look like insects in some ways. But there are three ways to tell a spider from an insect. Insects have six legs, and spiders have eight legs. Insects have antennae, but spiders do not. An insect's body is divided into three parts; a spider's body is divided into only two parts.

1. The main idea of this story is:

   Spiders are like insects.
   Spiders are like insects in some ways, but they are not insects.

2. What are three ways to tell a spider from an insect?

   1) ______________________________

   2) ______________________________

   3) ______________________________

Circle the correct answer.

3. Spiders are the same size as insects. True False

Drawing Conclusions

Directions: On the top line by each picture, write the word from the word box that describes the person in the picture. Then write a clue from the picture that helped you decide.

chef	astronaut	teacher

Answer: ______________________________

Clue: ______________________________

Answer: ______________________________

Clue: ______________________________

Answer: ______________________________

Clue: ______________________________

Making Inferences

Directions: Read the story. Then answer the questions.

Mrs. Sweet looked forward to a visit from her niece, Candy. In the morning, she cleaned her house. She also baked a cherry pie. An hour before Candy was to arrive, the phone rang. Mrs. Sweet said, "I understand." When she hung up the phone, she looked very sad.

1. Who do you think called Mrs. Sweet?

____

____

2. How do you know that?

____

____

3. Why is Mrs. Sweet sad?

____

____

Making Deductions: Sports

Children all over the world like to play sports. They like many different kinds of sports: football, soccer, basketball, softball, in-line skating, swimming and more.

Directions: Read the clues. Draw dots and **X**'s on the chart to match the children with their sports.

	swimming	football	soccer	basketball	baseball	in-line skating
J.J.						
Zoe						
Andy						
Amber						
Raul						
Sierra						

Clues

1. Zoe hates football.
2. Andy likes basketball.
3. Raul likes to pitch in his favorite sport.
4. J.J. likes to play what Zoe hates.
5. Amber is good at kicking the ball to her teammates.
6. Sierra needs a pool for her favorite sport.

Predicting: A Rainy Game

Predicting is telling what is likely to happen based on the facts.

Directions: Read the story. Then check each sentence below that tells how the story could end.

One cloudy day, Juan and his baseball team, the Bears, played the Crocodiles. It was the last half of the fifth inning, and it started to rain. The coaches and umpires had to decide what to do.

________ They kept playing until nine innings were finished.

________ They ran for cover and waited until the rain stopped.

________ Each player grabbed an umbrella and returned to the field to finish the game.

________ They canceled the game and played it another day.

________ They acted like crocodiles and slid around the wet bases.

________ The coaches played the game while the players sat in the dugout.

Sequencing/Predicting: A Game for Cats

Directions: Read about what cats like. Then follow the instructions.

Cats like to play with paper bags. Pull a paper bag open. Take everything out. Now, lay it on its side.

1. Write 1, 2 and 3 to put the pictures in order.

2. In box 4, draw what you think the cat will do.

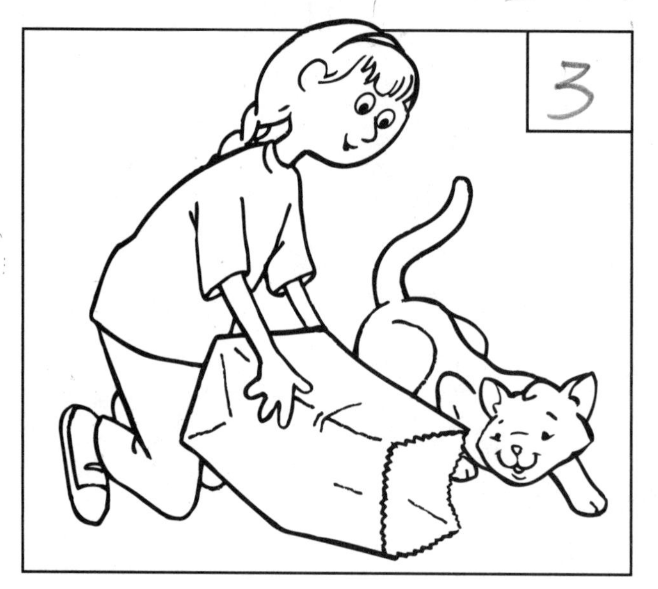

Predicting: Dog-Gone!

Directions: Read the story. Then follow the instructions.

Scotty and Simone were washing their dog, Willis. His fur was wet. Their hands were wet. Willis did NOT like to be wet. Scotty dropped the soap. Simone picked it up and let go of Willis. Uh-oh!

1. Write what happened next.

2. Draw what happened next.

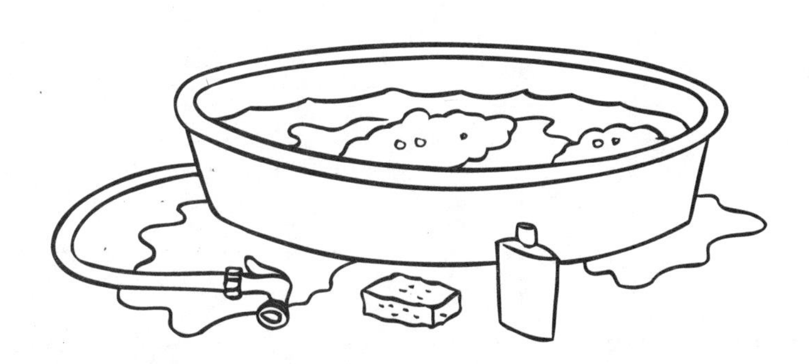

Predicting: Oops!

Directions: Look at the pictures on the left. On the right, draw and write what you predict will happen next.

Reading for Details

Directions: Draw a line from the sign to the sentence that tells about it.

1. If you see this sign, watch out for trains.

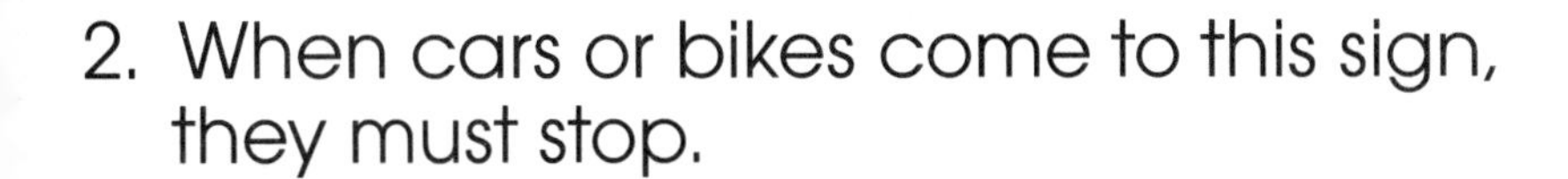

2. When cars or bikes come to this sign, they must stop.

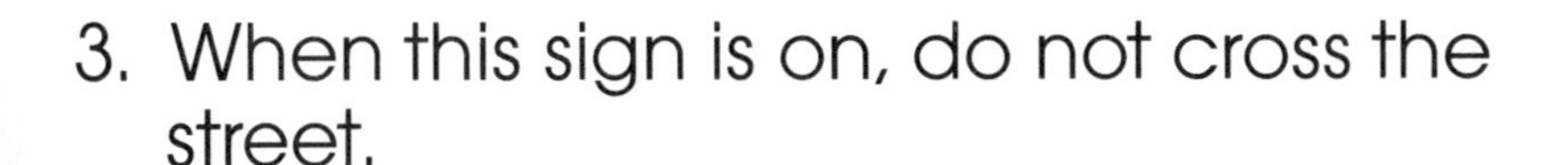

3. When this sign is on, do not cross the street.

4. This sign tells you to stay out of the yard.

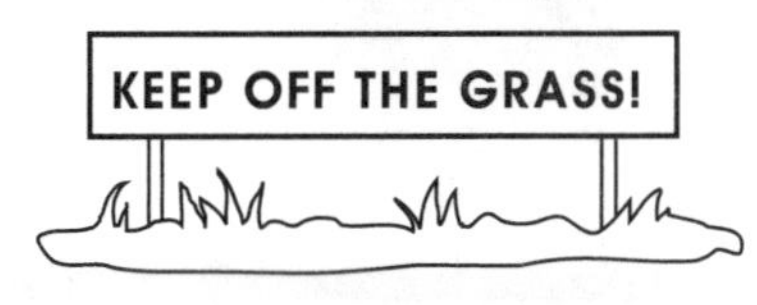

5. If you see this sign, do not eat or drink what is inside!

6. This sign warns you that it is not safe. Stay away!

7. This sign says you are not allowed to come in.

Comprehension: Fish Come in Many Colors

Directions: Read about the color of fish. Then follow the instructions.

All fish live in water. Fish that live at the top are blue, green or black. Fish that live down deep are silver or red. The colors make it hard to see the fish.

1. List the colors of fish at the top.

_____________________ _____________________ _____________________

2. List the two colors of fish that live down deep.

_____________________ _____________________

3. Color the top fish and the bottom fish the correct colors.

Reading for Details

Directions: Read the story about bike safety. Answer the questions below the story.

Mike has a red bike. He likes his bike. Mike wears a helmet. Mike wears knee pads and elbow pads. They keep him safe. Mike stops at signs. Mike looks both ways. Mike is safe on his bike.

1. What color is Mike's bike? ______________________________

2. Which sentence in the story tells why Mike wears pads and a helmet? Write it here.

   ____

3. What else does Mike do to keep safe?

   He ____________________ at signs and ____________________ both ways.

Recalling Details: Nikki's Pets

Directions: Read about Nikki's pets. Then answer the questions.

Nikki has two cats, Tiger and Sniffer, and two dogs, Spot and Wiggles. Tiger is an orange striped cat who likes to sleep under a big tree and pretend she is a real tiger. Sniffer is a gray cat who likes to sniff the flowers in Nikki's garden. Spot is a Dalmatian with many black spots. Wiggles is a big furry brown dog who wiggles all over when he is happy.

1. Which dog is brown and furry? ____________________

2. What color is Tiger? ____________________

3. What kind of dog is Spot? ____________________

4. Which cat likes to sniff flowers? ____________________

5. Where does Tiger like to sleep? ____________________

6. Who wiggles all over when he is happy? ____________________

Comprehension: How to Meet a Dog

Directions: Read about how to meet a dog. Then follow the instructions.

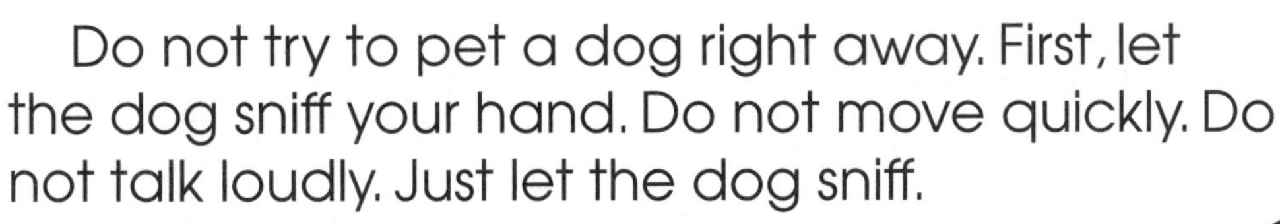

Do not try to pet a dog right away. First, let the dog sniff your hand. Do not move quickly. Do not talk loudly. Just let the dog sniff.

1. Predict what the dog will let you do if it likes you.

____

____

2. What should you let the dog do? ______________________

____

3. Name three things you should not do when you meet a dog.

1) ____

2) ____

3) ____

Reading Comprehension

Directions: Read the story. Then answer the questions.

You can grow a **citrus** (SIT-russ) plant in your home. Citrus fruits include lemons, oranges and grapefruits. Collect seeds from a piece of fruit. Wash the seeds with water and let them dry for three days. Next, fill a four-inch pot with potting soil. You can buy soil at a garden store. Plant the seeds about one-inch deep and water thoroughly.

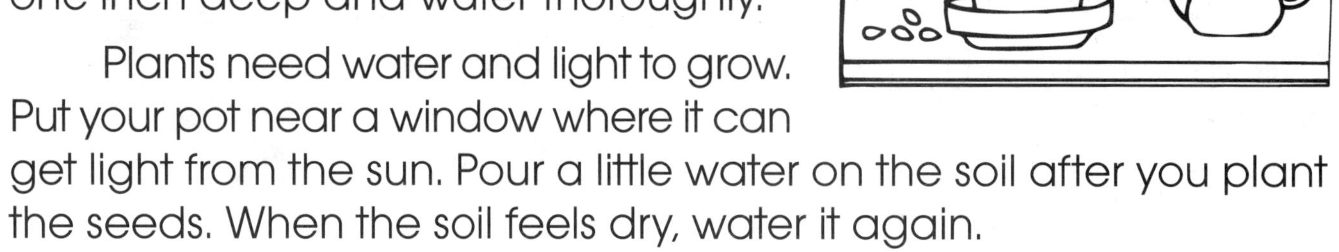

Plants need water and light to grow. Put your pot near a window where it can get light from the sun. Pour a little water on the soil after you plant the seeds. When the soil feels dry, water it again.

1. What are some kinds of citrus fruits? ______________________________

____

2. How deep should you plant the seeds in the soil? ______________

____

3. Name two things that plants need to grow.

   1) ______________________ 2) ______________________

4. How do you know when to water your plant? ________________

____

Reading Comprehension

Directions: Read the story. Then answer the questions.

Weed is the word used for any plant that grows where it is not wanted. Grasses that grow in your flower or vegetable garden are weeds. An unwanted flower growing in your lawn is also a weed. Dandelions are this kind of weed.

People do not plant weeds. They grow very fast. If you do not pull them out or kill them, weeds will crowd out the plants that you want to grow. The seeds of many kinds of weeds are spread by the wind. Birds and other animals also carry weed seeds.

1. A weed is any plant that grows ______________________________

____.

2. One kind of flowering weed is the ______________________________

____.

3. Two things that spread the seeds of weeds are

______________________ and ______________________.

Fact and Opinion: Games!

A **fact** is something that can be proven. An **opinion** is a feeling or belief about something and cannot be proven.

Directions: Read these sentences about different games. Then write **F** next to each fact and **O** next to each opinion.

_____ 1. Tennis is cool!

_____ 2. There are red and black markers in a Checkers game.

_____ 3. In football, a touchdown is worth six points.

_____ 4. Being a goalie in soccer is easy.

_____ 5. A yo-yo moves on a string.

_____ 6. June's sister looks like the queen on the card.

_____ 7. The six kids need three more players for a baseball team.

_____ 8. Table tennis is more fun than court tennis.

_____ 9. Hide-and-Seek is a game that can be played outdoors or indoors.

_____ 10. Play money is used in many board games.

Fact and Opinion: Recycling

Directions: Read about recycling. Then follow the instructions.

What do you throw away every day? What could you do with these things? You could change an old greeting card into a new card. You could make a puppet with an old paper bag. Old buttons make great refrigerator magnets. You can plant seeds in plastic cups. Cardboard tubes make perfect rockets. So, use your imagination!

1. Write **F** next to each fact and **O** next to each opinion.

_____ Cardboard tubes are ugly.

_____ Buttons can be made into refrigerator magnets.

_____ An old greeting card can be changed into a new card.

_____ Paper-bag puppets are cute.

_____ Seeds can be planted in plastic cups.

_____ Rockets can be made from cardboard tubes.

2. What could you do with a cardboard tube? ____________________

____

Fact and Opinion: A Bounty of Birds

Directions: Read the story. Then follow the instructions.

Tashi's family likes to go to the zoo. Her favorite animals are all the different kinds of birds. Tashi likes birds because they can fly, they have colorful feathers and they make funny noises.

Write **F** next to each fact and **O** next to each opinion.

_____ 1. Birds have two feet.

_____ 2. All birds lay eggs.

_____ 3. Parrots are too noisy.

_____ 4. All birds have feathers and wings.

_____ 5. It would be great to be a bird and fly south for the winter.

_____ 6. Birds have hard beaks or bills instead of teeth.

_____ 7. Pigeons are fun to watch.

_____ 8. Some birds cannot fly.

_____ 9. Parakeets make good pets.

_____ 10. A penguin is a bird.

Fantasy and Reality

Something that is **real** could actually happen. Something that is **fantasy** is not real. It could not happen.

Examples: Real: Dogs can bark.
Fantasy: Dogs can fly.

Directions: Look at the sentences below. Write **real** or **fantasy** next to each sentence.

1. My cat can talk to me. __________
2. Witches ride brooms and cast spells. __________
3. Dad can mow the lawn. __________
4. I ride a magic carpet to school. __________
5. I have a man-eating tree. __________
6. My sandbox has toys in it. __________
7. Mom can bake chocolate chip cookies. __________
8. Mark has tomatoes and corn in his garden. __________
9. Jack grows candy and ice cream in his garden. __________
10. I make my bed everyday. __________

Write your own **real** sentence. __________

____

Write your own **fantasy** sentence. __________

____

Fiction and Nonfiction: Which Is It?

Directions: Read about fiction and nonfiction books. Then follow the instructions.

There are many kinds of books. Some books have make-believe stories about princesses and dragons. Some books contain poetry and rhymes, like Mother Goose. These are fiction.

Some books contain facts about space and plants. And still other books have stories about famous people in history like Abraham Lincoln. These are nonfiction.

Write **F** for fiction and **NF** for nonfiction.

______ 1. nursery rhyme

______ 2. fairy tale

______ 3. true life story of a famous athlete

______ 4. Aesop's fables

______ 5. dictionary entry about foxes

______ 6. weather report

______ 7. story about a talking tree

______ 8. story about how a tadpole becomes a frog

______ 9. story about animal habitats

______ 10. riddles and jokes

Types of Books: Fiction and Nonfiction

Directions: Cut out the titles and place them in the correct category.

Fiction	Nonfiction

cut ✂ -

The Three Little Pigs	How to Grow a Garden
All About Trees	The Life of George Washington
Spaceboy Sammy	Jack and the Beanstalk
Curious Cammy	Farm Life
Arts and Crafts	Little Red Riding Hood

This page is blank for the cutting exercise
on the previous page.

Fiction/Nonfiction: Heavy Hitters

Fiction is a make-believe story. **Nonfiction** is a true story.

Directions: Read the stories about two famous baseball players. Then write **fiction** or **nonfiction** on the baseball bats.

In 1998, Mark McGwire played for the St. Louis Cardinals. He liked to hit home runs. On September 27, 1998, he hit home run number 70, to set a new record for the most home runs hit in one season. The old record was set in 1961 by Roger Maris, who later played for the St. Louis Cardinals (1967 to 1968), when he hit 61 home runs.

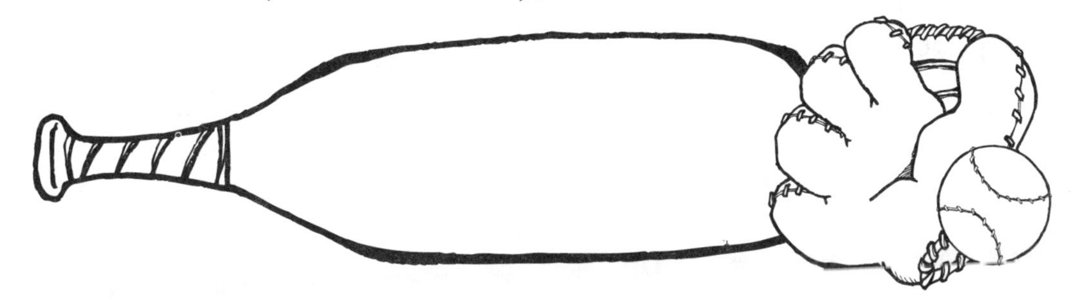

The Mighty Casey played baseball for the Mudville Nine and was the greatest of all baseball players. He could hit the cover off the ball with the power of a hurricane. But, when the Mudville Nine was behind 4 to 2 in the championship game, Mighty Casey struck out with the bases loaded. There was no joy in Mudville that day, because the Mudville Nine had lost the game.

Parts of a Book

A book has many parts. The title is the name of the book. The author is the person who wrote the words. The illustrator is the person who drew the pictures. The table of contents is located at the beginning to list what is in the book. The glossary is a little dictionary in the back to help you with unfamiliar words. Books are often divided into smaller sections of information called chapters.

Directions: Look at one of your books. Write the parts you see below.

The title of my book is ______________________________

The author is ______________________________

The illustrator is ______________________________

My book has a table of contents. Yes or No

My book has a glossary. Yes or No

My book is divided into chapters. Yes or No

Story Webs

All short stories have a plot, characters, a setting and a theme.

The **plot** is what the story is about.

The **characters** are the people or animals in the story.

The **setting** is where and when the story occurs.

The **theme** is the message or idea of the story.

Directions: Use the story "Snow White" to complete this story web.

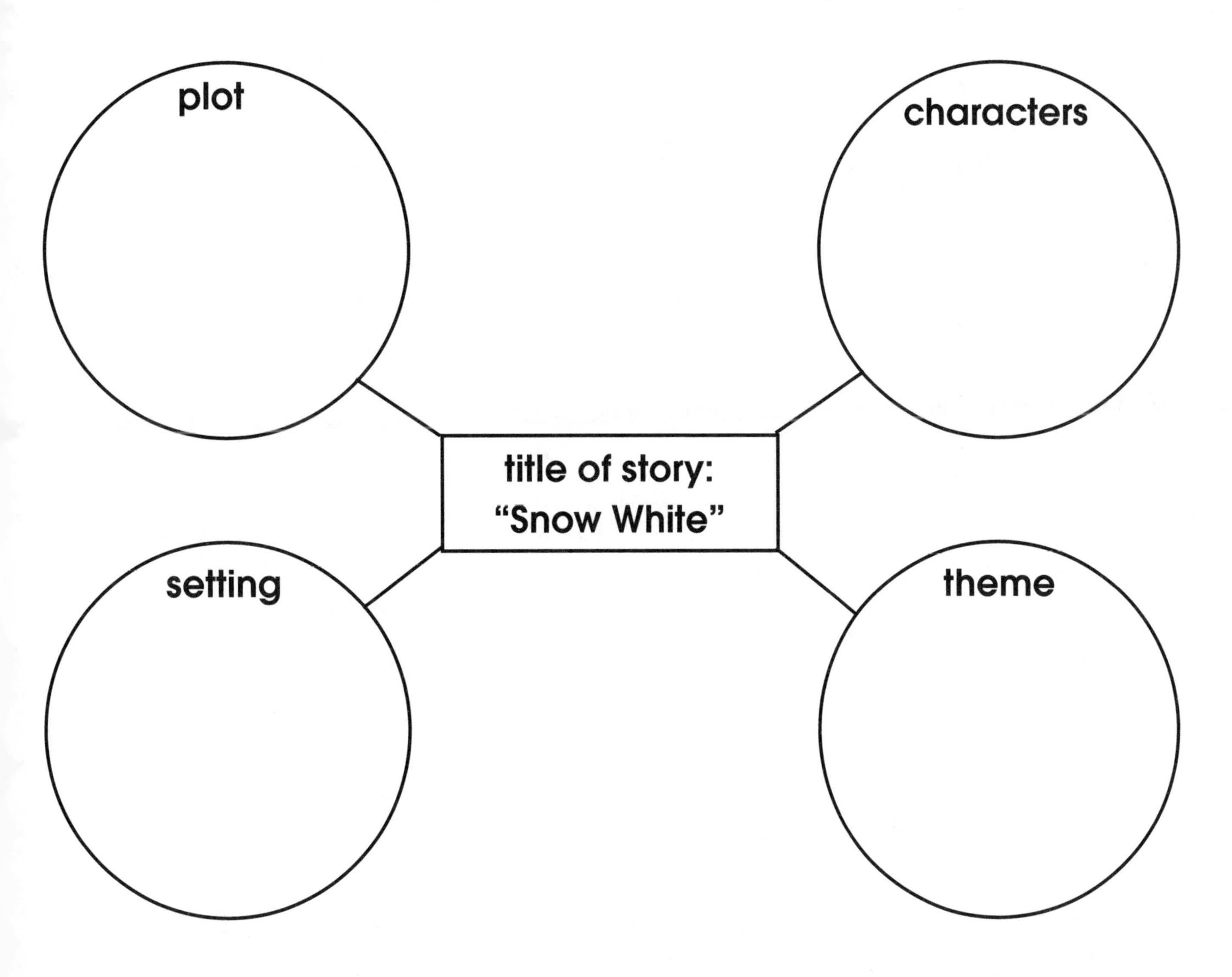

Tracking: Where Does She Go?

Every morning when Lisa wakes up, she goes somewhere. Find out where she goes.

Directions: Read the sentences. Follow the instructions.

1. On Monday, Lisa needs bread. Use a red crayon to mark her path from her house to that building. Where does she go? ___________________

2. On Tuesday, Lisa wants to read books. Use a green crayon to mark her path. Where does she go? ___________________

3. On Wednesday, Lisa wants to swing. Use a yellow crayon to mark her path. Where does she go? ___________________

4. On Thursday, Lisa wants to buy stamps. Use a black crayon to mark her path. Where does she go? ___________________

5. On Friday, Lisa wants to get money. Use a purple crayon to mark her path. Where does she go? ___________________

Tracking: Sequencing

Directions: Look at the paths you drew for Lisa on page 150. Number, in order, the places that Lisa went each day. Draw a line to connect the place with the day of the week.

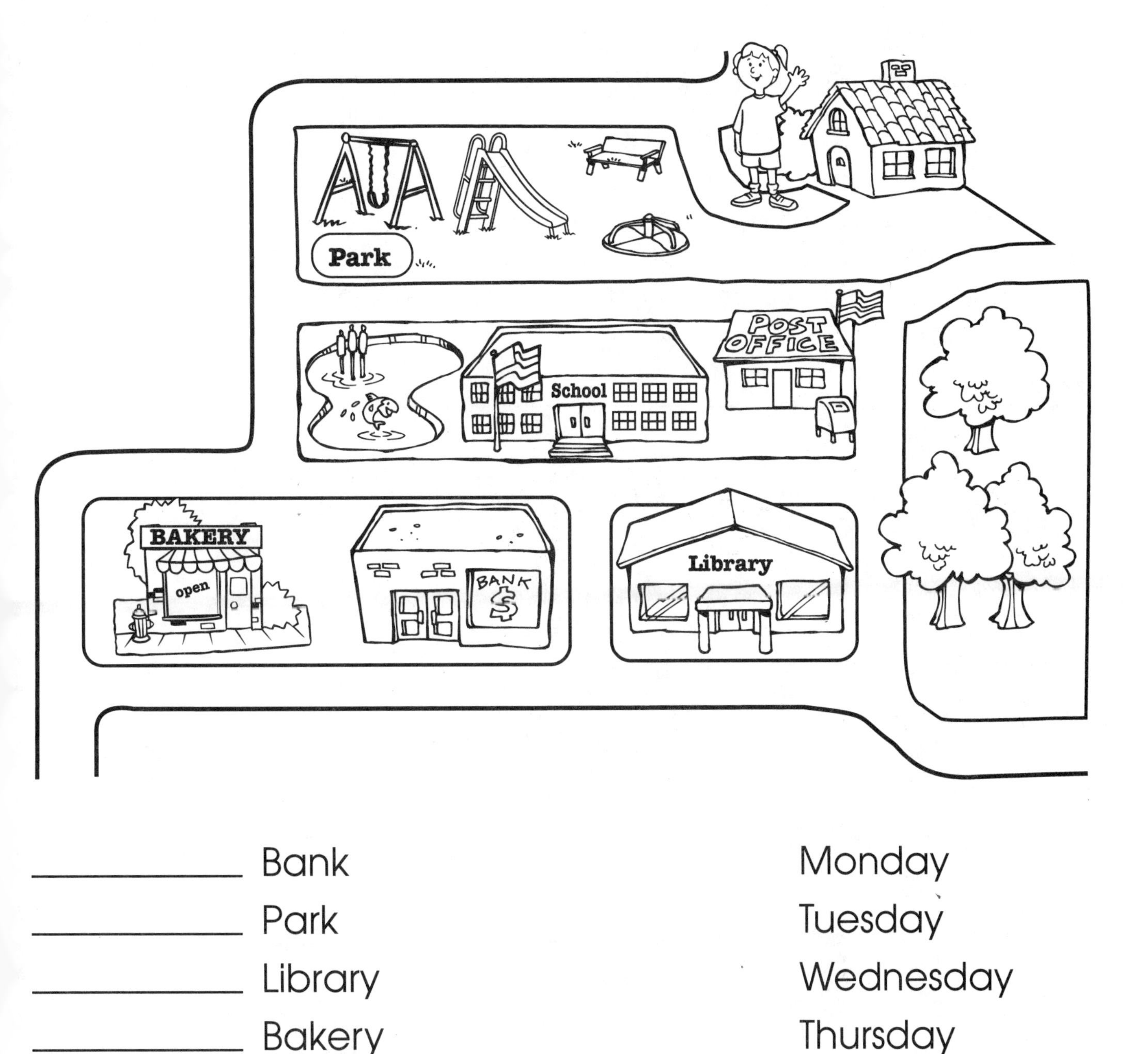

____________	Bank	Monday
____________	Park	Tuesday
____________	Library	Wednesday
____________	Bakery	Thursday
____________	Post Office	Friday

Tracking: With a Map

Tashi and Lamont are neighbors. Sometimes they walk to school together. One day, Tashi went to the library after school. She didn't walk home with Lamont.

Directions: Read the sentences. Draw Tashi's path in blue and Lamont's path in red.

Tashi left her house in the morning
and went to school.
She went to the library after school.
Then she went home.
Lamont left his house in the morning and went to school.
He went to the park.
Then he went home.

Directions

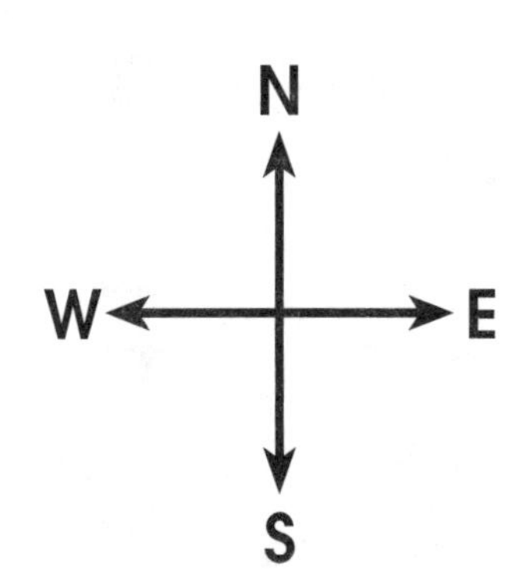

We give people directions using the terms north, south, east and west.

Directions: Follow the directions to help Patrick get to the park.

Go south to the church.

Go east to the pet store.

Go north to the bank.

Go east to the flower garden.

Go south to the park.

Tracking: With a Map

Directions: Study the map of the United States. Follow the instructions.

1. Draw a star on the state where you live.
2. Draw a line from your state to the Atlantic Ocean.
3. Draw a triangle in the Gulf of Mexico.
4. Draw a circle in the Pacific Ocean.
5. Color each state that borders your state a different color.

Learning Dictionary Skills

Directions: Look at this page from a picture dictionary. Then answer the questions.

table

Furniture with legs and a flat top.

tail

A slender part that is on the back of an animal.

teacher

A person who teaches lessons.

telephone

A machine that sends and receives sounds.

ticket

A paper slip or card.

tiger

An animal with stripes.

1. Who is a person who teaches lessons? ____________________

2. What is the name of an animal with stripes? ____________________

3. What is a piece of furniture with legs and a flat top? ____________

4. What is the definition of a ticket?

____

5. What is a machine that sends and receives sounds?

____

Learning Dictionary Skills

The guide words at the top of a page in a dictionary tell you what the first and last words on the page will be. Only words that come in ABC order between those two words will be on that page. Guide words help you find the page you need to look up a word.

Directions: Write each word from the box in ABC order between each pair of guide words.

faint	far	fence	feed	farmer
fan	feet	farm	family	face

face **fence**

______________________ ______________________

______________________ ______________________

______________________ ______________________

______________________ ______________________

______________________ ______________________

Learning Dictionary Skills

When words have more than one meaning, the meanings are numbered in a dictionary.

Directions: Read the meanings of **tag**. Write the number of the correct definition after each sentence.

tag

1. A small strip or tab attached to something else.
2. To label.
3. To follow closely and constantly.
4. A game of chase.

1. We will play a game of tag after we study. ____________________
2. I will tag this coat with its price. ____________________
3. My little brother will tag along with us. ____________________
4. My mother already took off the price tag. ____________________
5. The tag on the puppy said, "For Sale." ____________________
6. Do not tag that tree. ____________________

Library Skills

A library is a place filled with books. People can borrow the books and take them home. When they are finished reading them, people return the books to the library. Most libraries have two sections: One is for adult books and one is for children's books. A librarian is there to help people find books.

Directions: Read the title of each library book. On each line, write **A** if the book is written for an adult or **C** if it is written for a child.

1. *Sam Squirrel Goes to the City* ________
2. *Barney Beagle Plays Baseball* ________
3. *Sammy's Silly Poems* ________
4. *Understanding Your Child...* ________
5. *Learn to Play Guitar* ________
6. *Bake Bread in Five Easy Steps* ________
7. *The Selling of the President* ________
8. *Jenny's First Party* ________

MATH

Less Than, Greater Than

Directions: The open mouth points to the larger number. The small point goes to the smaller number. Draw the symbol **<** or **>** to the correct number.

Example: 5  3

This means that 5 is greater than 3, and 3 is less than 5.

12 ◯ 2

16 ◯ 6

16 ◯ 15

1 ◯ 2

7 ◯ 1

19 ◯ 5

9 ◯ 6

11 ◯ 13

Adding 3 or More Numbers

Directions: Add all the numbers to find the sum. Draw pictures to help or break up the problem into two smaller problems.

Examples:

1 ○	2 + 5 → 7
2 ○○	2 + 4 → +6
+3 ○○○	13
6	

3	8	3	8
6	5	1	2
+2	+4	+5	+9
11	17	9	19

2	3	4	6
8	6	1	7
4	5	2	3
+3	+2	+5	+1

Addition: Football Math

Directions: Follow the plays of your favorite team.

A touchdown is worth 6 points.
A field goal is worth 3 points.

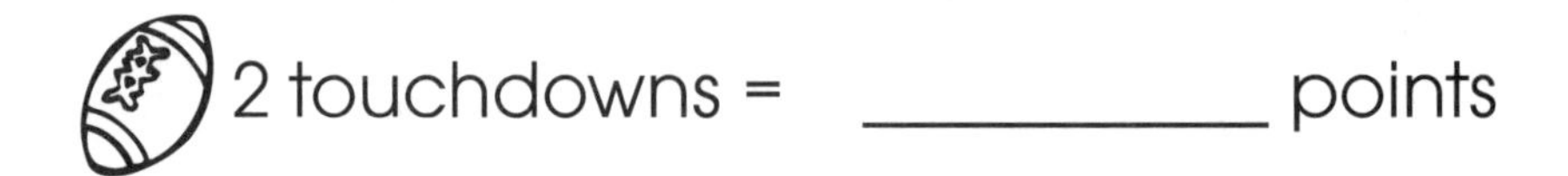
2 touchdowns = __________ points

1 touchdown + 2 field goals = __________ points

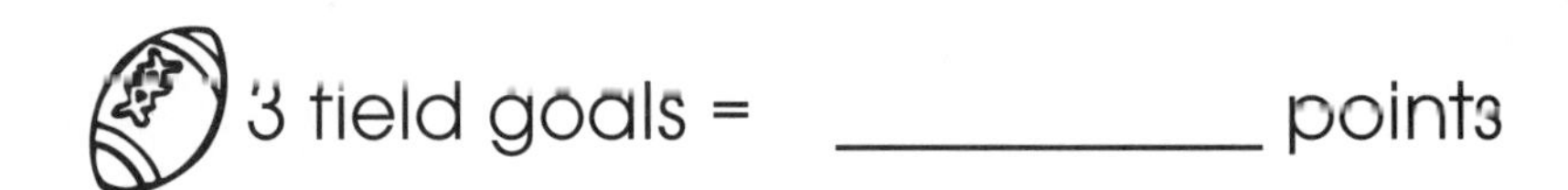
3 field goals = __________ points

1 field goal + 1 touchdown = __________ points

Your team won the game and made record-breaking points!
How many points did they score in all? __________

Addition Review

Directions: Fill in the blanks to solve the problems.

Example:

```
  1 2
+ 1 7
-----
  2 9
```

Think: What plus 7 equals 9?

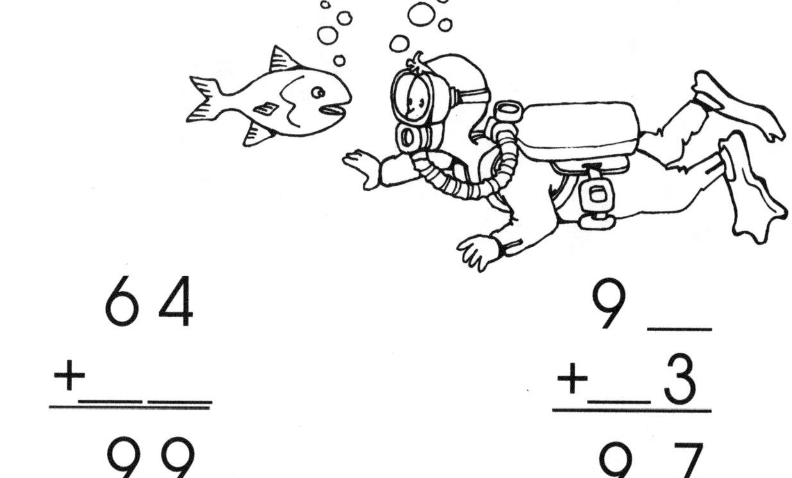

```
  3 __        6 4         9 __
+ __ 3      + __ __     + __ 3
------      -------     ------
  5 9         9 9         9 7
```

```
  4 __        5 __        2 __
+ 1 2       + __ 1      + __ 0
------      ------      ------
 __ 2         7 6         7 9
```

Subtraction

Subtraction means "taking away" or subtracting one number from another to find the difference. For example, **10 - 3 = 7**.

Directions: Subtract.

Example:

Subtract the ones.

$$\begin{array}{r} 39 \\ -24 \\ \hline 5 \end{array}$$

Subtract the tens.

$$\begin{array}{r} 39 \\ -24 \\ \hline 15 \end{array}$$

$$\begin{array}{r} 48 \\ -35 \\ \hline \end{array} \qquad \begin{array}{r} 95 \\ -22 \\ \hline \end{array} \qquad \begin{array}{r} 87 \\ -16 \\ \hline \end{array} \qquad \begin{array}{r} 55 \\ -43 \\ \hline \end{array}$$

$$\begin{array}{r} 37 \\ -14 \\ \hline \end{array} \qquad \begin{array}{r} 69 \\ -57 \\ \hline \end{array} \qquad \begin{array}{r} 44 \\ -23 \\ \hline \end{array} \qquad \begin{array}{r} 99 \\ -78 \\ \hline \end{array}$$

66 - 44 = ____

57 - 33 = ____

The yellow car traveled 87 miles per hour. The orange car traveled 66 miles per hour. How much faster was the yellow car traveling? ________

Subtraction Review

Directions: Fill in the blanks to solve the problems.

Example:

```
   2 _8_
-  _1_ 4
   -----
   1  4
```

Think: What minus 4 equals 4?

```
  ___ 8        2 ___       ___ 1
- 4 ___      - 1  4      - 7  0
  -----        -----       -----
  5   2       ___ 1        2 ___
```

```
  ___ 7        7 ___        6   3
- 3 ___      - ___ 4      - ___ ___
  -----        -----        -------
  5   5        1   3        4   0
```

Subtraction: Mental Math

Directions: Try to do these subtraction problems in your head without using paper and pencil.

9	12	7	5	15	2
- 3	- 6	- 6	-1	- 5	- 0
40	90	100	20	60	70
-20	- 80	- 50	-20	-10	- 40
450	500	250	690	320	900
-250	- 300	- 20	-100	- 20	- 600
1,000	8,000	7,000	4,000	9,500	5,000
- 400	- 500	- 900	-2,000	- 4,000	-2,000

Addition and Subtraction

Addition is "putting together" or adding two or more numbers to find the sum. Subtraction is "taking away" or subtracting one number from another to find the difference.

Directions: Add or subtract. Circle the answers that are less than 10.

Examples:

$$\begin{array}{r} 3 \\ +1 \\ \hline 4 \end{array}$$

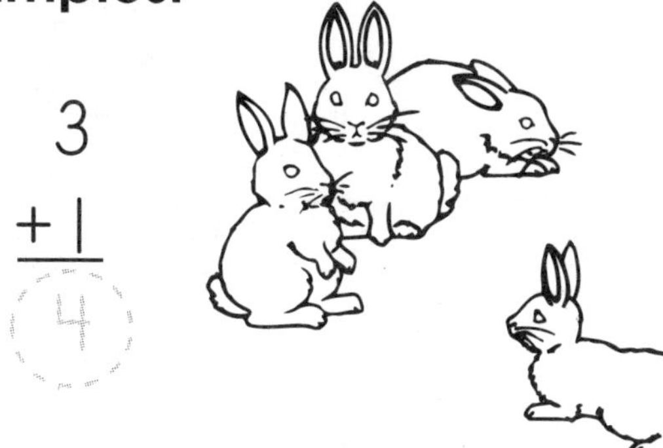

$$\begin{array}{r} 3 \\ -1 \\ \hline 2 \end{array}$$

$$\begin{array}{r} 9 \\ +3 \\ \hline \end{array} \qquad \begin{array}{r} 6 \\ -2 \\ \hline \end{array} \qquad \begin{array}{r} 12 \\ -1 \\ \hline \end{array} \qquad \begin{array}{r} 18 \\ +1 \\ \hline \end{array} \qquad \begin{array}{r} 15 \\ -6 \\ \hline \end{array}$$

$$\begin{array}{r} 7 \\ +6 \\ \hline \end{array} \qquad \begin{array}{r} 16 \\ -9 \\ \hline \end{array} \qquad \begin{array}{r} 10 \\ -3 \\ \hline \end{array} \qquad \begin{array}{r} 14 \\ +5 \\ \hline \end{array} \qquad \begin{array}{r} 16 \\ -8 \\ \hline \end{array}$$

$$\begin{array}{r} 8 \\ +7 \\ \hline \end{array} \qquad \begin{array}{r} 12 \\ +2 \\ \hline \end{array} \qquad \begin{array}{r} 13 \\ -4 \\ \hline \end{array} \qquad \begin{array}{r} 17 \\ +2 \\ \hline \end{array} \qquad \begin{array}{r} 9 \\ +9 \\ \hline \end{array}$$

Review

Directions: Fill in the missing numbers by counting by 10's.

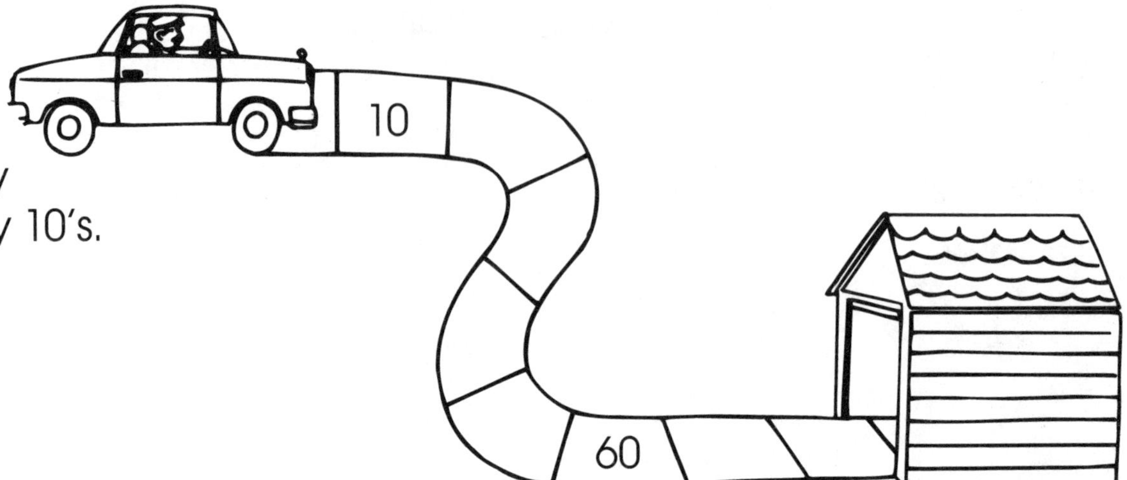

Directions: Draw a line to the correct numbers.

6 tens + 3 ones	45
4 tens + 5 ones	77
7 tens + 7 ones	63
9 tens + 3 ones	27
2 tens + 7 ones	93

Directions: Fill in the correct symbol, **+** or **–** .

12	7	15	14
__ 5	__ 3	__ 5	__ 4
17	4	10	18

Directions: Add or subtract.

3	8	12	10
+ 1	− 6	+ 7	+ 1

2-Digit Addition

Directions: Add the total points scored in each game. Remember to add **ones** first and **tens** second.

Example:

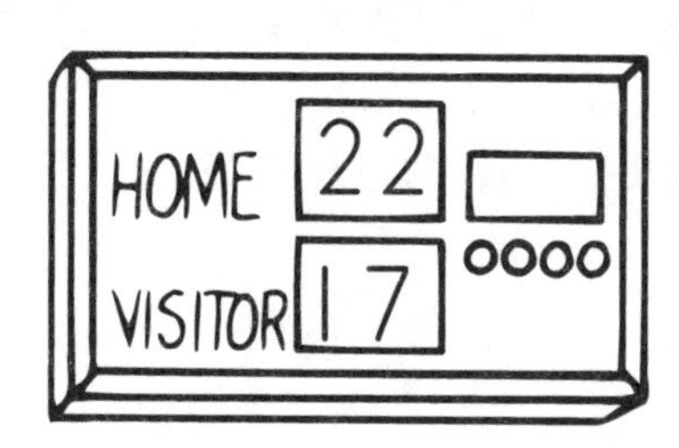

Total 39

HOME 28
VISITOR 30

Total ________

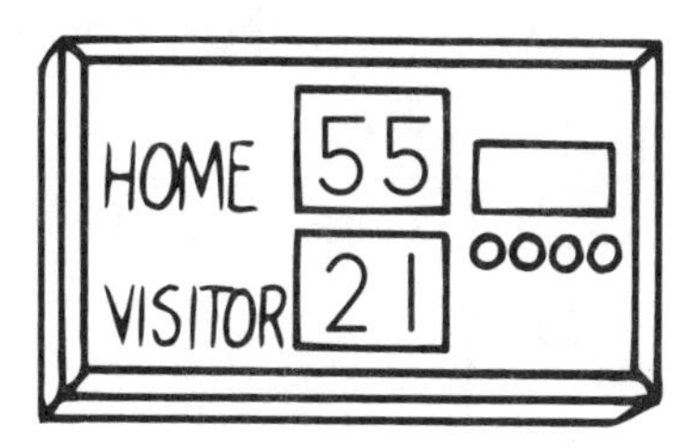

Total ________

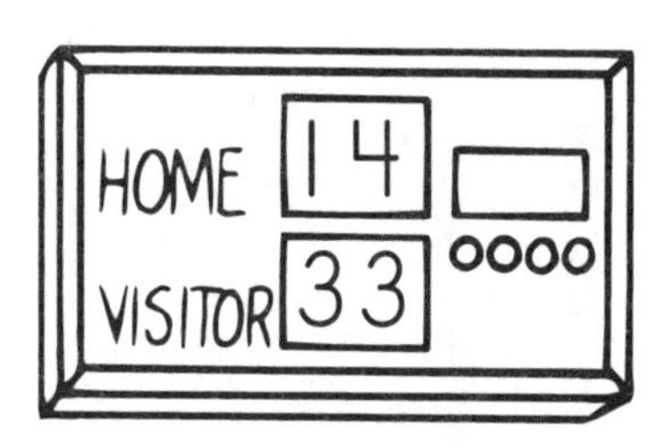

Total ________

Total ________

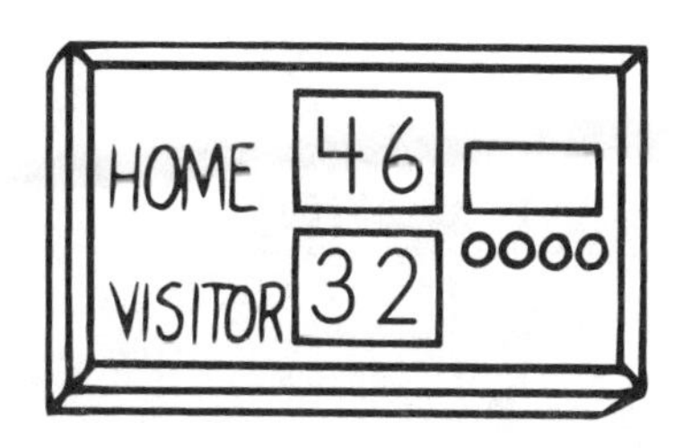

Total ________

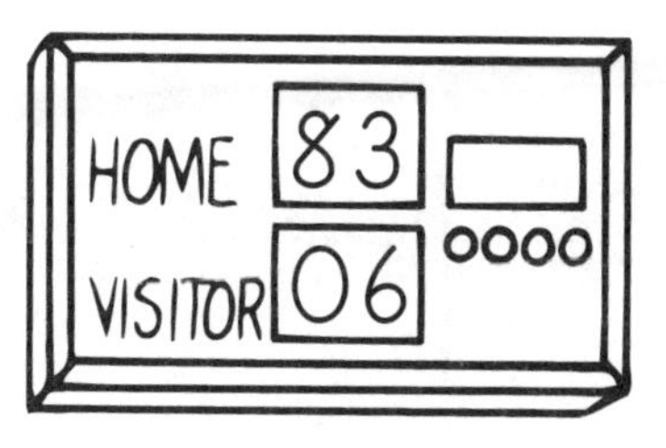

Total ________

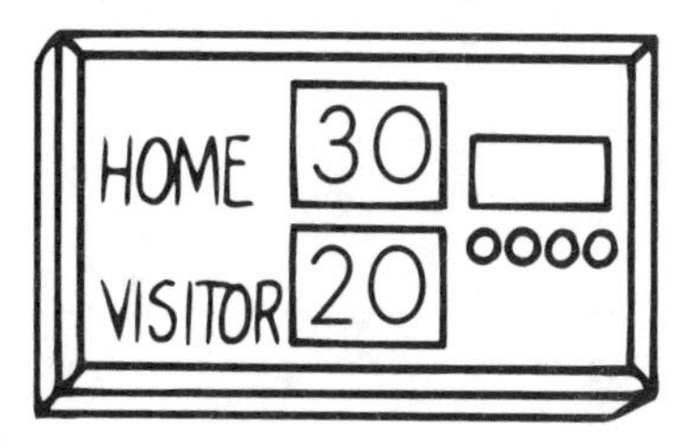

Total ________

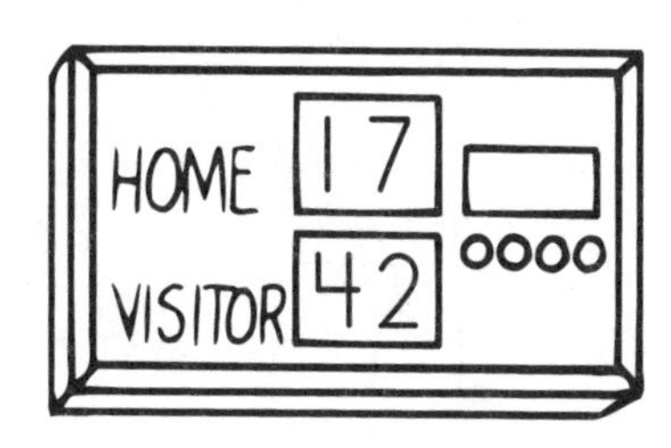

Total ________

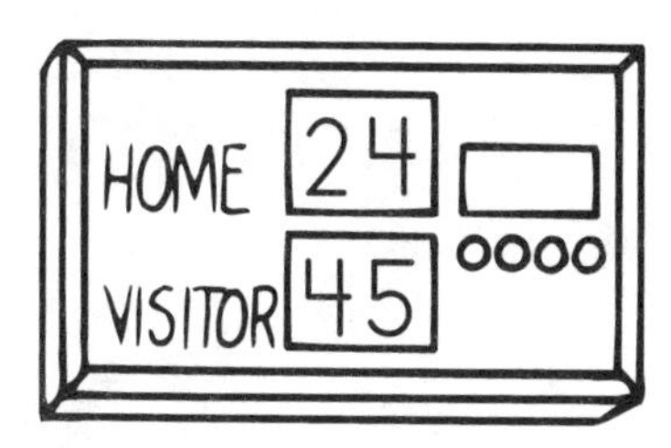

Total ________

2-Digit Addition: Regrouping

Addition is "putting together" or adding two or more numbers to find the sum. Regrouping is using **ten ones to form one ten, ten tens to form one 100, fifteen ones to form one ten and five ones** and so on.

Directions: Study the examples. Follow the steps to add.

Example:

$$\begin{array}{r} 14 \\ +8 \\ \hline \end{array}$$

Step 1: Add the ones.

tens	ones
1	4
+	8
	12

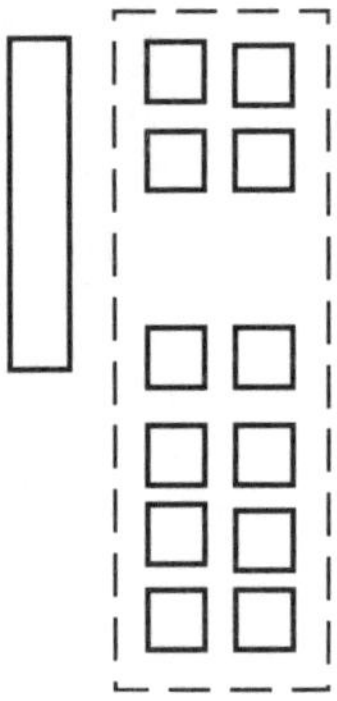

Step 2: Regroup the tens.

tens	ones
1	
1	4
+	8
	2

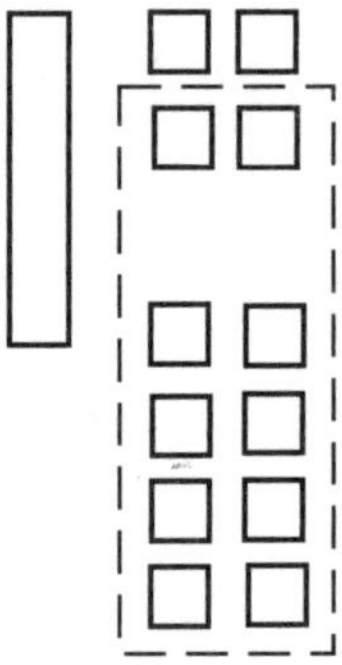

Step 3: Add the tens.

tens	ones
1	
1	4
+	8
2	2

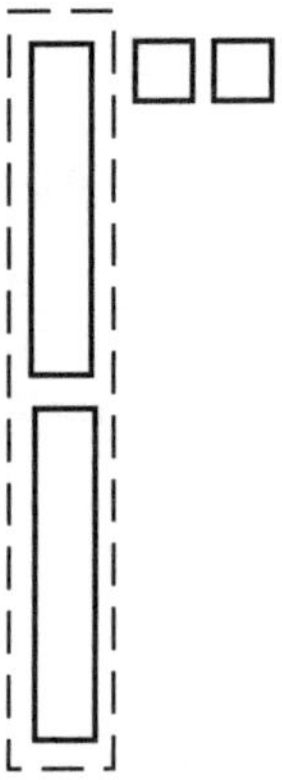

tens	ones
1	
1	6
+3	7
5	3

tens	ones
1	
3	8
+5	3
	1

tens	ones
1	
2	4
+4	7
	1

$$\begin{array}{r} 28 \\ +17 \\ \hline \end{array} \quad \begin{array}{r} 32 \\ +38 \\ \hline \end{array} \quad \begin{array}{r} 54 \\ +25 \\ \hline \end{array} \quad \begin{array}{r} 19 \\ +55 \\ \hline \end{array} \quad \begin{array}{r} 44 \\ +48 \\ \hline \end{array} \quad \begin{array}{r} 25 \\ +64 \\ \hline \end{array} \quad \begin{array}{r} 29 \\ +33 \\ \hline \end{array} \quad \begin{array}{r} 79 \\ +15 \\ \hline \end{array}$$

2-Digit Addition: Regrouping

Directions: Add the total points scored in the game. Remember to add the ones, regroup, and then add the tens.

Example:

Total 85

HOME 33
VISITOR 57

Total ________

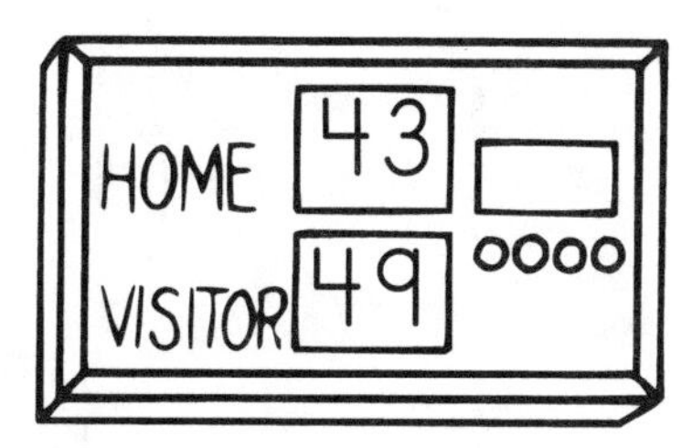

Total ________

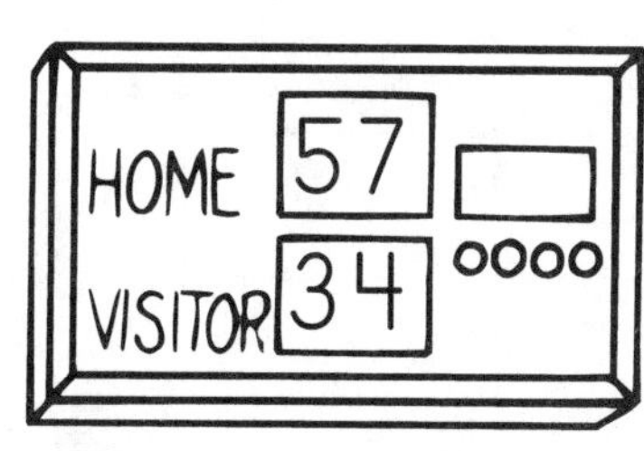

Total ________

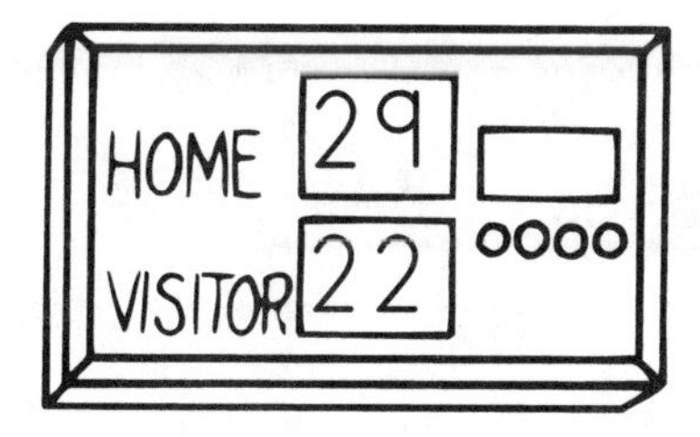

Total ________

Total ________

Total ________

HOME 66
VISITOR 26

Total ________

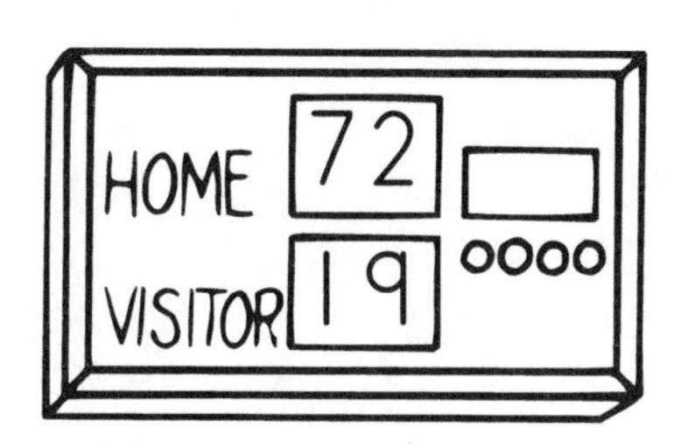

Total ________

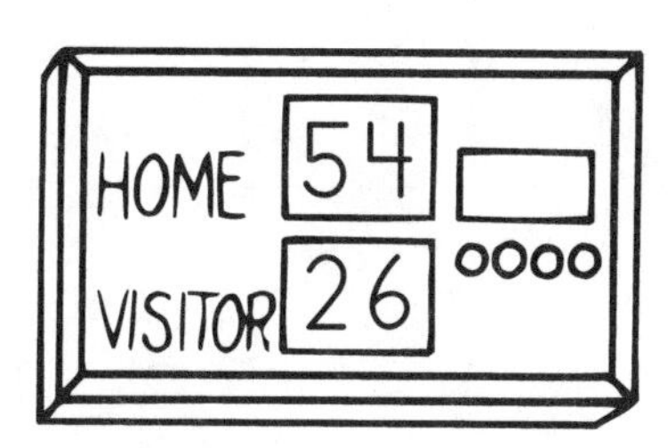

Total ________

2-Digit Subtraction: Regrouping

Subtraction is "taking away" or subtracting one number from another to find the difference. Regrouping is using **one ten to form ten ones, one 100 to form ten tens** and so on.

Directions: Study the examples. Follow the steps to subtract.

Example:

$$\begin{array}{r} 37 \\ -19 \\ \hline \end{array}$$

Step 1: Regroup.

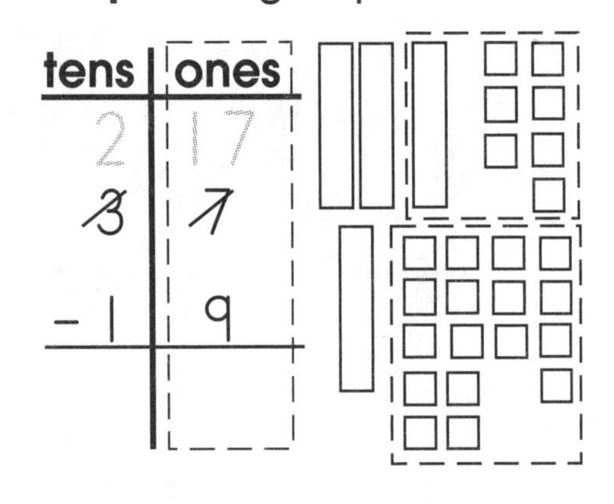

Step 2: Subtract the ones.

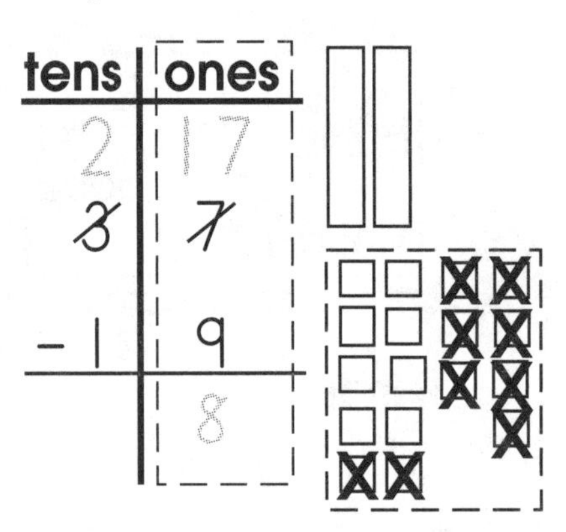

Step 3: Subtract the tens.

tens	ones
2	17
3	7
− 1	9
1	8

tens	ones
0	12
1	2
−	9
	3

tens	ones
2	14
3	4
− 1	6
1	8

tens	ones
3	15
4	5
− 2	9
1	6

$$\begin{array}{r} 28 \\ -19 \\ \hline \end{array} \quad \begin{array}{r} 46 \\ -18 \\ \hline \end{array} \quad \begin{array}{r} 12 \\ -\ 8 \\ \hline \end{array} \quad \begin{array}{r} 30 \\ -12 \\ \hline \end{array} \quad \begin{array}{r} 52 \\ -25 \\ \hline \end{array} \quad \begin{array}{r} 47 \\ -35 \\ \hline \end{array} \quad \begin{array}{r} 21 \\ -13 \\ \hline \end{array} \quad \begin{array}{r} 45 \\ -25 \\ \hline \end{array}$$

2-Digit Subtraction: Regrouping

Directions: Study the steps for subtracting. Solve the problems using the steps.

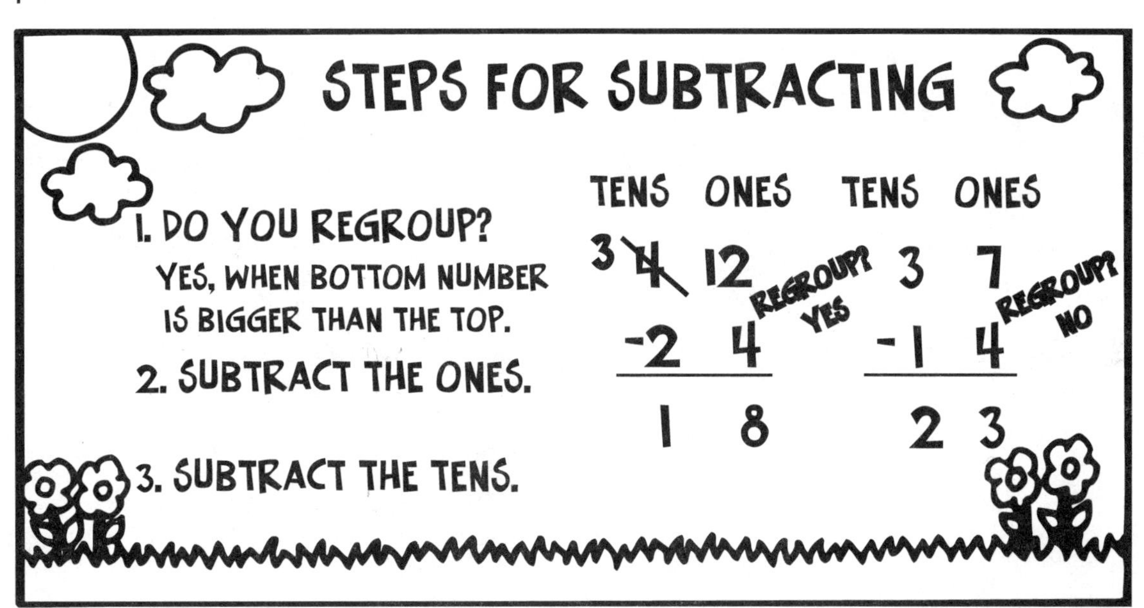
STEPS FOR SUBTRACTING
1. DO YOU REGROUP?
YES, WHEN BOTTOM NUMBER IS BIGGER THAN THE TOP.
2. SUBTRACT THE ONES.
3. SUBTRACT THE TENS.
TENS ONES TENS ONES
3 4 12
-2 4
1 8
REGROUP? YES
3 7
-1 4
2 3
REGROUP? NO

tens	ones
4	7
- 2	8

tens	ones
6	4
- 3	4

tens	ones
5	3
- 3	9

$$\begin{array}{r}56\\-27\\\hline\end{array}\quad\begin{array}{r}83\\-47\\\hline\end{array}\quad\begin{array}{r}43\\-39\\\hline\end{array}\quad\begin{array}{r}75\\-53\\\hline\end{array}\quad\begin{array}{r}91\\-18\\\hline\end{array}$$

$$\begin{array}{r}73\\-66\\\hline\end{array}\quad\begin{array}{r}35\\-14\\\hline\end{array}\quad\begin{array}{r}67\\-58\\\hline\end{array}\quad\begin{array}{r}26\\-7\\\hline\end{array}\quad\begin{array}{r}68\\-45\\\hline\end{array}$$

2-Digit Addition and Subtraction

Directions: Add or subtract using regrouping.

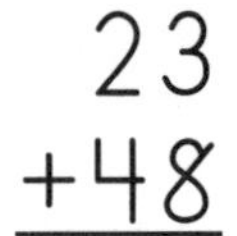

23	84	69	41
+48	-56	+29	-17
52	73	84	57
-28	+18	-27	-39
33	64	37	36
-15	+17	+58	-19
65	48	33	25
-28	-30	+18	+35

2-Digit Addition and Subtraction

Directions: Use the clues to subtract or add. Write your answers in the boxes.

Across

2. 52 + 32 = ______
4. 45 – 4 = ______
6. 58 – 47 = ______
7. 14 + 25 = ______
8. 25 + 50 = ______
9. 49 – 33 = ______
10. 71 – 12 = ______

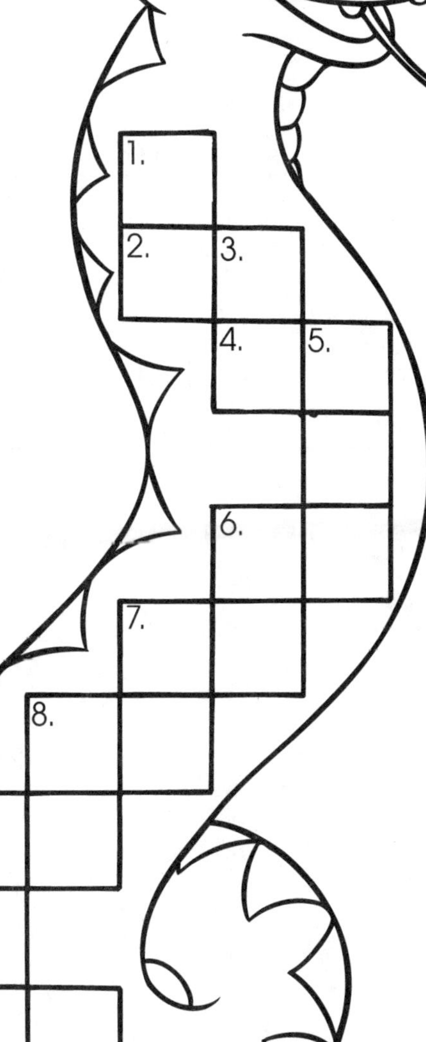

Down

1. 9 + 9 = ______
3. 18 + 26 = ______
5. 81 + 40 = ______
6. 21 – 2 = ______
7. 44 – 9 = ______
8. 39 + 37 = ______
9. 55 + 50 = ______

Place Value: Hundreds

Directions: Write the numbers for hundreds, tens and ones. Then add.

Example:

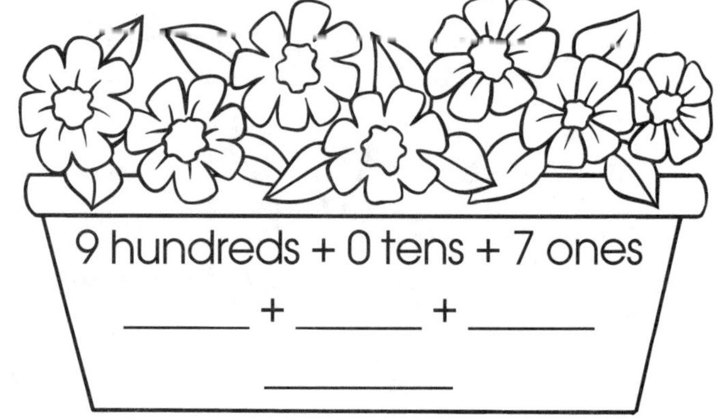

Rounding: The Nearest Ten

If the ones number is 5 or greater, "round up" to the nearest 10. If the ones number is 4 or less, the tens number stays the same and the ones number becomes a zero.

Examples: 15 round up to 20   23 round down to 20   47 round up to 50

7 ____   58 ____

12 ____   81 ____

33 ____   94 ____

27 ____   44 ____

73 ____   88 ____

25 ____   66 ____

39 ____   70 ____

Rounding: The Nearest Hundred

If the tens number is 5 or greater, "round up" to the nearest hundred. If the tens number is 4 or less, the hundreds number remains the same.

REMEMBER... Look at the number directly to the right of the place you are rounding to.

Example:

230 round down to 200

470 round up to 500

150 round up to 200

732 round down to 700

456 ____

120 ____

340 ____

923 ____

867 ____

550 ____

686 ____

231 ____

770 ____

492 ____

Front-End Estimation

Front-end estimation is useful when you don't need to know the exact amount, but a close answer will do.

When we use front-end estimation, we use only the first number. Then add the numbers together to get the estimate.

Example:

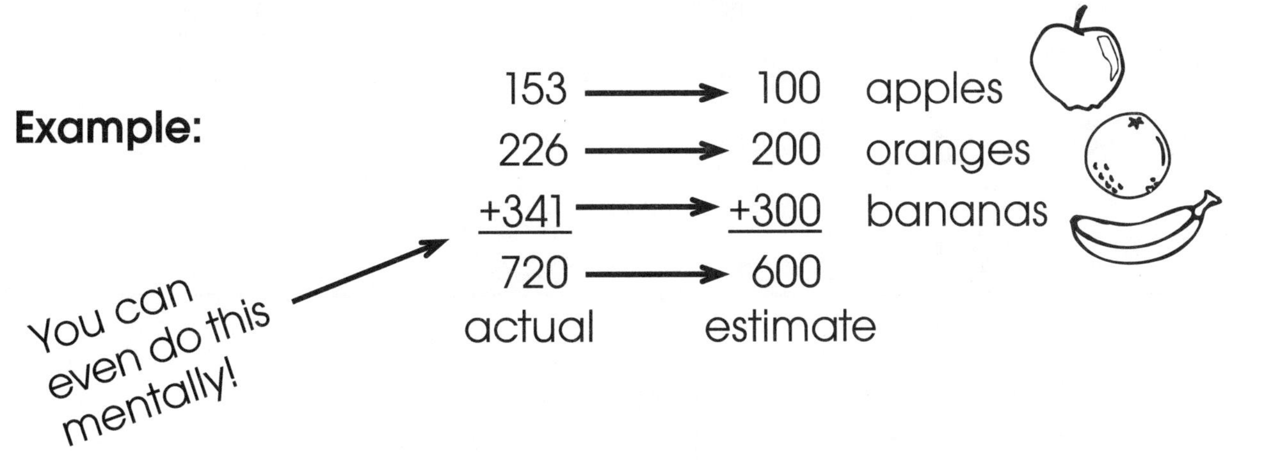

153 → 100 apples
226 → 200 oranges
+341 → +300 bananas
720 → 600
actual
estimate
You can even do this mentally!

Directions: Estimate the sum of these numbers.

456 →
121 →
+438 → + ____

910 →
280 →
+320 → + ____

686 →
307 →
+711 → + ____

3-Digit Addition: Regrouping

Directions: Study the examples. Follow the steps to add.

Example:

Step 1: Add the ones.

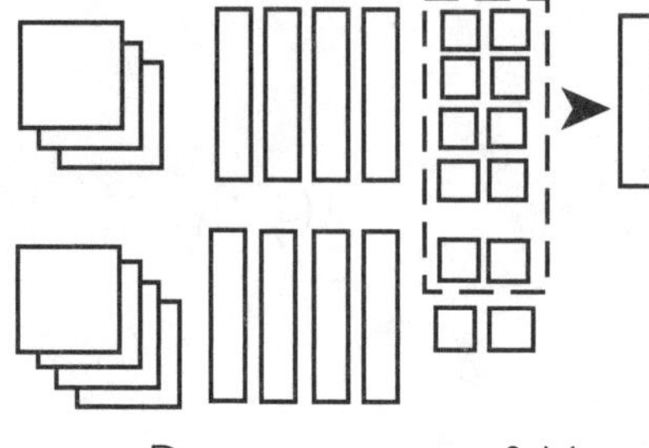

Do you regroup? Yes

Step 2: Add the tens.

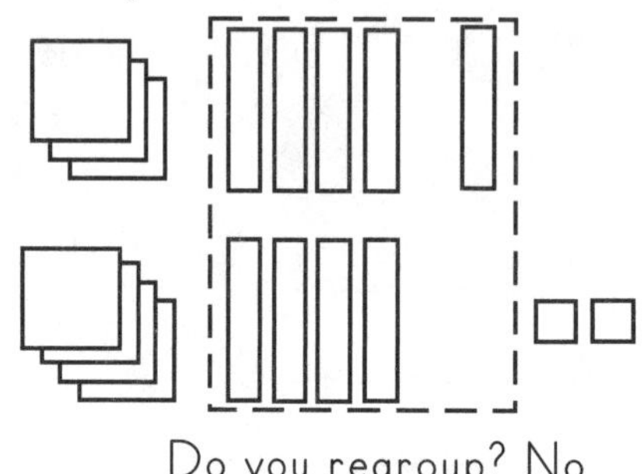

Do you regroup? No

Step 3: Add the hundreds.

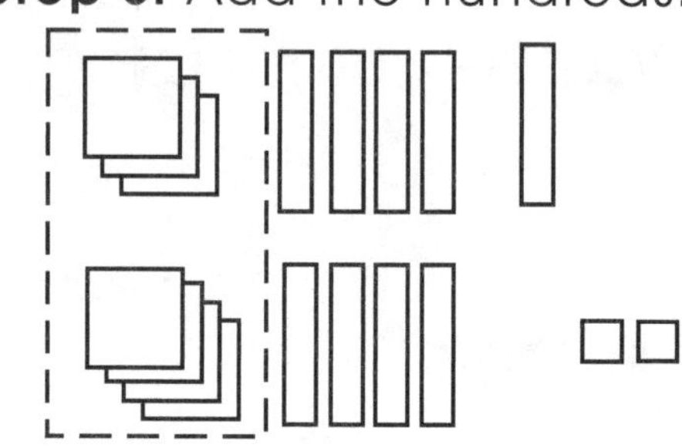

hundreds	tens	ones
	1	
3	4	8
+4	4	4
		2

hundreds	tens	ones
	1	
3	4	8
+4	4	4
	9	2

hundreds	tens	ones
	1	
3	4	8
+4	4	4
7	9	2

hundreds	tens	ones
	1	
2	1	4
+2	3	8
4	5	2

hundreds	tens	ones
	1	
3	6	8
+2	1	3
___	8	1

hundreds	tens	ones
	1	
1	1	9
+5	6	5
___	___	4

418	471	334	659	736	426	567	327
+323	+319	+528	+127	+145	+165	+228	+354

3-Digit Subtraction: Regrouping

Directions: Study the example. Follow the steps to subtract.

Step 1: Regroup ones.
Step 2: Subtract ones.
Step 3: Subtract tens.
Step 4: Subtract hundreds.

Example:

hundreds	tens	ones
	5	12
4	~~6~~	~~2~~
−2	5	3
2	0	9

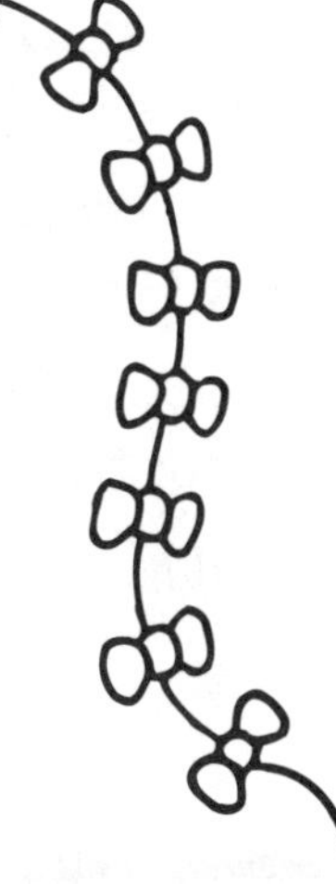

$$\begin{array}{r} 423 \\ -114 \\ \hline \end{array} \qquad \begin{array}{r} 562 \\ -349 \\ \hline \end{array}$$

$$\begin{array}{r} 478 \\ -239 \\ \hline \end{array} \qquad \begin{array}{r} 651 \\ -333 \\ \hline \end{array}$$

Directions: Draw a line to the correct answer. Color the kites.

$$\begin{array}{r} 347 \\ -218 \\ \hline \end{array} \quad \begin{array}{r} 144 \\ -135 \\ \hline \end{array} \quad \begin{array}{r} 963 \\ -748 \\ \hline \end{array} \quad \begin{array}{r} 762 \\ -553 \\ \hline \end{array} \quad \begin{array}{r} 287 \\ -179 \\ \hline \end{array} \quad \begin{array}{r} 427 \\ -398 \\ \hline \end{array}$$

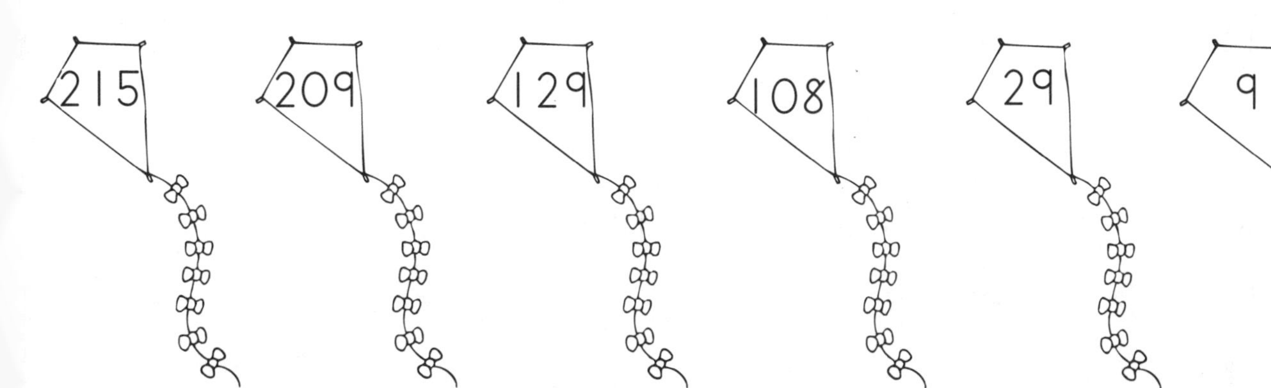

Subtraction: Regrouping

Directions: Study the example. Follow the steps. Subtract using regrouping. If you have to regroup to subtract ones and there are no tens, you must regroup twice.

Example:

$$\begin{array}{r} 300 \\ -182 \\ \hline 118 \end{array}$$

Steps:

1. Subtract ones. You cannot subtract 2 ones from 0 ones.
2. Regroup. No tens. Regroup hundreds (2 hundreds + 10 tens).
3. Regroup tens (9 tens + 10 ones).
4. Subtract 2 ones from ten ones.
5. Subtract 8 tens from 9 tens.
6. Subtract 1 hundred from 2 hundreds.

602 -423	306 -128	600 -263	807 -499	703 -328
800 -557	206 -137	400 -224	508 -379	909 -769
207 -138	604 -397	308 -199	700 -531	900 -278

Review

Directions: Add or subtract. Use the code to color the rocket.

If the answer has:

9 hundreds, color it gray.

7 tens, color it blue.

5 ones, color it orange.

4 ones, color it red.

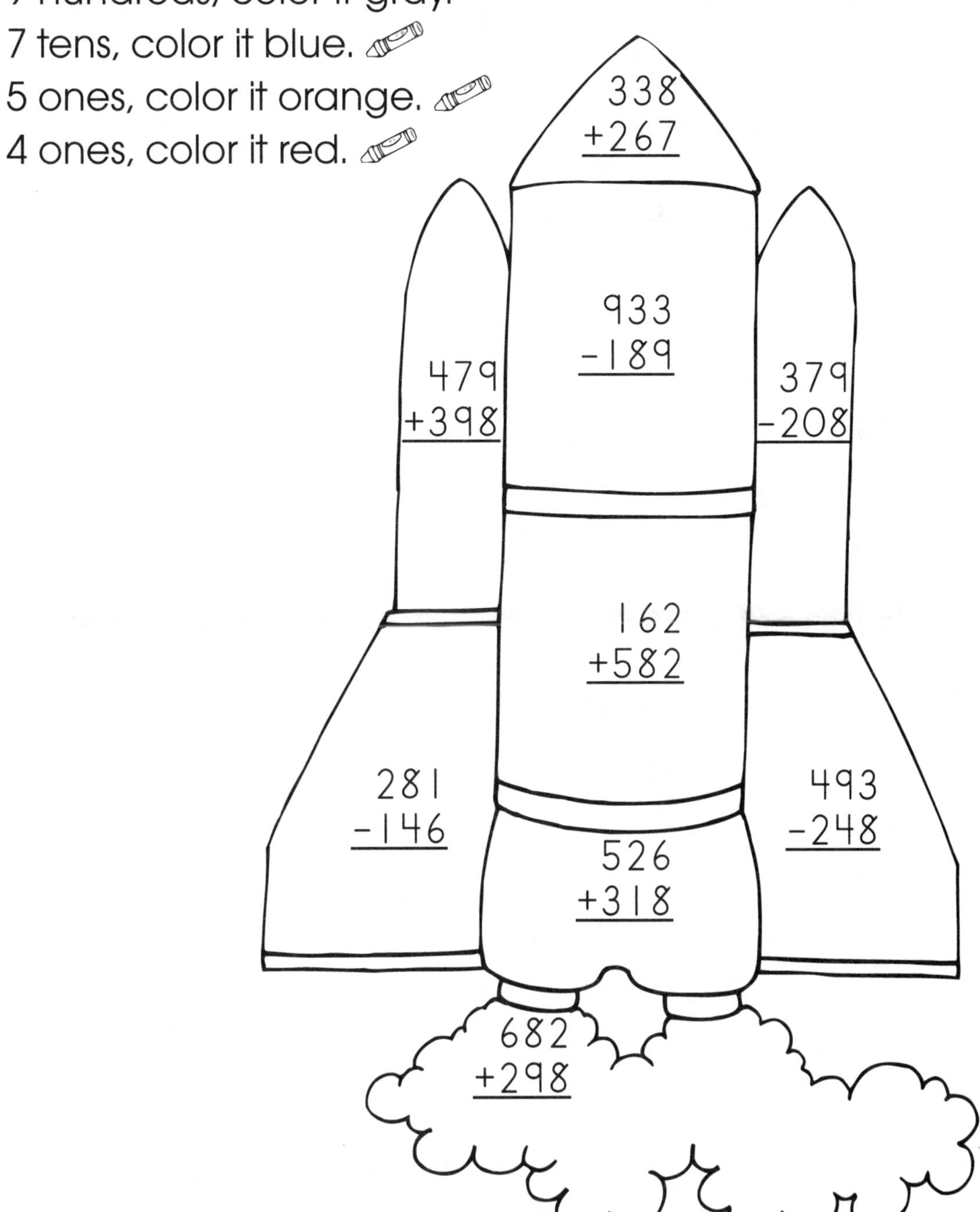

Place Value: Thousands

6,431

thousands	hundreds	tens	ones
6	4	3	1

Directions: Tell which number is in each place.

☆ Thousands place:

2,456	4,621	3,456
______	______	______

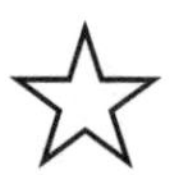 Hundreds place:

4,286	1,234	5,678
______	______	______

 Tens place:

6,321	3,210	7,871
______	______	______

 Ones place:

5,432	6,531	9,980
______	______	______

Place Value: Thousands

Directions: Study the example. Write the missing numbers.

Example:

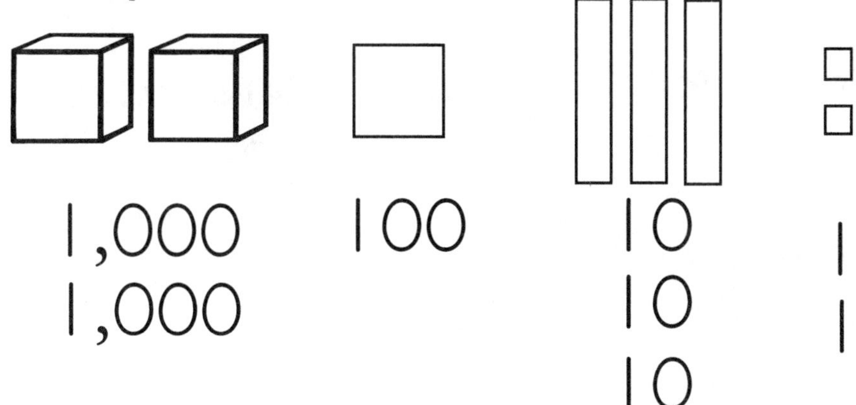

2 thousands + 1 hundred + __3__ tens + 2 ones = __2,132__

5,286 = ____ thousands + ____ hundreds + ____ tens + ____ ones

1,831 = ____ thousand + ____ hundreds + ____ tens + ____ one

8,972 = ____ thousands + ____ hundreds + ____ tens + ____ ones

4,528 = ____ thousands + ____ hundreds + ____ tens + ____ ones

3,177 = ____ thousands + ____ hundred + ____ tens + ____ ones

Directions: Draw a line to the number that has:

8 hundreds	7,103
5 ones	2,862
9 tens	5,996
7 thousands	1,485

Place Value

The place value of a digit, or numeral, is shown by where it is in the number. For example, in the number **1,234**, **1** has the place value of **thousands**, **2** is **hundreds**, **3** is **tens** and **4** is **ones**.

Hundred Thousands	Ten Thousands	Thousands	Hundreds	Tens	Ones
9	4	3	8	5	2

Directions: Match the numbers in Column A with the words in Column B.

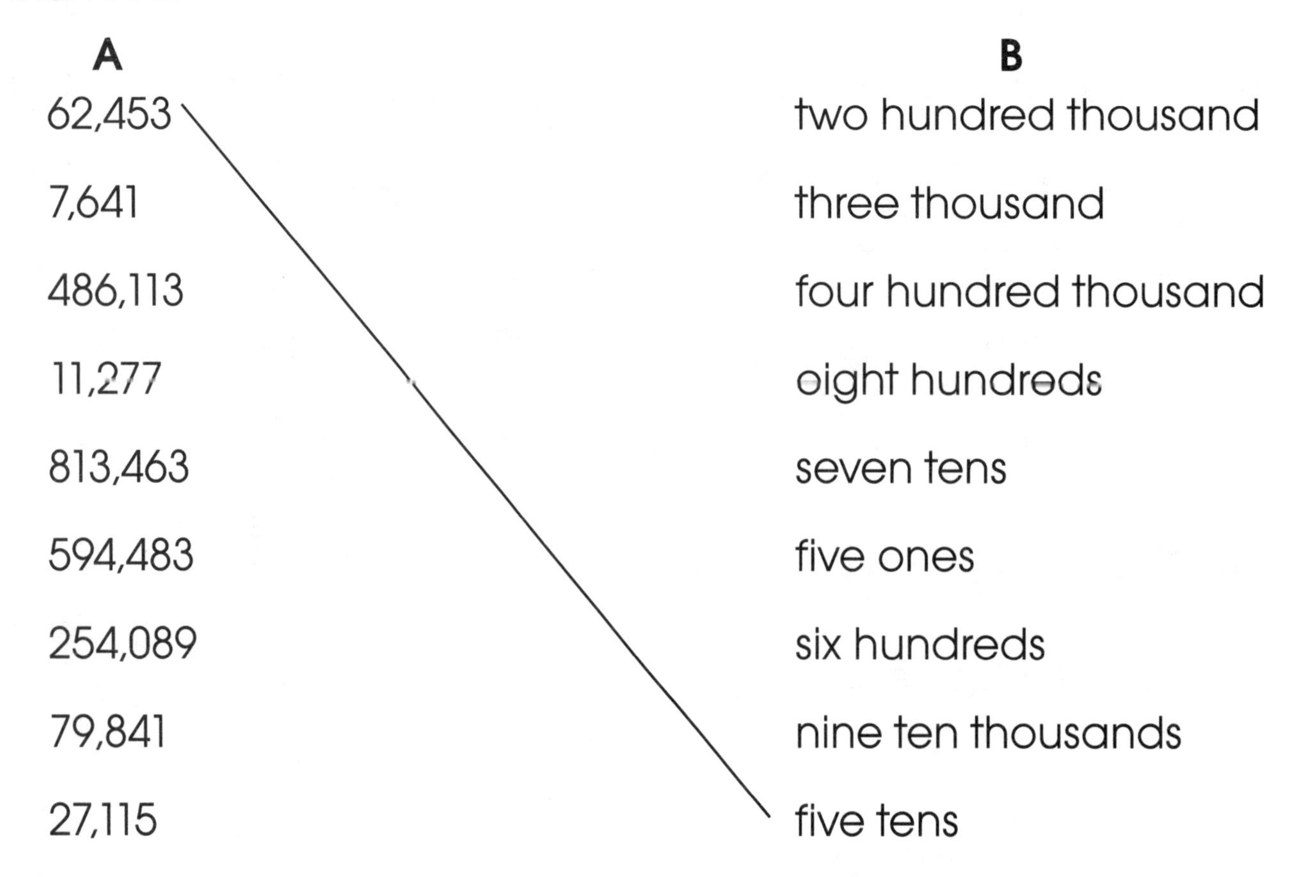

A	B
62,453	two hundred thousand
7,641	three thousand
486,113	four hundred thousand
11,277	eight hundreds
813,463	seven tens
594,483	five ones
254,089	six hundreds
79,841	nine ten thousands
27,115	five tens

Place Value

Directions: Use the code to color the rings.

If the number has:

7 ten thousands, color it red.

1 thousand, color it blue.

4 hundred thousands, color it green.

6 tens, color it brown.

8 ones, color it yellow.

Addition: Regrouping

Directions: Study the example. Add using regrouping.

Example:

Steps:

```
  5,356
 +3,976
  9,332
```

1. Add the ones.
2. Regroup the tens. Add the tens.
3. Regroup the hundreds. Add the hundreds.
4. Add the thousands.

```
  6,849        1,846        9,221
 +3,276       +8,384       +6,769
```

```
  2,758        5,299        7,932
 +3,663       +8,764       +6,879
```

A plane flew 1,838 miles on the first day. It flew 2,347 miles on the second day. How many miles did it fly in all? ________

Subtraction: Regrouping

Directions: Subtract. Regroup when necessary. The first one is done for you.

7,354 -5,295 2,059	4,214 -3,185	8,437 -5,338	6,837 -4,318
5,735 -3,826	1,036 - 947	6,735 -6,646	3,841 -1,953

Columbus discovered America in 1492. The pilgrims landed in America in 1620. How many years difference was there between these two events?

____

Multiplication

Multiplication is a short way to find the sum of adding the same number a certain amount of times. For example, **7 x 4 = 28** instead of **7 + 7 + 7 + 7 = 28**.

Directions: Study the example. Solve the problems.

Example:

3 + 3 + 3 = 9
3 threes = 9
3 x 3 = 9

7 + 7 = 14
2 sevens = 14
2 x 7 = 14

4 + 4 + 4 + 4 = ____
4 fours = ____
4 x ____ = ____

5 + 5 = ____
2 fives = ____
2 x ____ = ____

 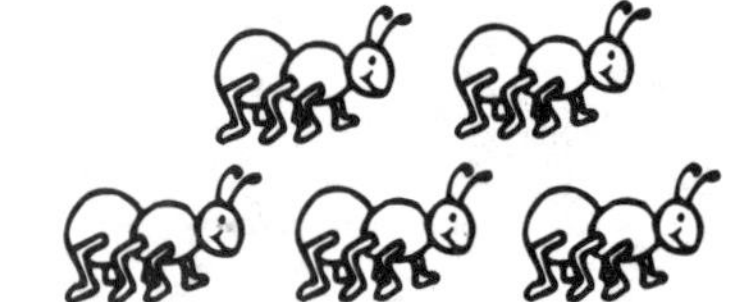

2 + 2 + 2 + 2 = ____
4 twos = ____
4 x ____ = ____

6 + 6 = ____
2 sixes = ____
2 x ____ = ____

Multiplication

Multiplication is a short way to find the sum of adding the same number a certain amount of times. For example, we write 7 x 4 = 28 instead of 7 + 7 + 7 + 7 = 28.

Directions: Study the example. Multiply.

Example:

There are two groups of seashells.
There are 3 seashells in each group.
How many seashells are there in all?

2 x 3 = 6

4 + 4 = _____

2 x 4 = _____

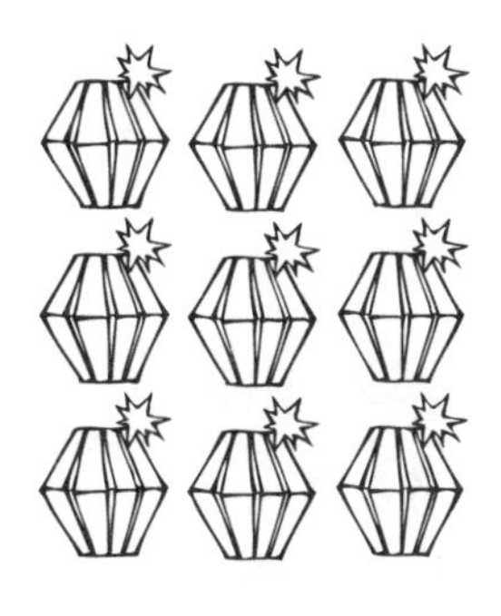

3 + 3 + 3 = _____

3 x 3 = _____

2	3	4	6	7
x3	x5	x3	x2	x3

5	6	4	7	8
x2	x3	x2	x2	x3

5	9	8	6	9
x5	x4	x5	x6	x3

Multiplication

Directions: Multiply.

$$\begin{array}{r} 3 \\ \underline{\times 5} \end{array} \quad \begin{array}{r} 4 \\ \underline{\times 6} \end{array} \quad \begin{array}{r} 3 \\ \underline{\times 8} \end{array}$$

$$\begin{array}{r} 5 \\ \underline{\times 5} \end{array} \quad \begin{array}{r} 4 \\ \underline{\times 8} \end{array} \quad \begin{array}{r} 5 \\ \underline{\times 4} \end{array}$$

$$\begin{array}{r} 6 \\ \underline{\times 7} \end{array} \quad \begin{array}{r} 3 \\ \underline{\times 9} \end{array} \quad \begin{array}{r} 2 \\ \underline{\times 8} \end{array} \quad \begin{array}{r} 7 \\ \underline{\times 6} \end{array} \quad \begin{array}{r} 9 \\ \underline{\times 4} \end{array}$$

$$\begin{array}{r} 6 \\ \underline{\times 8} \end{array} \quad \begin{array}{r} 5 \\ \underline{\times 6} \end{array} \quad \begin{array}{r} 7 \\ \underline{\times 7} \end{array} \quad \begin{array}{r} 5 \\ \underline{\times 3} \end{array} \quad \begin{array}{r} 8 \\ \underline{\times 9} \end{array}$$

A river boat makes 3 trips a day every day.
How many trips does it make in a week? __________

Multiplication: Zero And One

Any number multiplied by zero equals zero. One multiplied by any number equals that number. Study the example. Multiply.

Example:

How many full sails are there in all?

2 boats x **1** sail on each boat = **2** sails

How many full sails are there now?

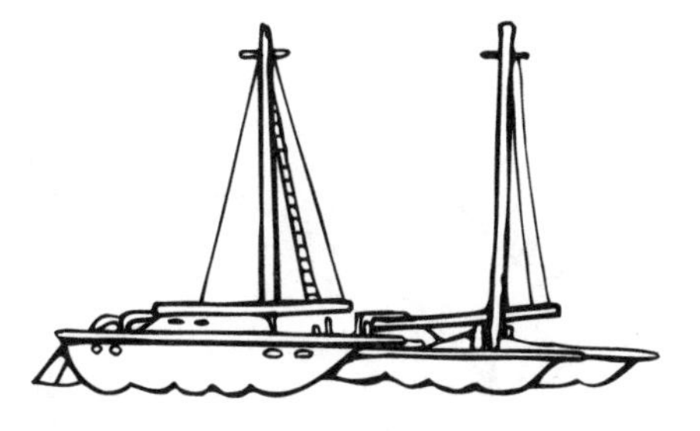

2 boats x **0** sails = **0** sails

Directions: Multiply.

1	2	3	4	0	7
x5	x1	x0	x1	x6	x0

9	8	3	4	7	6
x1	x0	x1	x0	x1	x1

Multiplication

Directions: Use the code to color the rainbow.

If the answer is:

6, color it green.
8, color it purple.
9, color it red.
16, color it pink.
18, color it white.
21, color it brown.
25, color it orange.
27, color it blue.

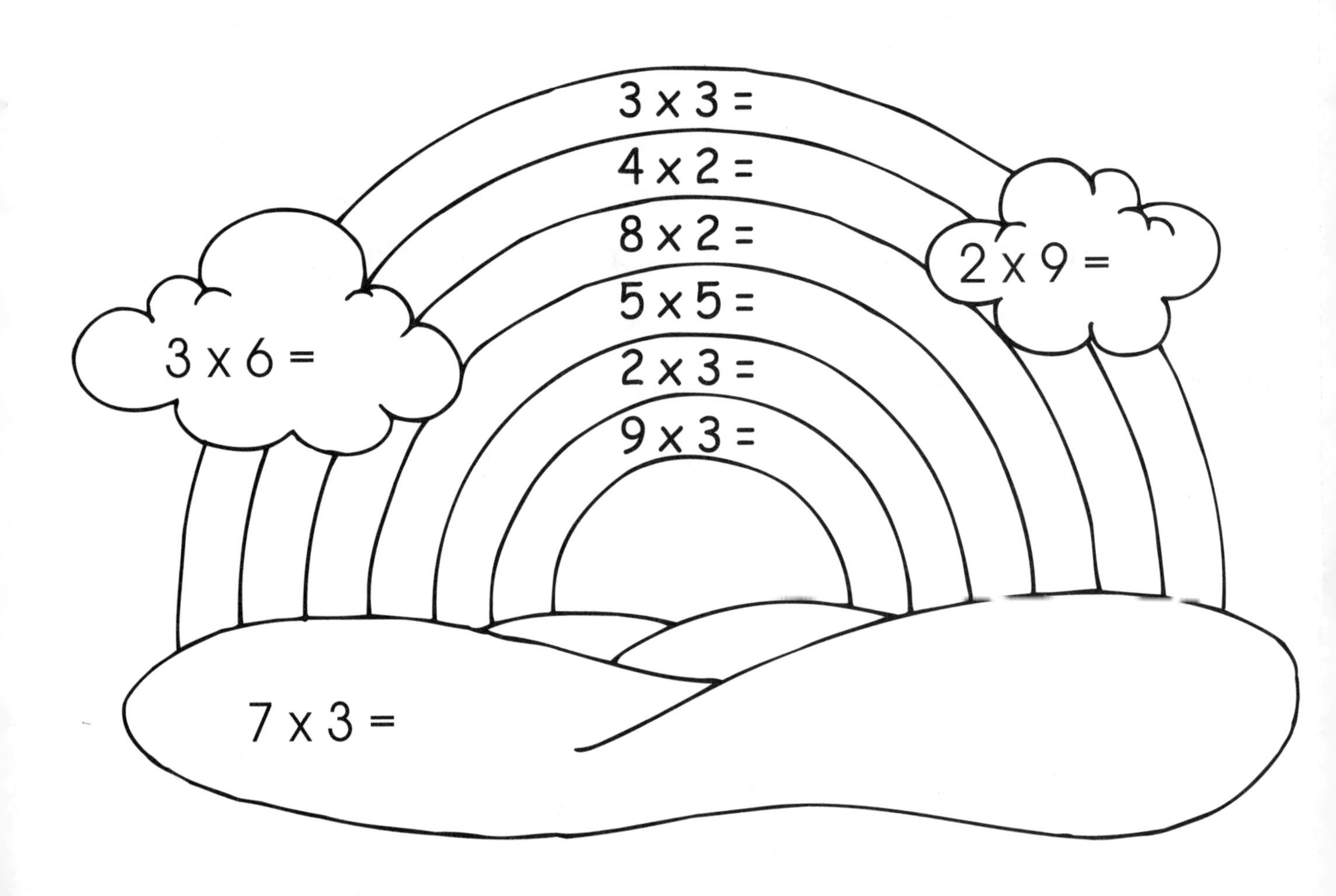

Review

Directions: Draw a line to the number that has:

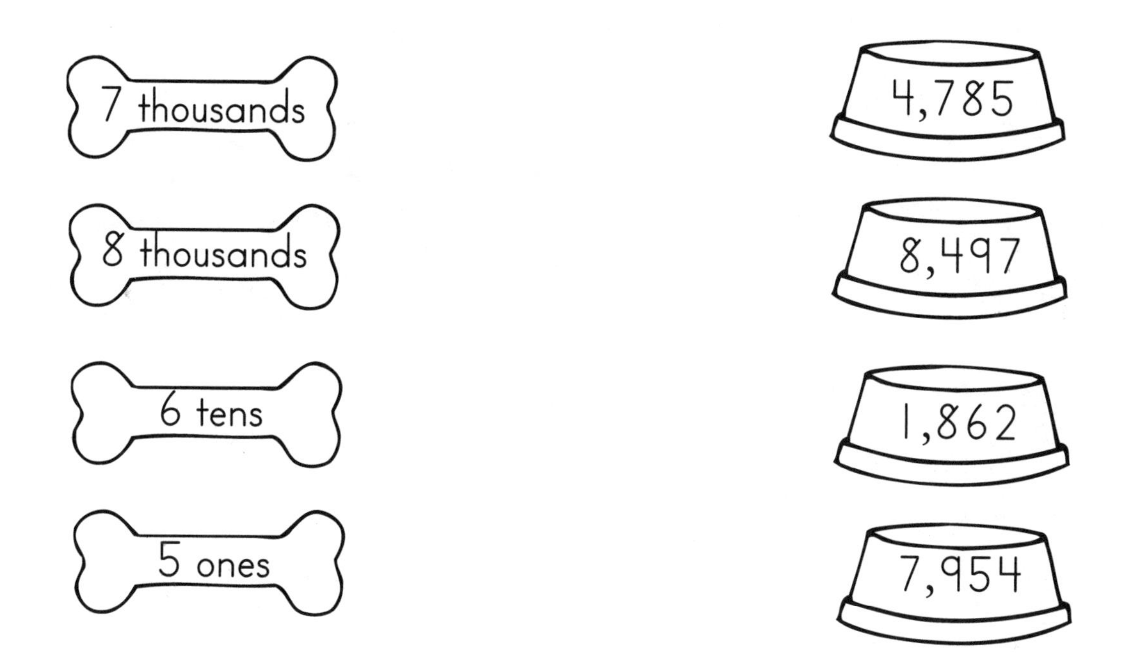

Directions: Draw a line from the problem to its answer.

Multiplication

Directions: Time yourself as you multiply. How quickly can you complete this page?

3 x2	8 x7	1 x0	1 x6	3 x4	0 x4
4 x1	4 x4	2 x5	9 x3	9 x9	5 x3
0 x8	2 x6	9 x6	8 x5	7 x3	4 x2
3 x5	2 x0	4 x6	1 x3	0 x0	3 x3

Multiplication Table

Directions: Complete the multiplication table. Use it to practice your multiplication facts.

X	0	1	2	3	4	5	6	7	8	9	10
0	0										
1		1									
2			4								
3				9							
4					16						
5						25					
6							36				
7								49			
8									64		
9										81	
10											100

Division

Division is a way to find out how many times one number is contained in another number. For example, **28 ÷ 4 = 7** means that there are seven groups of four in 28.

Directions: Study the example. Divide.

Example:

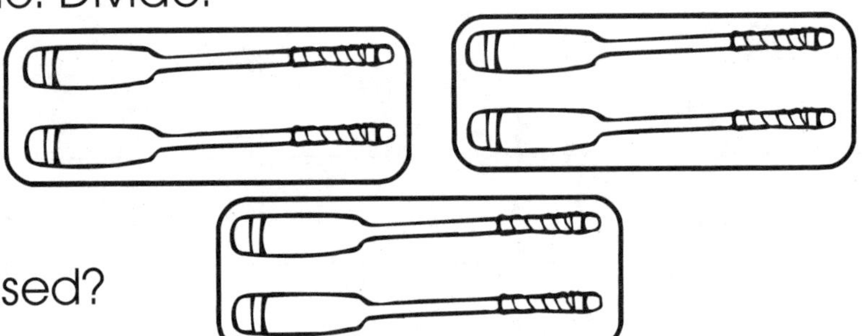

There are 6 oars.
Each canoe needs 2 oars.
How many canoes can be used?

Circle groups of 2.
There are 3 groups of 2.

6	÷	2	=	3
oars		number of oars needed per canoe		canoes

9 ÷ 3 = _____   8 ÷ 2 = _____   16 ÷ 4 = _____

15 ÷ 5 = _____   18 ÷ 2 = _____   20 ÷ 4 = _____

21 ÷ 7 = _____   24 ÷ 6 = _____   12 ÷ 2= _____

Division

Directions: Divide. Draw a line from the boat to the sail with the correct answer.

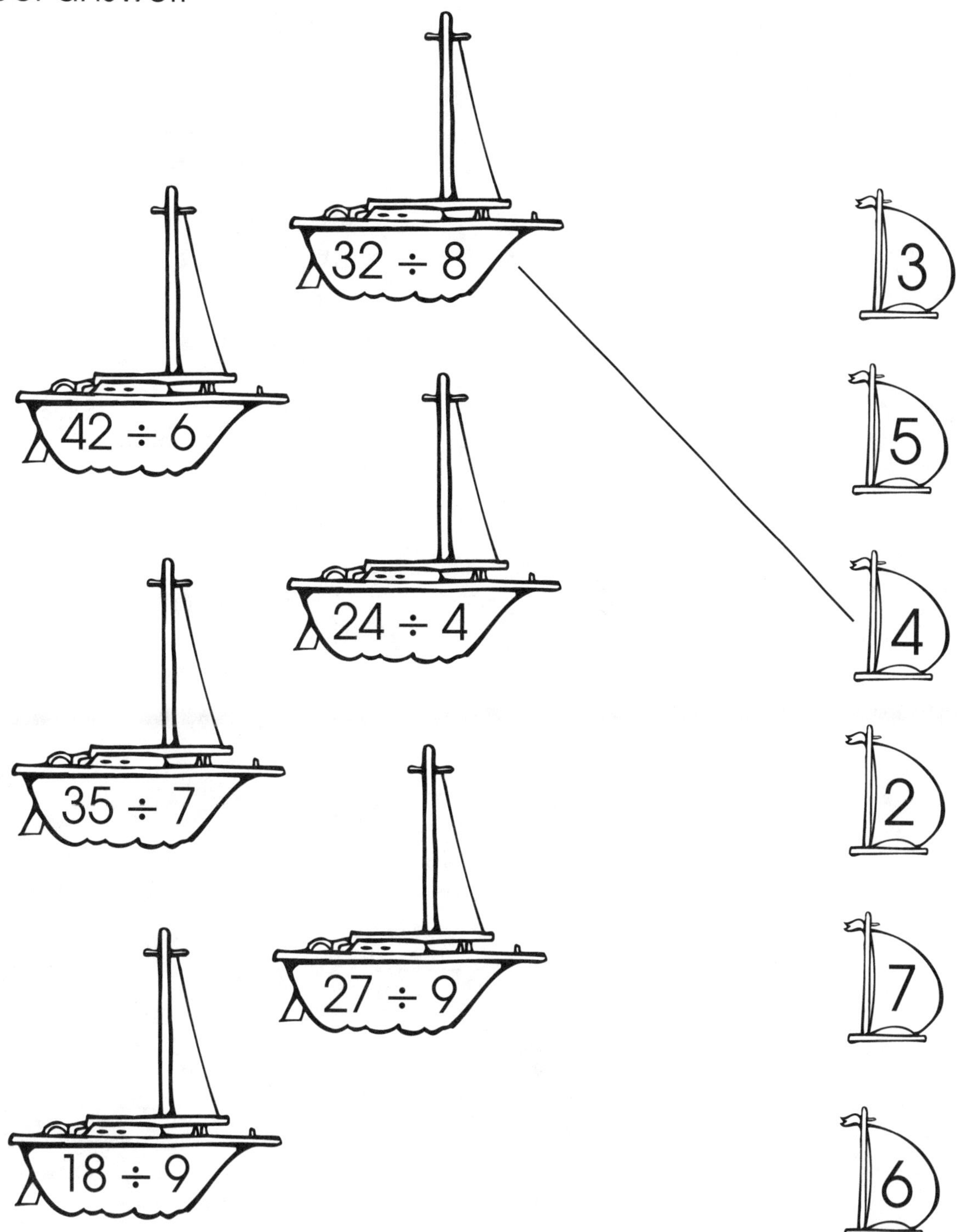

Review

Directions: Multiply or divide. Fill in the blanks with the missing numbers or x or ÷ signs. The first one is done for you.

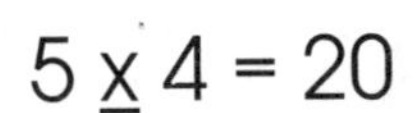

5 x 4 = 20   6 x 8 = ____   7 x ____ = 14

3 _ 6 = 18   7 x 2 = ____   ____ x 3 = 24

6 _ 2 = 3   24 ÷ 6 = ____   6 x 5 = ____

25 _ 5 = 5   49 ÷ 7 = ____   8 x ____ = 32

3 _ 8 = 24   18 ÷ 3 = ____   9 x 5 = ____

12 _ 3 = 4   9 x 8 = ____   6 x ____ = 36

Fractions

A **fraction** is a number that names part of a whole, such as $\frac{1}{2}$ or $\frac{1}{3}$.

Directions: Write the fraction that tells what part of each figure is colored. The first one is done for you.

Example:

$\underline{2}$ parts shaded
5 parts in the whole figure

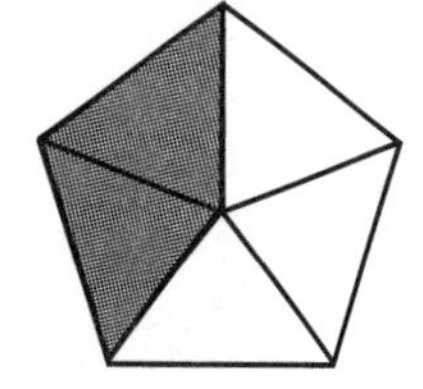

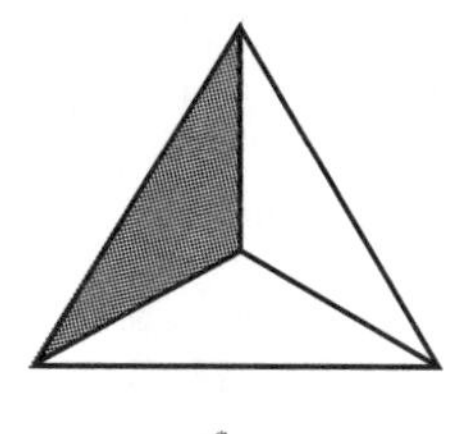

$\frac{1}{3}$

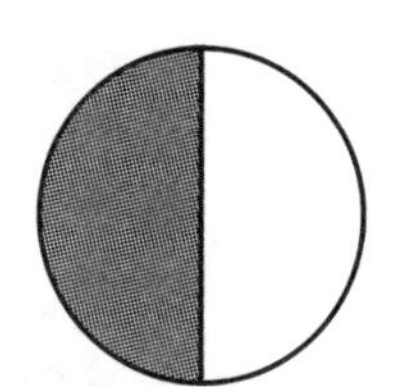

______

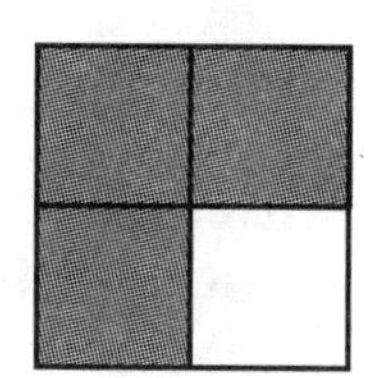

______

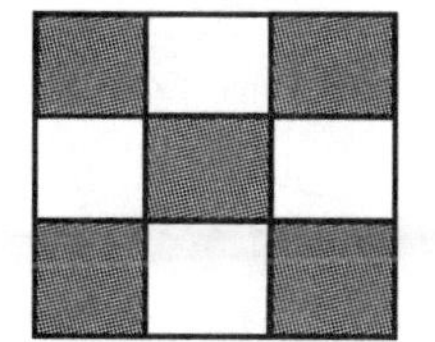

______

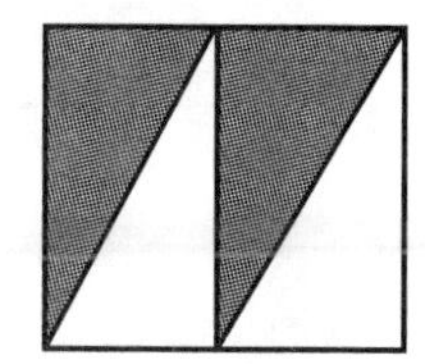

______

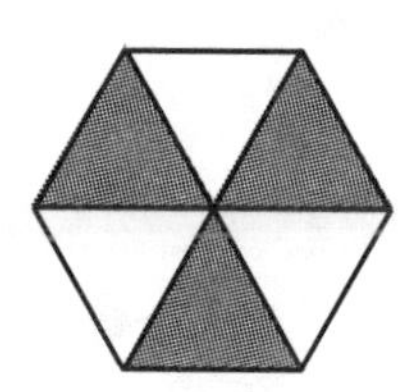

______

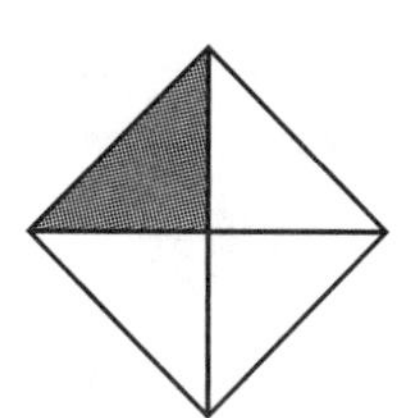

______

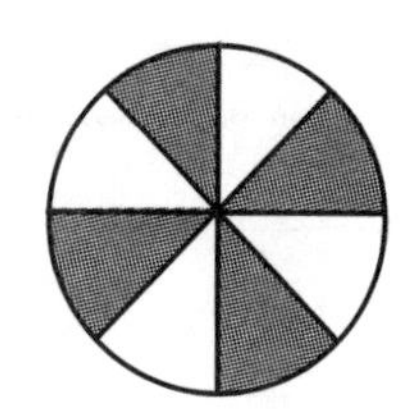

______

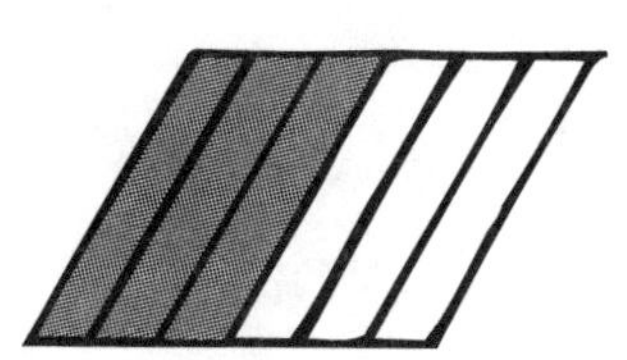

______

Fractions: Half, Third, Fourth

A fraction is a number that names part of a whole, such as $\frac{1}{2}$ or $\frac{1}{3}$.

Directions: Study the examples. Color the correct fraction of each shape.

Examples:

shaded part 1
equal parts 2
$\frac{1}{2}$ (one-half) shaded

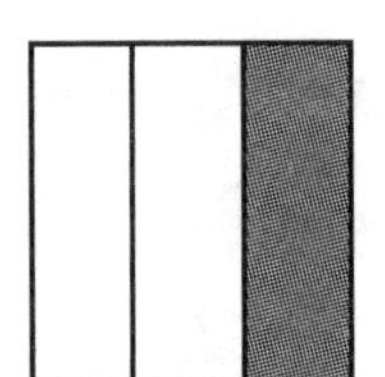

shaded part 1
equal parts 3
$\frac{1}{3}$ (one-third) shaded

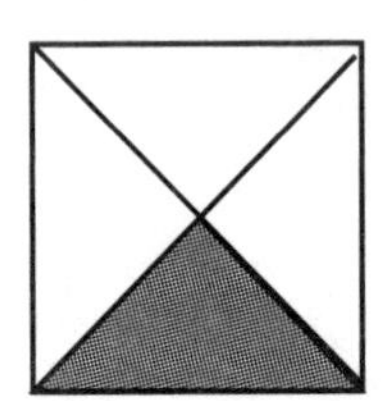

shaded part 1
equal parts 4
$\frac{1}{4}$ (one-fourth) shaded

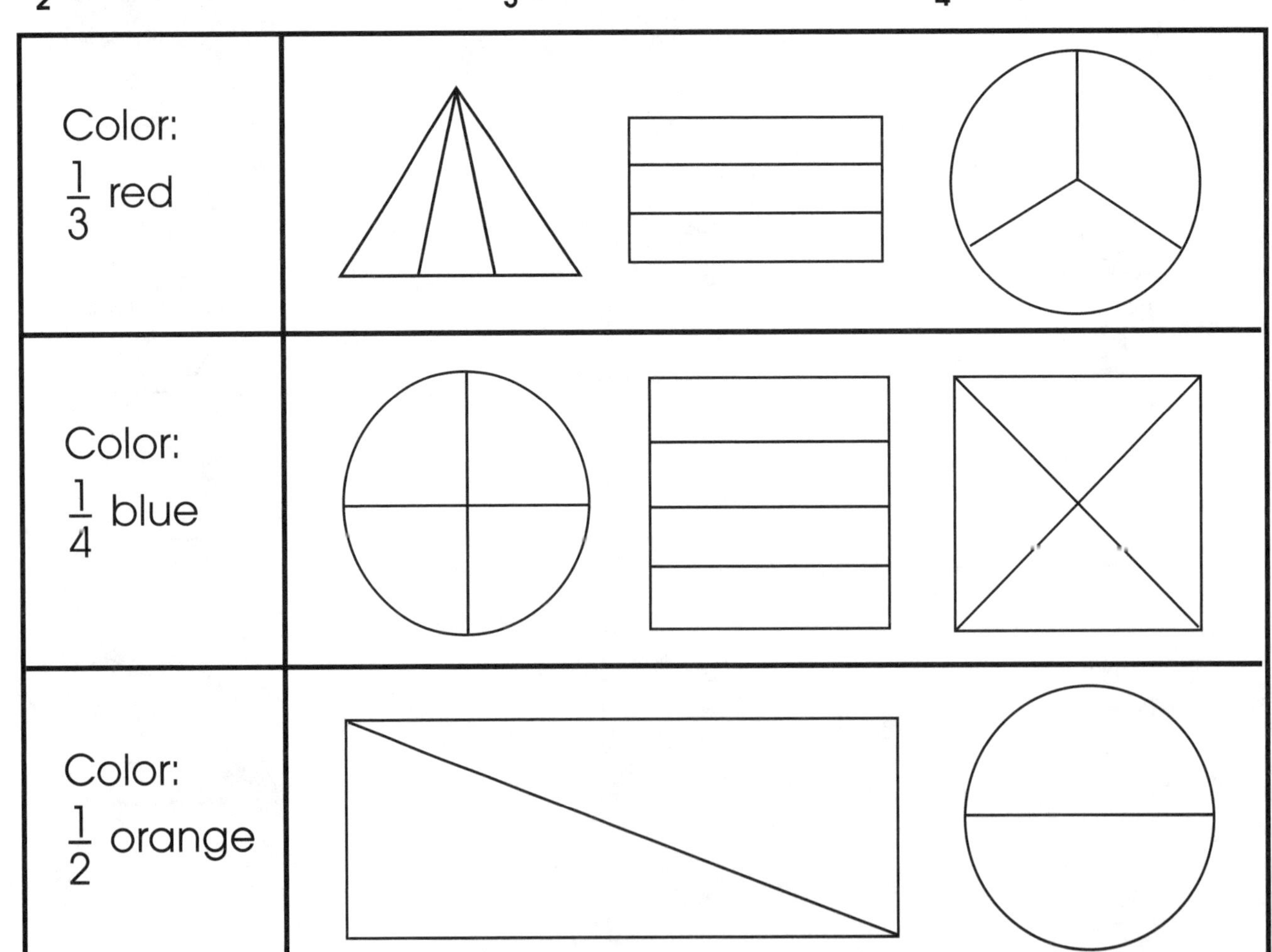

Color: $\frac{1}{3}$ red
Color: $\frac{1}{4}$ blue
Color: $\frac{1}{2}$ orange

Fractions: Half, Third, Fourth

Directions: Draw a line from the fraction to the correct shape.

$\frac{1}{4}$ shaded

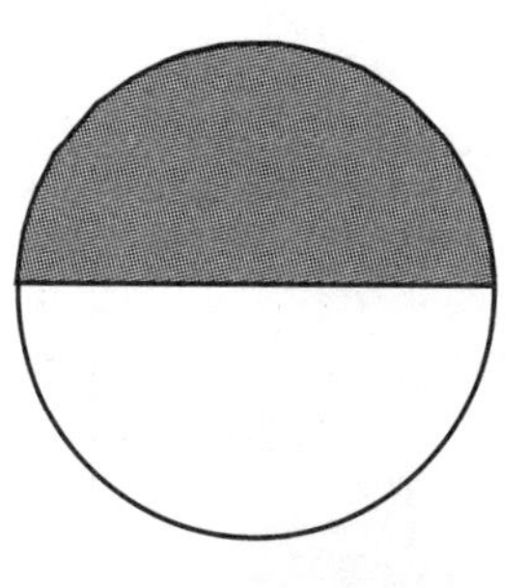

$\frac{2}{4}$ shaded

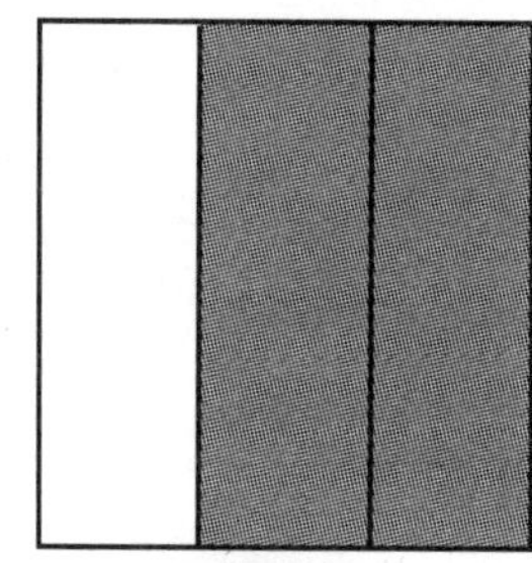

$\frac{1}{2}$ shaded

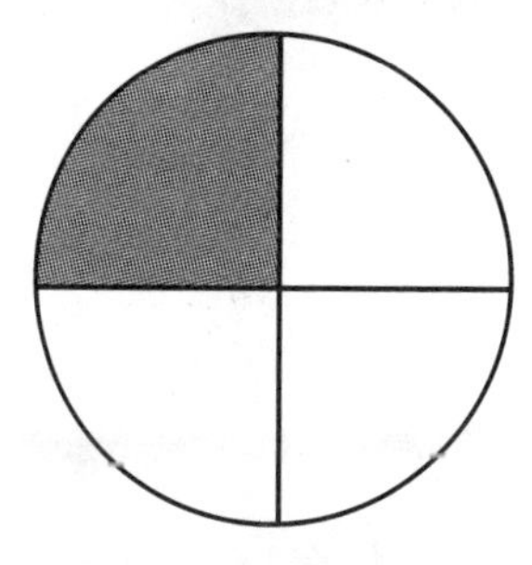

$\frac{1}{3}$ shaded

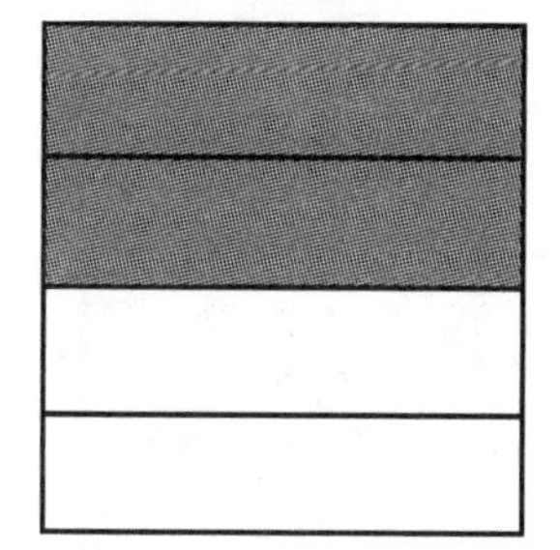

$\frac{2}{3}$ shaded

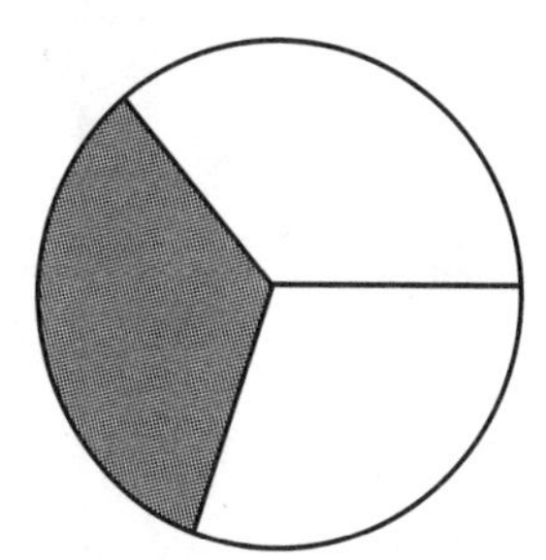

Fractions: Half, Third, Fourth

Directions: Study the examples. Circle the fraction that shows the shaded part. Then circle the fraction that shows the white part.

Examples:

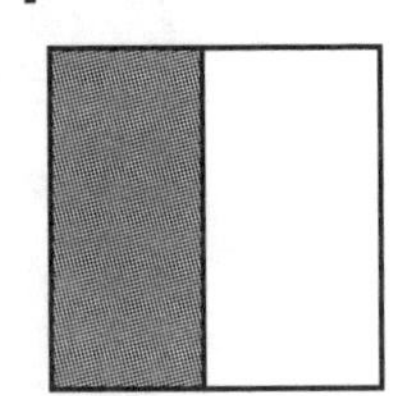

shaded $\frac{1}{4}$ $\frac{1}{3}$ $\frac{1}{2}$ **white** $\frac{1}{3}$ $\frac{1}{2}$ $\frac{1}{4}$

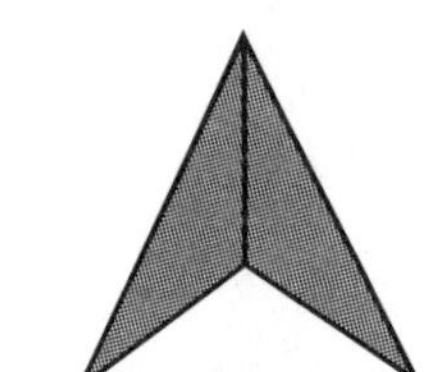

shaded $\frac{1}{2}$ $\frac{2}{3}$ $\frac{3}{4}$ **white** $\frac{2}{3}$ $\frac{1}{2}$ $\frac{1}{3}$

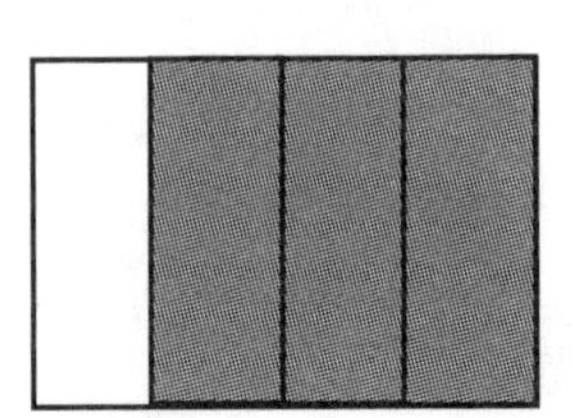

shaded $\frac{1}{4}$ $\frac{1}{2}$ $\frac{3}{4}$ **white** $\frac{1}{4}$ $\frac{2}{3}$ $\frac{1}{2}$

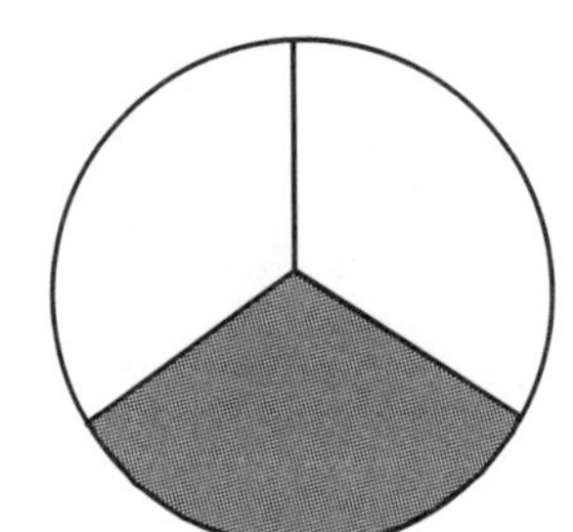

shaded $\frac{1}{4}$ $\frac{1}{3}$ $\frac{1}{2}$ **white** $\frac{2}{4}$ $\frac{2}{3}$ $\frac{2}{2}$

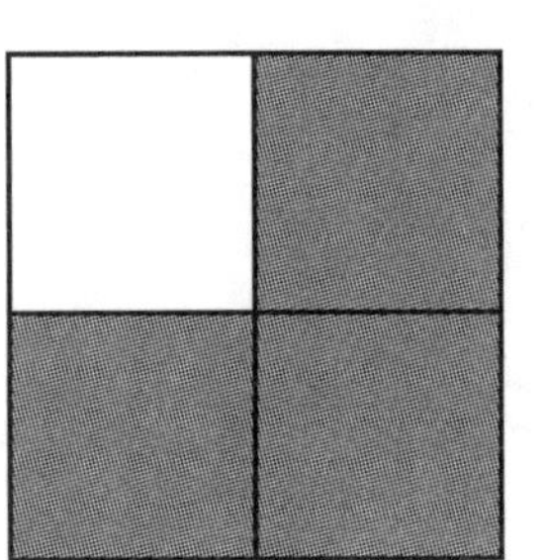

shaded $\frac{3}{4}$ $\frac{1}{3}$ $\frac{3}{2}$ **white** $\frac{1}{2}$ $\frac{1}{4}$ $\frac{1}{3}$

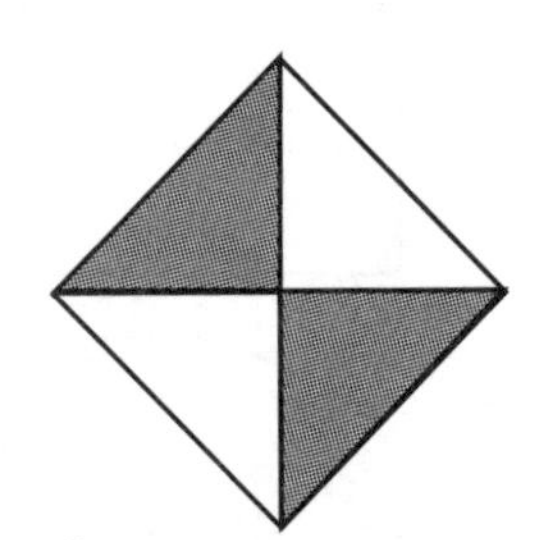

shaded $\frac{2}{3}$ $\frac{2}{4}$ $\frac{2}{2}$ **white** $\frac{1}{3}$ $\frac{2}{4}$ $\frac{2}{2}$

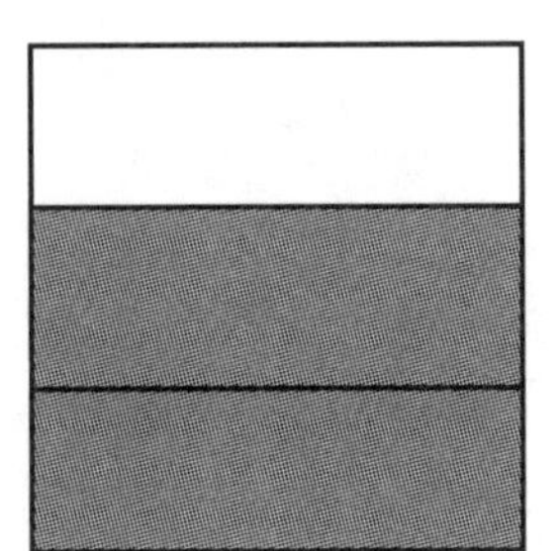

shaded $\frac{2}{4}$ $\frac{2}{3}$ $\frac{2}{2}$ **white** $\frac{1}{2}$ $\frac{1}{4}$ $\frac{1}{3}$

Fractions: Comparing

Directions: Circle the fraction in each pair that is larger.

Example:

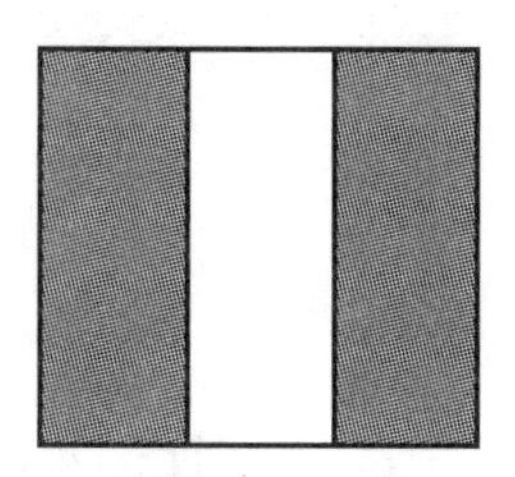

$\frac{2}{3}$

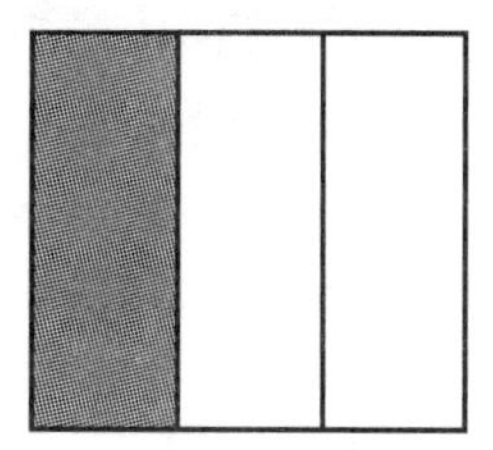

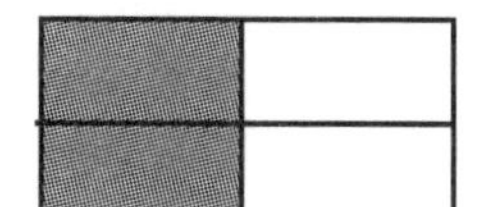

$\frac{2}{4}$

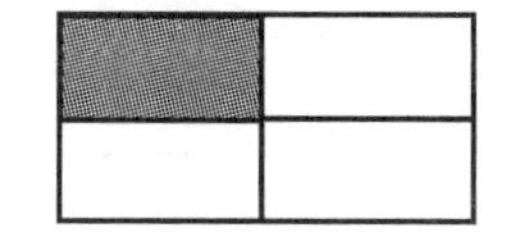

$\frac{1}{4}$

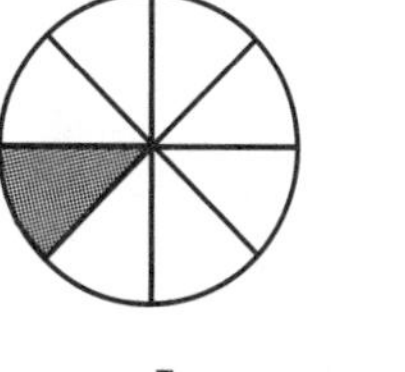

$\frac{1}{8}$

$\frac{2}{8}$

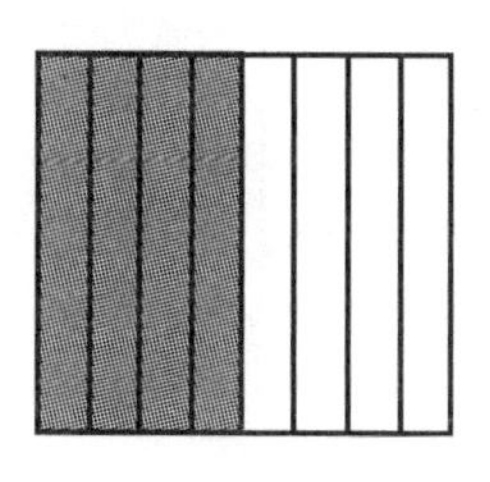

$\frac{1}{2}$

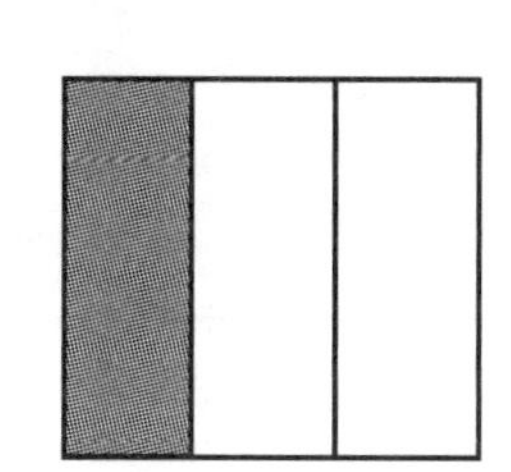

$\frac{1}{3}$

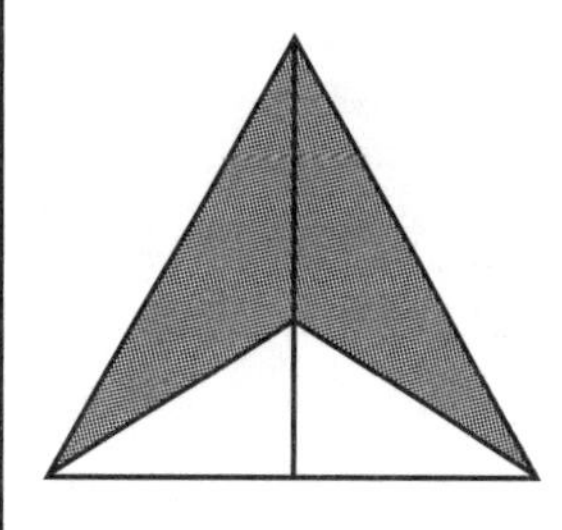

$\frac{2}{3}$

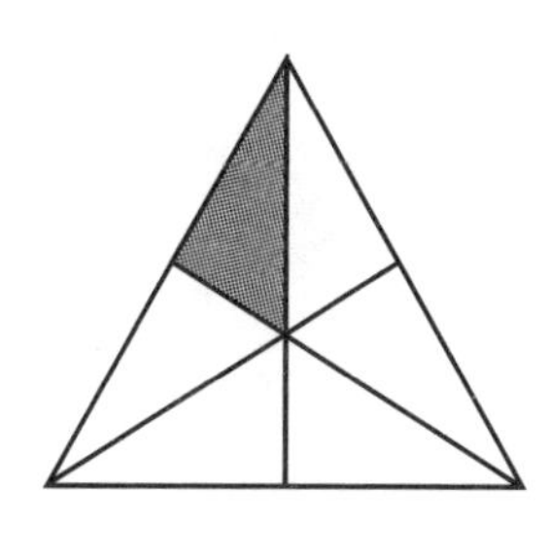

$\frac{1}{6}$

$\frac{1}{4}$ or $\frac{1}{6}$

$\frac{1}{5}$ or $\frac{1}{7}$

$\frac{1}{8}$ or $\frac{1}{4}$

Decimals

A **decimal** is a number with one or more numbers to the right of a decimal point. A **decimal point** is a dot placed between the ones place and the tens place of a number, such as 2.5.

Example:

$\frac{3}{10}$ can be written as 0.3 They are both read as three-tenths.

Directions: Write the answer as a decimal for the shaded parts.

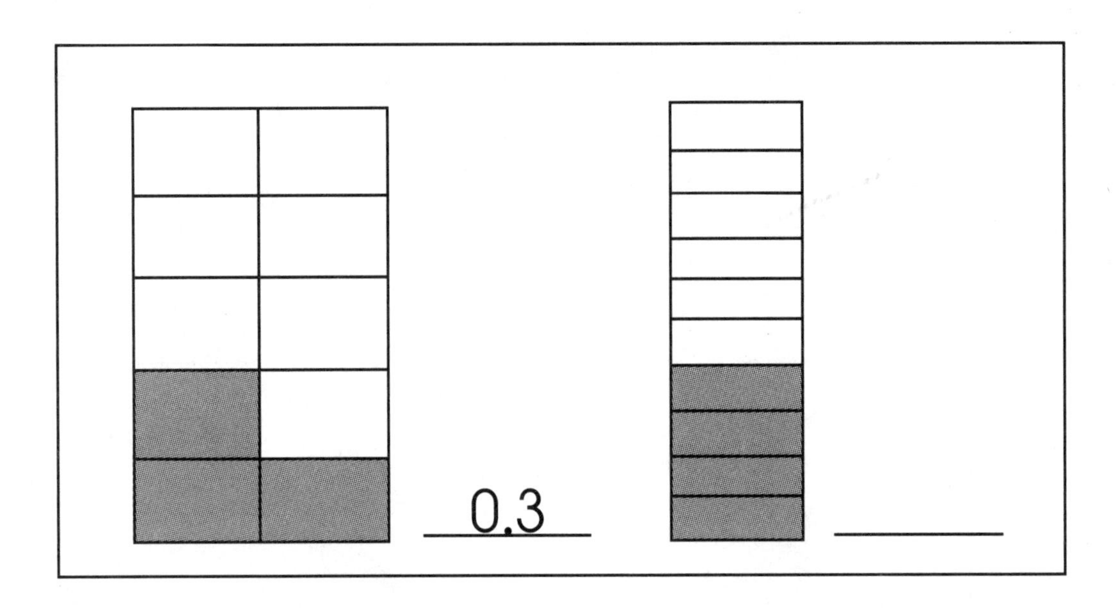

Directions: Color parts of each object to match the decimals given.

0.7

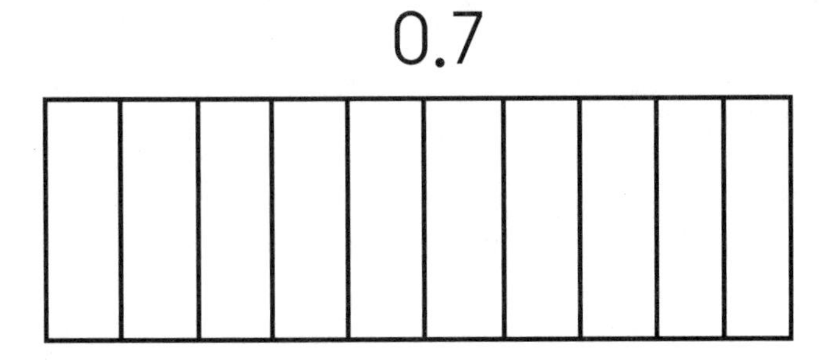

0.6

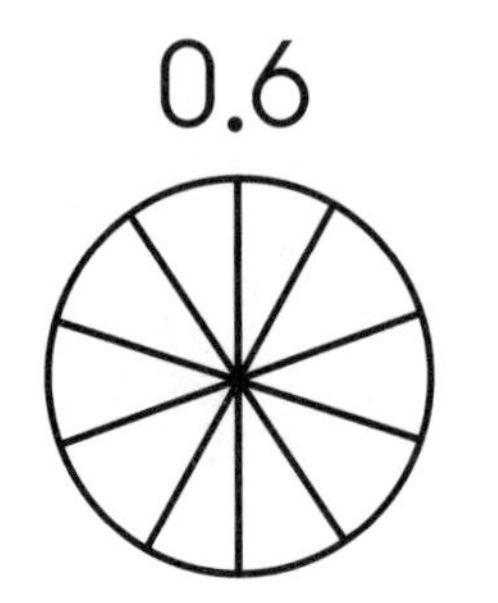

0.5

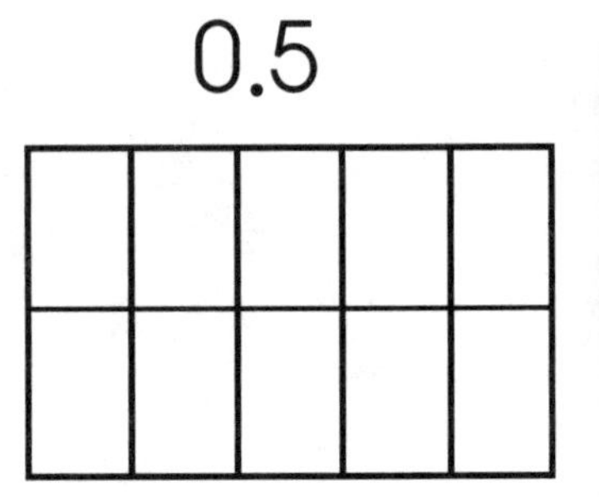

Graphs

Directions: Count the fish. Color the bowls to make a graph that shows the number of fish.

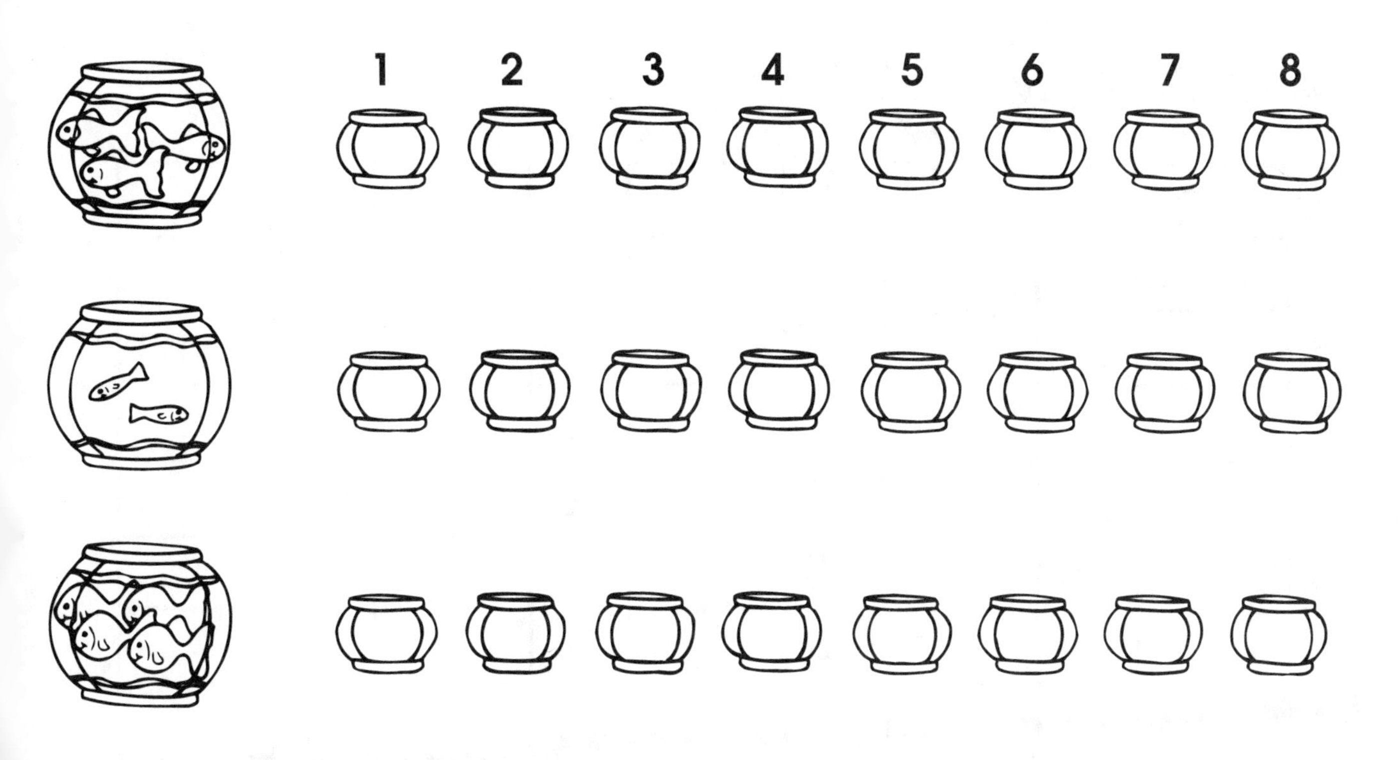

Directions: Use your fishbowl graphs to find the answers to the following questions. Draw a line to the correct bowl.

The most fish

The fewest fish

Graphs

Directions: Count the bananas in each row. Color the boxes to show how many have been eaten by the monkeys.

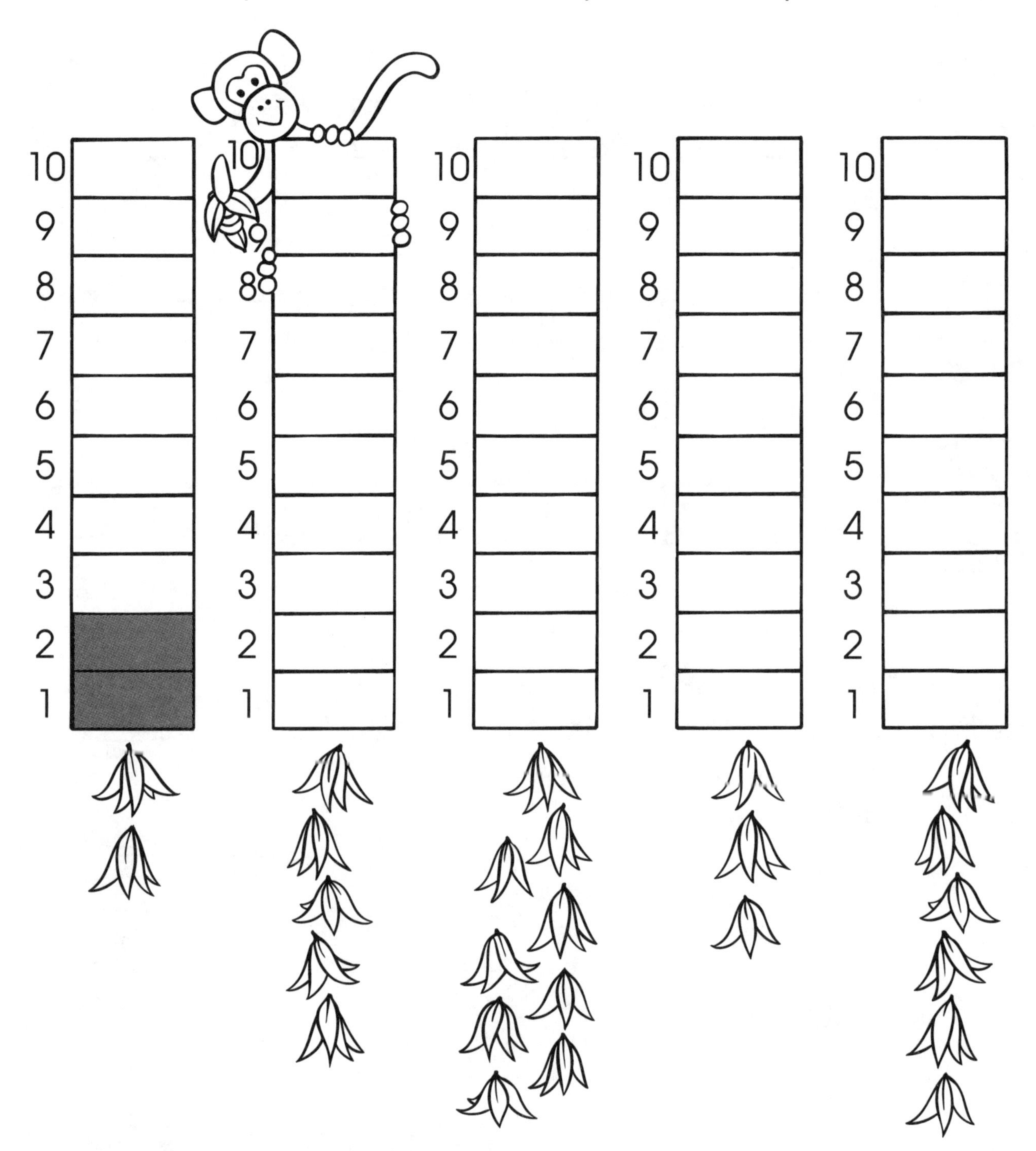

Graphs

A graph is a drawing that shows information about numbers.

Directions: Color the picture. Then tell how many there are of each object by completing the graph.

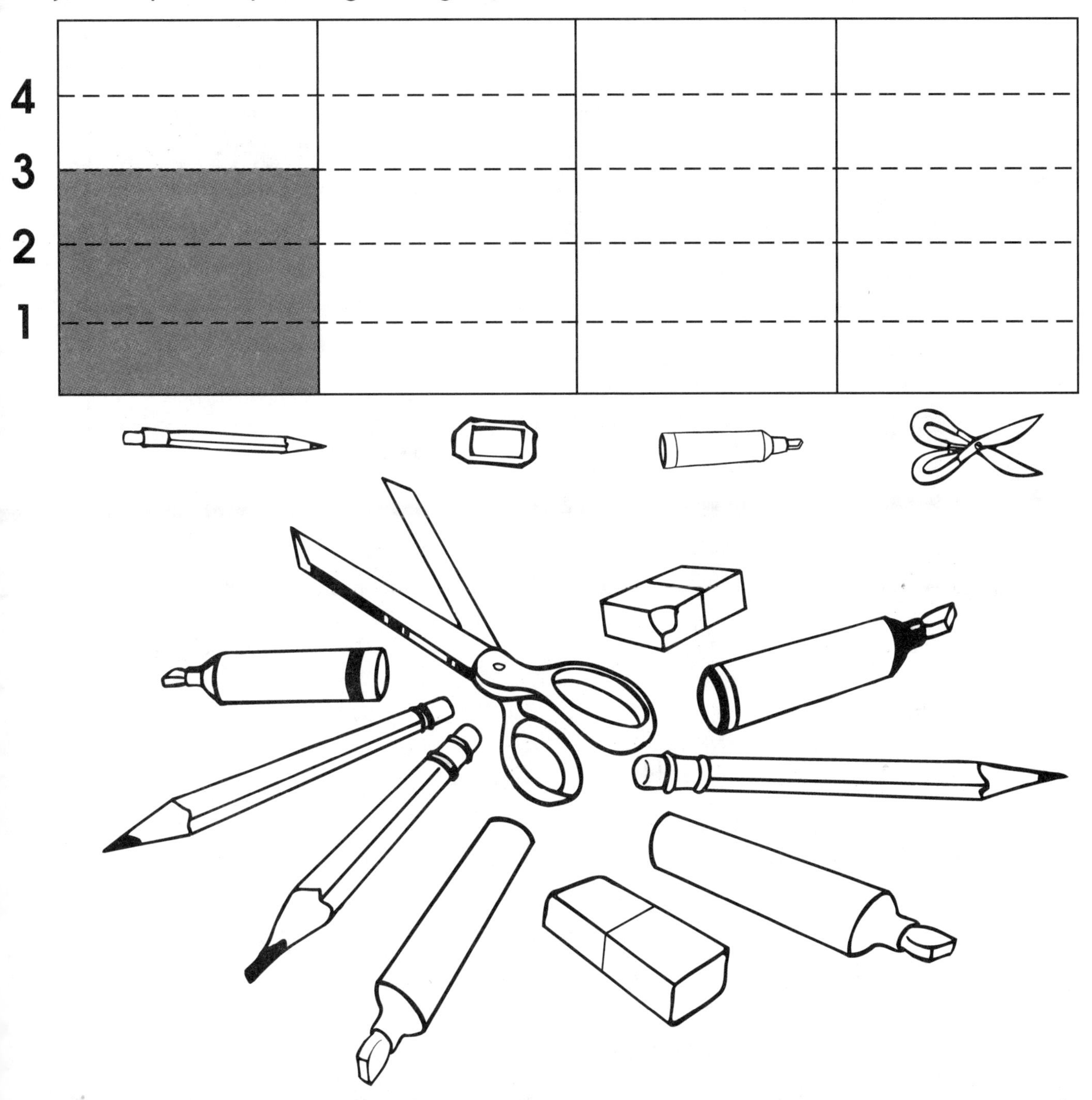

Graphs

Directions: Answer the questions about the graph.

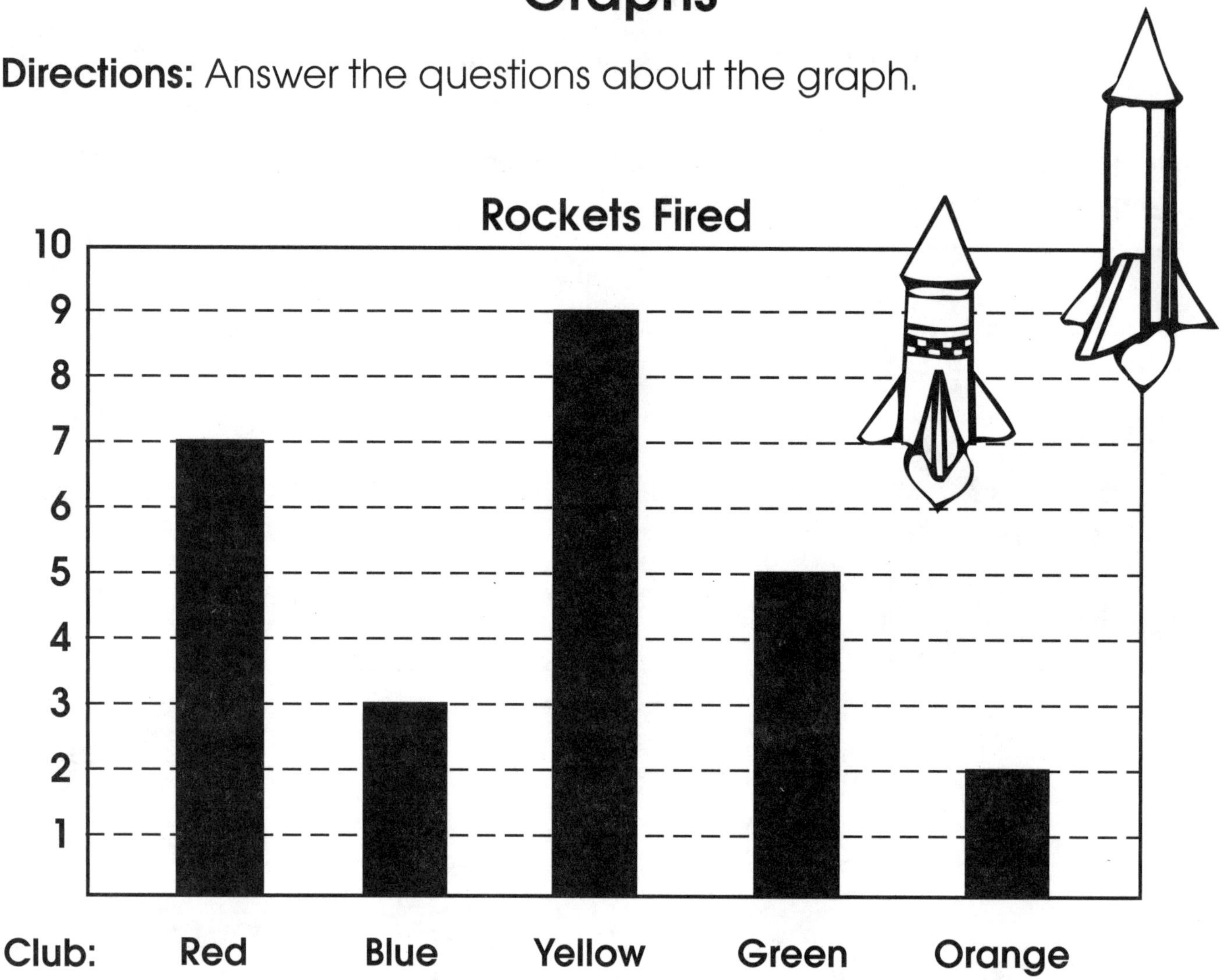

Rockets Fired

10
9
8
7
6
5
4
3
2
1

Club: **Red** **Blue** **Yellow** **Green** **Orange**

How many rockets did the Red Club fire? __________

How many rockets did the Green Club fire? __________

The Yellow Club fired 9 rockets. How many more rockets did it fire than the Blue Club? __________

How many rockets were fired in all? __________

Geometry

Geometry is mathematics that has to do with lines and shapes.

Directions: Color the shapes.

Color the triangles blue.
Color the circles red.
Color the squares green.
Color the rectangles pink.

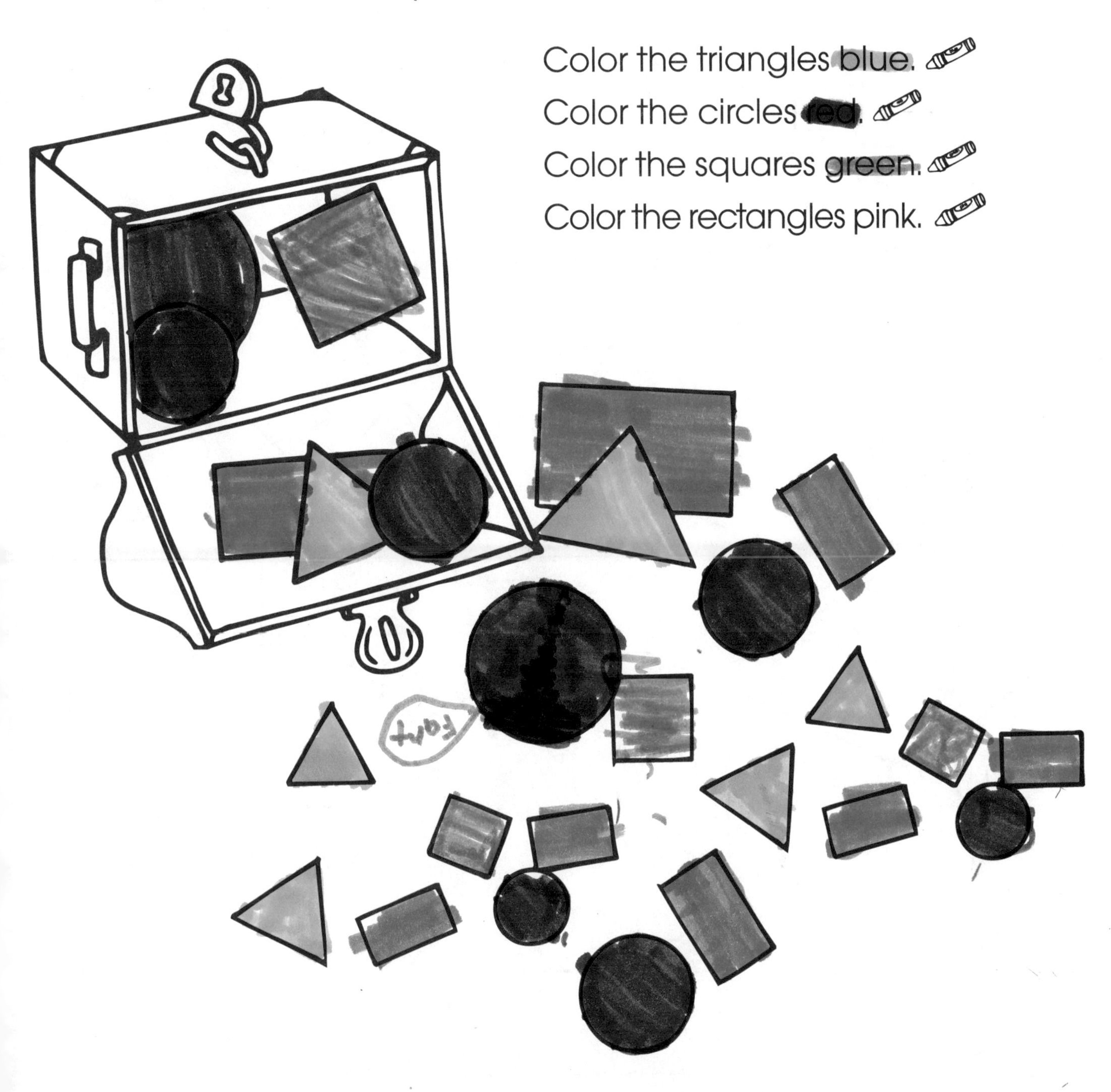

Geometry

Closed figures are figures whose lines connect. **Open figures** are figures whose lines do not connect.

Example:

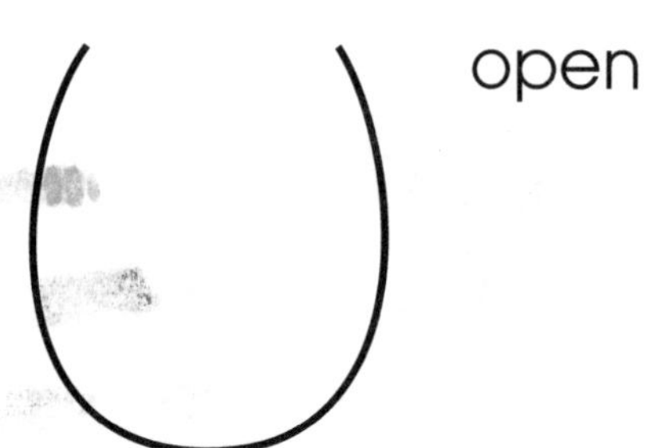

open

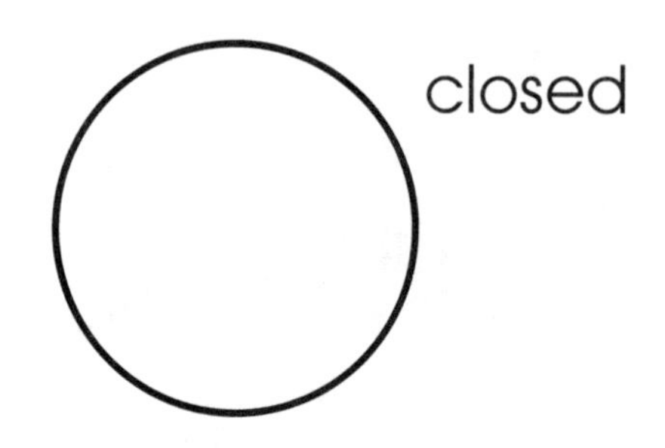

closed

Directions: Draw an **X** on the open figures and circle the closed figures.

Geometry

Directions: Answer the questions.

How many triangles do you see? ____

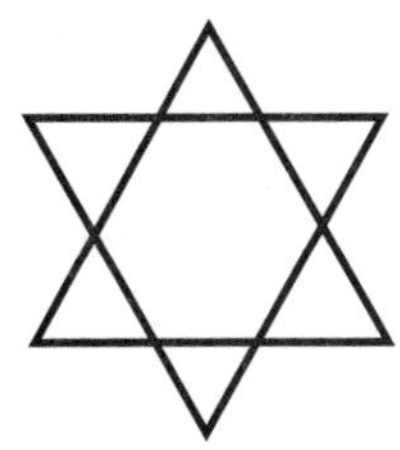

How many squares in this figure? ____

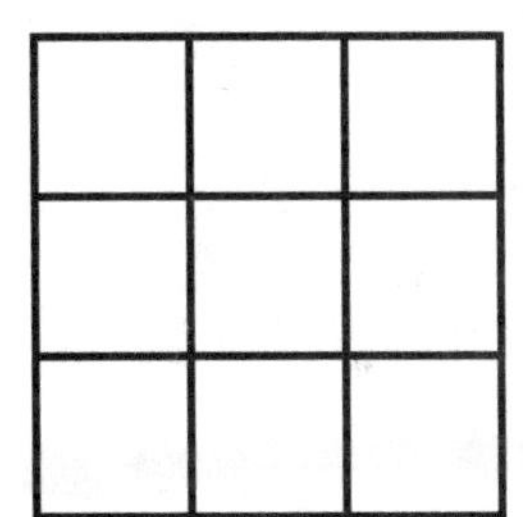

How many line segments can be drawn to connect the four dots? ____

Geometry

You have learned about shapes such as circles, square, triangles and rectangles. You will recognize these shapes in the three-dimensional figures shown below.

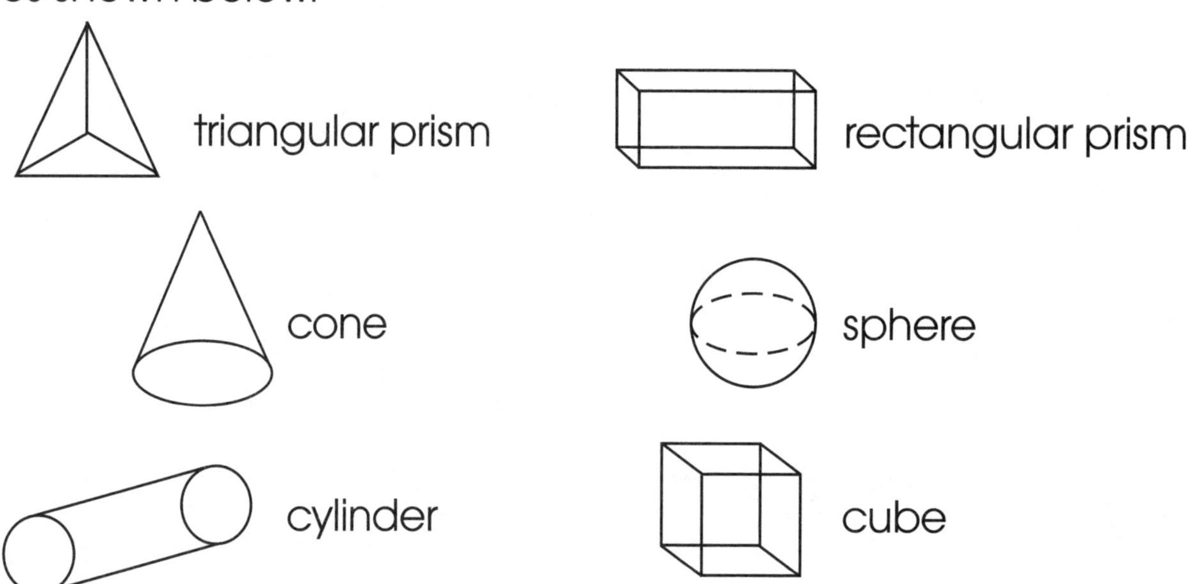

Directions: Draw a picture of an object you know which looks like each figure.

cube:

cone:

triangular prism:

cylinder:

rectangular prism:

sphere:

Tangram

Directions: Cut out the tangram below. Use the shapes to make a cat, a chicken, a boat and a large triangle.

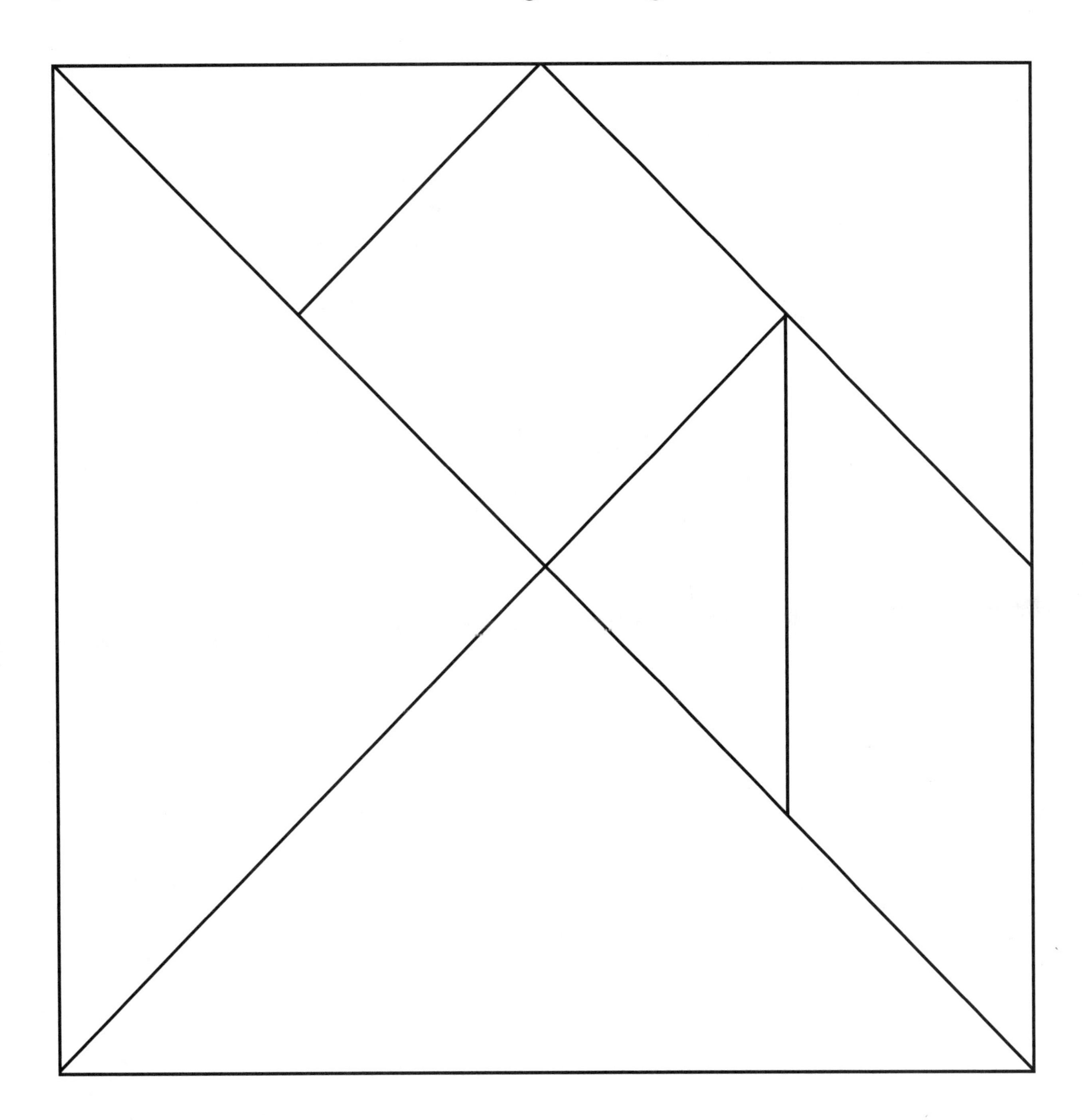

This page is blank for the cutting exercise
on the previous page.

Time: Hour, Half-Hour

An hour is sixty minutes. The short hand of a clock tells the hour. It is written **0:00**, such as **5:00**. A half-hour is thirty minutes. When the long hand of the clock is pointing to the six, the time is on the half-hour. It is written **:30**, such as **5:30**.

Directions: Study the examples.
Tell what time it is on each clock.

Examples:

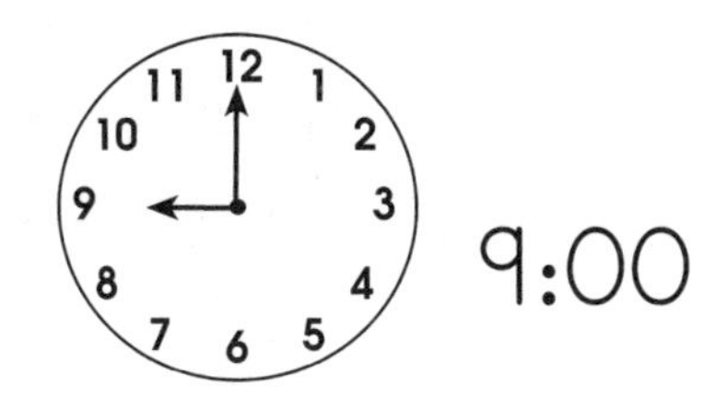

The minute hand is on the 12.
The hour hand is on the 9.
It is 9 o'clock.

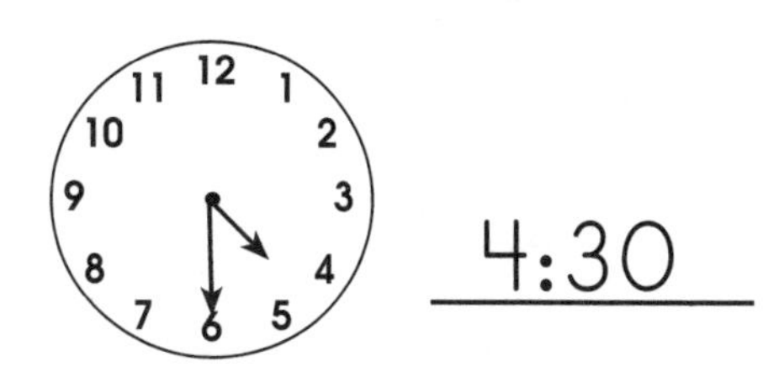

The minute hand is *on* the 6.
The hour hand is *between* the 4 and 5.
It is 4:30.

 ______

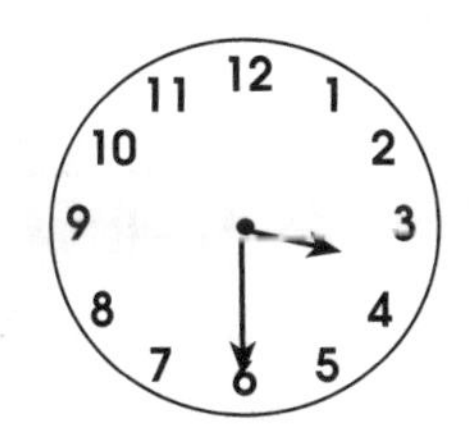 ______

 ______

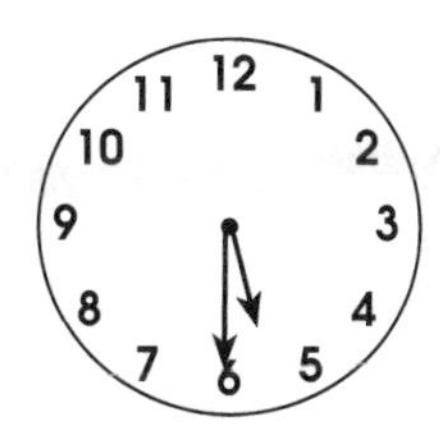 ______

 ______

 ______

 ______

 ______

 ______

 ______

Time: Hour, Half-Hour

Directions: Draw lines between the clocks that show the same time.

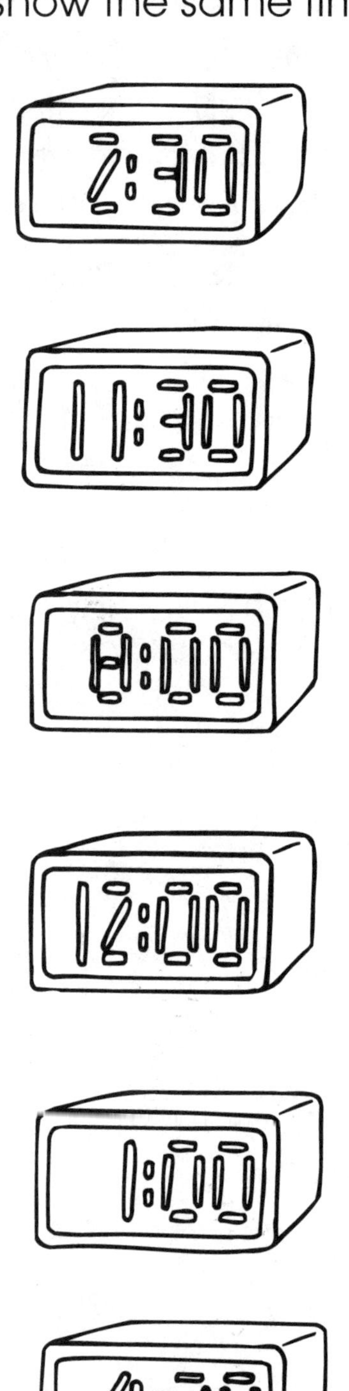

Time: Quarter-Hours

Time can also be shown as fractions. 30 minutes = $\frac{1}{2}$ hour.

Directions: Shade the fraction of each clock and tell how many minutes you have shaded.

Example:

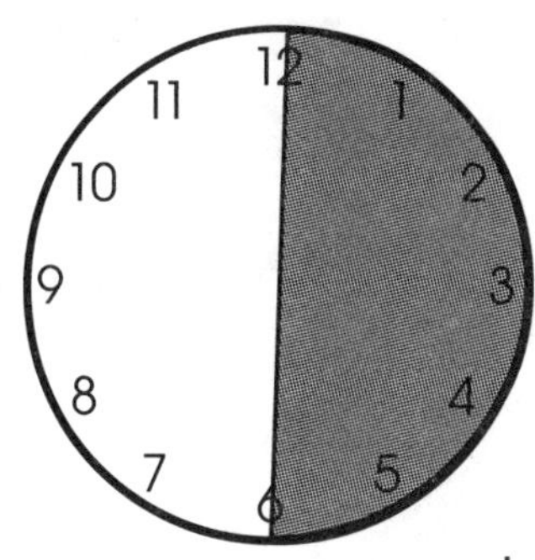

$\frac{1}{2}$ hour

30 minutes

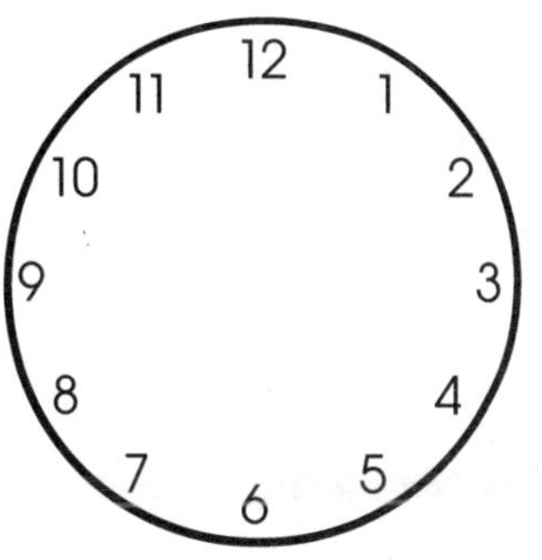

$\frac{1}{4}$ hour

____ minutes

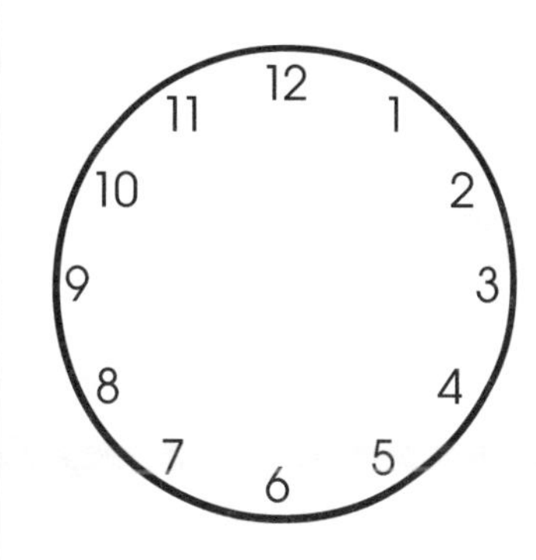

$\frac{2}{4}$ hour

____ minutes

12 1 2 3 4 5 6 7 8 9 10 11

$\frac{3}{4}$ hour

____ minutes

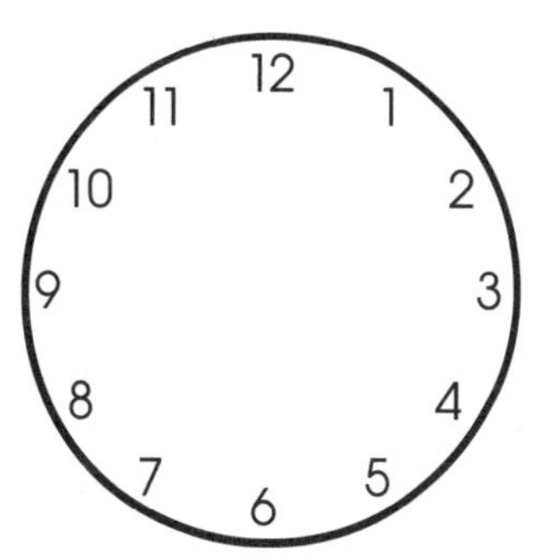

$\frac{1}{2}$ hour

____ minutes

Time: Counting by 5's

The minute hand of a clock takes 5 minutes to move from one number to the next. Start at the 12 and count by fives to tell how many minutes it is past the hour.

Directions: Study the examples. Tell what time is on each clock.

Examples:

9:10

8:25

____

____

____

____

____

____

____

____

____

Time: a.m. and p.m.

In telling time, the hours between 12:00 midnight and 12:00 noon are a.m. hours. The hours between 12:00 noon and 12:00 midnight are p.m. hours.

Directions: Draw a line between the times that are the same.

Examples:

7:30 in the morning — 7:30 a.m.
half-past seven a.m.
seven thirty in the morning

9:00 in the evening - - - 9:00 p.m.
nine o'clock at night

six o'clock in the evening	8:00 a.m.
3:30 a.m.	six o'clock in the morning
4:15 p.m.	6:00 p.m.
eight o'clock in the morning	eleven o'clock in the evening
quarter past five in the evening	three thirty in the morning
11:00 p.m.	four fifteen in the evening
6:00 a.m.	5:15 p.m.

Time: Addition

Directions: Add the hours and minutes together.
(Remember, 1 hour equals 60 minutes.)

Examples:

2 hours 10 minutes
\+ 1 hour 50 minutes
3 hours 60 minutes
(1 hour)
4 hours

4 hours 20 minutes
\+ 2 hours 10 minutes
6 hours 30 minutes

9 hours
\+ 2 hours

1 hour
\+ 5 hours

6 hours
\+ 3 hours

6 hours 15 minutes
\+ 1 hour 15 minutes

10 hours 30 minutes
\+ 1 hour 10 minutes

3 hours 40 minutes
\+ 8 hours 20 minutes

11 hours 15 minutes
\+ 1 hour 30 minutes

4 hours 15 minutes
\+ 5 hours 45 minutes

7 hours 10 minutes
\+ 1 hour 30 minutes

Time: Subtraction

Directions: Subtract the hours and minutes.
(Remember, 1 hour equals 60 minutes.)
"Borrow" from the "hours" if you need to.

Example:

5 70
~~6~~ hours ~~10~~ minutes
- 2 hours 30 minutes
3 hours 40 minutes

12 hours
- 2 hours

5 hour
- 3 hours

2 hours
- 1 hour

5 hours 30 minutes
- 2 hours 15 minutes

9 hours 45 minutes
- 3 hours 15 minutes

11 hours 50 minutes
- 4 hours 35 minutes

12 hours
- 6 hours 30 minutes

7 hours 15 minutes
- 5 hours 30 minutes

8 hours 10 minutes
- 4 hours 40 minutes

Money: Penny, Nickel, Dime

Penny **1¢** Nickel **5¢** Dime **10¢**

Directions: Count the coins and write the amount.

16 ¢

_______ ¢

_______ ¢

_______ ¢

_______ ¢

Money: Penny, Nickel, Dime

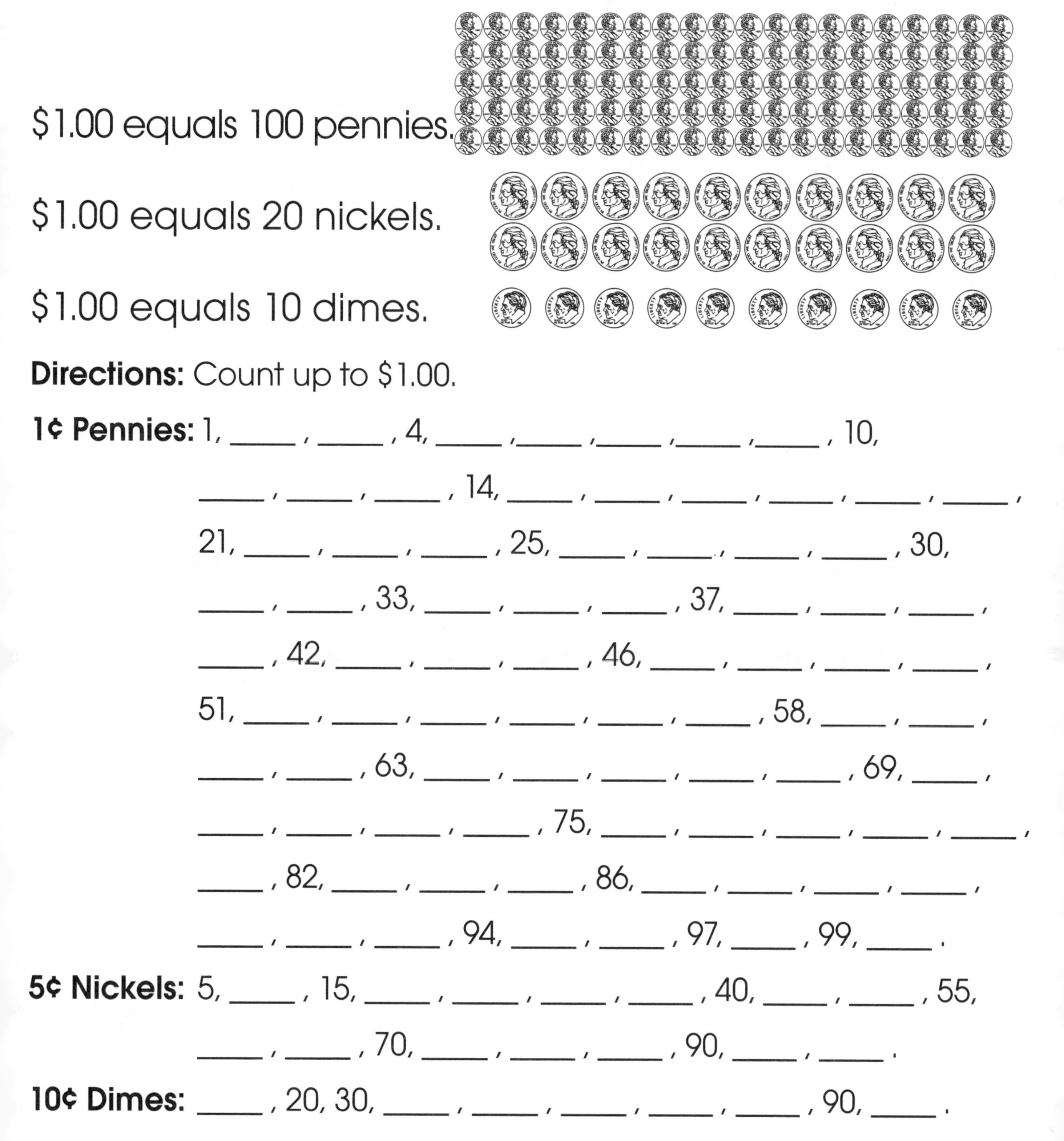

$1.00 equals 100 pennies.

$1.00 equals 20 nickels.

$1.00 equals 10 dimes.

Directions: Count up to $1.00.

1¢ Pennies: 1, ____, ____, 4, ____, ____, ____, ____, ____, 10,

____, ____, ____, 14, ____, ____, ____, ____, ____, ____,

21, ____, ____, ____, 25, ____, ____, ____, ____, 30,

____, ____, 33, ____, ____, ____, 37, ____, ____, ____,

____, 42, ____, ____, ____, 46, ____, ____, ____, ____,

51, ____, ____, ____, ____, ____, ____, 58, ____, ____,

____, ____, 63, ____, ____, ____, ____, ____, 69, ____,

____, ____, ____, ____, 75, ____, ____, ____, ____, ____,

____, 82, ____, ____, ____, 86, ____, ____, ____, ____,

____, ____, ____, 94, ____, ____, 97, ____, 99, ____.

5¢ Nickels: 5, ____, 15, ____, ____, ____, ____, 40, ____, ____, 55,

____, ____, 70, ____, ____, ____, 90, ____, ____.

10¢ Dimes: ____, 20, 30, ____, ____, ____, ____, ____, 90, ____.

Money: Penny, Nickel, Dime

Directions: Draw a line from the toy to the amount of money it costs.

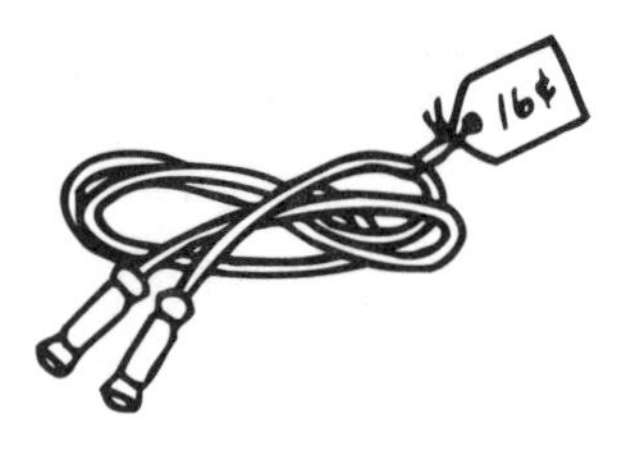

Money: Penny, Nickel, Dime

Directions: Draw a line to match the amounts of money.

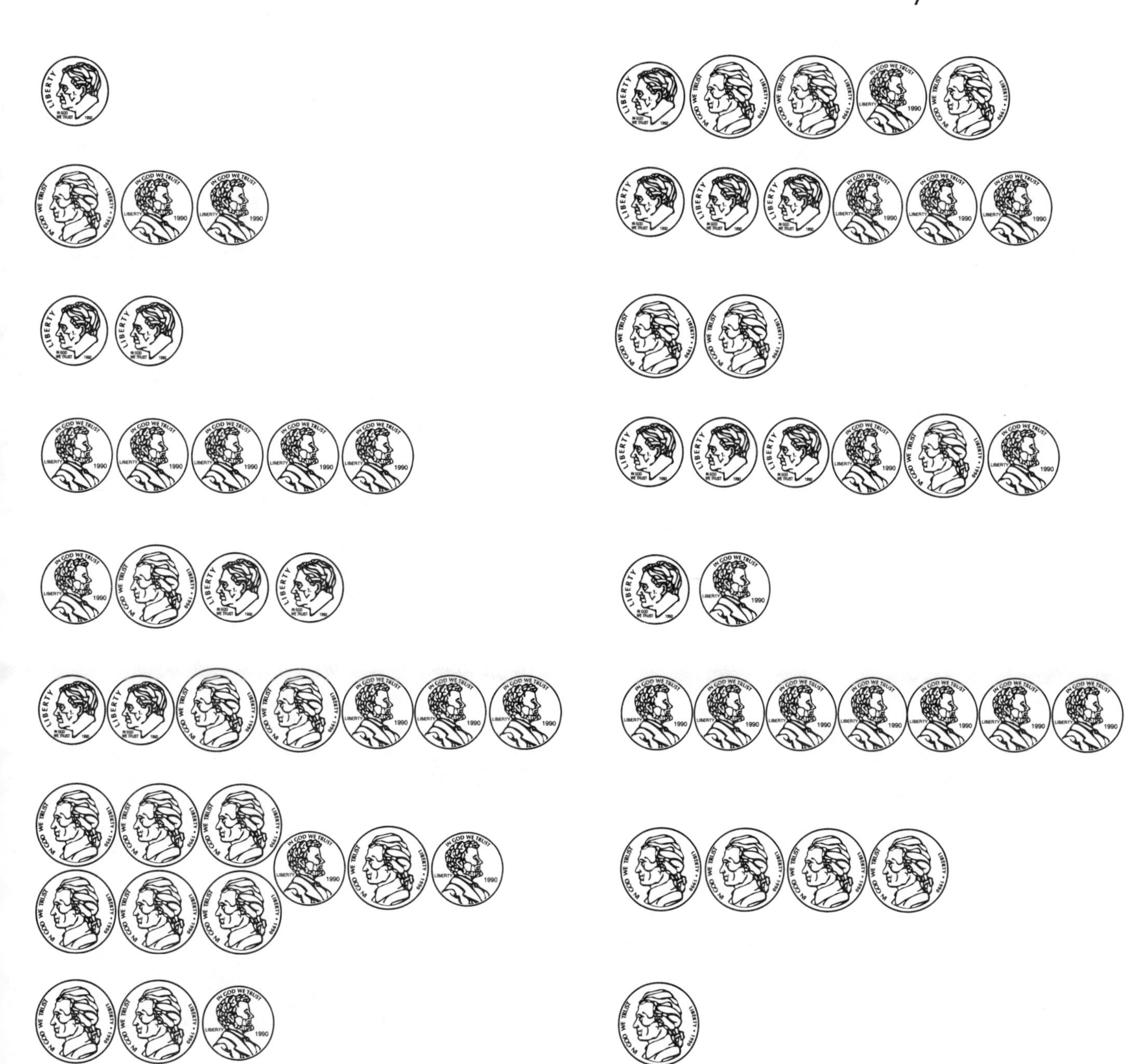

Money: Quarter

A quarter is worth 25¢.

Directions: Count the coins and write the amounts.

______ ¢

______ ¢

______ ¢

______ ¢

______ ¢

______ ¢

______ ¢

______ ¢

Money: Dollar

One dollar equals 100 cents. It is written $1.00.

Directions: Count the money and write the amounts.

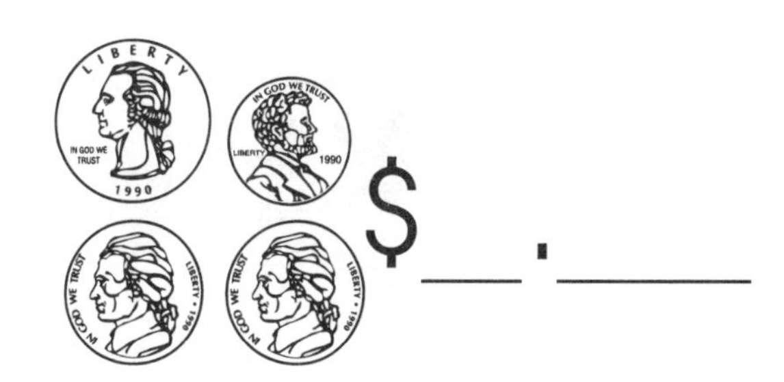

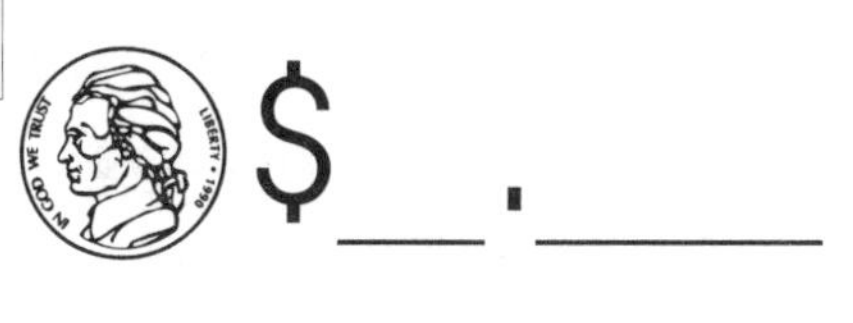

Adding Money

Directions: Write each amount of money as a decimal. Then add to find the total amount.

Example:

$1.00
+ .25
$1.25

$ ____ . ______
$ ____ . ______
+ $ ____ . ______
$ ____ . ______

$ ____ . ______
$ ____ . ______
+ $ ____ . ______
$ ____ . ______

$ ____ . ______
$ ____ . ______
$ ____ . ______
+ $ ____ . ______
$ ____ . ______

$ ____ . ______
$ ____ . ______
$ ____ . ______
+ $ ____ . ______
$ ____ . ______

Money: Practice

Directions: Draw a line from each food item to the correct amount of money.

$1.59

$.89

$1.27

$1.09

$.77

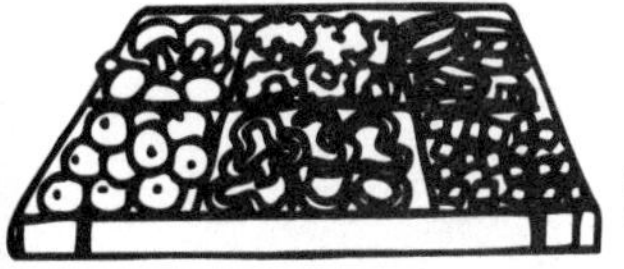

$1.95

Money: Five-Dollar Bill and Ten-Dollar Bill

Directions: Write the amount for each group of money shown. Use a dollar sign and decimal point. The first one is done for you.

Five-dollar bill =
5 one-dollar bills

Ten-dollar bill =
2 five-dollar bills or
10 one-dollar bills

$15.00

____

____

____

7 one-dollar bills, 2 quarters __________

2 five-dollar bills, 3 one-dollar bills, half-dollar __________

3 ten-dollar bills, 1 five-dollar bill, 3 quarters__________

Money: Counting Change

Directions: Subtract the money using decimals to show how much change a person would receive in each of the following.

Example:

Bill had 3 dollars. $3.00

He bought a baseball for $2.83. -$2.83

How much change did he receive? $ .17

Paid 2 dollars.

____

Paid 1 dollar.

____

Paid 5 dollars.

____

Paid 10 dollars.

____

Paid 4 dollars.

____

Paid 7 dollars.

____

Review

Directions: Complete each clock to show the time written below it.

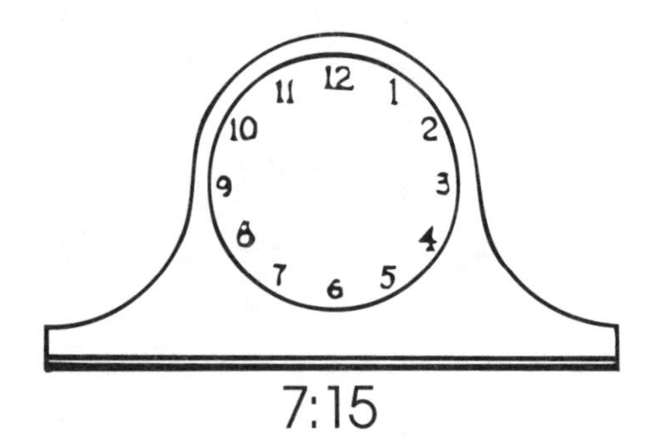

7:15

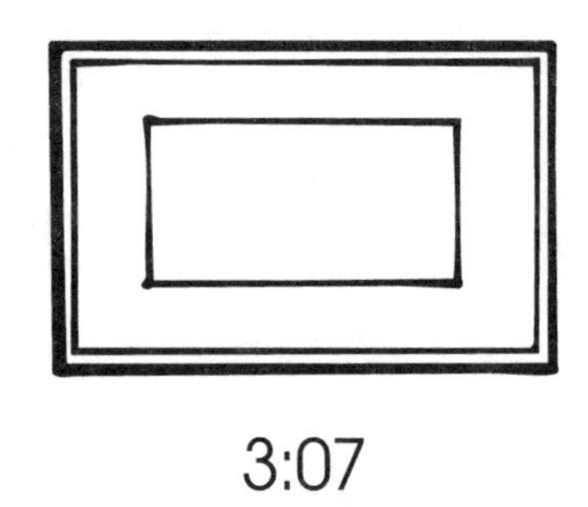

3:07

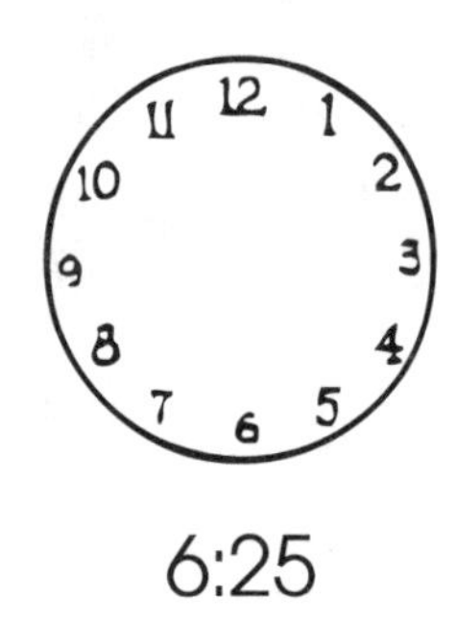

6:25

Directions: Write the time using a.m. or p.m.

seven twenty-two in the evening ______________________

three fifteen in the morning ______________________

eight thirty at night ______________________

Directions: Write the correct amount of money.

____

____

Joey paid $4.67 for a model car. He gave the clerk a five-dollar bill. How much change should he receive? __________

Measurement: Inches

An **inch** is a unit of length in the standard measurement system.

Directions: Use a ruler to measure each object to the nearest $\frac{1}{4}$ inch. Write **in.** to stand for inch.

Example:

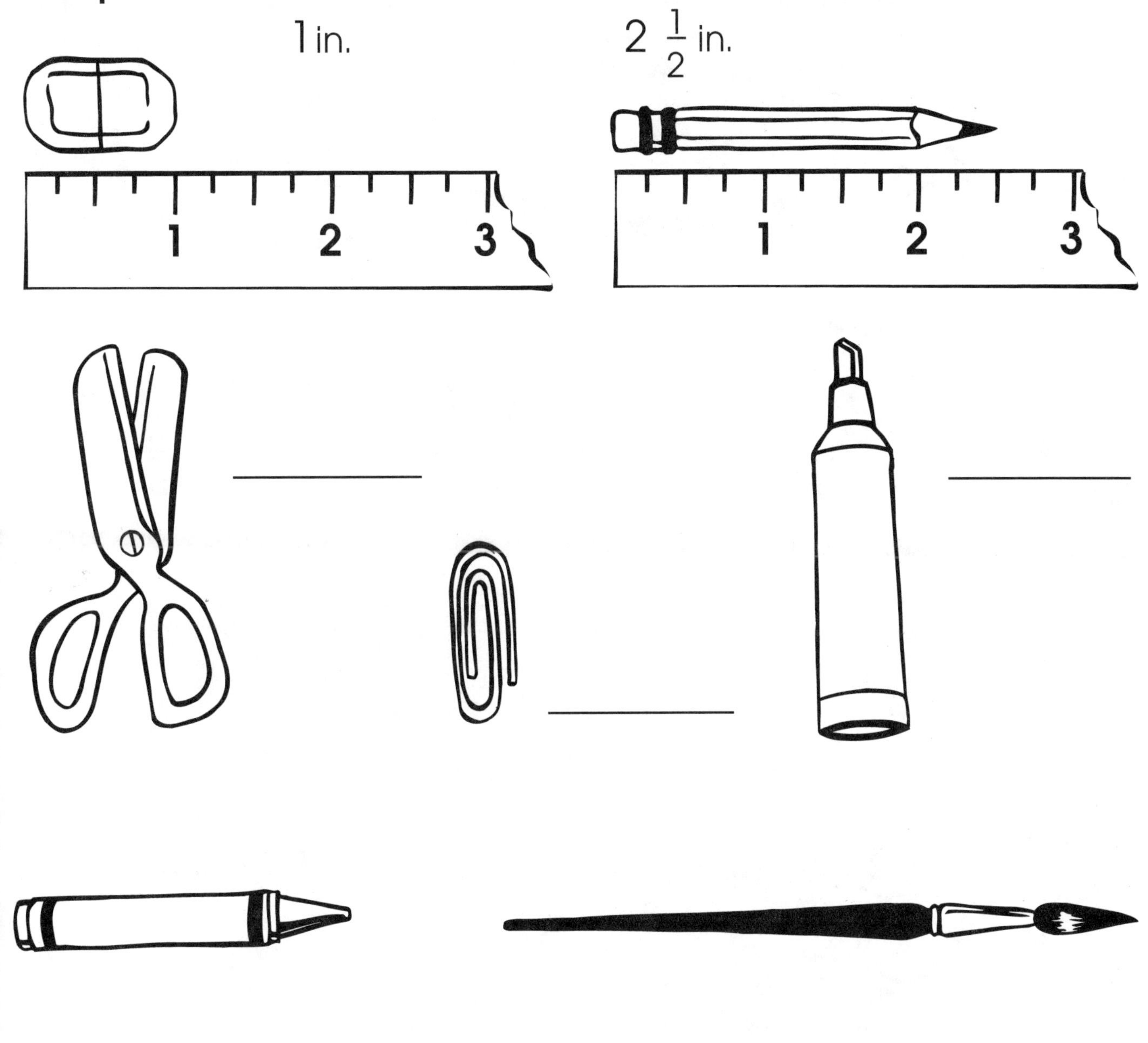

Measurement: Inches

Directions: Use the ruler to measure the fish to the nearest inch.

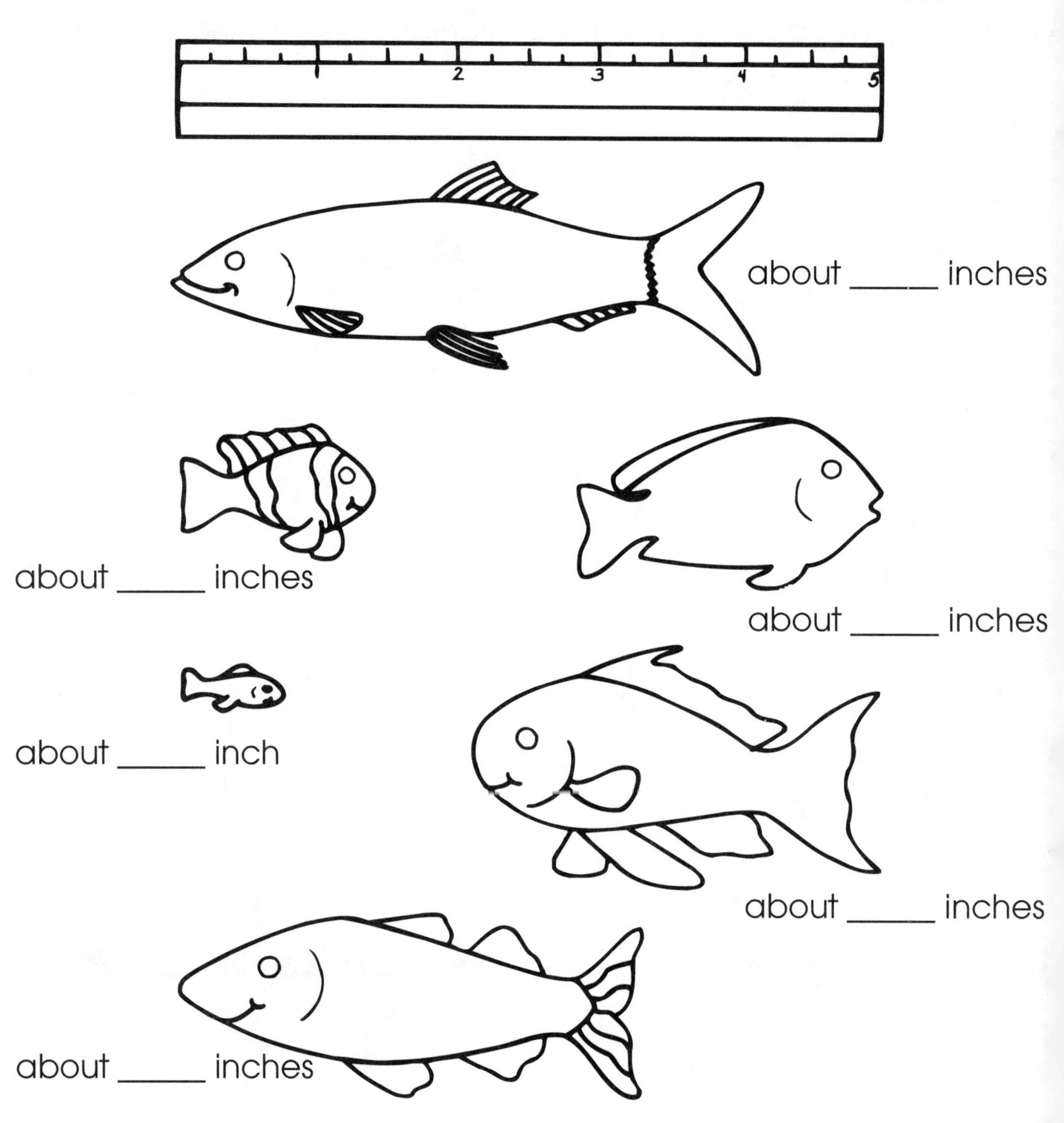

Measurement: Inches

Directions: Cut out the ruler. Measure each object to the nearest inch.

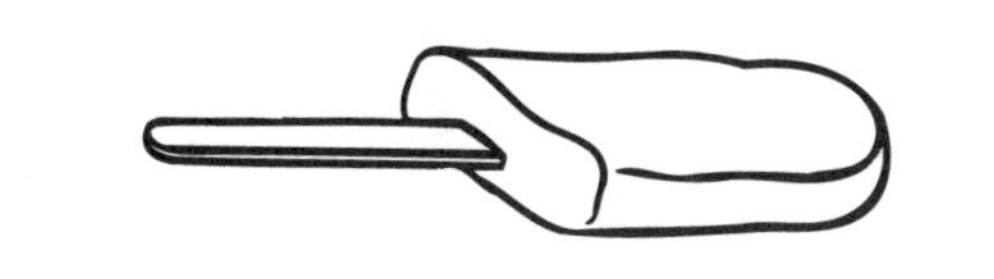

_______ inches

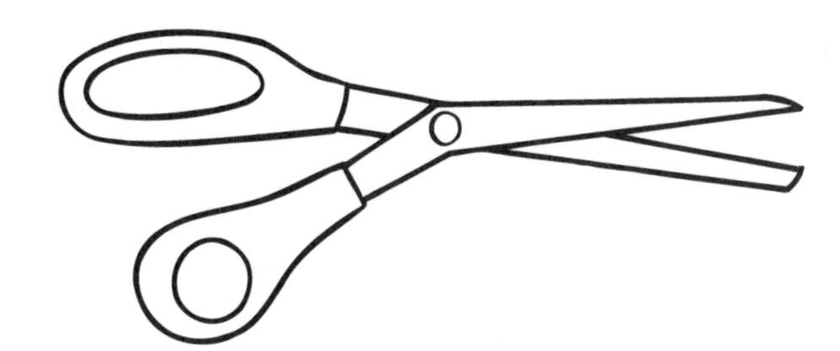

_______ inches

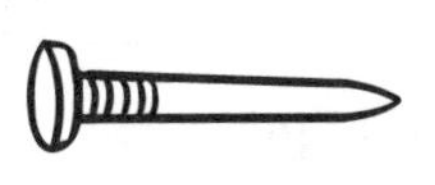

_______ inch

cut out

8 7 6 5 4 3 2 1

Measurement

Directions: Measure objects around your house. Write the measurement to the nearest inch.

can of soup _______ inches

pen _______ inches

toothbrush _______ inches

paper clip _______ inch

small toy _______ inches

This page is blank for the cutting exercise
on the previous page.

Measurement: Foot, Yard, Mile

Directions: Decide whether you would use foot, yard or mile to measure each object.

1 foot = 12 inches
1 yard = 36 inches or 3 feet
1 mile = 1,760 yards

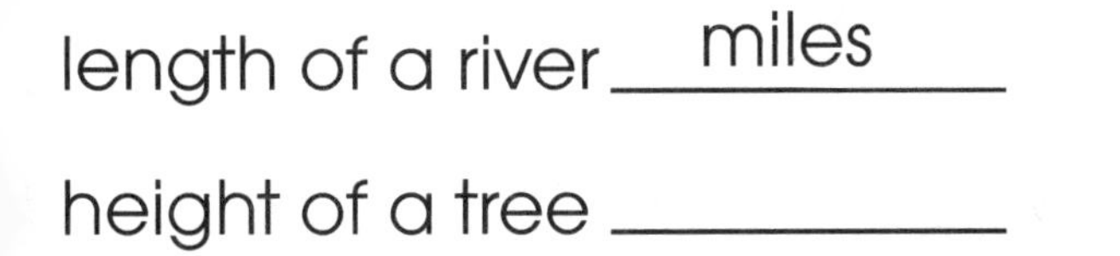

length of a river miles

height of a tree ____________

width of a room ____________

length of a football field ____________

height of a door ____________

length of a dress ____________

length of a race ____________

height of a basketball hoop ____________

width of a window ____________

distance a plane travels ____________

Directions: Solve the problem.

Tara races Tom in the 100-yard dash. Tara finishes 10 yards in front of Tom. How many feet did Tara finish in front of Tom? ____________

Measurement: Centimeters

A **centimeter** is a unit of length in the metric system. There are 2.54 centimeters in an inch.

Directions: Use a centimeter ruler to measure the crayons to the nearest centimeter.

Example: The first crayon is about 7 centimeters long.

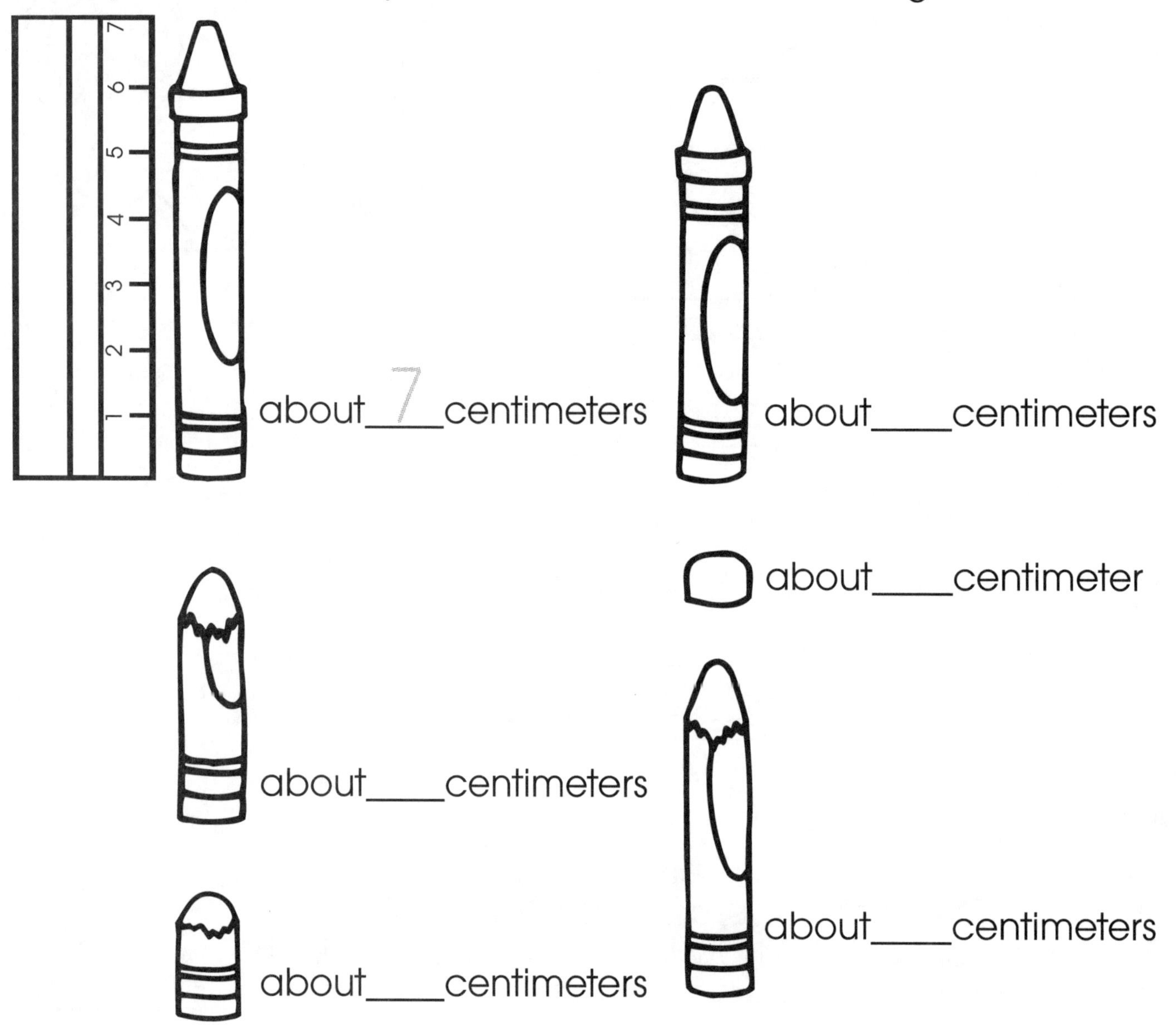

Measurement: Centimeter

A centimeter is a unit of length in the metric system. There are 2.54 centimeters in an inch.

Directions: Use a centimeter ruler to measure each object to the nearest half of a centimeter. Write **cm** to stand for centimeter.

Examples:

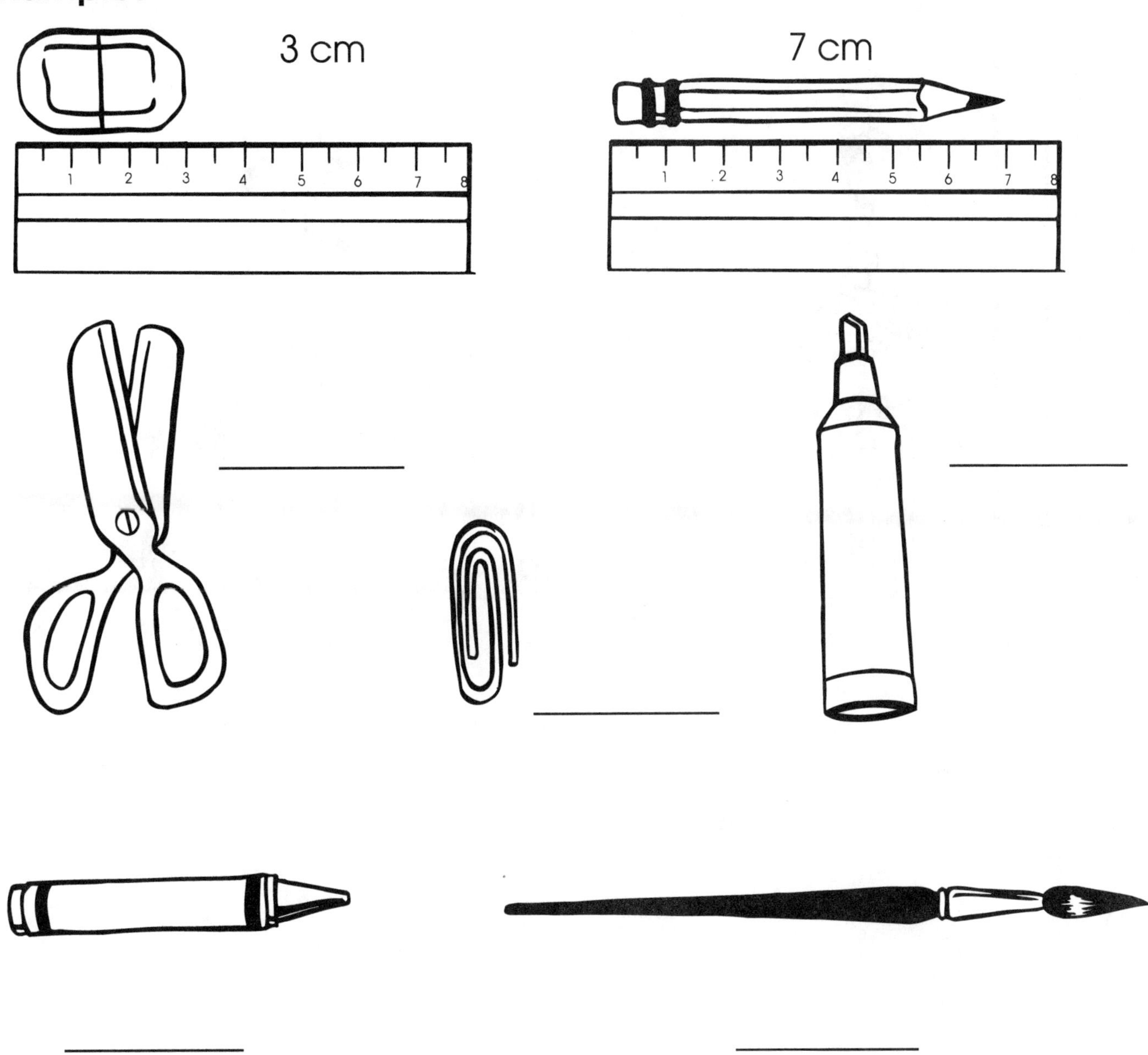

Measurement: Centimeters

Directions: The giraffe is about 8 centimeters high. How many centimeters (cm) high are the trees? Write your answers in the blanks.

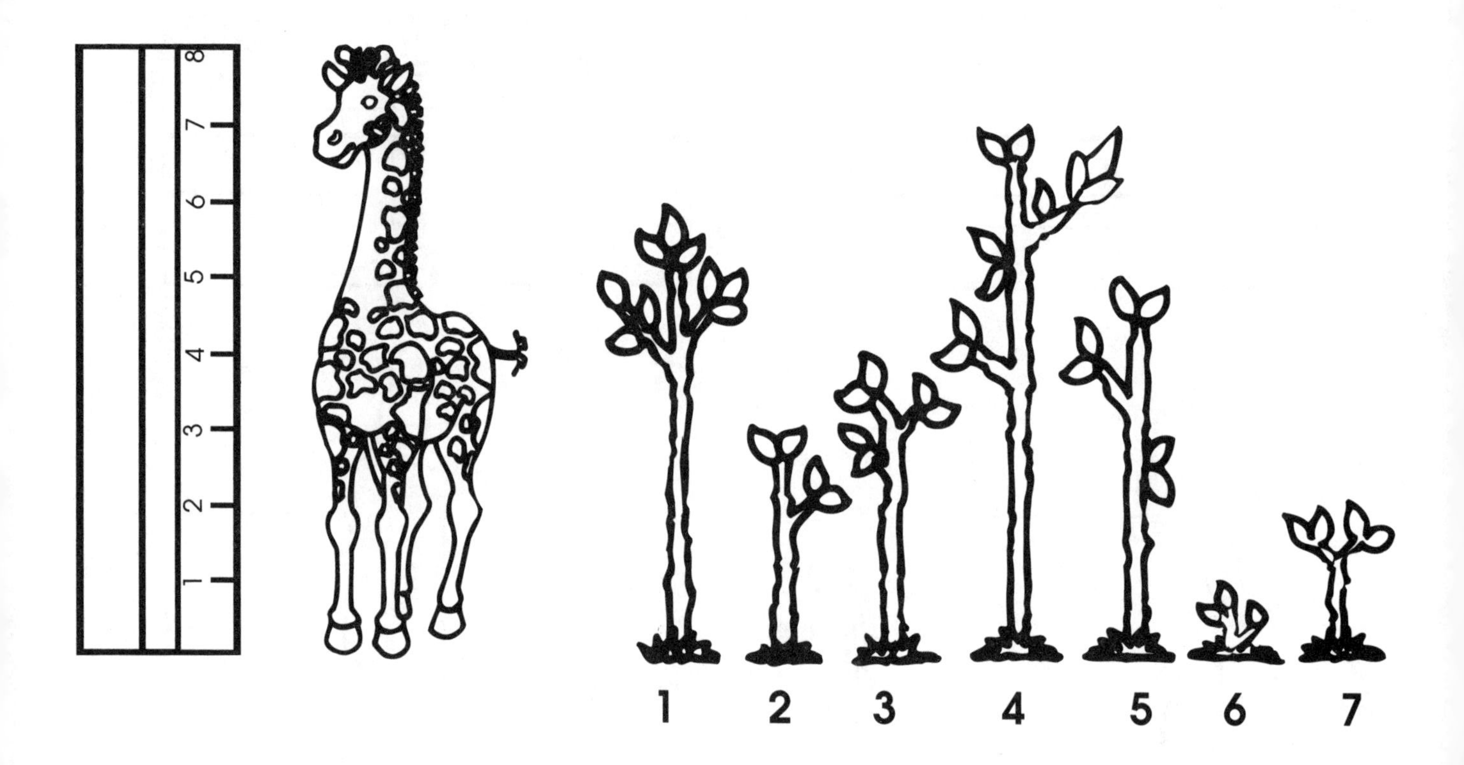

1)_____cm 2)_____cm 3)_____cm

4)_____cm 5)_____cm 6)_____cm 7)_____cm

Measurement: Meter and Kilometer

Meters and **kilometers** are units of length in the metric system. A meter is equal to 39.37 inches. A kilometer is equal to about $\frac{5}{8}$ of a mile.

Directions: Decide whether you would use meter or kilometer to measure each object.

1 meter = 100 centimeters
1 kilometer = 1,000 meters

length of a river kilometer

height of a tree ____________

width of a room ____________

length of a football field ____________

height of a door ____________

length of a dress ____________

length of a race ____________

height of a basketball pole ____________

width of a window ____________

distance a plane travels ____________

Directions: Solve the problem.

Tara races Tom in the 100-meter dash. Tara finishes 10 meters in front of Tom. How many centimeters did Tara finish in front of Tom? ____________

Measurement: Ounce and Pound

Ounces and pounds are measurements of weight in the standard measurement system. The ounce is used to measure the weight of very light objects. The pound is used to measure the weight of heavier objects. 16 ounces = 1 pound.

Example:

8 ounces  15 pounds

Directions: Decide if you would use ounces or pounds to measure the weight of each object. Circle your answer.

ounce pound

ounce pound

ounce pound

ounce pound

a chair: ounce pound

a table: ounce pound

a shoe: ounce pound

a shirt: ounce pound

Problem Solving

Directions: Tell whether you should add or subtract. "In all" is a clue to add. "Left" is a clue to subtract. Draw pictures to help you.

Example:

Jane's dog has 5 bones. He ate 3 bones. How many bones are left?

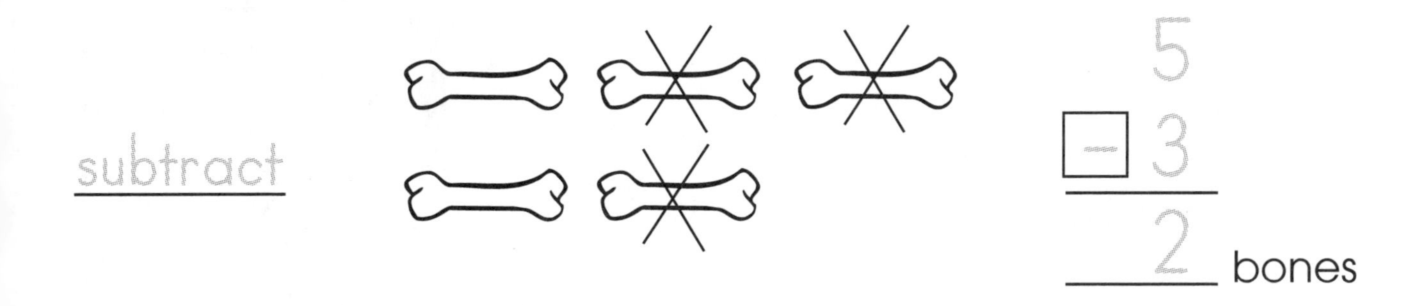

Lucky the cat had 5 mice. She got 4 more for her birthday. How many mice did she have in all?

__________ ☐ ______

______ mice

Sam bought 6 fish. She gave 2 fish to a friend. How many fish does she have left?

__________ ☐ ______

______ fish

Problem Solving: Addition, Subtraction, Multiplication

Directions: Tell if you add, subtract or multiply. Then write the answer. **Hints**: "In all" means to add. "Left" means to subtract. "In each" means to multiply.

Example:

There are 6 red birds and 7 blue birds. How many birds in all?

add 13 birds

The pet store had 25 goldfish, but 10 were sold. How many goldfish are left?

__________ _____ goldfish

There are 5 cages of bunnies. There are 2 bunnies in each cage. How many bunnies are there in the store?

__________ _____ bunnies

The store had 18 puppies this morning. It sold 7 puppies today. How many puppies are left?

__________ _____ puppies

Problem Solving: Addition, Subtraction, Multiplication

Directions: Tell if you add, subtract or multiply. Then write the answer.

Example:
There were 12 frogs sitting on a log by a pond, but 3 frogs hopped away. How many frogs are left?

Subtract ___9___ frogs

There are 9 flowers growing by the pond.
Each flower has 2 leaves.
How many leaves are there?

________________ ______ leaves

A tree had 7 squirrels playing in it.
Then 8 more came along.
How many squirrels are there in all?

________________ ______ squirrels

There were 27 birds living in the trees around the pond, but 9 flew away.
How many birds are left?

________________ ______ birds

Problem Solving: Fractions

A **fraction** is a number that names part of a whole, such as $\frac{1}{2}$ or $\frac{1}{3}$.
Directions: Read each problem. Use the pictures to help you solve the problem. Write the fraction that answers the question.

Simon and Jessie shared a pizza.
Together they ate $\frac{3}{4}$ of the pizza.
How much of the pizza is left? ______

Sylvia baked a cherry pie. She gave $\frac{1}{3}$ to her grandmother and $\frac{1}{3}$ to a friend.
How much of the pie did she keep? ______

Timmy erased $\frac{1}{2}$ of the blackboard before the bell rang for recess.
How much of the blackboard does he have left to erase? ______

Directions: Read the problem. Draw your own picture to help you solve the problem. Write the fraction that answers the question.

Sarah mowed $\frac{1}{4}$ of the yard before lunch.
How much does she have left to mow? ______

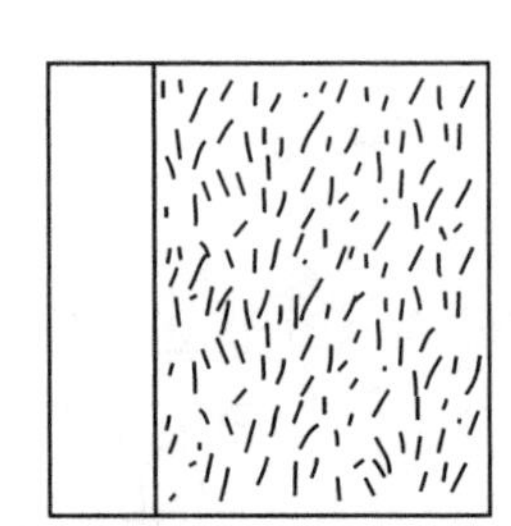

Review

Place Value

Directions: Write the number's value in each place: **678,421**.

_____	ones	_____	hundred thousands
_____	thousands	_____	hundreds
_____	tens	_____	ten thousands

Addition and Subtraction

Directions: Add or subtract. Remember to regroup, if you need to.

88	46	75	93	76
- 19	+ 39	+ 24	- 68	- 59

		84	97	
683	855	49	54	9,731
- 496	+ 138	+ 62	+ 361	- 4,664

Rounding

Directions: Round to the nearest 10, 100 or 1,000.

72 _____	49 _____	31 _____	66 _____
151 _____	296 _____	917 _____	621 _____

Review

Multiplication

Directions: Solve the problems. Draw groups if necessary.

$$\begin{array}{r} 2 \\ \times 8 \\ \hline \end{array} \quad \begin{array}{r} 6 \\ \times 4 \\ \hline \end{array} \quad \begin{array}{r} 3 \\ \times 2 \\ \hline \end{array} \quad \begin{array}{r} 8 \\ \times 4 \\ \hline \end{array} \quad \begin{array}{r} 5 \\ \times 3 \\ \hline \end{array} \quad \begin{array}{r} 2 \\ \times 2 \\ \hline \end{array}$$

Fractions

Directions: Circle the correct fraction of each shape's white part.

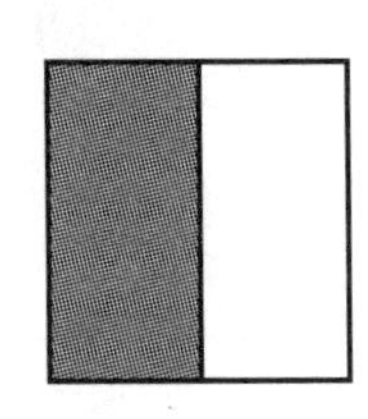

$\frac{1}{2}$ $\frac{1}{3}$ $\frac{1}{4}$

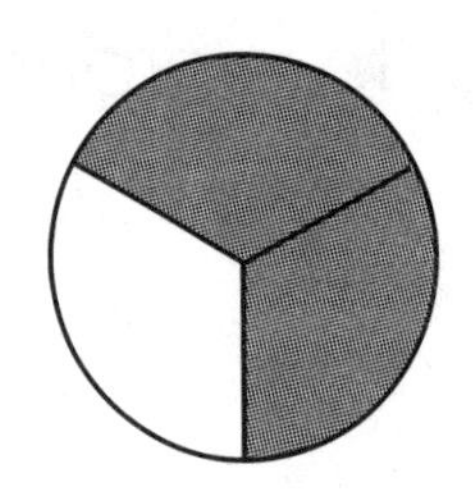

$\frac{1}{4}$ $\frac{1}{3}$ $\frac{1}{2}$

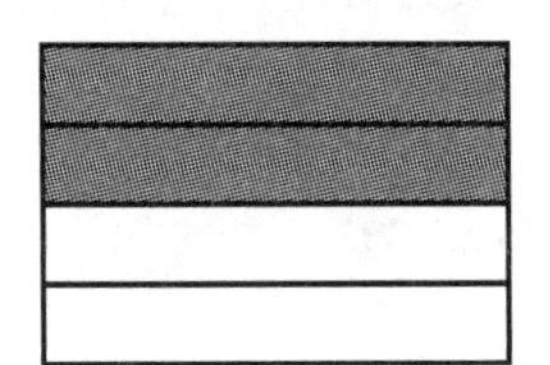

$\frac{2}{3}$ $\frac{2}{4}$ $\frac{1}{3}$

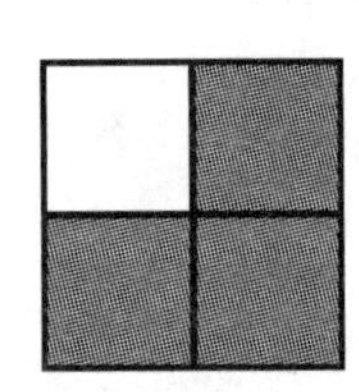

$\frac{1}{4}$ $\frac{1}{2}$ $\frac{3}{4}$

Graphs

Directions: Count the flowers. Color the pots to make a graph that shows the number of flowers.

1 2 3 4 5 6 7 8

Review

Geometry

Directions: Match the shapes.

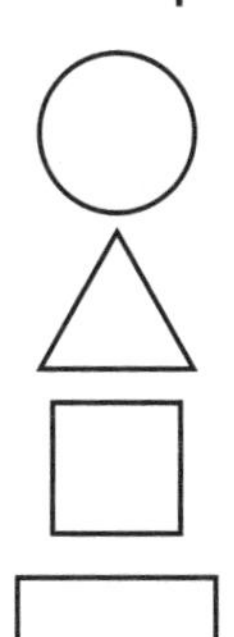

rectangle

square

circle

triangle

Measurement

Directions: Look at the ruler. Measure the objects to the nearest inch.

1 2 3 4 5

_______ inches

_______ inches

_______ inches

Time

Directions: Tell what time is on each clock.

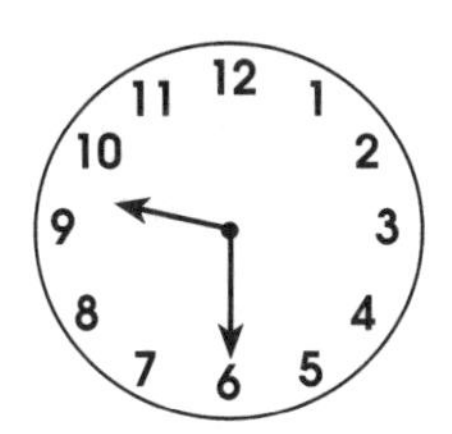

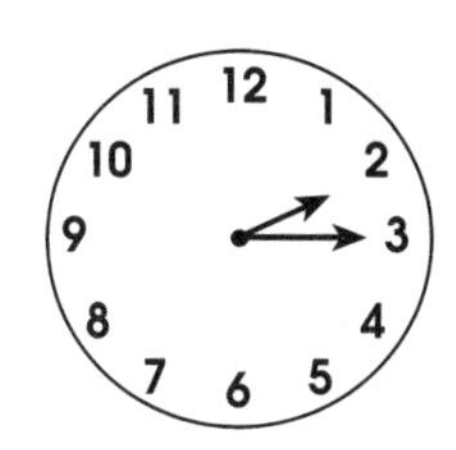

_______________ _______________ _______________ _______________

Review

Money

Directions: Match the correct amounts.

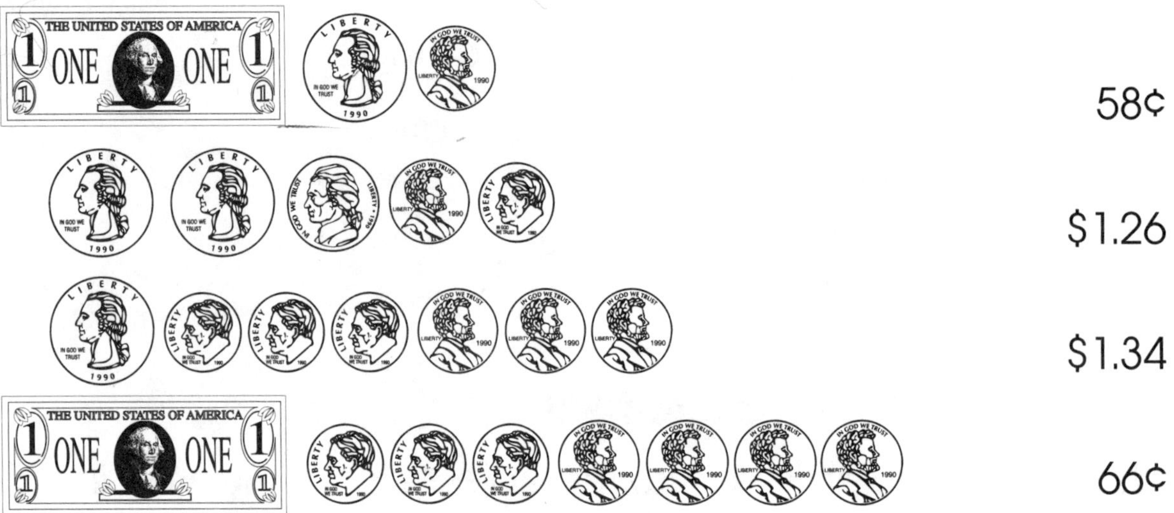

58¢

$1.26

$1.34

66¢

Problem Solving

Directions: Tell if you add or subtract, then write the answer.

Katarina had 5 dolls. She gave 2 dolls to Lexie. How many are left?

____________ ______ dolls

Jacob caught 12 butterflies. Jessica caught 7 more butterflies. How many did they catch in all?

____________ ______ butterflies

Answer Key

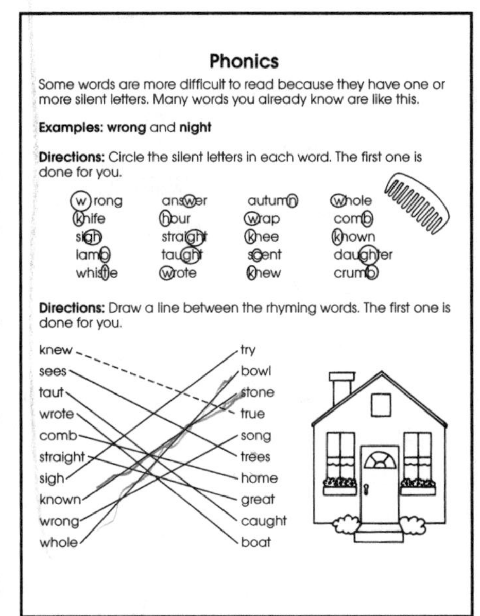
Phonics

Some words are more difficult to read because they have one or more silent letters. Many words you already know are like this.

Examples: wrong and **night**

Directions: Circle the silent letters in each word. The first one is done for you.

wrong	answer	autumn	whole
knife	hour	wrap	comb
sigh	straight	knee	known
lamb	taught	scent	daughter
whistle	wrote	knew	crumb

Directions: Draw a line between the rhyming words. The first one is done for you.

knew	try
sees	bowl
taut	stone
wrote	true
comb	song
straight	trees
sigh	home
known	great
wrong	caught
whole	boat

4

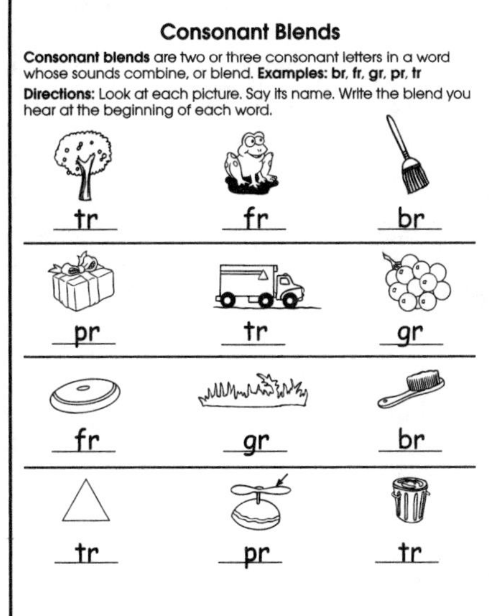
Consonant Blends

Consonant blends are two or three consonant letters in a word whose sounds combine, or blend. **Examples: br, fr, gr, pr, tr**

Directions: Look at each picture. Say its name. Write the blend you hear at the beginning of each word.

tr fr br

pr tr gr

fr gr br

tr pr tr

5

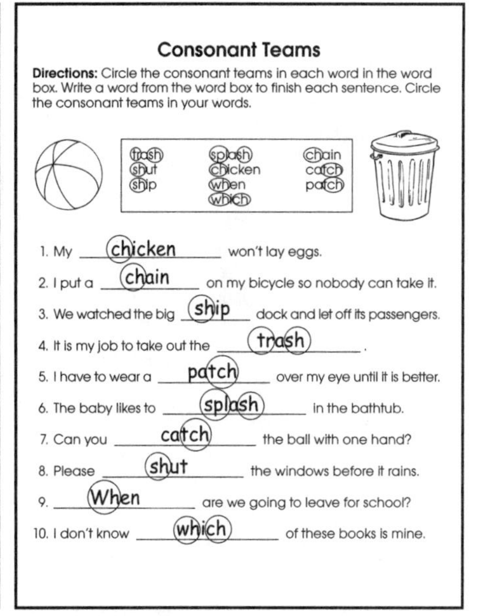
Consonant Teams

Directions: Circle the consonant teams in each word in the word box. Write a word from the word box to finish each sentence. Circle the consonant teams in your words.

trash	splash	chain
shut	chicken	catch
ship	when	patch
	which	

1. My chicken won't lay eggs.
2. I put a chain on my bicycle so nobody can take it.
3. We watched the big ship dock and let off its passengers.
4. It is my job to take out the trash.
5. I have to wear a patch over my eye until it is better.
6. The baby likes to splash in the bathtub.
7. Can you catch the ball with one hand?
8. Please shut the windows before it rains.
9. When are we going to leave for school?
10. I don't know which of these books is mine.

6

Consonant Teams

Directions: Look at the words in the word box. Write all of the words that end with the **ng** sound in the column under the picture of the **ring**. Write all of the words that end with the **nk** sound under the picture of the **sink**. Finish the sentences with words from the word box.

strong	rank	bring	bank	honk	hang	thank
long	hunk	song	stung	bunk	sang	junk

ng	nk
strong	rank
long	hunk
bring	bank
song	honk
stung	bunk
hang	thank
sang	junk

1. Honk your horn when you get to my house.
2. He was stung by a bumblebee.
3. We are going to put our money in a bank.
4. I want to thank you for the birthday present.
5. My brother and I sleep in bunk beds.

7

Phonics

There are several consonants that make the **k** sound: **c** when followed by **a**, **o** or **u** as in **cow** or **cup**; the letter **k** as in **milk**; the letters **ch** as in **Christmas** and **ck** as in **black**.

Directions: Read the following words. Circle the letters that make the **k** sound. The first one is done for you.

ache	school	market	comb
camera	deck	darkness	Christmas
necklace	doctor	stomach	crack
nickel	skin	thick	escape

Directions: Use your own words to finish the following sentences. Use words with the **k** sound.

1. If I had a nickel, I would Answers will vary.
2. My doctor is very
3. We bought ripe, juicy tomatoes at the
4. If I had a camera now, I would take a picture of
5. When my stomach aches,

8

Hard and Soft c

When **c** is followed by **e**, **i** or **y**, it usually has a **soft** sound. The **soft c** sounds like **s**. For example, **c**ircle and fen**c**e. When **c** is followed by **a** or **u**, it usually has a **hard** sound. The **hard c** sounds like **k**.

Examples: cup and **c**art

Directions: Read the words in the word box. Write the words in the correct lists. Write a word from the word box to finish each sentence.

pencil	cookie
dance	cent
popcorn	circus
lucky	mice
tractor	card

Words with soft c	Words with hard c
pencil	popcorn
dance	lucky
cent	tractor
mice	cookie
circus	card

1. Another word for a penny is a cent.
2. A cat likes to chase mice.
3. You will see animals and clowns at the circus.
4. We like to dance to the music.
5. Will you please sharpen my pencil?

9

Answer Key

Hard and Soft g

When **g** is followed by **e**, **i** or **y**, it usually has a **soft** sound. The **soft g** sounds like **j**. **Example:** change and gentle. The **hard g** sounds like the **g** in girl or gate.

Directions: Read the words in the word box. Write the words in the correct lists. Write a word from the box to finish each sentence.

engine	glove	cage	magic	frog
giant	flag	large	glass	goose

Words with soft g	Words with hard g
engine	glove
giant	flag
cage	glass
large	frog
magic	goose

1. Our bird lives in a cage.
2. Pulling a rabbit from a hat is a good magic trick.
3. A car needs an engine to run.
4. A giant is a huge person.
5. An elephant is a very large animal.

10

Phonics

The **sh** sound is usually made by the letters **sh**. Sometimes it is made by the letters **ci** as in **musician**, **si** as in **possession** or **ti** as in **station**.

Directions: Read the following words. Circle the letters that make the **sh** sound.

wash	nation	delicious
action	rush	shine
special	attention	vacation	permission

Directions: Use the word box above to find the words hidden in the puzzle below. One is done for you.

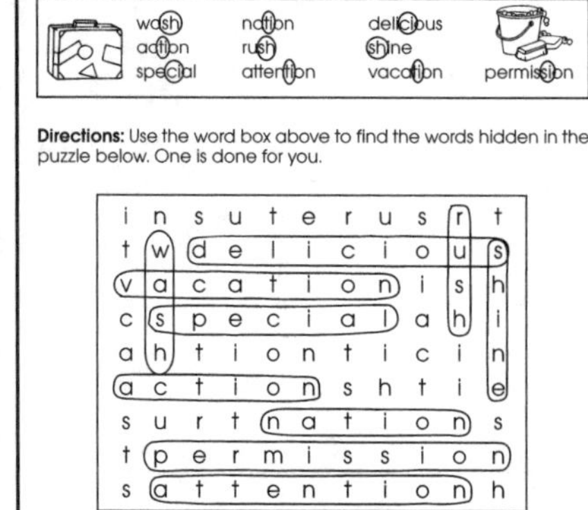

i	n	s	u	t	e	r	u	s	r	t
t	w	d	e	l	i	c	i	o	u	s
v	a	c	a	t	i	o	n	i	s	h
c	s	p	e	c	i	a	l	a	h	i
a	h	t	i	o	n	t	i	c	i	n
a	c	t	i	o	n	s	h	t	i	e
s	u	r	t	n	a	t	i	o	n	s
t	p	e	r	m	i	s	s	i	o	n
s	a	t	t	e	n	t	i	o	n	h

11

Short Vowels

Directions: Say the name of each picture and listen for the short vowel sounds. Read the sentences below. Circle the words that have the same short vowel sound as the letter at the beginning of the sentence.

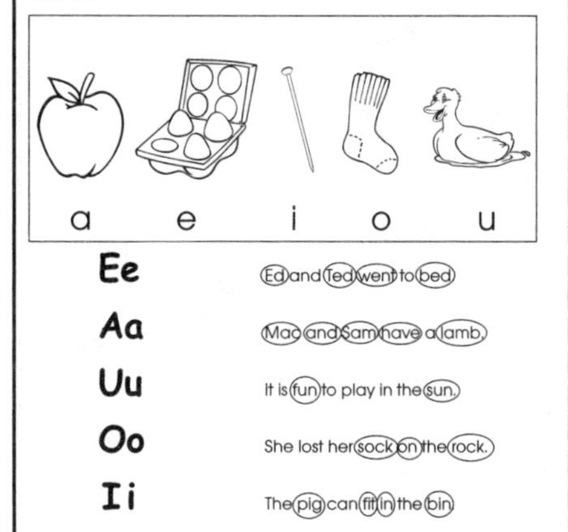

a e i o u

Ee Ed and Ted went to bed.

Aa Mac and Sam have a lamb.

Uu It is fun to play in the sun.

Oo She lost her sock on the rock.

Ii The pig can fit in the bin.

12

Short Vowels

Directions: Use the word box below. Write each word on the vowel which has its sound. Say each word as you write it.

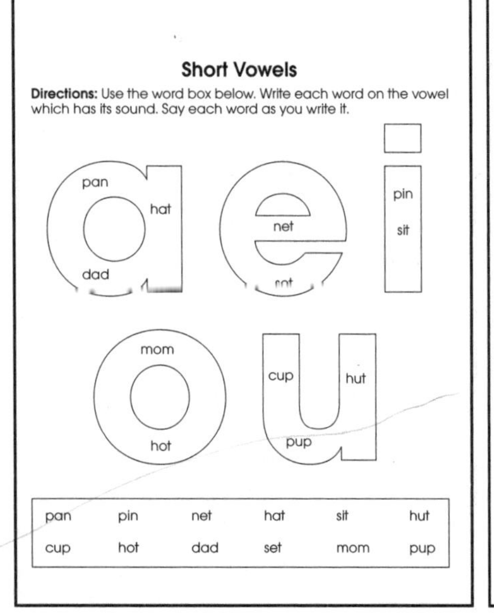

pan	pin	net	hat	sit	hut
cup	hot	dad	set	mom	pup

13

Long Vowels

Long vowel sounds have the same sound as their names. When a **Super Silent e** comes at the end of a word, you can't hear it, but it changes the short vowel sound to a long vowel sound.

Examples: rope, skate, bee, pie, cute

Directions: Say the name of the pictures. Listen for the long vowel sounds. Write the missing long vowel sound under each picture.

c a ke

h i ke

n o se

a pe

c u be

gr a pe

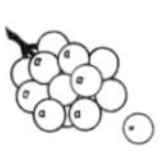

r a ke

b o ne

k i te

14

Long Vowels

Directions: Use the word list below. Write each word on the vowel which has its sound. Say each word as you write it.

a: rake, stake
e: team, jeep, bean
i: pile, time
o: boat, hose, phone
u: mule, cube

team	rake	cube	mule	bean	pile
boat	time	phone	hose	stake	jeep

15

Answer Key

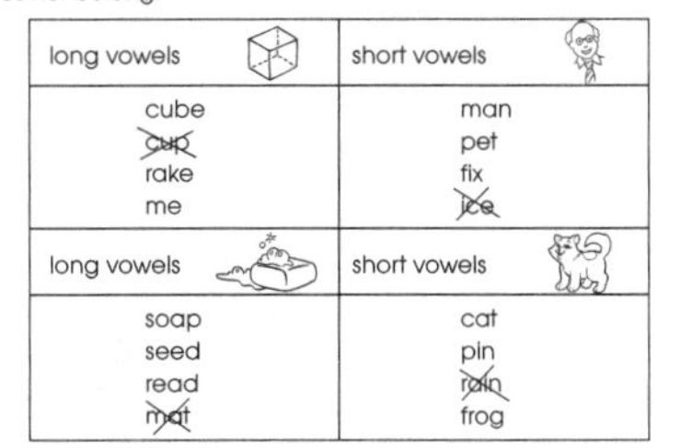

Review

Directions: Read the words in each box. Cross out the word that does not belong.

long vowels	short vowels
cube ~~cup~~ rake me	man pet fix ~~ice~~
long vowels	**short vowels**
soap seed read ~~mat~~	cat pin ~~rain~~ frog

Directions: Write **short** or **long** to label the words in each box.

long vowels	short vowels
hose take bead cube eat see	frog hot sled lap block sit

16

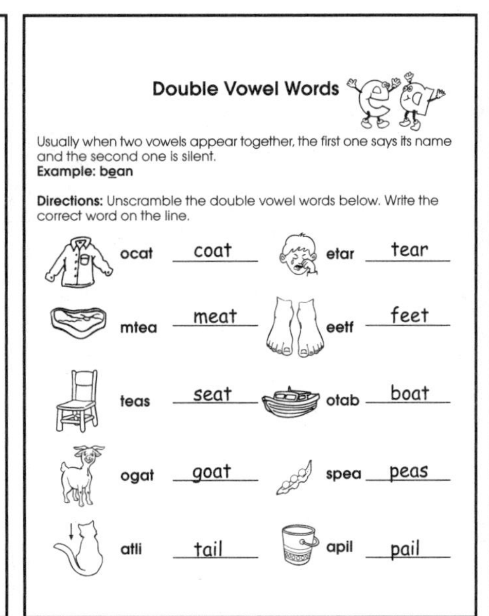

Double Vowel Words

Usually when two vowels appear together, the first one says its name and the second one is silent.
Example: bean

Directions: Unscramble the double vowel words below. Write the correct word on the line.

ocat coat — etar tear
mtea meat — eetf feet
teas seat — otab boat
ogat goat — spea peas
atli tail — apil pail

17

Vowel Teams

The vowel team **ie** makes the long **e** sound like in **believe**. The team **ei** also makes the long **e** sound like in **either**. But **ei** can also make a long **a** sound like in **eight**.
Directions: Circle the **ei** words with the long **a** sound.

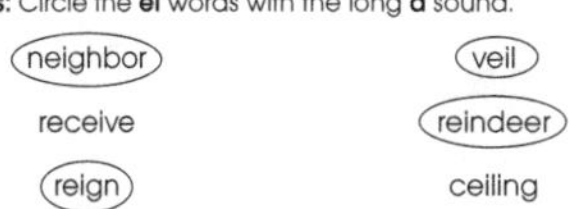

(neighbor) (veil)
receive (reindeer)
(reign) ceiling

The teams **eigh** and **ey** also make the long **a** sound.
Directions: Finish the sentences with words from the word box.

chief	sleigh	obey	weigh	thief	field	ceiling

1. Eight reindeer pull Santa's sleigh.
2. Rules are for us to obey.
3. The bird got out of its cage and flew up to the ceiling.
4. The leader of a Native American tribe is the chief.
5. How much do you weigh?
6. They caught the thief who took my bike.
7. Corn grows in a field.

18

Y as a Vowel

When **y** comes at the end of a word, it is a vowel. When **y** is the only vowel at the end of a one-syllable word, it has the sound of a long **i** (like in **my**). When **y** is the only vowel at the end of a word with more than one syllable, it has the sound of a long **e** (like in **baby**).

Directions: Look at the words in the word box. If the word has the sound of a long **i**, write it under the word **my**. If the word has the sound of a long **e**, write it under the word **baby**. Write the word from the word box that answers each riddle.

happy	penny	fry	try	sleepy	dry
bunny	why	windy	sky	party	fly

my	baby
why	happy
fry	bunny
try	penny
sky	windy
dry	sleepy
fly	party

1. It takes five of these to make a nickel. penny
2. This is what you call a baby rabbit. bunny
3. It is often blue and you can see it if you look up. sky
4. You might have one of these on your birthday. party
5. It is the opposite of wet. dry
6. You might use this word to ask a question. why

19

Phonics

Sometimes, vowels have unusual sounds that are neither short nor long. For example, often when an **a** is followed by an **l**, instead of the short **a** sound, as in **apple**, it has the sound in **ball**. Sometimes an **o** has the sound of short **u**, as in **done**.

Directions: Read the words in the following word "families." Write another word in each group.

Answers will vary.

The **al** and **all** families:
also, always, ball, small, tall,

The **alk** family:
chalk, stalk, talk,

The **alt** family:
halt, malt,

The **o** family:
done, come, other,

Directions: Draw lines to match the rhyming words.

glove	call
pull	halt
wall	shove
salt	talk
walk	full

20

Vowel Teams

The vowel teams **ou** and **ow** can have the same sound. You can hear it in the words **clown** and **cloud**. The vowel teams **au** and **aw** have the same sound. You hear it in the words **because** and **law**.

Directions: Look at the pictures. Write the correct vowel team to complete the words. The first one is done for you. You may need to use a dictionary to help you with the correct spelling.

au to — cl ow n — h ou se
fl ow er — s aw — ow l
p ow der — m ou th — j aw
p aw — m ou se — cl ou d

21

Answer Key

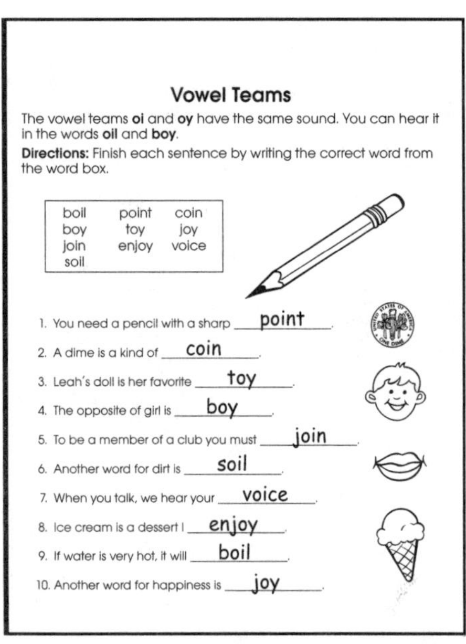

Vowel Teams

The vowel teams **oi** and **oy** have the same sound. You can hear it in the words **oil** and **boy**.

Directions: Finish each sentence by writing the correct word from the word box.

boil	point	coin
boy	toy	joy
join	enjoy	voice
soil		

1. You need a pencil with a sharp point.
2. A dime is a kind of coin.
3. Leah's doll is her favorite toy.
4. The opposite of girl is boy.
5. To be a member of a club you must join.
6. Another word for dirt is soil.
7. When you talk, we hear your voice.
8. Ice cream is a dessert I enjoy.
9. If water is very hot, it will boil.
10. Another word for happiness is joy.

22

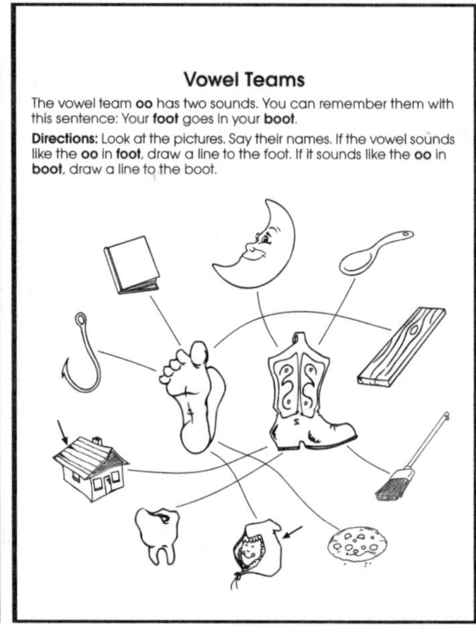

Vowel Teams

The vowel team **oo** has two sounds. You can remember them with this sentence: Your **foot** goes in your **boot**.

Directions: Look at the pictures. Say their names. If the vowel sounds like the **oo** in **foot**, draw a line to the foot. If it sounds like the **oo** in **boot**, draw a line to the boot.

23

Vowel Teams

The vowel team **ea** can have a short **e** sound like in **head** or a long **e** sound like in **bead**. An **ea** followed by an **r** makes a sound like the one in **ear** or like the one in **heard**.

Directions: Read the story. Listen for the sound **ea** makes in the bold words.

Have you ever **read** a book or **heard** a story about a **bear**? You might have **learned** that bears sleep through the winter. Some bears may sleep the whole **season**. Sometimes they look almost **dead**! But they are very much alive. As the cold winter passes and the spring **weather** comes **near**, they wake up. After such a nice rest, they must be **ready** to **eat** a **really** big **meal**!

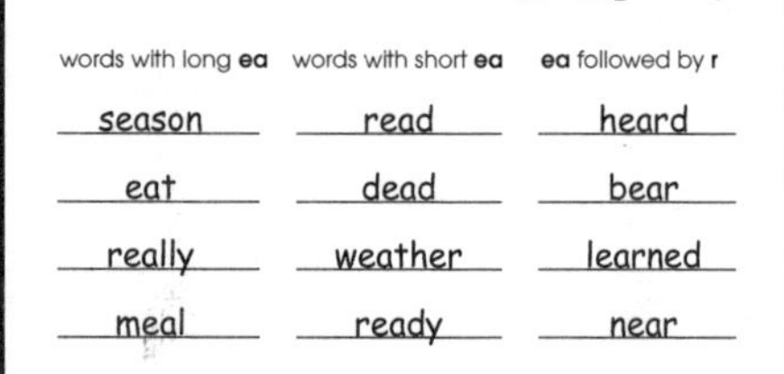

words with long **ea**	words with short **ea**	**ea** followed by **r**
season	read	heard
eat	dead	bear
really	weather	learned
meal	ready	near

24

R-Controlled Vowels

When a vowel is followed by the letter **r**, it has a different sound.

Example: he and **her**

Directions: Write a word from the word box to finish each sentence. Notice the sound of the vowel followed by an **r**.

park	chair	horse	bark	bird
hurt	girl	hair	store	ears

1. A dog likes to bark.
2. You buy food at a store.
3. Children like to play at the park.
4. An animal you can ride is a horse.
5. You hear with your ears.
6. A robin is a kind of bird.
7. If you fall down, you might get hurt.
8. The opposite of a boy is a girl.
9. You comb and brush your hair.
10. You sit down on a chair.

25

Syllables

One way to help you read a word you don't know is to divide it into parts called **syllables**. Every syllable has a vowel sound.

Directions: Say the words. Write the number of syllables. The first one is done for you.

bird	1	rabbit	2
apple	2	elephant	3
balloon	2	family	3
basketball	3	fence	1
breakfast	2	ladder	2
block	1	open	2
candy	2	puddle	2
popcorn	2	Saturday	3
yellow	2	wind	1
understand	3	butterfly	3

26

Syllables

When a double consonant is used in the middle of a word, the word can usually be divided between the consonants.

Directions: Look at the words in the word box. Divide each word into two syllables. Leave space between each syllable. One is done for you.

butter	puppy	kitten	yellow
dinner	chatter	ladder	happy
pillow	letter	mitten	summer

but ter	chat ter	mit ten
din ner	let ter	yel low
pil low	kit ten	hap py
pup py	lad der	sum mer

Many words are divided between two consonants that are not alike.

Directions: Look at the words in the word box. Divide each word into two syllables. One is done for you.

window	doctor	number	carpet
mister	winter	pencil	candle
barber	sister	picture	under

win dow	win ter	pic ture
mis ter	Sis ter	car pet
bar ber	num ber	can dle
doc tor	pen cil	un der

27

Answer Key

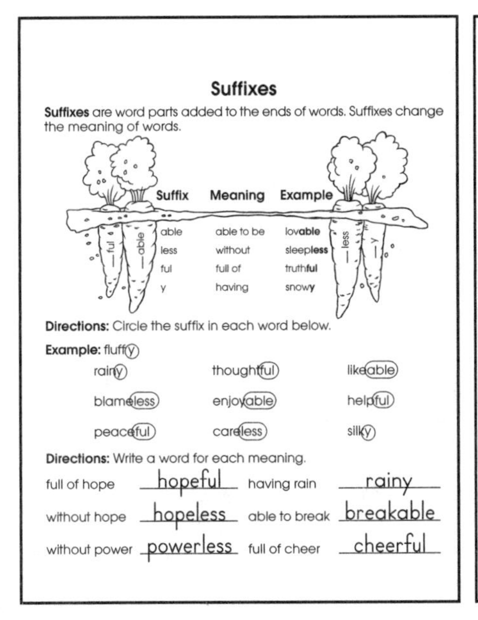

Suffixes

Suffixes are word parts added to the ends of words. Suffixes change the meaning of words.

Suffix	Meaning	Example
able	able to be	lov**able**
less	without	sleep**less**
ful	full of	truth**ful**
y	having	snow**y**

Directions: Circle the suffix in each word below.

Example: fluff(y)

rain(y) thought(ful) like(able)

blame(less) enjoy(able) help(ful)

peace(ful) care(less) silk(y)

Directions: Write a word for each meaning.

full of hope hopeful having rain rainy

without hope hopeless able to break breakable

without power powerless full of cheer cheerful

28

Suffixes

A **suffix** is a syllable added to the end of a word which changes its meaning, as in small, small**er**, small**est**. The word you start with is called the root word. Some root words change their spelling before adding **er** and **est**. **Example:** in the word **big**, another **g** is added to make the words big**ger** and big**gest**. In the word **pretty**, the **y** changes to an **i** to make the words prett**ier** and prett**iest**.

Directions: Use words from the word box to help you add **er** and **est** to the root words.

prettier	happier	luckiest	busiest	tinier
luckier	silliest	greener	busier	busier
prettiest	funnier	tiniest	happiest	bigger
biggest	greenest	sillier	maddest	funniest

	er	est
happy	happier	happiest
busy	busier	busiest
tiny	tinier	tiniest
pretty	prettier	prettiest
lucky	luckier	luckiest
big	bigger	biggest
silly	sillier	silliest
green	greener	greenest
mad	madder	maddest
funny	funnier	funniest

29

Suffixes

Adding **ing** to a word means that it is happening now. Adding **ed** to a word means it happened in the past.

Directions: Look at the words in the word box. Underline the root word in each one. Write a word to complete each sentence.

snowing	wished	played	looking	crying
talking	walked	eating	going	doing

1. We like to play. We played yesterday.
2. Is that snow? Yes, it is snowing.
3. Do you want to go with me? No, I am going with my friend.
4. The baby will cry if we leave. The baby is crying.
5. We will walk home from school. We walked to school this morning.
6. Did you wish for a new bike? Yes, I wished for one.
7. Who is going to do it while we are away? I am doing it.
8. Did you talk to your friend? Yes, we are talking now.
9. Will you look at my book? I am looking at it now.
10. I like to eat pizza. We are eating it today.

30

Review

Directions: Read the word in bold in each sentence and circle each suffix. Write the root word on the line. Remember that some root words are changed when an ending is added.

Example: silliness → silly

1. Sue and Tim were **danc(ing)** at the party. dance
2. The children were **care(ful)** not to play in the street. care
3. We made a mistake and put the door on **back(ward)**. back
4. This is the **funn(iest)** movie I ever saw. funny
5. A new baby is **help(less)**. help
6. I **ask(ed)** Mike to bring his wagon to my house. ask
7. I'm really tired today because I had a **sleep(less)** night. sleep
8. My teacher is **real(ly)** nice. real
9. The book I am **read(ing)** is good. read
10. Everyone wants to find **happi(ness)**. happy
11. The game isn't **like(ly)** to end soon. like
12. My plant seems to grow **tall(er)** every day. tall
13. Don't be **care(less)** with your nice toys. care

31

Prefixes

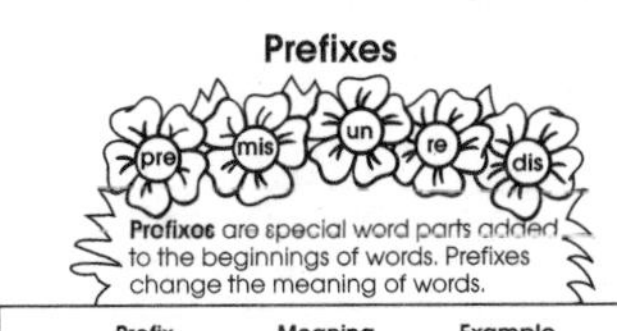

Prefixes are special word parts added to the beginnings of words. Prefixes change the meaning of words.

Prefix	Meaning	Example
un	not	**un**happy
re	again	**re**do
pre	before	**pre**view
mis	wrong	**mis**understanding
dis	opposite	**dis**obey

Directions: Circle the word that begins with a prefix. Then write the prefix and the root word.

1. The dog was (unhappy.) un + happy
2. The movie (preview) was interesting. pre + view
3. The referee called an (unfair) penalty. un + fair
4. Please do not (misbehave.) mis + behave
5. My parents (disapprove) of that show. dis + approve
6. I had to (redo) the assignment. re + do

32

Prefixes

Directions: Read the prefix and its meaning. Add each prefix to a root word to make a new word. Write the new word. Finish the sentences using the words you just wrote.

Prefixes	(Meaning)	Root Word	New Word
bi	(two)	cycle	bicycle
dis	(away from)	appear	disappear
ex	(out of)	change	exchange
im	(not)	polite	impolite
in	(within)	side	inside
mis	(wrong)	place	misplace
non	(not)	sense	nonsense
pre	(before)	school	preschool
re	(again)	build	rebuild
un	(not)	happy	unhappy

1. Did you go to preschool before kindergarten?
2. The magician made the rabbit disappear.
3. Put your things where they belong so you don't misplace them.
4. Can you ride a bicycle?
5. Do you want to exchange your shirt for one that fits?

33

Answer Key

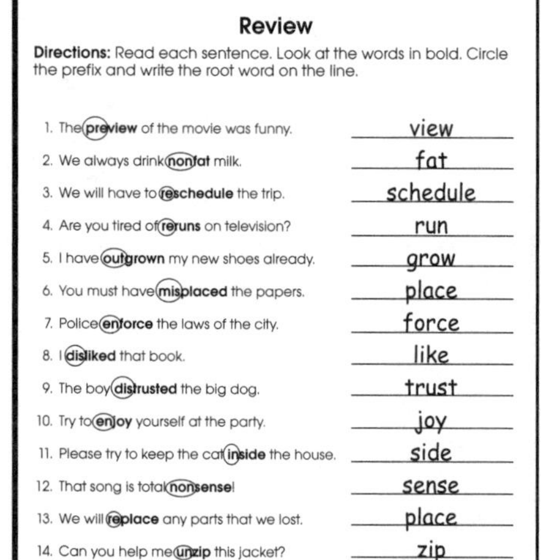

Review

Directions: Read each sentence. Look at the words in bold. Circle the prefix and write the root word on the line.

1. The **preview** of the movie was funny. view
2. We always drink **nonfat** milk. fat
3. We will have to **reschedule** the trip. schedule
4. Are you tired of **reruns** on television? run
5. I have **outgrown** my new shoes already. grow
6. You must have **misplaced** the papers. place
7. Police **enforce** the laws of the city. force
8. I **disliked** that book. like
9. The boy **distrusted** the big dog. trust
10. Try to **enjoy** yourself at the party. joy
11. Please try to keep the cat **inside** the house. side
12. That song is total **nonsense**! sense
13. We will **replace** any parts that we lost. place
14. Can you help me **unzip** this jacket? zip
15. Let's **rework** today's arithmetic problems. work

34

ABC Order

Directions: Put the words in ABC order on the bags.

grapes, bread, soup, apples — apples, bread, grapes, soup

napkins, rolls, ice cream, pizza — ice cream, napkins, pizza, rolls

milk, carrots, treats, potatoes — carrots, milk, potatoes, treats

meat, soda, cups, rice — cups, meat, rice, soda

35

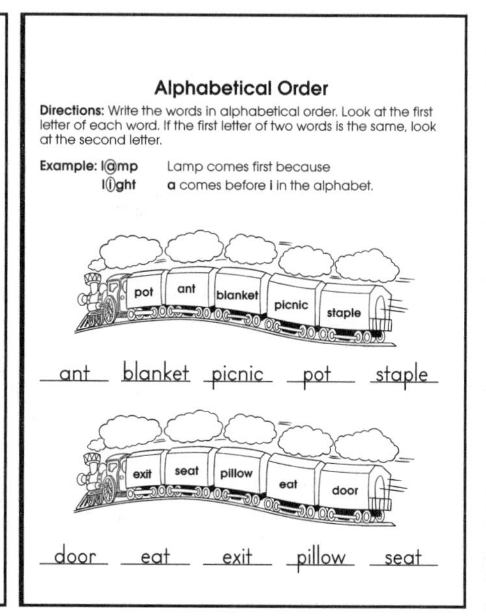

Alphabetical Order

Directions: Write the words in alphabetical order. Look at the first letter of each word. If the first letter of two words is the same, look at the second letter.

Example: l**a**mp l**i**ght — Lamp comes first because **a** comes before **i** in the alphabet.

ant blanket picnic pot staple

door eat exit pillow seat

36

Sequencing: ABC Order

If the first letters of two words are the same, look at the second letters in both words. If the second letters are the same, look at the third letters.

Directions: Write 1, 2, 3 or 4 on the lines in each row to put the words in ABC order.

Example:

1. 1 candy 2 carrot 4 duck 3 dance
2. 2 cold 4 hot 1 carry 3 hit
3. 2 flash 1 fan 3 fun 4 garden
4. 2 seat 4 sun 1 saw 3 sit
5. 3 row 1 ring 2 rock 4 run
6. 2 truck 3 turn 4 twin 1 talk
7. 1 seven 2 shoe 4 soup 3 smell

37

Compound Words

Compound words are two words that are put together to make one new word.

Example: **nut** + **shell** = **nutshell**

Directions: Choose a word from the box to make compound words in the sentences below.

board	bone	ground	prints	shake	house
brush	man	top	shell	ball	hive

Example:

The bird built its nest in the **treetop**.

1. We pitched our tent at the camp ground.
2. You would not be able to stand up without your back bone.
3. The police officer looked for finger prints.
4. She placed the hair brush in her purse.
5. It is important to have a firm hand shake.
6. The teacher wrote on the chalk board.
7. The egg shell is cracked.
8. Our whole family plays foot ball together.
9. Be sure to put a top hat on the snow man.
10. Spot never sleeps in his dog house.
11. The beekeeper must check the bee hive today.

38

Compound Words

Directions: Cut out the words below. Glue them together in the box to make compound words.

COMPOUND WORDS

sunflower football
mailbox watermelon
classroom airplane
livingroom bodyguard

Can you think of any more compound words?

39

Answer Key

Compound Words

Directions: Read the compound words in the word box. Then use them to answer the questions. The first one is done for you.

sailboat	blueberry	bookcase	tablecloth	beehive
dishpan	pigpen	classroom	playground	bedtime
broomstick	treetop	fireplace	newspaper	sunburn

Which compound word means . . .

1. a case for books? bookcase
2. a berry that is blue? blueberry
3. a hive for bees? beehive
4. a place for fires? fireplace
5. a pen for pigs? pigpen
6. a room for a class? classroom
7. a pan for dishes? dishpan
8. a boat to sail? sailboat
9. a paper for news? newspaper
10. a burn from the sun? sunburn
11. the top of a tree? treetop
12. a stick for a broom? broomstick
13. the time to go to bed? bedtime
14. a cloth for the table? tablecloth
15. ground to play on? playground

41

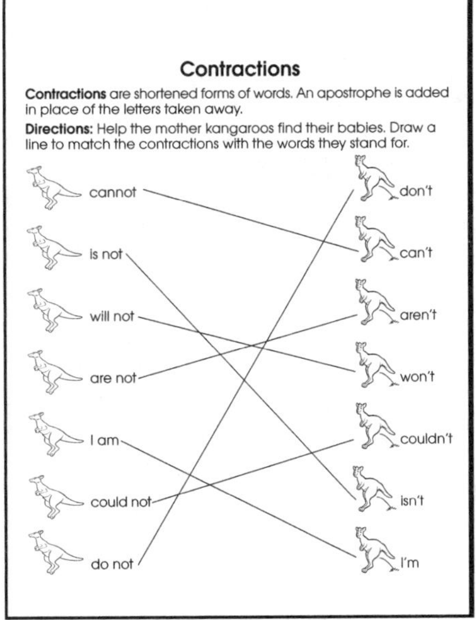

Contractions

Contractions are shortened forms of words. An apostrophe is added in place of the letters taken away.

Directions: Help the mother kangaroos find their babies. Draw a line to match the contractions with the words they stand for.

cannot	don't
is not	can't
will not	aren't
are not	won't
I am	couldn't
could not	isn't
do not	I'm

42

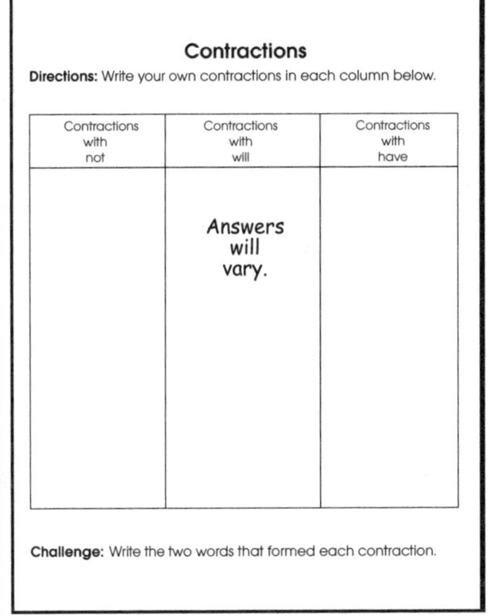

Contractions

Directions: Write your own contractions in each column below.

Contractions with not	Contractions with will	Contractions with have
	Answers will vary.	

Challenge: Write the two words that formed each contraction.

43

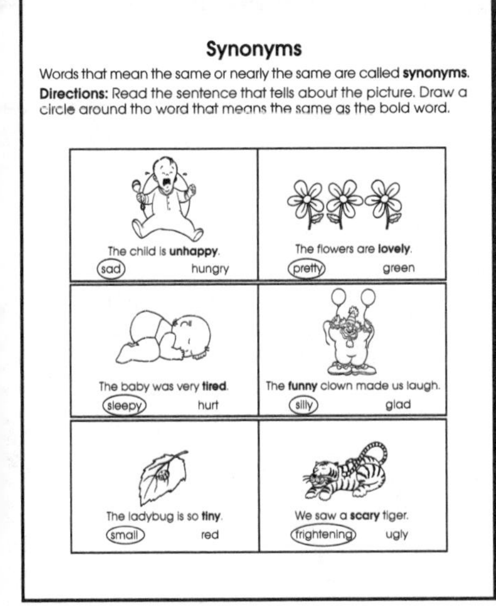

Synonyms

Words that mean the same or nearly the same are called **synonyms**.

Directions: Read the sentence that tells about the picture. Draw a circle around the word that means the same as the bold word.

The child is **unhappy**. (sad) hungry

The flowers are **lovely**. (pretty) green

The baby was very **tired**. (sleepy) hurt

The **funny** clown made us laugh. (silly) glad

The ladybug is so **tiny**. (small) red

We saw a **scary** tiger. (frightening) ugly

44

Synonyms

Directions: Read each sentence. Fill in the blanks with the synonyms.

friend	tired	story
presents	little	

I want to go to bed because I am very sleepy. tired

On my birthday I like to open my gifts. presents

My pal and I like to play together. friend

My favorite tale is *Cinderella*. story

The mouse was so tiny that it was hard to catch him. little

45

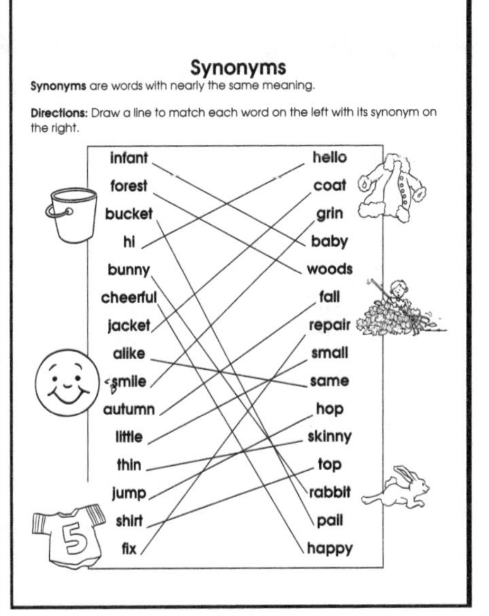

Synonyms

Synonyms are words with nearly the same meaning.

Directions: Draw a line to match each word on the left with its synonym on the right.

infant	hello
forest	coat
bucket	grin
hi	baby
bunny	woods
cheerful	fall
jacket	repair
alike	small
smile	same
autumn	hop
little	skinny
thin	top
jump	rabbit
shirt	pail
fix	happy

46

Answer Key

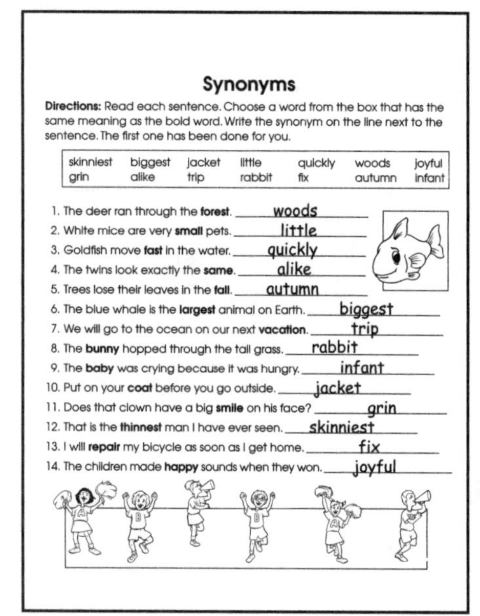

Synonyms

Directions: Read each sentence. Choose a word from the box that has the same meaning as the bold word. Write the synonym on the line next to the sentence. The first one has been done for you.

skinniest	biggest	jacket	little	quickly	woods	joyful
grin	alike	trip	rabbit	fix	autumn	infant

1. The deer ran through the **forest**. woods
2. White mice are very **small** pets. little
3. Goldfish move **fast** in the water. quickly
4. The twins look exactly the **same**. alike
5. Trees lose their leaves in the **fall**. autumn
6. The blue whale is the **largest** animal on Earth. biggest
7. We will go to the ocean on our next **vacation**. trip
8. The **bunny** hopped through the tall grass. rabbit
9. The **baby** was crying because it was hungry. infant
10. Put on your **coat** before you go outside. jacket
11. Does that clown have a big **smile** on his face? grin
12. That is the **thinnest** man I have ever seen. skinniest
13. I will **repair** my bicycle as soon as I get home. fix
14. The children made **happy** sounds when they won. joyful

47

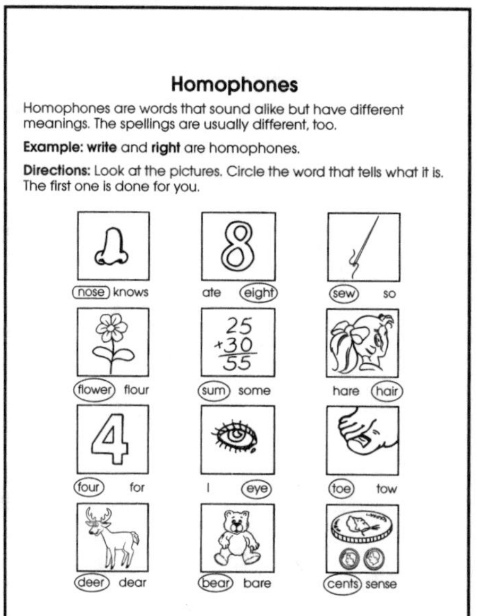

Homophones

Homophones are words that sound alike but have different meanings. The spellings are usually different, too.

Example: write and **right** are homophones.

Directions: Look at the pictures. Circle the word that tells what it is. The first one is done for you.

(nose) knows — ate (eight) — (sew) so

(flower) flour — (sum) some — hare (hair)

(four) for — I (eye) — (toe) tow

(deer) dear — (bear) bare — (cents) sense

48

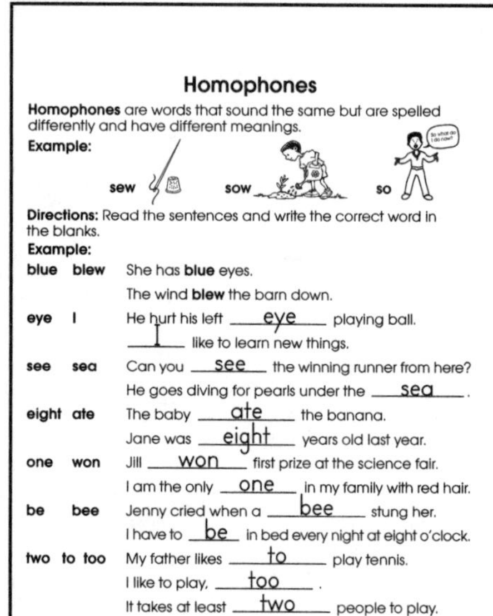

Homophones

Homophones are words that sound the same but are spelled differently and have different meanings.

Example:

sew — sow — so

Directions: Read the sentences and write the correct word in the blanks.

Example:

blue blew — She has **blue** eyes. The wind **blew** the barn down.

eye I — He hurt his left eye playing ball. I like to learn new things.

see sea — Can you see the winning runner from here? He goes diving for pearls under the sea.

eight ate — The baby ate the banana. Jane was eight years old last year.

one won — Jill won first prize at the science fair. I am the only one in my family with red hair.

be bee — Jenny cried when a bee stung her. I have to be in bed every night at eight o'clock.

two to too — My father likes to play tennis. I like to play, too. It takes at least two people to play.

49

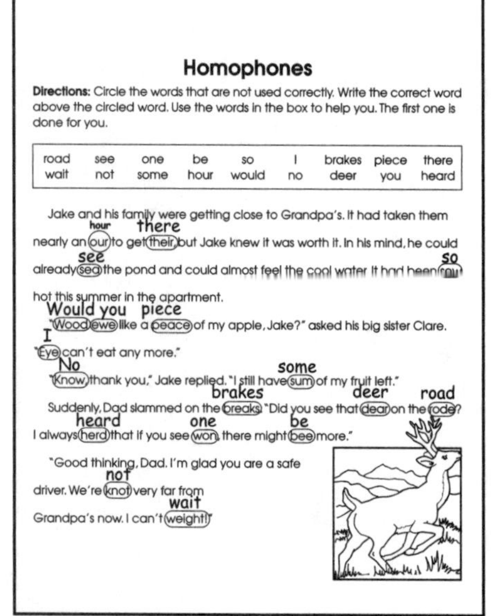

Homophones

Directions: Circle the words that are not used correctly. Write the correct word above the circled word. Use the words in the box to help you. The first one is done for you.

road	see	one	be	so	I	brakes	piece	there
wait	not	some	hour	would	no	deer	you	heard

Jake and his family were getting close to Grandpa's. It had taken them nearly an (our) hour to get (their) there but Jake knew it was worth it. In his mind, he could already (sea) see the pond and could almost feel the cool water. It had been (sew) so hot this summer in the apartment.

"(Wood) Would (ewe) you like a (peace) piece of my apple, Jake?" asked his big sister Clare.

"(Eye) I can't eat any more."

"(Know) No thank you," Jake replied. "I still have (sum) some of my fruit left."

Suddenly, Dad slammed on the (breaks) brakes. "Did you see that (dear) deer on the (rode) road? I always (herd) heard that if you see (won) one, there might (bee) be more."

"Good thinking, Dad. I'm glad you are a safe driver. We're (knot) not very far from Grandpa's now. I can't (weight) wait!"

50

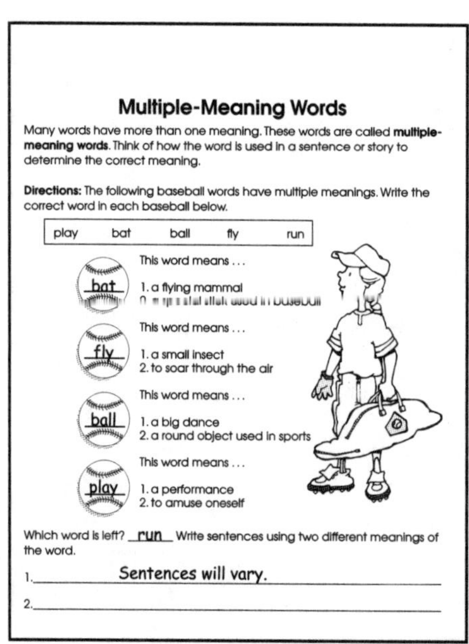

Multiple-Meaning Words

Many words have more than one meaning. These words are called **multiple-meaning words**. Think of how the word is used in a sentence or story to determine the correct meaning.

Directions: The following baseball words have multiple meanings. Write the correct word in each baseball below.

play	bat	ball	fly	run

bat — This word means . . . 1. a flying mammal 2. [illegible]

fly — This word means . . . 1. a small insect 2. to soar through the air

ball — This word means . . . 1. a big dance 2. a round object used in sports

play — This word means . . . 1. a performance 2. to amuse oneself

Which word is left? run Write sentences using two different meanings of the word.

1. Sentences will vary.
2.

51

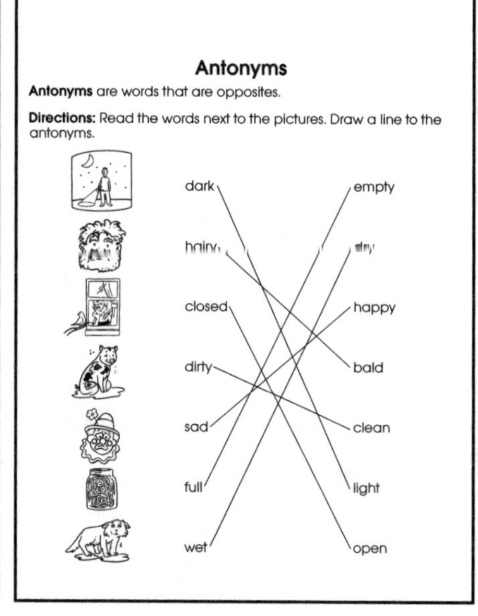

Antonyms

Antonyms are words that are opposites.

Directions: Read the words next to the pictures. Draw a line to the antonyms.

dark — light

hairy — bald

closed — open

dirty — clean

sad — happy

full — empty

wet — dry

52

Answer Key

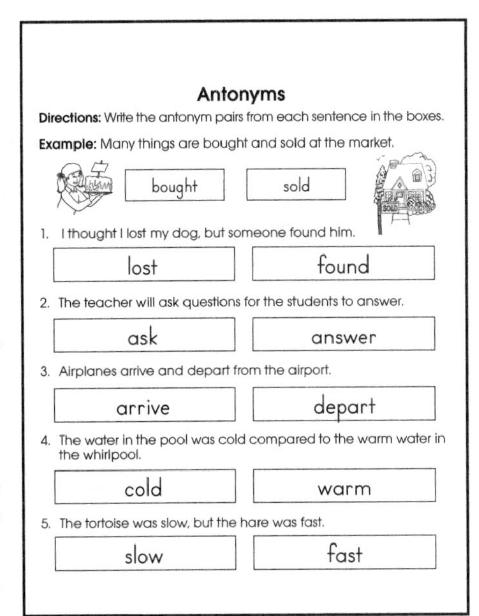

Antonyms

Directions: Write the antonym pairs from each sentence in the boxes.

Example: Many things are bought and sold at the market.

bought	sold

1. I thought I lost my dog, but someone found him.

lost	found

2. The teacher will ask questions for the students to answer.

ask	answer

3. Airplanes arrive and depart from the airport.

arrive	depart

4. The water in the pool was cold compared to the warm water in the whirlpool.

cold	warm

5. The tortoise was slow, but the hare was fast.

slow	fast

53

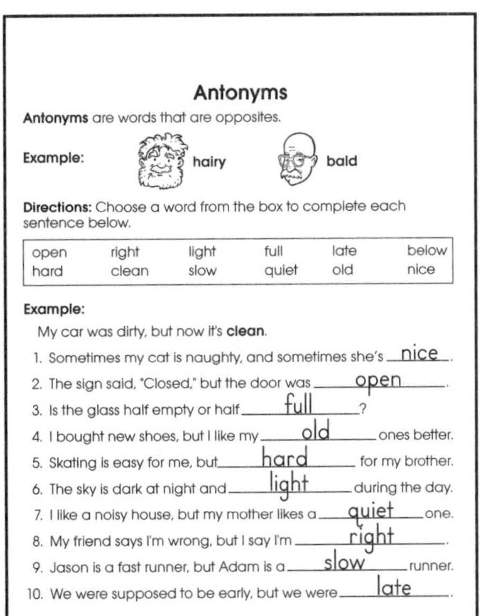

Antonyms

Antonyms are words that are opposites.

Example: hairy bald

Directions: Choose a word from the box to complete each sentence below.

open	right	light	full	late	below
hard	clean	slow	quiet	old	nice

Example:
My car was dirty, but now it's **clean**.

1. Sometimes my cat is naughty, and sometimes she's nice.
2. The sign said, "Closed," but the door was open.
3. Is the glass half empty or half full?
4. I bought new shoes, but I like my old ones better.
5. Skating is easy for me, but hard for my brother.
6. The sky is dark at night and light during the day.
7. I like a noisy house, but my mother likes a quiet one.
8. My friend says I'm wrong, but I say I'm right.
9. Jason is a fast runner, but Adam is a slow runner.
10. We were supposed to be early, but we were late.

54

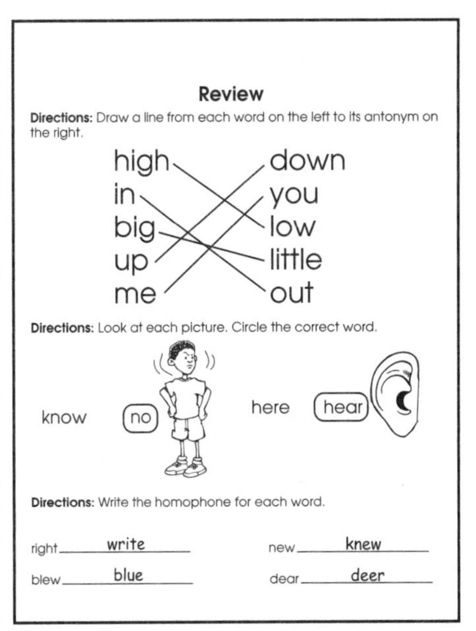

Review

Directions: Draw a line from each word on the left to its antonym on the right.

high	down
in	you
big	low
up	little
me	out

Directions: Look at each picture. Circle the correct word.

know (no) here (hear)

Directions: Write the homophone for each word.

right write new knew

blew blue dear deer

55

Common Nouns

Common nouns are nouns that name any member of a group of people, places or things, rather than specific people, places or things.

Directions: Read the sentences below and write the common noun found in each sentence.

Example: socks My socks do not match.

COMMON NOUNS

1. bird The bird could not fly.
2. jelly beans Ben likes to eat jelly beans.
3. mother I am going to meet my mother.
4. lake We will go swimming in the lake tomorrow.
5. flowers I hope the flowers will grow quickly.
6. eggs We colored eggs together.
7. bicycle It is easy to ride a bicycle.
8. cousin My cousin is very tall.
9. boat Ted and Jane went fishing in their boat.
10. prize They won a prize yesterday.
11. ankle She fell down and twisted her ankle.
12. brother My brother was born today.
13. slide She went down the slide.
14. doctor Ray went to the doctor today.

56

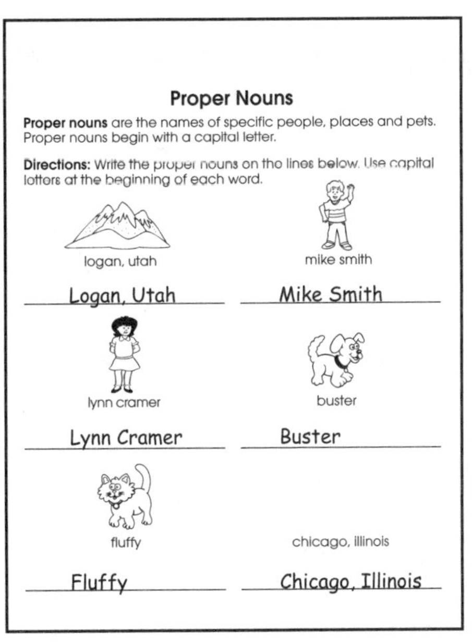

Proper Nouns

Proper nouns are the names of specific people, places and pets. Proper nouns begin with a capital letter.

Directions: Write the proper nouns on the lines below. Use capital letters at the beginning of each word.

logan, utah — Logan, Utah

mike smith — Mike Smith

lynn cramer — Lynn Cramer

buster — Buster

fluffy — Fluffy

chicago, illinois — Chicago, Illinois

57

Proper Nouns

Directions: Read the sentences and circle the proper nouns.

How do you get to Minneapolis?
MAP

1. My mom, (Carol) lives in (Wisconsin).
2. (Aunt Lorraine) lives in (Minneapolis).
3. (Jack) and (Jill) eat at (Dawn's) house.
4. (Dr. Saxton) gave (Ron) a sticker.
5. Movie stars live in (Hollywood, California).
6. (Andrea) went to (Hawaii) on her vacation.
7. (George Washington) was the first president of the (United States).

58

Answer Key

Proper Nouns

The days of the week and the months of the year are always capitalized.

Directions: Circle the words that are written correctly. Write the words that need capital letters on the lines below.

sunday	July	Wednesday	may	december
friday	tuesday	june	august	Monday
january	February	March	Thursday	April
September	saturday	October		

Days of the Week	Months of the Year
1. Sunday	1. January
2. Friday	2. June
3. Tuesday	3. May
4. Saturday	4. August
	5. December

59

Common and Proper Nouns

Directions: Look at the list of nouns in the box. Write the common nouns under the kite. Write the proper nouns under the balloon. Remember to capitalize the first letter of each proper noun.

lisa smith, cats, shoelace, saturday, dr. martin, whistle, teddy bears, main street, may, boy, lawn chair, mary stewart, bird, florida, school, apples, washington, d.c., pine cone, elizabeth jones, charley reynolds

Kite (common)	Balloon (proper)
cats	Lisa Smith
shoelace	Saturday
whistle	Dr. Martin
teddy bears	Main Street
boy	Mary Stewart
lawn chair	Florida
bird	Washington, D.C.
school	May
apples	Elizabeth Jones
pine cone	Charley Reynolds

60

Nouns

Nouns can also name ideas. **Ideas** are things we cannot see or touch such as bravery, beauty or honesty.

Directions: Underline the "idea" nouns in each sentence.

1. Respect is something that must be earned.
2. Truth and justice are two things that are highly valued.
3. The beauty of the flower garden was breathtaking.
4. Skills must be learned in order to master new things.
5. His courage impressed everyone.

61

Plural Nouns

A **plural** is more than one person, place or thing. We usually add an **s** to show that a noun names more than one. If a noun ends in **x**, **ch**, **sh** or **s**, we add an **es** to the word.

Example: pizza 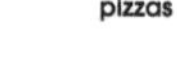 pizzas  

Directions: Write the plural of the words below.

Example: dog + s = dogs		**Example: peach + es = peaches**	
cat	cats	lunch	lunches
boot	boots	bunch	bunches
house	houses	punch	punches
Example: ax + es = axes		**Example: glass + es = glasses**	
fox	foxes	mess	messes
tax	taxes	guess	guesses
box	boxes	class	classes

Example: dish + es = dishes

bush — bushes
ash — ashes
brush — brushes

walrus
walruses

62

Plural Nouns

Directions: Write the plural of each noun to complete the sentences below. Remember to change the **y** to **ie** before you add **s**!

1. I am going to two birthday parties (party) this week.
2. Sandy picked some cherries (cherry) for Mom's pie.
3. At the store, we saw lots of bunnies (bunny).
4. My change at the candy store was three pennies (penny).
5. All the ladies (lady) baked cookies for the bake sale.
6. Thanksgiving is a special time for families (family) to gather together.
7. Boston and New York are very large cities (city).

63

Plural Nouns

Some words have special plural forms.

Example: leaf leaves

tooth	teeth
child	children
foot	feet
mouse	mice
woman	women
man	men

Directions: Some of the words in the box are special plurals. Complete each sentence with a plural from the box. Then write the letters from the boxes in the blanks below to solve the puzzle.

1. I lost my two front t e e t h!
2. My sister has two pet m i c e.
3. Her favorite book is Little W o m e n.
4. The circus clown had big f e e t.
5. The teacher played a game with the c h i l d r e n.

Take good care of this pearly plural!

t e e t h
1 2 3 4 5

64

Answer Key

Singular Nouns

Directions: The **singular form** of a word shows one person, place or thing. Write the singular form of each noun on the lines below.

cherries cherry
lunches lunch
countries country
leaves leaf
churches church
arms arm
boxes box
men man
wheels wheel
pictures picture
cities city
places place
ostriches ostrich
glasses glass

65

Possessive Nouns

Possessive nouns tell who or what is the owner of something. With singular nouns, we use an apostrophe **before** the **s**. With plural nouns, we use an apostrophe **after** the **s**.

Example:
singular: one elephant
The **elephant's** dance was wonderful.
plural: more than one elephant
The **elephants'** dance was wonderful.

Directions: Put the apostrophe in the correct place in each bold word. Then write the word in the blank.

1. The **lions** cage was big. lion's or lions'
2. The **bears'**costumes were purple. bears'
3. One **boys** laughter was very loud. boy's
4. The **trainers** dogs were dancing about. trainer's or trainers'
5. The **mans** popcorn was tasty and good. man's
6. **Marks** cotton candy was delicious. Mark's
7. A little **girls** balloon burst in the air. girl's
8. The big **clowns** tricks were very funny. clown's or clowns'
9. **Lauras** sister clapped for the clowns. Laura's
10. The **womans** money was lost in the crowd. woman's
11. **Kellys** mother picked her up early. Kelly's

66

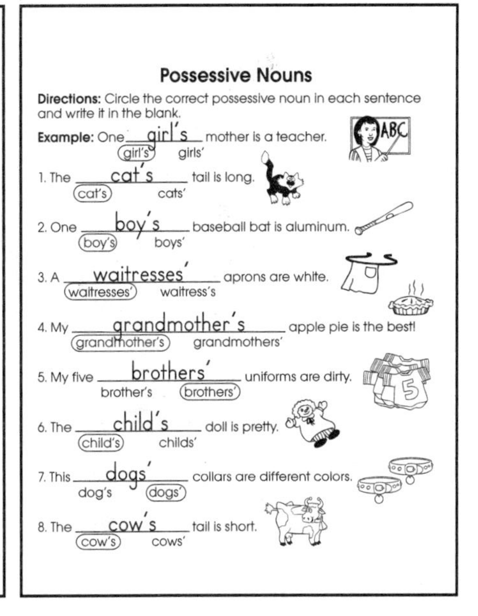

Possessive Nouns

Directions: Circle the correct possessive noun in each sentence and write it in the blank.

Example: One girl's mother is a teacher. (girl's) girls'

1. The cat's tail is long. (cat's) cats'
2. One boy's baseball bat is aluminum. (boy's) boys'
3. A waitresses' aprons are white. (waitresses') waitress's
4. My grandmother's apple pie is the best! (grandmother's) grandmothers'
5. My five brothers' uniforms are dirty. brother's (brothers')
6. The child's doll is pretty. (child's) childs'
7. This dogs' collars are different colors. dog's (dogs')
8. The cow's tail is short. (cow's) cows'

67

Pronouns

Pronouns are words that are used in place of nouns.
Examples: he, she, it, they, him, them, her, him

Directions: Read each sentence. Write the pronoun that takes the place of each noun.

Example:
The **monkey** dropped the banana. It

1. **Dad** washed the car last night. He
2. **Mary and David** took a walk in the park. They
3. **Peggy** spent the night at her grandmother's house. She
4. The **baseball players** lost their game. they
5. **Mike Van Meter** is a great soccer player. He
6. The **parrot** can say five different words. It
7. **Megan** wrote a story in class today. She
8. They gave a party for **Teresa**. her
9. Everyone in the class was happy for **Ted**. him
10. The children petted the **giraffe**. it
11. Linda put the **kittens** near the warm stove. them
12. **Gina** made a chocolate cake for my birthday. She
13. **Pete and Matt** played baseball on the same team. They
14. Give the books to **Herbie**. him

68

Pronouns

We use the pronouns **I** and **we** when talking about the person or people doing the action.

Example: I can roller skate. **We** can roller skate.

We use **me** and **us** when talking about something that is happening to a person or people.

Example: They gave **me** the roller skates.
They gave **us** the roller skates.

Directions: Circle the correct pronoun and write it in the blank.

Example:
We are going to the picnic together. (We) Us

1. I am finished with my science project. (I), Me
2. Eric passed the football to me. (me), I
3. They ate dinner with us last night. we, (us)
4. I like spinach better than ice cream. (I), Me
5. Mom came in the room to tell me good night. (me), I
6. We had a pizza party in our backyard. Us, (We)
7. They told us the good news. (us), we
8. Tom and I went to the store. me, (I)
9. She is taking me with her to the movies. I, (me)
10. Katie and I are good friends. (I), me

69

Possessive Pronouns

Possessive pronouns show ownership.
Examples: his hat, **her** shoes, **our** dog
We can use these pronouns before a noun:
my, our, you, his, her, its, their
Example: That is **my** bike.
We can use these pronouns on their own:
mine, yours, ours, his, hers, theirs, its
Example: That is **mine.**

Directions: Write each sentence again, using a pronoun instead of the words in bold letters. Be sure to use capitals and periods.

Example:
My **dog's** bowl is brown. **Its** bowl is brown.

1. That is **Lisa's** book. That is her book.
2. This is **my pencil**. This is mine.
3. This hat is **your hat**. This hat is yours.
4. Fifi is **Kevin's** cat. Fifi is his cat.
5. That beautiful house is **our home**.
That beautiful house is ours.
6. **The gerbil's** cage is too small.
Its cage is too small.

70

Answer Key

Pronouns

Singular Pronouns	Plural Pronouns
I me my mine	we us our ours
you your yours	you your yours
he she it her	they them their theirs
hers his its him	

Directions: Underline the pronouns in each sentence.

1. Mom told us to wash our hands.
2. Did you go to the store?
3. We should buy him a present.
4. I called you about their party.
5. Our house had damage on its roof.
6. They want to give you a prize at our party.
7. My cat ate her sandwich.
8. Your coat looks like his coat.

71

Articles

Articles are small words that help us to better understand nouns. **A** and **an** are articles. We use **an** before a word that begins with a vowel. We use **a** before a word that begins with a consonant.

Example: We looked in **a** nest. It had **an** eagle in it.

Directions: Read the sentences. Write **a** or **an** in the blank.

1. I found __a__ book.
2. It had a story about __an__ ant in it.
3. In the story, __a__ lion gave three wishes to __an__ ant.
4. The ant's first wish was to ride __an__ elephant.
5. The second wish was to ride __an__ alligator.
6. The last wish was __a__ wish for three more wishes.

72

Adjectives

Adjectives are words that tell more about a person, place or thing.

Examples: cold, fuzzy, dark

Directions: Circle the adjectives in the sentences.

1. The (juicy) apple is on the plate.

2. The (furry) dog is eating a bone.

3. It was a (sunny) day.

4. The kitten drinks (warm) milk.

5. The baby has a (loud) cry.

73

Adjectives

Directions: Think of your own adjectives. Write a story about Fluffy the cat.

1. Fluffy is a ______________ cat.
2. The color of his fur is ______________ .
3. He likes to chew on my______________ shoes.
4. He likes to eat ______________ cat food.
5. I like Fluffy because he is so______________.

Answers will vary.

74

Verbs

A **verb** is the action word in a sentence. Verbs tell what something does or that something exists.

Example: **Run**, **sleep** and **jump** are verbs.

Directions: Circle the verbs in the sentences below.

1. We (play) baseball every day.
2. Susan (pitches) the ball very well.
3. Mike (swings) the bat harder than anyone.
4. Chris (slides) into home base.
5. Laura (hit) a home run.

75

Verbs

We use verbs to tell when something happens. Sometimes we add an **ed** to verbs that tell us if something has already happened.

Example: Today, we will **play**. Yesterday, we **played**.

Directions: Write the correct verb in the blank.

1. Today, I will __wash__ my dog, Fritz. (wash) washed
2. Last week, Fritz __cried__ when we said, "Bath time, Fritz." cry (cried)
3. My sister likes to __help__ wash Fritz. (help) helped
4. One time she __cleaned__ Fritz by herself. clean (cleaned)
5. Fritz will __look__ a lot better after his bath. (look) looked

76

Answer Key

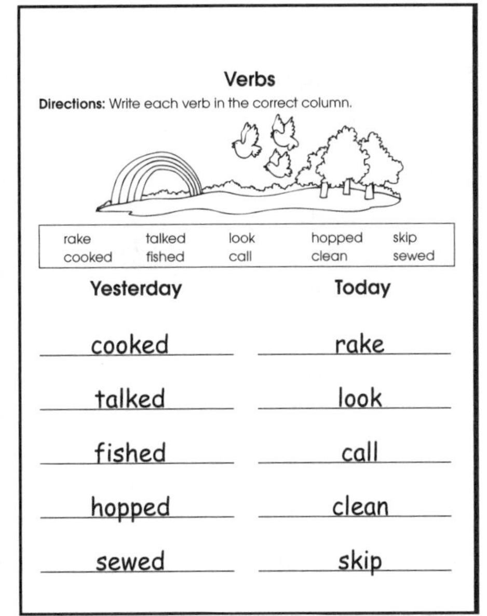

Verbs

Directions: Write each verb in the correct column.

rake	talked	look	hopped	skip
cooked	fished	call	clean	sewed

Yesterday	Today
cooked	rake
talked	look
fished	call
hopped	clean
sewed	skip

77

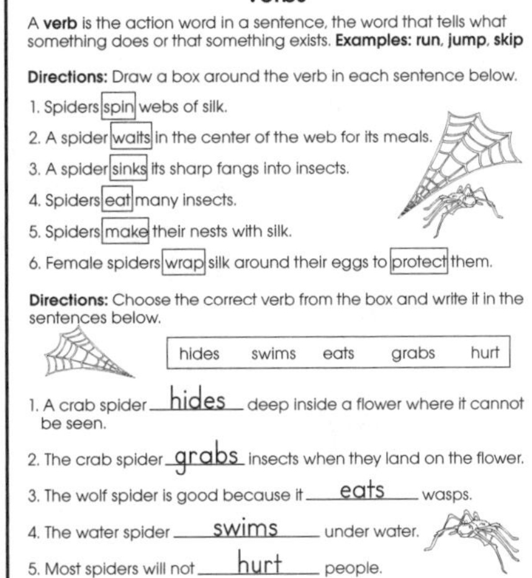

Verbs

A **verb** is the action word in a sentence, the word that tells what something does or that something exists. **Examples: run, jump, skip**

Directions: Draw a box around the verb in each sentence below.

1. Spiders [spin] webs of silk.
2. A spider [waits] in the center of the web for its meals.
3. A spider [sinks] its sharp fangs into insects.
4. Spiders [eat] many insects.
5. Spiders [make] their nests with silk.
6. Female spiders [wrap] silk around their eggs to [protect] them.

Directions: Choose the correct verb from the box and write it in the sentences below.

hides	swims	eats	grabs	hurt

1. A crab spider hides deep inside a flower where it cannot be seen.
2. The crab spider grabs insects when they land on the flower.
3. The wolf spider is good because it eats wasps.
4. The water spider swims under water.
5. Most spiders will not hurt people.

78

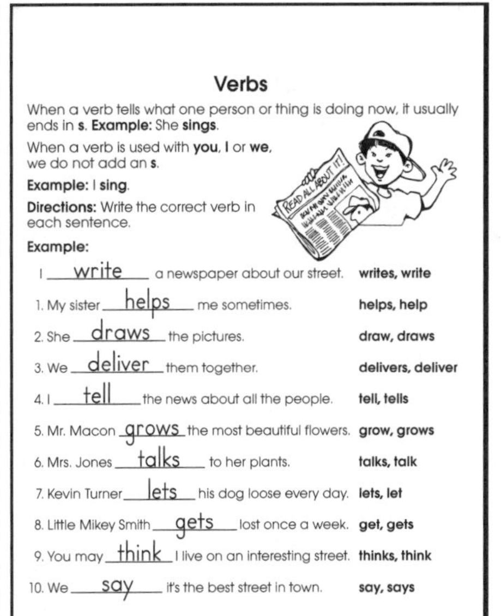

Verbs

When a verb tells what one person or thing is doing now, it usually ends in **s**. **Example:** She **sings**.

When a verb is used with **you**, **I** or **we**, we do not add an **s**.

Example: I **sing**.

Directions: Write the correct verb in each sentence.

Example:

I write a newspaper about our street. **writes, write**

1. My sister helps me sometimes. **helps, help**
2. She draws the pictures. **draw, draws**
3. We deliver them together. **delivers, deliver**
4. I tell the news about all the people. **tell, tells**
5. Mr. Macon grows the most beautiful flowers. **grow, grows**
6. Mrs. Jones talks to her plants. **talks, talk**
7. Kevin Turner lets his dog loose every day. **lets, let**
8. Little Mikey Smith gets lost once a week. **get, gets**
9. You may think I live on an interesting street. **thinks, think**
10. We say it's the best street in town. **say, says**

79

Is, Are and Am

Is, **are** and **am** are special action words that tell us something is happening now.

Use **am** with **I**. **Example:** I **am**.
Use **is** to tell about one person or thing. **Example:** He **is**.
Use **are** to tell about more than one. **Example:** We **are**.
Use **are** with **you**. **Example:** You **are**.

Directions: Write **is**, **are** or **am** in the sentences below.

1. My friends are helping me build a tree house.
2. It is in my backyard.
3. We are using hammers, wood and nails.
4. It is a very hard job.
5. I am lucky to have good friends.

80

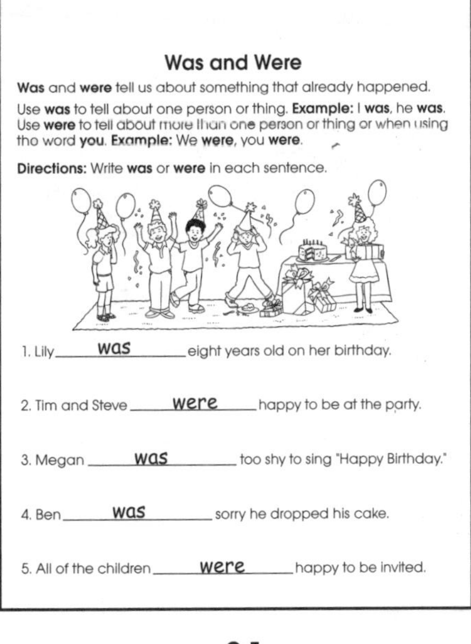

Was and Were

Was and **were** tell us about something that already happened.

Use **was** to tell about one person or thing. **Example:** I **was**, he **was**.
Use **were** to tell about more than one person or thing or when using the word **you**. **Example:** We **were**, you **were**.

Directions: Write **was** or **were** in each sentence.

1. Lily was eight years old on her birthday.
2. Tim and Steve were happy to be at the party.
3. Megan was too shy to sing "Happy Birthday."
4. Ben was sorry he dropped his cake.
5. All of the children were happy to be invited.

81

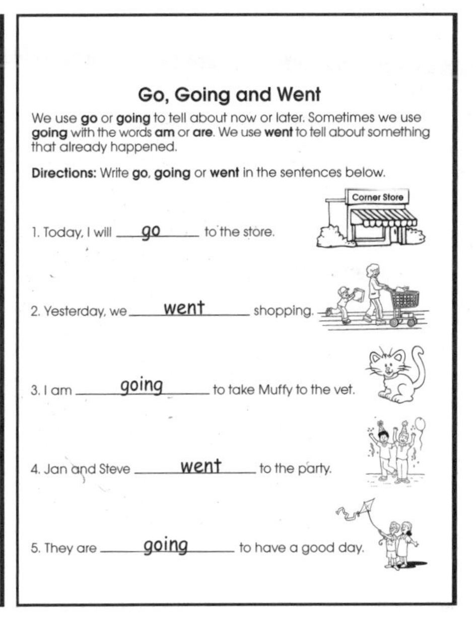

Go, Going and Went

We use **go** or **going** to tell about now or later. Sometimes we use **going** with the words **am** or **are**. We use **went** to tell about something that already happened.

Directions: Write **go**, **going** or **went** in the sentences below.

1. Today, I will go to the store.
2. Yesterday, we went shopping.
3. I am going to take Muffy to the vet.
4. Jan and Steve went to the party.
5. They are going to have a good day.

82

Answer Key

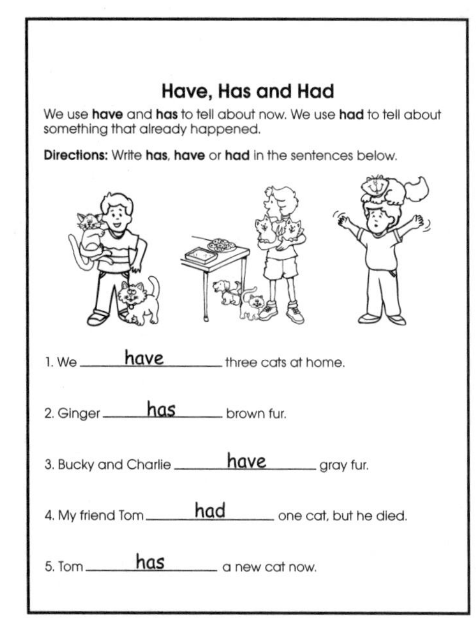

Have, Has and Had

We use **have** and **has** to tell about now. We use **had** to tell about something that already happened.

Directions: Write **has, have** or **had** in the sentences below.

1. We ___have___ three cats at home.
2. Ginger ___has___ brown fur.
3. Bucky and Charlie ___have___ gray fur.
4. My friend Tom ___had___ one cat, but he died.
5. Tom ___has___ a new cat now.

83

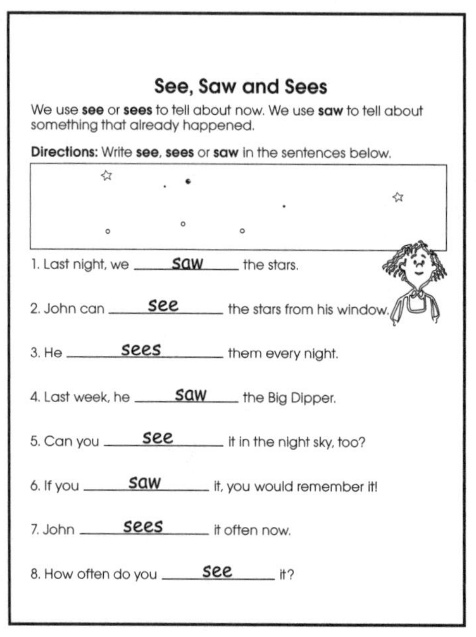

See, Saw and Sees

We use **see** or **sees** to tell about now. We use **saw** to tell about something that already happened.

Directions: Write **see, sees** or **saw** in the sentences below.

1. Last night, we ___saw___ the stars.
2. John can ___see___ the stars from his window.
3. He ___sees___ them every night.
4. Last week, he ___saw___ the Big Dipper.
5. Can you ___see___ it in the night sky, too?
6. If you ___saw___ it, you would remember it!
7. John ___sees___ it often now.
8. How often do you ___see___ it?

84

Eat, Eats and Ate

We use **eat** or **eats** to tell about now. We use **ate** to tell about what already happened.

Directions: Write **eat, eats** or **ate** in the sentences below.

1. We like to ___eat___ in the lunchroom.
2. Today, my teacher will ___eat___ in a different room.
3. She ___eats___ with the other teachers.
4. Yesterday, we ___ate___ pizza, pears and peas.
5. Today, we will ___eat___ turkey and potatoes.

85

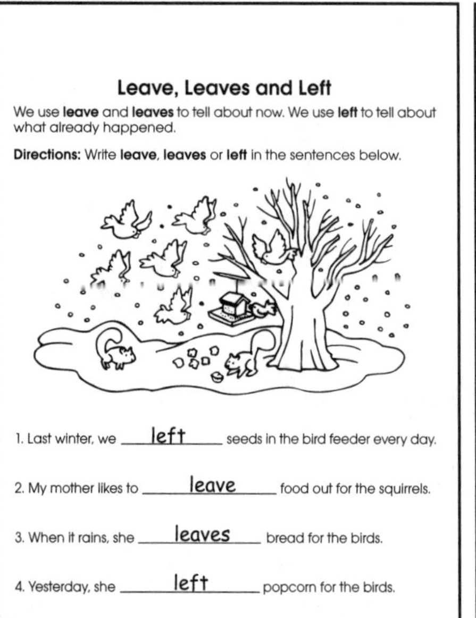

Leave, Leaves and Left

We use **leave** and **leaves** to tell about now. We use **left** to tell about what already happened.

Directions: Write **leave, leaves** or **left** in the sentences below.

1. Last winter, we ___left___ seeds in the bird feeder every day.
2. My mother likes to ___leave___ food out for the squirrels.
3. When it rains, she ___leaves___ bread for the birds.
4. Yesterday, she ___left___ popcorn for the birds.

86

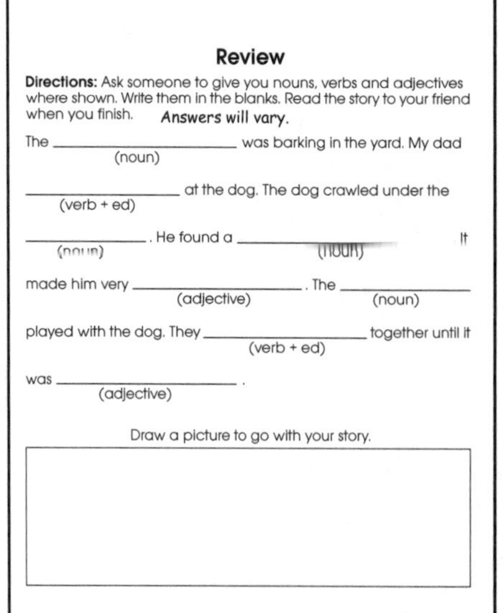

Review

Directions: Ask someone to give you nouns, verbs and adjectives where shown. Write them in the blanks. Read the story to your friend when you finish. *Answers will vary.*

The ________ (noun) was barking in the yard. My dad ________ (verb + ed) at the dog. The dog crawled under the ________ (noun). He found a ________ (noun). It made him very ________ (adjective). The ________ (noun) played with the dog. They ________ (verb + ed) together until it was ________ (adjective).

Draw a picture to go with your story.

87

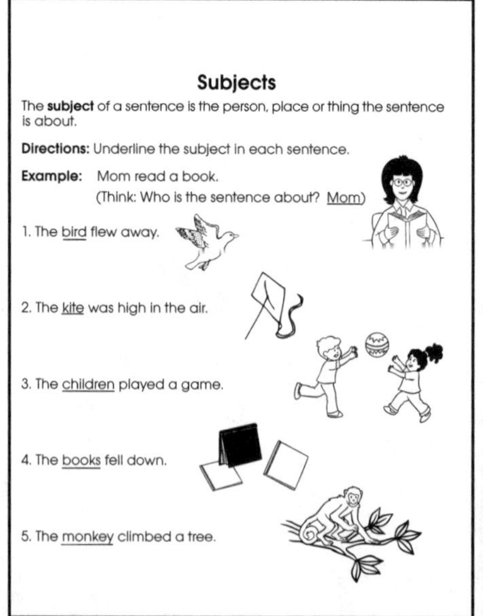

Subjects

The **subject** of a sentence is the person, place or thing the sentence is about.

Directions: Underline the subject in each sentence.

Example: Mom read a book.
(Think: Who is the sentence about? Mom)

1. The bird flew away.
2. The kite was high in the air.
3. The children played a game.
4. The books fell down.
5. The monkey climbed a tree.

88

Answer Key

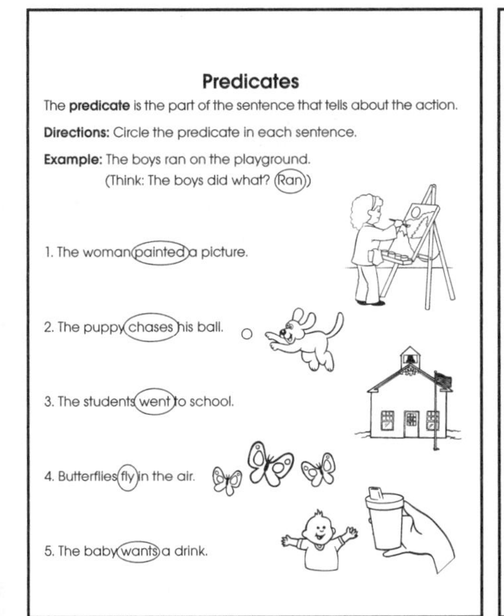

Predicates

The **predicate** is the part of the sentence that tells about the action.

Directions: Circle the predicate in each sentence.

Example: The boys ran on the playground.
(Think: The boys did what? Ran)

1. The woman painted a picture.
2. The puppy chases his ball.
3. The students went to school.
4. Butterflies fly in the air.
5. The baby wants a drink.

89

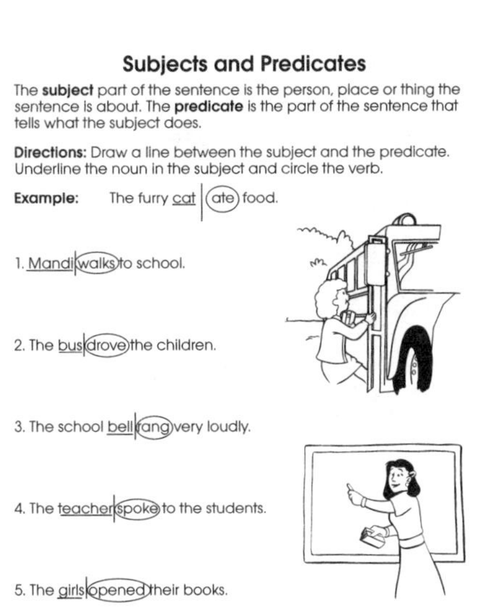

Subjects and Predicates

The **subject** part of the sentence is the person, place or thing the sentence is about. The **predicate** is the part of the sentence that tells what the subject does.

Directions: Draw a line between the subject and the predicate. Underline the noun in the subject and circle the verb.

Example: The furry cat | ate food.

1. Mandi | walks to school.
2. The bus | drove the children.
3. The school bell | rang very loudly.
4. The teacher | spoke to the students.
5. The girls | opened their books.

90

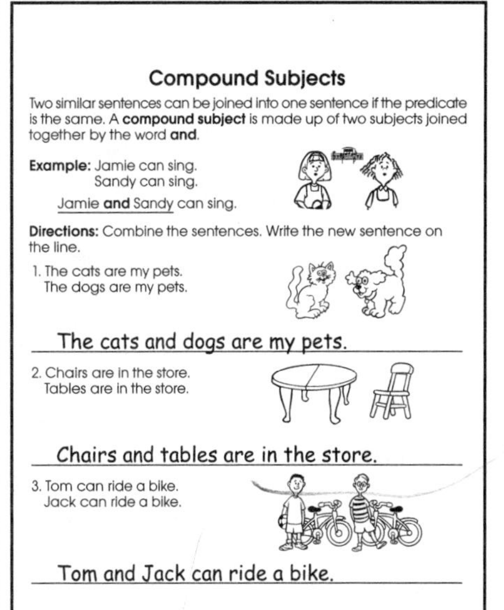

Compound Subjects

Two similar sentences can be joined into one sentence if the predicate is the same. A **compound subject** is made up of two subjects joined together by the word **and**.

Example: Jamie can sing.
Sandy can sing.
Jamie **and** Sandy can sing.

Directions: Combine the sentences. Write the new sentence on the line.

1. The cats are my pets.
The dogs are my pets.
The cats and dogs are my pets.
2. Chairs are in the store.
Tables are in the store.
Chairs and tables are in the store.
3. Tom can ride a bike.
Jack can ride a bike.
Tom and Jack can ride a bike.

91

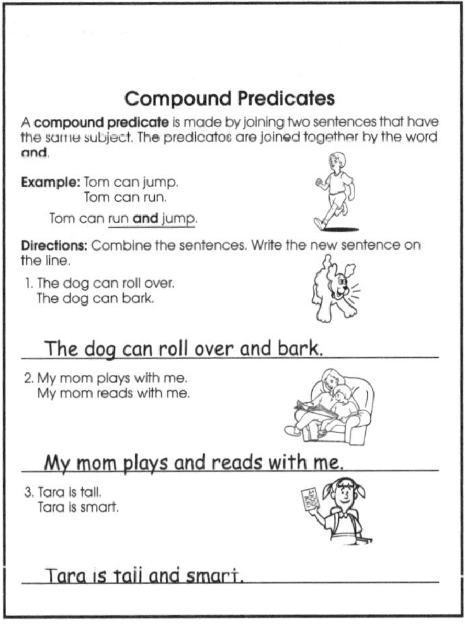

Compound Predicates

A **compound predicate** is made by joining two sentences that have the same subject. The predicates are joined together by the word **and**.

Example: Tom can jump.
Tom can run.
Tom can run **and** jump.

Directions: Combine the sentences. Write the new sentence on the line.

1. The dog can roll over.
The dog can bark.
The dog can roll over and bark.
2. My mom plays with me.
My mom reads with me.
My mom plays and reads with me.
3. Tara is tall.
Tara is smart.
Tara is tall and smart.

92

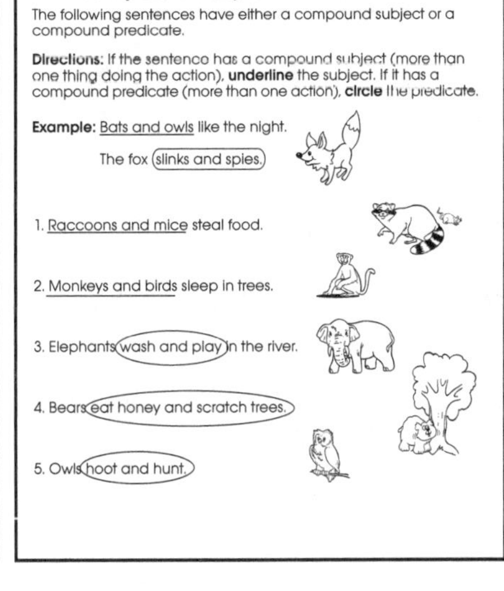

Compound Subjects and Predicates

The following sentences have either a compound subject or a compound predicate.

Directions: If the sentence has a compound subject (more than one thing doing the action), **underline** the subject. If it has a compound predicate (more than one action), **circle** the predicate.

Example: Bats and owls like the night.
The fox slinks and spies.

1. Raccoons and mice steal food.
2. Monkeys and birds sleep in trees.
3. Elephants wash and play in the river.
4. Bears eat honey and scratch trees.
5. Owls hoot and hunt.

93

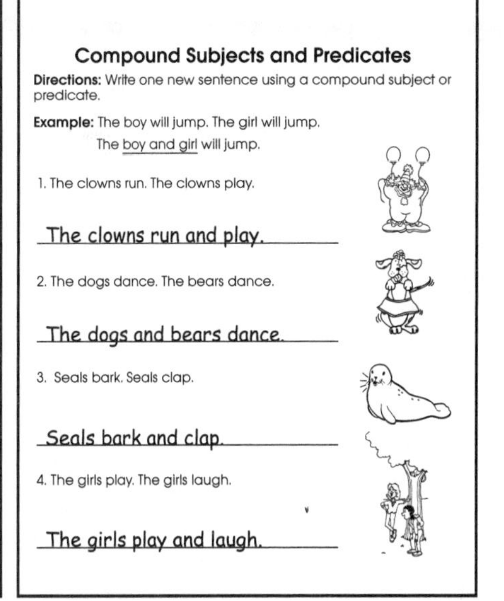

Compound Subjects and Predicates

Directions: Write one new sentence using a compound subject or predicate.

Example: The boy will jump. The girl will jump.
The boy and girl will jump.

1. The clowns run. The clowns play.
The clowns run and play.
2. The dogs dance. The bears dance.
The dogs and bears dance.
3. Seals bark. Seals clap.
Seals bark and clap.
4. The girls play. The girls laugh.
The girls play and laugh.

94

Answer Key

Word Order

Word order is the logical order of words in sentences.

Directions: Put the words in order so that each sentence tells a complete idea.

Example: outside put cat the

Put the cat outside.

1. mouse the ate snake the
   The snake ate the mouse.
2. dog John his walk took a for
   John took his dog for a walk.
3. birthday Maria the present wrapped
   Maria wrapped the birthday present.
4. escaped parrot the cage its from
   The parrot escaped from its cage.
5. to soup quarts water three of add the
   Add three quarts of water to the soup.
6. bird the bushes into the chased cat the
   The cat chased the bird into the bushes.

96

Sentences and Non-Sentences

A **sentence** tells a complete idea. It has a noun and a verb. It begins with a capital letter and has punctuation at the end.

Directions: Circle the group of words if it is a sentence.

1. (Grass is a green plant.)
2. Mowing the lawn.
3. (Grass grows in fields and lawns.)
4. Tickle the feet.
5. (Sheep, cows and horses eat grass.)
6. We like to play in.
7. (My sister likes to mow the lawn.)
8. A picnic on the grass.
9. (My dog likes to roll in the grass.)
10. Plant flowers around.

97

Statements

Statements are sentences that tell us something. They begin with a capital letter and end with a period.

Directions: Write the sentences on the lines below. Begin each sentence with a capital letter and end it with a period.

1. we like to ride our bikes
   We like to ride our bikes.
2. we go down the hill very fast
   We go down the hill very fast.
3. we keep our bikes shiny and clean
   We keep our bikes shiny and clean.
4. we know how to change the tires
   We know how to change the tires.

98

Questions

Questions are sentences that ask something. They begin with a capital letter and end with a question mark.

Directions: Write the questions on the lines below. Begin each sentence with a capital letter and end it with a question mark.

1. will you be my friend
   Will you be my friend?
2. what is your name
   What is your name?
3. are you eight years old
   Are you eight years old?
4. do you like rainbows
   Do you like rainbows?

99

Surprising Sentences

Surprising sentences tell a strong feeling and end with an exclamation point. A surprising sentence may be only one or two words showing fear, surprise or pain. **Example: Oh, no!**

Directions: Put a period at the end of the sentences that tell something. Put an exclamation point at the end of the sentences that tell a strong feeling. Put a question mark at the end of the sentences that ask a question.

1. The cheetah can run very fast .
2. Wow !
3. Look at that cheetah go !
4. Can you run fast ?
5. Oh, my !
6. You're faster than I am .
7. Let's run together .
8. We can run as fast as a cheetah .
9. What fun !
10. Do you think cheetahs get tired ?

100

Commands

Commands tell someone to do something. **Example: "Be careful."** It can also be written as "Be careful!" if it tells a strong feeling.

Directions: Put a period at the end of the command sentences. Use an exclamation point if the sentence tells a strong feeling. Write your own commands on the lines below.

1. Clean your room .
2. Now !
3. Be careful with your goldfish .
4. Watch out !
5. Be a little more careful .

Answers will vary.

101

Answer Key

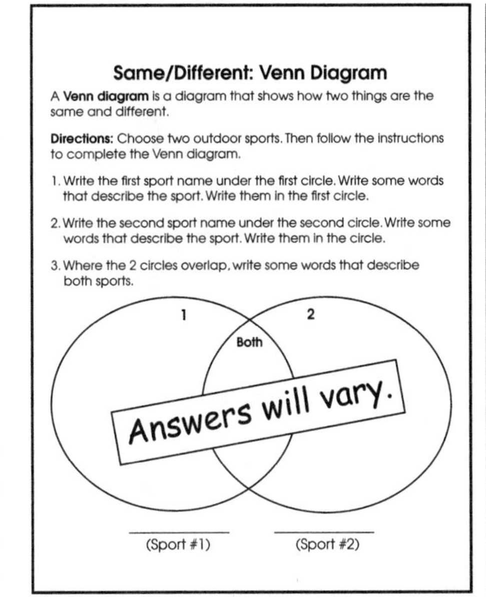

Same/Different: Venn Diagram

A **Venn diagram** is a diagram that shows how two things are the same and different.

Directions: Choose two outdoor sports. Then follow the instructions to complete the Venn diagram.

1. Write the first sport name under the first circle. Write some words that describe the sport. Write them in the first circle.
2. Write the second sport name under the second circle. Write some words that describe the sport. Write them in the circle.
3. Where the 2 circles overlap, write some words that describe both sports.

102

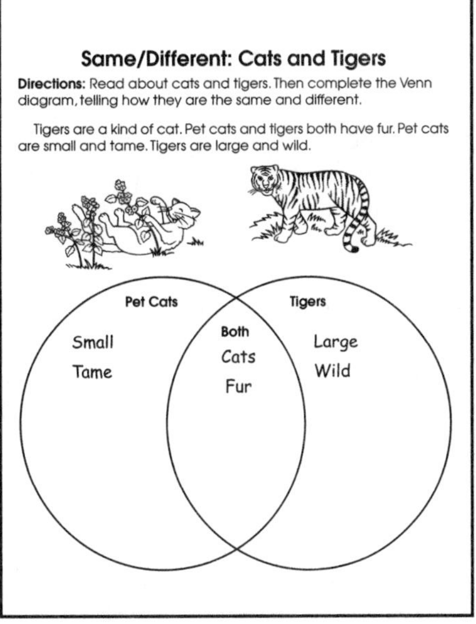

Same/Different: Cats and Tigers

Directions: Read about cats and tigers. Then complete the Venn diagram, telling how they are the same and different.

Tigers are a kind of cat. Pet cats and tigers both have fur. Pet cats are small and tame. Tigers are large and wild.

103

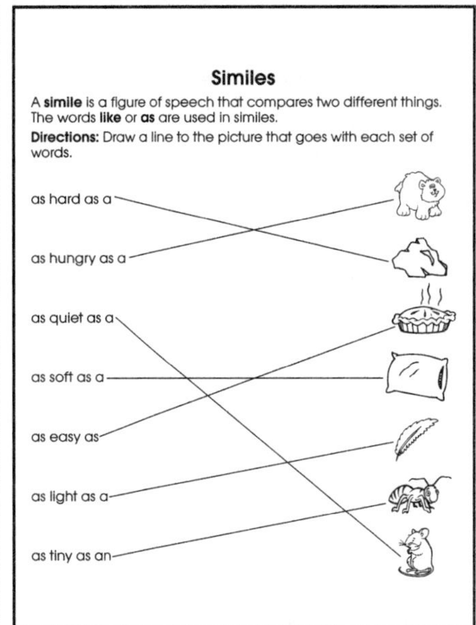

Similes

A **simile** is a figure of speech that compares two different things. The words **like** or **as** are used in similes.

Directions: Draw a line to the picture that goes with each set of words.

as hard as a

as hungry as a

as quiet as a

as soft as a

as easy as

as light as a

as tiny as an

104

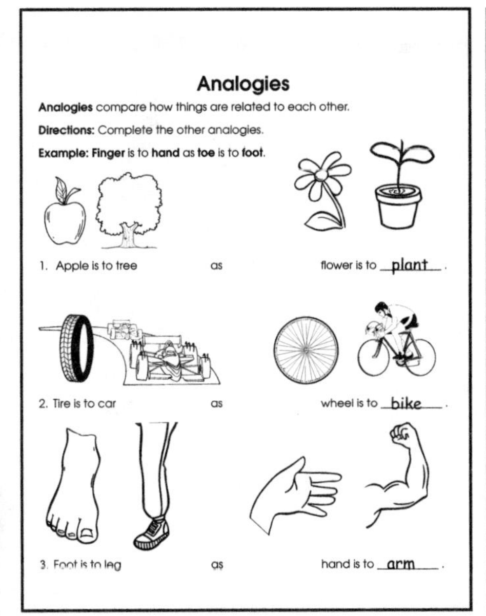

Analogies

Analogies compare how things are related to each other.

Directions: Complete the other analogies.

Example: Finger is to **hand** as **toe** is to **foot**.

1. Apple is to tree as flower is to plant.
2. Tire is to car as wheel is to bike.
3. Foot is to leg as hand is to arm.

105

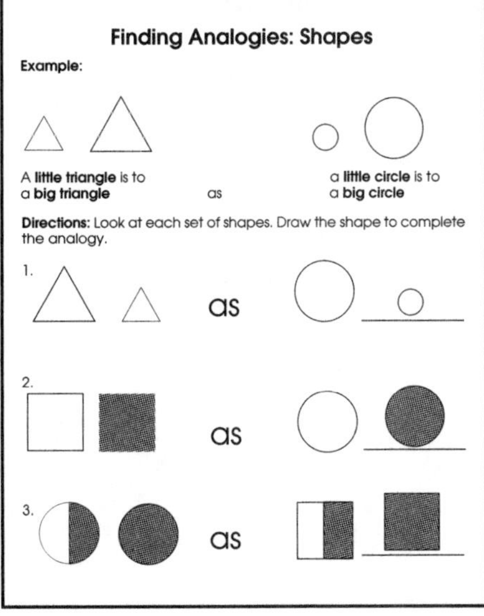

Finding Analogies: Shapes

Example:

A **little triangle** is to a **big triangle** as a **little circle** is to a **big circle**

Directions: Look at each set of shapes. Draw the shape to complete the analogy.

1. as
2. as
3. as

106

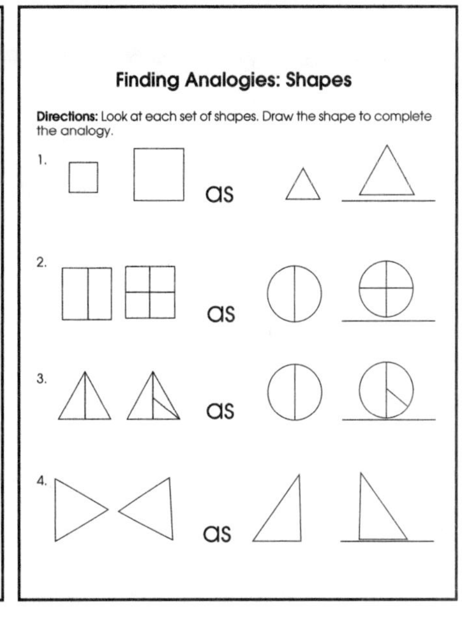

Finding Analogies: Shapes

Directions: Look at each set of shapes. Draw the shape to complete the analogy.

1. as
2. as
3. as
4. as

107

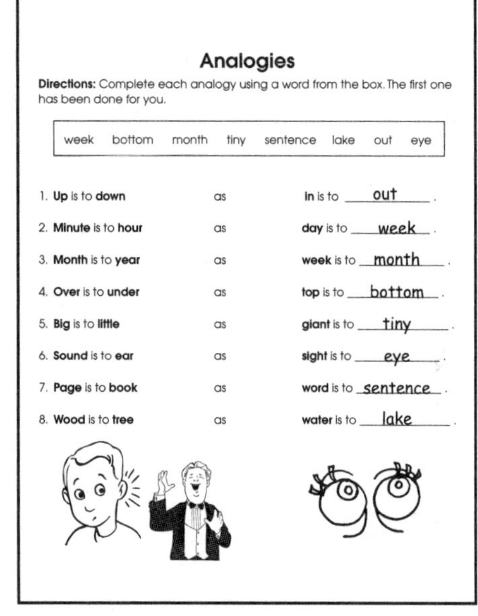

Analogies

Directions: Complete each analogy using a word from the box. The first one has been done for you.

week bottom month tiny sentence lake out eye

1. **Up** is to **down** as **In** is to out.
2. **Minute** is to **hour** as **day** is to week.
3. **Month** is to **year** as **week** is to month.
4. **Over** is to **under** as **top** is to bottom.
5. **Big** is to **little** as **giant** is to tiny.
6. **Sound** is to **ear** as **sight** is to eye.
7. **Page** is to **book** as **word** is to sentence.
8. **Wood** is to **tree** as **water** is to lake.

108

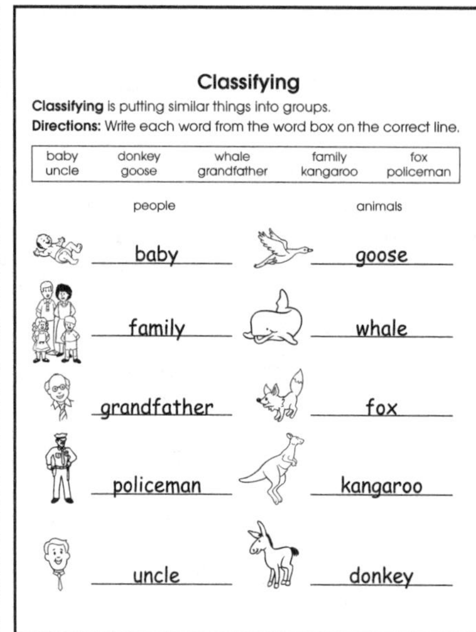

Classifying

Classifying is putting similar things into groups.

Directions: Write each word from the word box on the correct line.

baby donkey whale family fox uncle goose grandfather kangaroo policeman

people	animals
baby	goose
family	whale
grandfather	fox
policeman	kangaroo
uncle	donkey

109

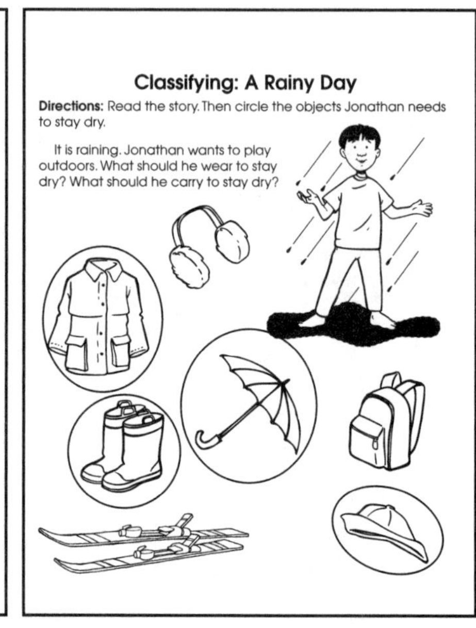

Classifying: A Rainy Day

Directions: Read the story. Then circle the objects Jonathan needs to stay dry.

It is raining. Jonathan wants to play outdoors. What should he wear to stay dry? What should he carry to stay dry?

110

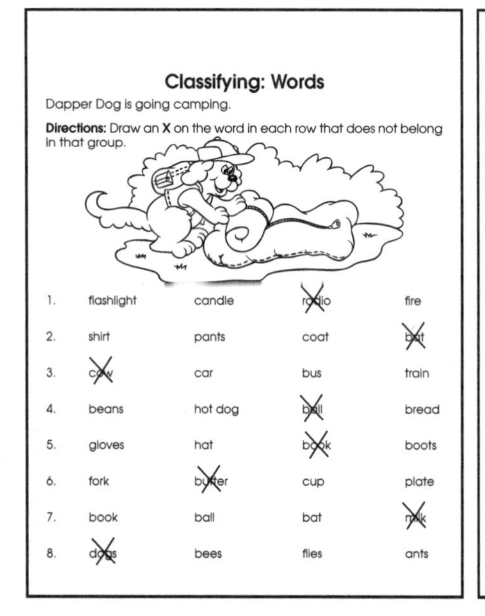

Classifying: Words

Dapper Dog is going camping.

Directions: Draw an **X** on the word in each row that does not belong in that group.

1.	flashlight	candle	radio (X)	fire
2.	shirt	pants	coat	bat (X)
3.	cow (X)	car	bus	train
4.	beans	hot dog	ball (X)	bread
5.	gloves	hat	book (X)	boots
6.	fork	butter (X)	cup	plate
7.	book	ball	bat	milk (X)
8.	dogs (X)	bees	flies	ants

111

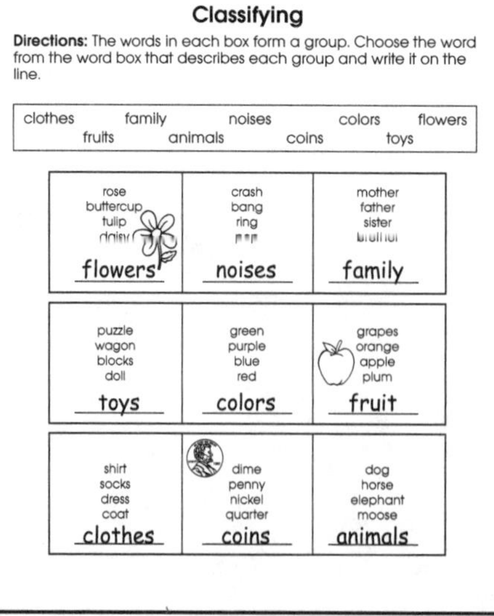

Classifying

Directions: The words in each box form a group. Choose the word from the word box that describes each group and write it on the line.

clothes family noises colors flowers fruits animals coins toys

rose, buttercup, tulip, daisy — flowers	crash, bang, ring, pop — noises	mother, father, sister, brother — family
puzzle, wagon, blocks, doll — toys	green, purple, blue, red — colors	grapes, orange, apple, plum — fruit
shirt, socks, dress, coat — clothes	dime, penny, nickel, quarter — coins	dog, horse, elephant, moose — animals

112

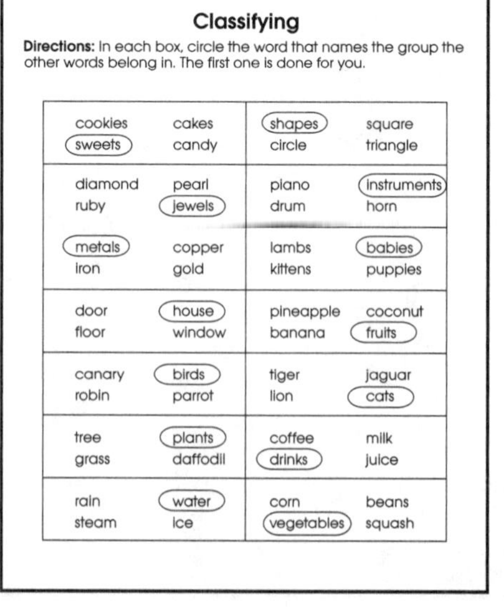

Classifying

Directions: In each box, circle the word that names the group the other words belong in. The first one is done for you.

cookies, cakes, (sweets), candy	(shapes), square, circle, triangle
diamond, pearl, ruby, (jewels)	piano, (instruments), drum, horn
(metals), copper, iron, gold	lambs, (babies), kittens, puppies
door, (house), floor, window	pineapple, coconut, banana, (fruits)
canary, (birds), robin, parrot	tiger, jaguar, lion, (cats)
tree, (plants), grass, daffodil	coffee, milk, (drinks), juice
rain, (water), steam, ice	corn, beans, (vegetables), squash

113

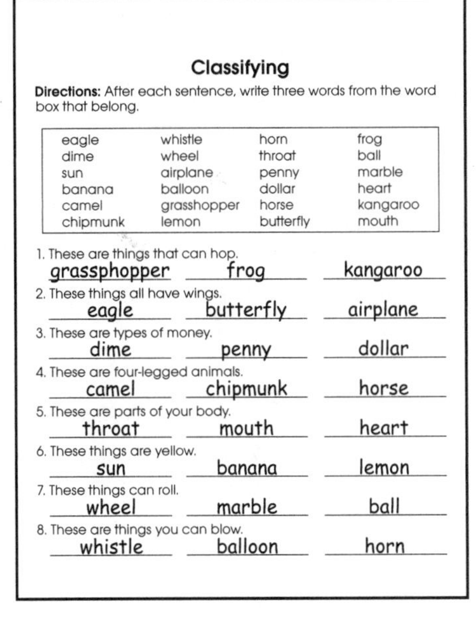

Classifying

Directions: After each sentence, write three words from the word box that belong.

eagle	whistle	horn	frog
dime	wheel	throat	ball
sun	airplane	penny	marble
banana	balloon	dollar	heart
camel	grasshopper	horse	kangaroo
chipmunk	lemon	butterfly	mouth

1. These are things that can hop.
   grassphopper frog kangaroo
2. These things all have wings.
   eagle butterfly airplane
3. These are types of money.
   dime penny dollar
4. These are four-legged animals.
   camel chipmunk horse
5. These are parts of your body.
   throat mouth heart
6. These things are yellow.
   sun banana lemon
7. These things can roll.
   wheel marble ball
8. These are things you can blow.
   whistle balloon horn

114

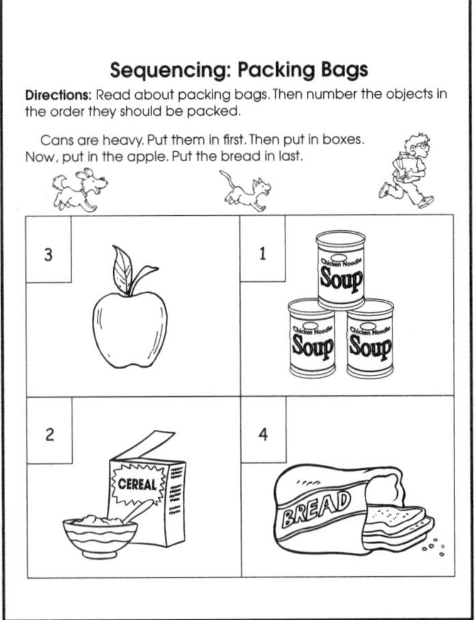

Sequencing: Packing Bags

Directions: Read about packing bags. Then number the objects in the order they should be packed.

Cans are heavy. Put them in first. Then put in boxes. Now, put in the apple. Put the bread in last.

3 (apple) 1 (soup cans) 2 (cereal) 4 (bread)

115

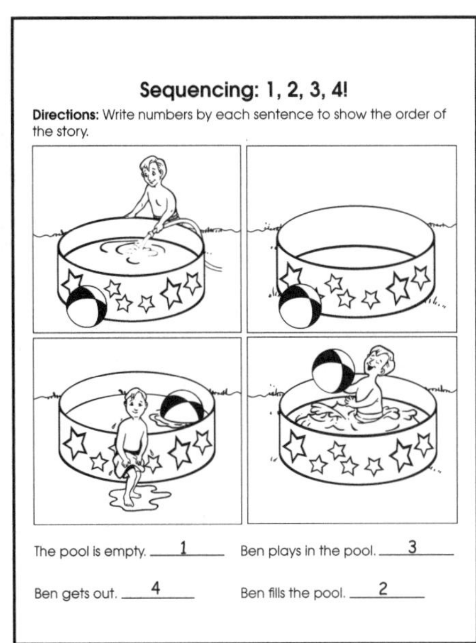

Sequencing: 1, 2, 3, 4!

Directions: Write numbers by each sentence to show the order of the story.

The pool is empty. 1 Ben plays in the pool. 3

Ben gets out. 4 Ben fills the pool. 2

116

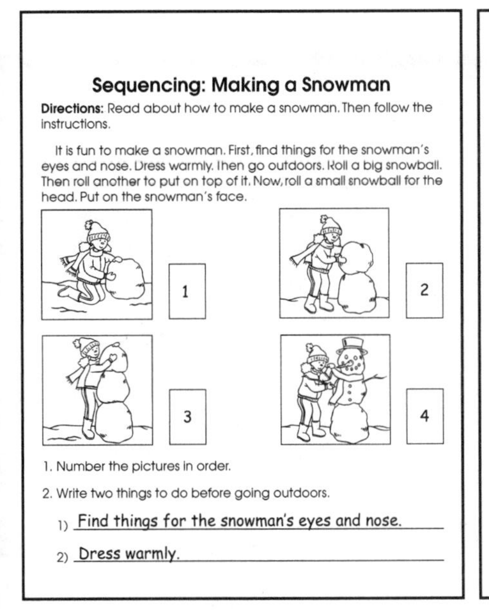

Sequencing: Making a Snowman

Directions: Read about how to make a snowman. Then follow the instructions.

It is fun to make a snowman. First, find things for the snowman's eyes and nose. Dress warmly. Then go outdoors. Roll a big snowball. Then roll another to put on top of it. Now, roll a small snowball for the head. Put on the snowman's face.

1 2 3 4

1. Number the pictures in order.
2. Write two things to do before going outdoors.
   1) Find things for the snowman's eyes and nose.
   2) Dress warmly.

117

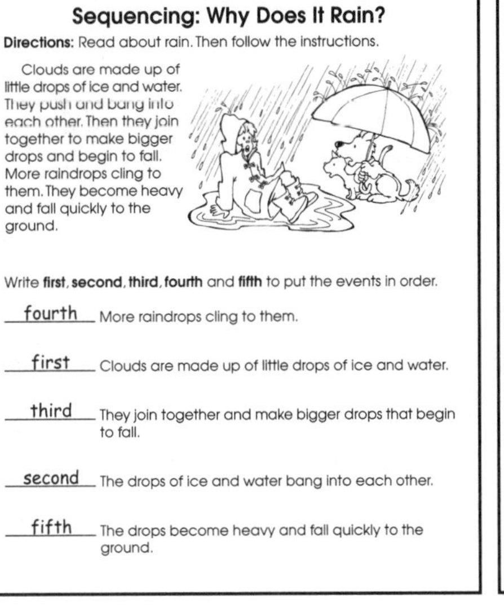

Sequencing: Why Does It Rain?

Directions: Read about rain. Then follow the instructions.

Clouds are made up of little drops of ice and water. They push and bang into each other. Then they join together to make bigger drops and begin to fall. More raindrops cling to them. They become heavy and fall quickly to the ground.

Write **first**, **second**, **third**, **fourth** and **fifth** to put the events in order.

fourth More raindrops cling to them.

first Clouds are made up of little drops of ice and water.

third They join together and make bigger drops that begin to fall.

second The drops of ice and water bang into each other.

fifth The drops become heavy and fall quickly to the ground.

118

Following Directions: Draw a House

Nick and Miguel like to draw pictures using shapes. You can help them draw a house.

Directions: Follow the instructions to create a geometric house in the bubble.

1. Draw a big square in the middle of the bubble.
2. On top of the square, draw a big triangle.
3. Inside the square, draw small squares on the left and right sides.
4. Between the two small squares, draw an upright rectangle.
5. On the rectangle, draw a small hexagon at the top.
6. Draw your face looking out the hexagon window.

120

Answer Key

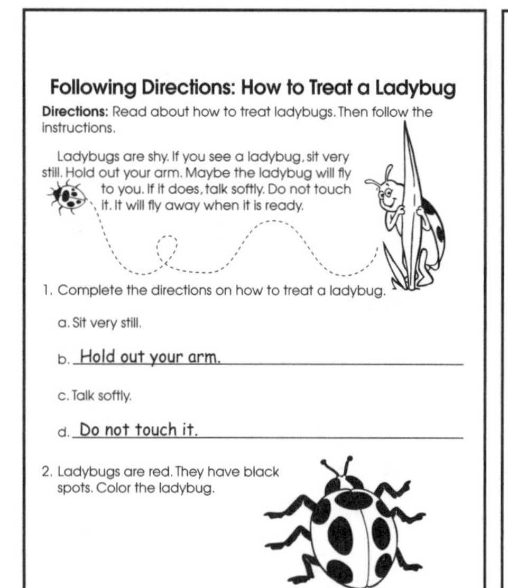

Following Directions: How to Treat a Ladybug

Directions: Read about how to treat ladybugs. Then follow the instructions.

Ladybugs are shy. If you see a ladybug, sit very still. Hold out your arm. Maybe the ladybug will fly to you. If it does, talk softly. Do not touch it. It will fly away when it is ready.

1. Complete the directions on how to treat a ladybug.
   a. Sit very still.
   b. Hold out your arm.
   c. Talk softly.
   d. Do not touch it.
2. Ladybugs are red. They have black spots. Color the ladybug.

121

Following Directions

Directions: Read the story. Answer the questions. Try the recipe.

Cows Give Us Milk

Cows live on a farm. The farmer milks the cow to get milk. Many things are made from milk. We make ice cream, sour cream, cottage cheese and butter from milk. Butter is fun to make! You can learn to make your own butter. First, you need cream. Put the cream in a jar and shake it. Then you need to pour off the liquid. Next, you put the butter in a bowl. Add a little salt and stir! Finally, spread it on crackers and eat!

1. What animal gives us milk? cow
2. What 4 things are made from milk? ice cream sour cream cottage cheese butter
3. What did the story teach you to make? butter
4. Put the steps in order. Place 1, 2, 3 or 4 by the sentence.
   4 Spread the butter on crackers and eat!
   2 Shake cream in a jar.
   1 Start with cream.
   3 Add salt to the butter.

122

Comprehension: Types of Tops

The **main idea** is the most important point or idea in a story.

Directions: Read about tops. Then answer the questions.

Tops come in all sizes. Some tops are made of wood. Some tops are made of tin. All tops do the same thing. They spin! Do you have a top?

1. Circle the main idea:
   (There are many kinds of tops.)
   Some tops are made of wood.
2. What are some tops made of? wood, tin
3. What do all tops do? spin

123

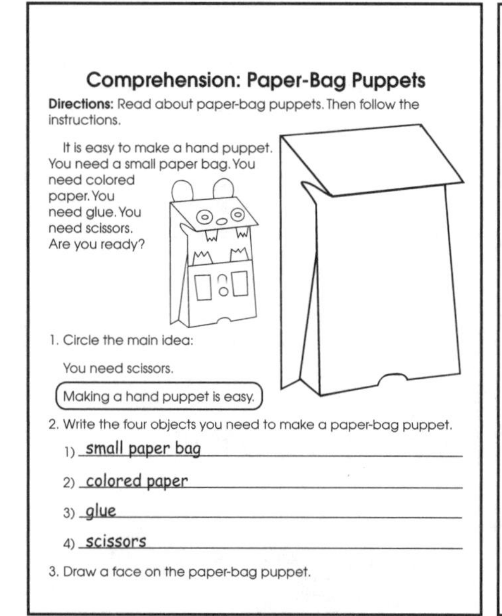

Comprehension: Paper-Bag Puppets

Directions: Read about paper-bag puppets. Then follow the instructions.

It is easy to make a hand puppet. You need a small paper bag. You need colored paper. You need glue. You need scissors. Are you ready?

1. Circle the main idea:
   You need scissors.
   (Making a hand puppet is easy.)
2. Write the four objects you need to make a paper-bag puppet.
   1) small paper bag
   2) colored paper
   3) glue
   4) scissors
3. Draw a face on the paper-bag puppet.

124

Main Idea

Directions: Read about spiders. Then answer the questions.

Many people think spiders are insects, but they are not. Spiders are the same size as insects, and they look like insects in some ways. But there are three ways to tell a spider from an insect. Insects have six legs, and spiders have eight legs. Insects have antennae, but spiders do not. An insect's body is divided into three parts; a spider's body is divided into only two parts.

1. The main idea of this story is:
   Spiders are like insects.
   (Spiders are like insects in some ways, but they are not insects.)
2. What are three ways to tell a spider from an insect?
   1) Spiders have eight legs; insects have six.
   2) Insects have antennae; spiders do not.
   3) Insects have three body parts; spiders have two

Circle the correct answer.

3. Spiders are the same size as insects. (True) False

125

Drawing Conclusions

Directions: On the top line by each picture, write the word from the word box that describes the person in the picture. Then write a clue from the picture that helped you decide.

chef	astronaut	teacher

Answer: astronaut
Clue: answers will vary.

Answer: teacher
Clue: answers will vary.

Answer: chef
Clue: answers will vary.

126

Answer Key

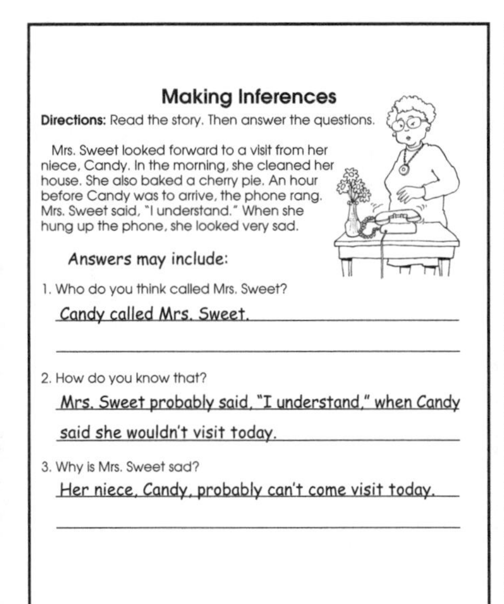

Making Inferences

Directions: Read the story. Then answer the questions.

Mrs. Sweet looked forward to a visit from her niece, Candy. In the morning, she cleaned her house. She also baked a cherry pie. An hour before Candy was to arrive, the phone rang. Mrs. Sweet said, "I understand." When she hung up the phone, she looked very sad.

Answers may include:

1. Who do you think called Mrs. Sweet?

Candy called Mrs. Sweet.

2. How do you know that?

Mrs. Sweet probably said, "I understand," when Candy said she wouldn't visit today.

3. Why is Mrs. Sweet sad?

Her niece, Candy, probably can't come visit today.

127

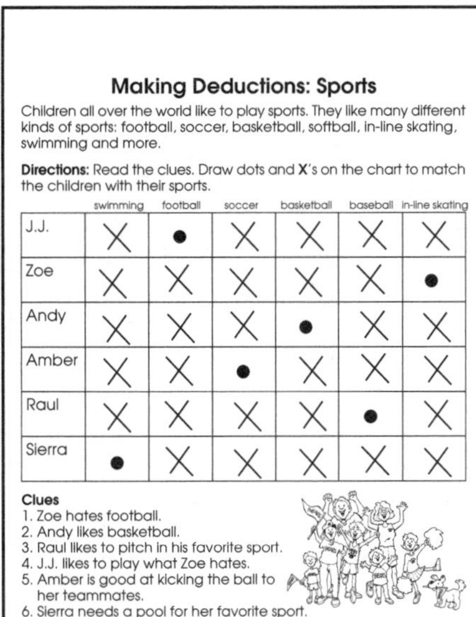

Making Deductions: Sports

Children all over the world like to play sports. They like many different kinds of sports: football, soccer, basketball, softball, in-line skating, swimming and more.

Directions: Read the clues. Draw dots and **X**'s on the chart to match the children with their sports.

	swimming	football	soccer	basketball	baseball	in-line skating
J.J.	X	•	X	X	X	X
Zoe	X	X	X	X	X	•
Andy	X	X	X	•	X	X
Amber	X	X	•	X	X	X
Raul	X	X	X	X	•	X
Sierra	•	X	X	X	X	X

Clues

1. Zoe hates football.
2. Andy likes basketball.
3. Raul likes to pitch in his favorite sport.
4. J.J. likes to play what Zoe hates.
5. Amber is good at kicking the ball to her teammates.
6. Sierra needs a pool for her favorite sport.

128

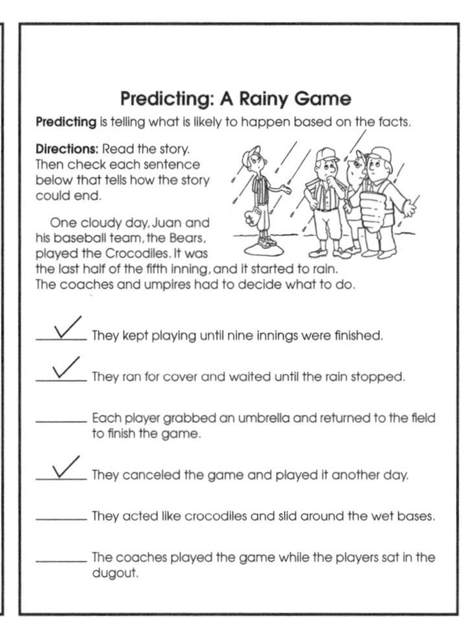

Predicting: A Rainy Game

Predicting is telling what is likely to happen based on the facts.

Directions: Read the story. Then check each sentence below that tells how the story could end.

One cloudy day, Juan and his baseball team, the Bears, played the Crocodiles. It was the last half of the fifth inning, and it started to rain. The coaches and umpires had to decide what to do.

✓ They kept playing until nine innings were finished.

✓ They ran for cover and waited until the rain stopped.

____ Each player grabbed an umbrella and returned to the field to finish the game.

✓ They canceled the game and played it another day.

____ They acted like crocodiles and slid around the wet bases.

____ The coaches played the game while the players sat in the dugout.

129

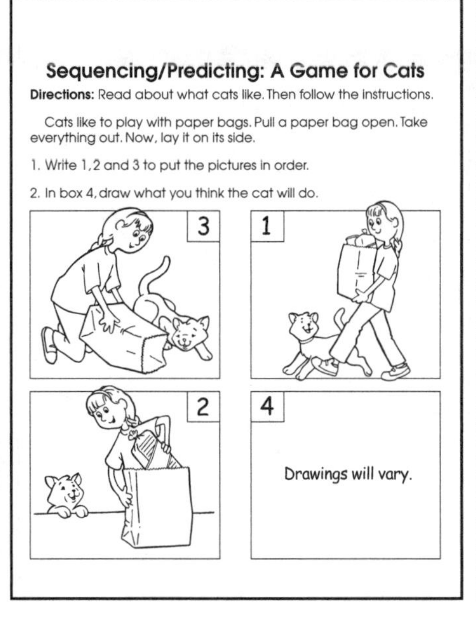

Sequencing/Predicting: A Game for Cats

Directions: Read about what cats like. Then follow the instructions.

Cats like to play with paper bags. Pull a paper bag open. Take everything out. Now, lay it on its side.

1. Write 1, 2 and 3 to put the pictures in order.
2. In box 4, draw what you think the cat will do.

3 | 1 | 2 | 4

Drawings will vary.

130

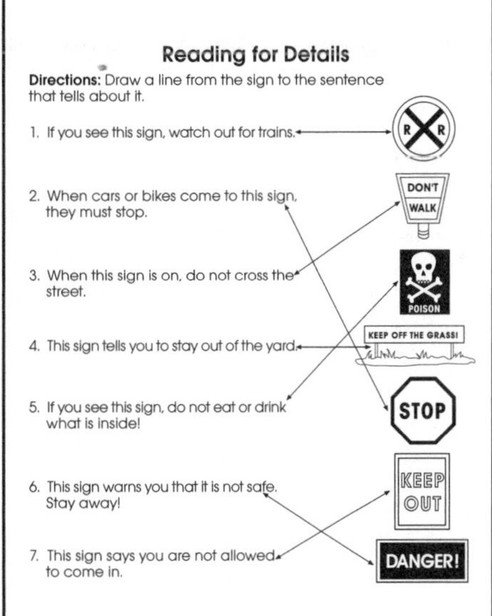

Reading for Details

Directions: Draw a line from the sign to the sentence that tells about it.

1. If you see this sign, watch out for trains.
2. When cars or bikes come to this sign, they must stop.
3. When this sign is on, do not cross the street.
4. This sign tells you to stay out of the yard.
5. If you see this sign, do not eat or drink what is inside!
6. This sign warns you that it is not safe. Stay away!
7. This sign says you are not allowed to come in.

133

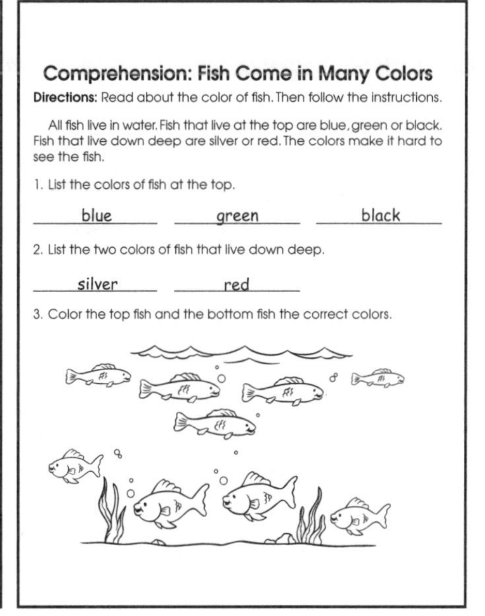

Comprehension: Fish Come in Many Colors

Directions: Read about the color of fish. Then follow the instructions.

All fish live in water. Fish that live at the top are blue, green or black. Fish that live down deep are silver or red. The colors make it hard to see the fish.

1. List the colors of fish at the top.

blue green black

2. List the two colors of fish that live down deep.

silver red

3. Color the top fish and the bottom fish the correct colors.

134

Answer Key

Reading for Details

Directions: Read the story about bike safety. Answer the questions below the story.

Mike has a red bike. He likes his bike. Mike wears a helmet. Mike wears knee pads and elbow pads. They keep him safe. Mike stops at signs. Mike looks both ways. Mike is safe on his bike.

1. What color is Mike's bike? red
2. Which sentence in the story tells why Mike wears pads and a helmet? Write it here.
   They keep him safe.
3. What else does Mike do to keep safe?
   He stops at signs and looks both ways.

135

Recalling Details: Nikki's Pets

Directions: Read about Nikki's pets. Then answer the questions.

Nikki has two cats, Tiger and Sniffer, and two dogs, Spot and Wiggles. Tiger is an orange striped cat who likes to sleep under a big tree and pretend she is a real tiger. Sniffer is a gray cat who likes to sniff the flowers in Nikki's garden. Spot is a Dalmatian with many black spots. Wiggles is a big furry brown dog who wiggles all over when he is happy.

1. Which dog is brown and furry? Wiggles
2. What color is Tiger? orange with stripes
3. What kind of dog is Spot? Dalmation
4. Which cat likes to sniff flowers? Sniffer
5. Where does Tiger like to sleep? under a big tree
6. Who wiggles all over when he is happy? Wiggles

136

Comprehension: How to Meet a Dog

Directions: Read about how to meet a dog. Then follow the instructions.

Do not try to pet a dog right away. First, let the dog sniff your hand. Do not move quickly. Do not talk loudly. Just let the dog sniff.

1. Predict what the dog will let you do if it likes you.
   Pet it.
2. What should you let the dog do?
   Sniff your hand.
3. Name three things you should not do when you meet a dog.
   1) try to pet it
   2) move quickly
   3) talk loudly

137

Reading Comprehension

Directions: Read the story. Then answer the questions.

You can grow a **citrus** (SIT-russ) plant in your home. Citrus fruits include lemons, oranges and grapefruits. Collect seeds from a piece of fruit. Wash the seeds with water and let them dry for three days. Next, fill a four-inch pot with potting soil. You can buy soil at a garden store. Plant the seeds about one-inch deep and water thoroughly.

Plants need water and light to grow. Put your pot near a window where it can get light from the sun. Pour a little water on the soil after you plant the seeds. When the soil feels dry, water it again.

1. What are some kinds of citrus fruits? lemons, oranges and grapefruits.
2. How deep should you plant the seeds in the soil?
   one-inch deep
3. Name two things that plants need to grow.
   1) water 2) light
4. How do you know when to water your plant? when the soil feels dry.

138

Reading Comprehension

Directions: Read the story. Then answer the questions.

Weed is the word used for any plant that grows where it is not wanted. Grasses that grow in your flower or vegetable garden are weeds. An unwanted flower growing in your lawn is also a weed. Dandelions are this kind of weed.

People do not plant weeds. They grow very fast. If you do not pull them out or kill them, weeds will crowd out the plants that you want to grow. The seeds of many kinds of weeds are spread by the wind. Birds and other animals also carry weed seeds.

1. A weed is any plant that grows where it is not wanted.
2. One kind of flowering weed is the dandelion
3. Two things that spread the seeds of weeds are wind and birds and other animals.

139

Fact and Opinion: Games!

A **fact** is something that can be proven. An **opinion** is a feeling or belief about something and cannot be proven.

Directions: Read these sentences about different games. Then write **F** next to each fact and **O** next to each opinion.

O 1. Tennis is cool!
F 2. There are red and black markers in a Checkers game.
F 3. In football, a touchdown is worth six points.
O 4. Being a goalie in soccer is easy.
F 5. A yo-yo moves on a string.
O 6. June's sister looks like the queen on the card.
F 7. The six kids need three more players for a baseball team.
O 8. Table tennis is more fun than court tennis.
F 9. Hide-and-Seek is a game that can be played outdoors or indoors.
F 10. Play money is used in many board games.

140

Fact and Opinion: Recycling

Directions: Read about recycling. Then follow the instructions.

What do you throw away every day? What could you do with these things? You could change an old greeting card into a new card. You could make a puppet with an old paper bag. Old buttons make great refrigerator magnets. You can plant seeds in plastic cups. Cardboard tubes make perfect rockets. So, use your imagination!

1. Write **F** next to each fact and **O** next to each opinion.

O Cardboard tubes are ugly.

F Buttons can be made into refrigerator magnets.

F An old greeting card can be changed into a new card.

O Paper-bag puppets are cute.

F Seeds can be planted in plastic cups.

F Rockets can be made from cardboard tubes.

2. What could you do with a cardboard tube? Make a rocket.

141

Fact and Opinion: A Bounty of Birds

Directions: Read the story. Then follow the instructions.

Tashi's family likes to go to the zoo. Her favorite animals are all the different kinds of birds. Tashi likes birds because they can fly, they have colorful feathers and they make funny noises.

Write **F** next to each fact and **O** next to each opinion.

F 1. Birds have two feet.

F 2. All birds lay eggs.

O 3. Parrots are too noisy.

F 4. All birds have feathers and wings.

O 5. It would be great to be a bird and fly south for the winter.

F 6. Birds have hard beaks or bills instead of teeth.

O 7. Pigeons are fun to watch.

F 8. Some birds cannot fly.

O 9. Parakeets make good pets.

F 10. A penguin is a bird.

142

Fantasy and Reality

Something that is **real** could actually happen. Something that is **fantasy** is not real. It could not happen.

Examples: Real: Dogs can bark.
Fantasy: Dogs can fly.

Directions: Look at the sentences below. Write **real** or **fantasy** next to each sentence.

1. My cat can talk to me. fantasy
2. Witches ride brooms and cast spells. fantasy
3. Dad can mow the lawn. real
4. I ride a magic carpet to school. fantasy
5. I have a man-eating tree. fantasy
6. My sandbox has toys in it. real
7. Mom can bake chocolate chip cookies. real
8. Mark has tomatoes and corn in his garden. real
9. Jack grows candy and ice cream in his garden. fantasy
10. I make my bed everyday. real

Write your own **real** sentence. Answers will vary.

Write your own **fantasy** sentence. Answers will vary.

143

Fiction and Nonfiction: Which Is It?

Directions: Read about fiction and nonfiction books. Then follow the instructions.

There are many kinds of books. Some books have make-believe stories about princesses and dragons. Some books contain poetry and rhymes, like Mother Goose. These are fiction.

Some books contain facts about space and plants. And still other books have stories about famous people in history like Abraham Lincoln. These are nonfiction.

Write **F** for fiction and **NF** for nonfiction.

F 1. nursery rhyme

F 2. fairy tale

NF 3. true life story of a famous athlete

F 4. Aesop's fables

NF 5. dictionary entry about foxes

NF 6. weather report

F 7. story about a talking tree

NF 8. story about how a tadpole becomes a frog

NF 9. story about animal habitats

F 10. riddles and jokes

144

Types of Books: Fiction and Nonfiction

Directions: Cut out the titles and place them in the correct category.

Fiction	Nonfiction
The Three Little Pigs	All About Trees
Curious Cammy	Arts and Crafts
Spaceboy Sammy	Farm Life
Jack and the Beanstalk	How to Grow a Garden
Little Red Riding Hood	The Life of George Washington

145

Fiction/Nonfiction: Heavy Hitters

Fiction is a make-believe story. **Nonfiction** is a true story.

Directions: Read the stories about two famous baseball players. Then write **fiction** or **nonfiction** on the baseball bats.

In 1998, Mark McGwire played for the St. Louis Cardinals. He liked to hit home runs. On September 27, 1998, he hit home run number 70, to set a new record for the most home runs hit in one season. The old record was set in 1961 by Roger Maris, who later played for the St. Louis Cardinals (1967 to 1968), when he hit 61 home runs.

The Mighty Casey played baseball for the Mudville Nine and was the greatest of all baseball players. He could hit the cover off the ball with the power of a hurricane. But, when the Mudville Nine was behind 4 to 2 in the championship game, Mighty Casey struck out with the bases loaded. There was no joy in Mudville that day, because the Mudville Nine had lost the game.

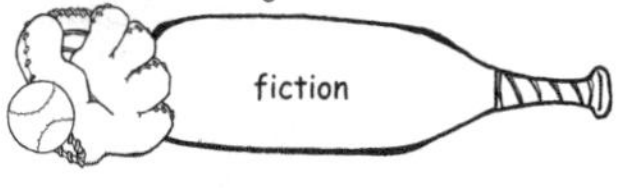

147

Answer Key

Parts of a Book

A book has many parts. The title is the name of the book. The author is the person who wrote the words. The illustrator is the person who drew the pictures. The table of contents is located at the beginning to list what is in the book. The glossary is a little dictionary in the back to help you with unfamiliar words. Books are often divided into smaller sections of information called chapters.

Directions: Look at one of your books. Write the parts you see below.

Answers will vary.

The title of my book is ____________________

The author is ____________________

The illustrator is ____________________

My book has a table of contents. Yes or No

My book has a glossary. Yes or No

My book is divided into chapters. Yes or No

148

Story Webs

All short stories have a plot, characters, a setting and a theme.

The **plot** is what the story is about.
The **characters** are the people or animals in the story.
The **setting** is where and when the story occurs.
The **theme** is the message or idea of the story.

Directions: Use the story "Snow White" to complete this story web.

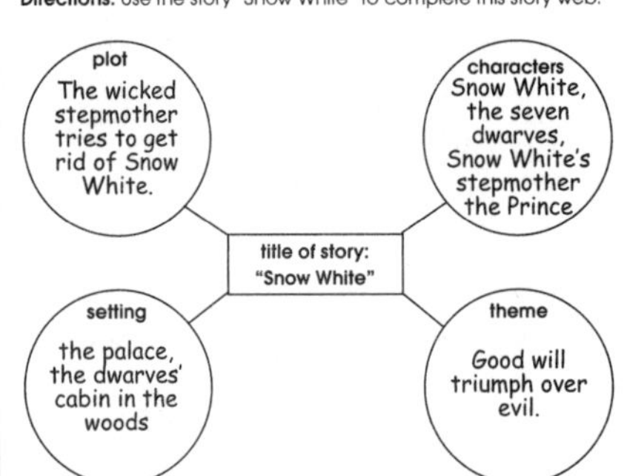

149

Tracking: Where Does She Go?

Every morning when Lisa wakes up, she goes somewhere. Find out where she goes.

Directions: Read the sentences. Follow the instructions.

1. On Monday, Lisa needs bread. Use a red crayon to mark her path from her house to that building. Where does she go? __bakery__
2. On Tuesday, Lisa wants to read books. Use a green crayon to mark her path. Where does she go? __library__
3. On Wednesday, Lisa wants to swing. Use a yellow crayon to mark her path. Where does she go? __park__
4. On Thursday, Lisa wants to buy stamps. Use a black crayon to mark her path. Where does she go? __post office__
5. On Friday, Lisa wants to get money. Use a purple crayon to mark her path. Where does she go? __bank__

150

Tracking: Sequencing

Directions: Look at the paths you drew for Lisa on page 150. Number, in order, the places that Lisa went each day. Draw a line to connect the place with the day of the week.

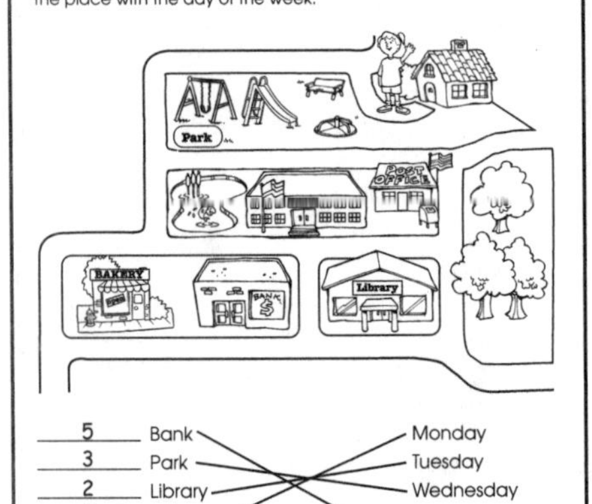

__5__ Bank — Friday
__3__ Park — Wednesday
__2__ Library — Tuesday
__1__ Bakery — Monday
__4__ Post Office — Thursday

151

Tracking: With a Map

Tashi and Lamont are neighbors. Sometimes they walk to school together. One day, Tashi went to the library after school. She didn't walk home with Lamont.

Directions: Read the sentences. Draw Tashi's path in blue and Lamont's path in red.

Tashi left her house in the morning and went to school.
She went to the library after school.
Then she went home.
Lamont left his house in the morning and went to school.
He went to the park.
Then he went home.

152

Directions

We give people directions using the terms north, south, east and west.

N
W E
S

Directions: Follow the directions to help Patrick get to the park.

PET STORE

Go south to the church.
Go east to the pet store.
Go north to the bank.
Go east to the flower garden.
Go south to the park.

153

Answer Key

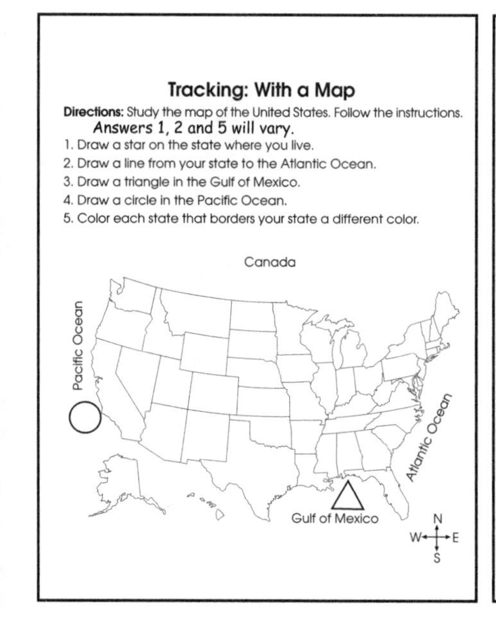

Tracking: With a Map

Directions: Study the map of the United States. Follow the instructions.

Answers 1, 2 and 5 will vary.

1. Draw a star on the state where you live.
2. Draw a line from your state to the Atlantic Ocean.
3. Draw a triangle in the Gulf of Mexico.
4. Draw a circle in the Pacific Ocean.
5. Color each state that borders your state a different color.

154

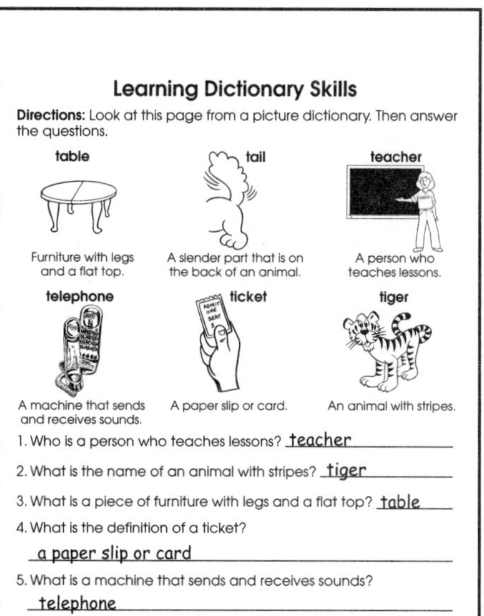

Learning Dictionary Skills

Directions: Look at this page from a picture dictionary. Then answer the questions.

table — Furniture with legs and a flat top.

tail — A slender part that is on the back of an animal.

teacher — A person who teaches lessons.

telephone — A machine that sends and receives sounds.

ticket — A paper slip or card.

tiger — An animal with stripes.

1. Who is a person who teaches lessons? teacher
2. What is the name of an animal with stripes? tiger
3. What is a piece of furniture with legs and a flat top? table
4. What is the definition of a ticket?
   a paper slip or card
5. What is a machine that sends and receives sounds?
   telephone

155

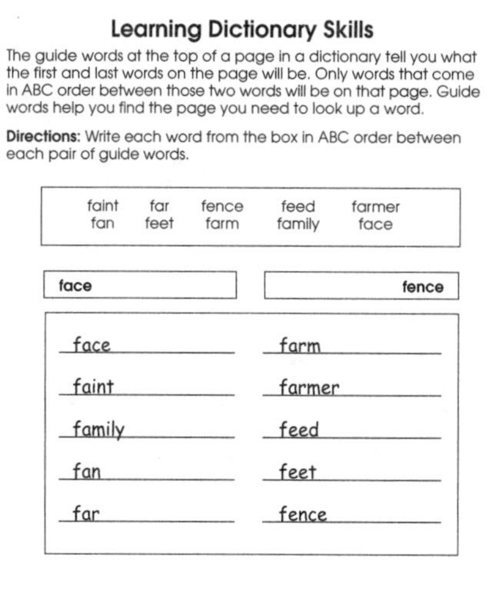

Learning Dictionary Skills

The guide words at the top of a page in a dictionary tell you what the first and last words on the page will be. Only words that come in ABC order between those two words will be on that page. Guide words help you find the page you need to look up a word.

Directions: Write each word from the box in ABC order between each pair of guide words.

faint	far	fence	feed	farmer
fan	feet	farm	family	face

face — **fence**

face	farm
faint	farmer
family	feed
fan	feet
far	fence

156

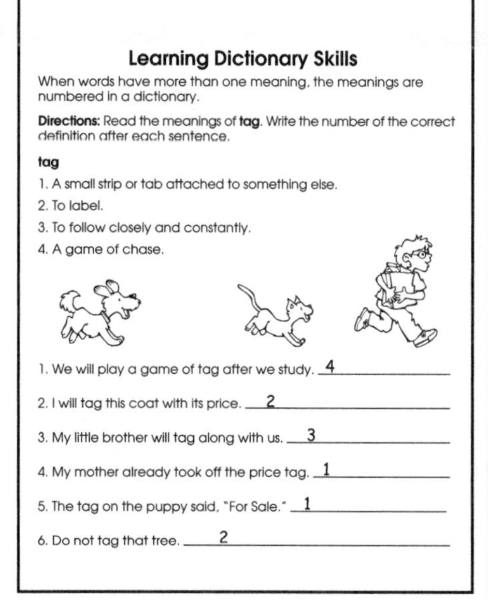

Learning Dictionary Skills

When words have more than one meaning, the meanings are numbered in a dictionary.

Directions: Read the meanings of **tag**. Write the number of the correct definition after each sentence.

tag

1. A small strip or tab attached to something else.
2. To label.
3. To follow closely and constantly.
4. A game of chase.

1. We will play a game of tag after we study. 4
2. I will tag this coat with its price. 2
3. My little brother will tag along with us. 3
4. My mother already took off the price tag. 1
5. The tag on the puppy said, "For Sale." 1
6. Do not tag that tree. 2

157

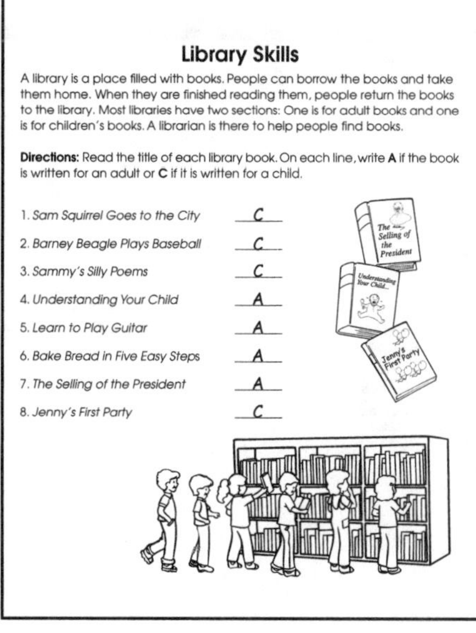

Library Skills

A library is a place filled with books. People can borrow the books and take them home. When they are finished reading them, people return the books to the library. Most libraries have two sections: One is for adult books and one is for children's books. A librarian is there to help people find books.

Directions: Read the title of each library book. On each line, write **A** if the book is written for an adult or **C** if it is written for a child.

1. *Sam Squirrel Goes to the City* C
2. *Barney Beagle Plays Baseball* C
3. *Sammy's Silly Poems* C
4. *Understanding Your Child* A
5. *Learn to Play Guitar* A
6. *Bake Bread in Five Easy Steps* A
7. *The Selling of the President* A
8. *Jenny's First Party* C

158

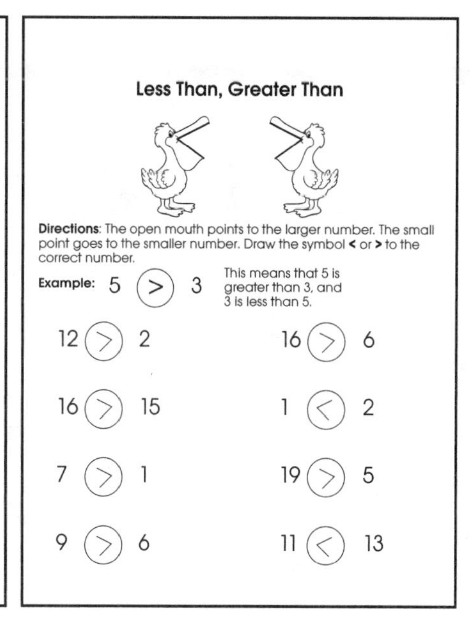

Less Than, Greater Than

Directions: The open mouth points to the larger number. The small point goes to the smaller number. Draw the symbol **<** or **>** to the correct number.

Example: 5 (>) 3 — This means that 5 is greater than 3, and 3 is less than 5.

12 (>) 2	16 (>) 6
16 (>) 15	1 (<) 2
7 (>) 1	19 (>) 5
9 (>) 6	11 (<) 13

160

Answer Key

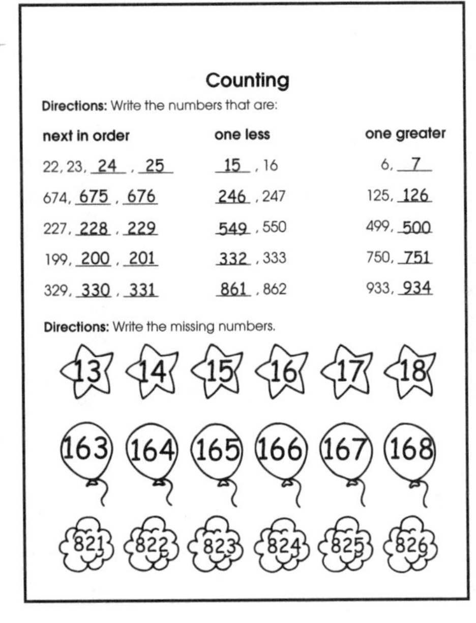

Counting

Directions: Write the numbers that are:

next in order	one less	one greater
22, 23, 24, 25	15, 16	6, 7
674, 675, 676	246, 247	125, 126
227, 228, 229	549, 550	499, 500
199, 200, 201	332, 333	750, 751
329, 330, 331	861, 862	933, 934

Directions: Write the missing numbers.

13 14 15 16 17 18

163 164 165 166 167 168

821 822 823 824 825 826

161

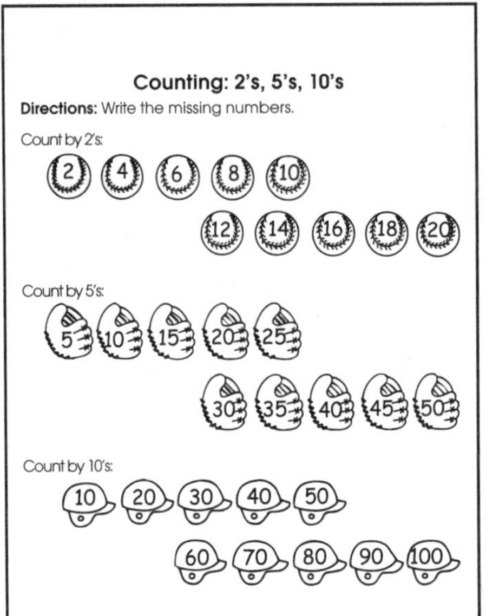

Counting: 2's, 5's, 10's

Directions: Write the missing numbers.

Count by 2's:

2 4 6 8 10 12 14 16 18 20

Count by 5's:

5 10 15 20 25 30 35 40 45 50

Count by 10's:

10 20 30 40 50 60 70 80 90 100

162

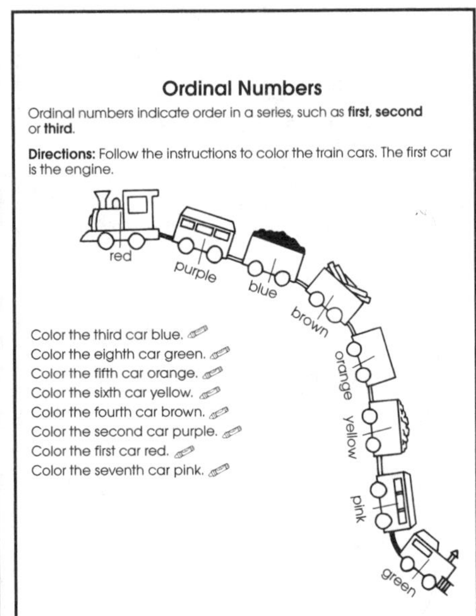

Ordinal Numbers

Ordinal numbers indicate order in a series, such as **first**, **second** or **third**.

Directions: Follow the instructions to color the train cars. The first car is the engine.

Color the third car blue.
Color the eighth car green.
Color the fifth car orange.
Color the sixth car yellow.
Color the fourth car brown.
Color the second car purple.
Color the first car red.
Color the seventh car pink.

163

Ordinal Numbers

Directions: Follow the instructions.

Draw glasses on the second one.
Put a hat on the fourth one.
Color blonde hair on the third one.
Draw a tie on the first one.
Draw ears on the fifth one.
Draw black hair on the seventh one.
Put a bow on the head of the sixth one.

164

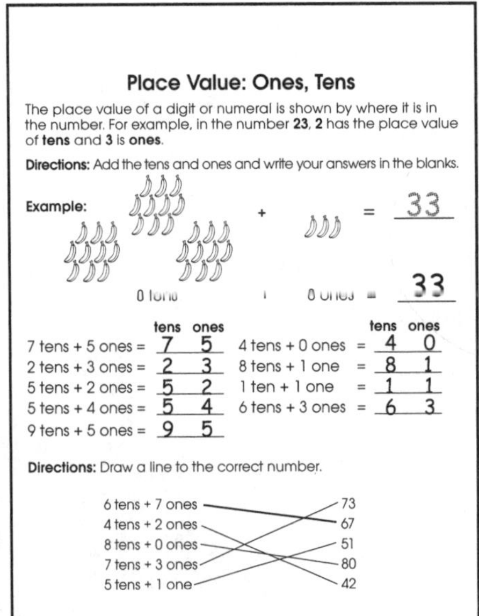

Place Value: Ones, Tens

The place value of a digit or numeral is shown by where it is in the number. For example, in the number **23**, **2** has the place value of **tens** and **3** is **ones**.

Directions: Add the tens and ones and write your answers in the blanks.

Example: + = 33

0 tens + 0 ones = 33

	tens	ones		tens	ones
7 tens + 5 ones =	7	5	4 tens + 0 ones =	4	0
2 tens + 3 ones =	2	3	8 tens + 1 one =	8	1
5 tens + 2 ones =	5	2	1 ten + 1 one =	1	1
5 tens + 4 ones =	5	4	6 tens + 3 ones =	6	3
9 tens + 5 ones =	9	5			

Directions: Draw a line to the correct number.

6 tens + 7 ones — 67
4 tens + 2 ones — 42
8 tens + 0 ones — 80
7 tens + 3 ones — 73
5 tens + 1 one — 51

165

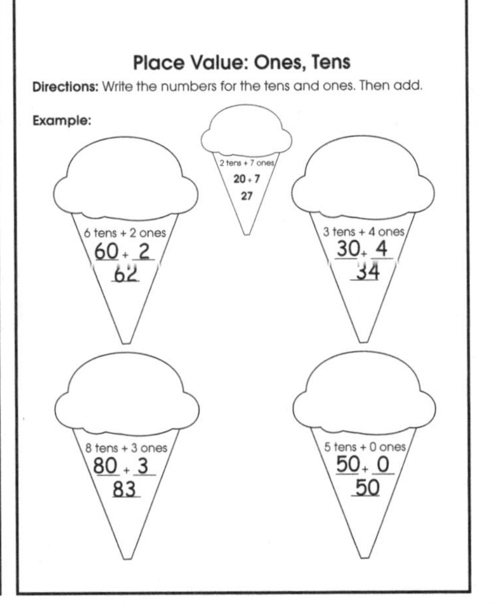

Place Value: Ones, Tens

Directions: Write the numbers for the tens and ones. Then add.

Example: 2 tens + 7 ones: 20 + 7 = 27

6 tens + 2 ones: 60 + 2 = 62

3 tens + 4 ones: 30 + 4 = 34

8 tens + 3 ones: 80 + 3 = 83

5 tens + 0 ones: 50 + 0 = 50

166

Addition: Commutative Property

The commutative property of addition states that even if the order of the numbers is changed in an addition sentence, the sum will stay the same.

Example: **2 + 3 = 5**
3 + 2 = 5

Directions: Look at the addition sentences below. Complete the addition sentences by writing the missing numerals.

5 + 4 = 9 | 3 + 1 = 4 | 2 + 6 = 8
4 + 5 = 9 | 1 + 3 = 4 | 6 + 2 = 8

6 + 1 = 7 | 4 + 3 = 7 | 1 + 9 = 10
1 + 6 = 7 | 3 + 4 = 7 | 9 + 1 = 10

Now try these:

6 + 3 = 9 | 10 + 2 = 12 | 8 + 3 = 11
3 + 6 = 9 | 2 + 10 = 12 | 3 + 8 = 11

Look at these sums. Can you think of two number sentences that would show the commutative property of addition?

__ + __ = 7 | __ + __ = 11 | __ + __ = 9
__ + __ = 7 | __ + __ = 11 | __ + __ = 9

Answers will vary.

167

Addition

Directions: Add.
Example:

Add the ones. 26 + 21 = 7
Add the tens. 26 + 21 = 47

18 + 11 = 29 | 24 + 35 = 59 | 38 + 21 = 59 | 49 + 50 = 99 | 52 + 33 = 85

75 + 12 = 87 | 83 + 16 = 99 | 67 + 32 = 99 | 44 + 25 = 69 | 28 + 41 = 69

68 + 20 = 88 | 54 + 25 = 79 | 71 + 17 = 88

The Lions scored 42 points. The Clippers scored 21 points. How many points were scored in all? 63

168

Adding 3 or More Numbers

Directions: Add all the numbers to find the sum. Draw pictures to help or break up the problem into two smaller problems.

Example: 1 + 2 + 3 = 6 | 2 + 5 = 7, 2 + 4 = 6, 7 + 6 = 13

3 + 6 + 2 = 11 | 8 + 5 + 4 = 17 | 3 + 1 + 5 = 9 | 8 + 2 + 9 = 19

2 + 8 = 10, 4 + 3 = 7, 10 + 7 = 17 | 3 + 6 = 9, 5 + 2 = 7, 9 + 7 = 16 | 4 + 1 = 5, 2 + 5 = 7, 5 + 7 = 12 | 6 + 7 = 13, 3 + 1 = 4, 13 + 4 = 17

169

Addition: Football Math

Directions: Follow the plays of your favorite team.

A touchdown is worth 6 points.
A field goal is worth 3 points.

2 touchdowns = 12 points

1 touchdown + 2 field goals = 12 points

3 field goals = 9 points

1 field goal + 1 touchdown = 9 points

Your team won the game and made record-breaking points! How many points did they score in all? 42

170

Addition Table

Directions: Fill in the blanks to complete the table.

+	0	1	2	3	4	5	6	7	8	9	10
0	0	1	2	3	4	5	6	7	8	9	10
1	1	2	3	4	5	6	7	8	9	10	11
2	2	3	4	5	6	7	8	9	10	11	12
3	3	4	5	6	7	8	9	10	11	12	13
4	4	5	6	7	8	9	10	11	12	13	14
5	5	6	7	8	9	10	11	12	13	14	15
6	6	7	8	9	10	11	12	13	14	15	16
7	7	8	9	10	11	12	13	14	15	16	17
8	8	9	10	11	12	13	14	15	16	17	18
9	9	10	11	12	13	14	15	16	17	18	19
10	10	11	12	13	14	15	16	17	18	19	20

What number patterns do you see in the Addition Table?

171

Addition: Mental Math

Directions: Try to do these addition problems in your head without using paper and pencil.

7 + 4 = 11 | 6 + 3 = 9 | 8 + 1 = 9 | 10 + 2 = 12 | 2 + 9 = 11 | 6 + 6 = 12

10 + 20 = 30 | 40 + 20 = 60 | 80 + 100 = 180 | 60 + 30 = 90 | 50 + 70 = 140 | 100 + 40 = 160

350 + 150 = 500 | 300 + 500 = 800 | 400 + 800 = 1,200 | 450 + 10 = 460 | 680 + 100 = 780 | 900 + 70 = 970

1,000 + 200 = 1,200 | 4,000 + 400 + 30 = 4,430 | 300 + 200 + 80 = 580 | 8,000 + 500 + 60 = 8,560 | 9,800 + 150 = 9,950 | 7,000 + 300 + 30 = 7,330

172

Answer Key

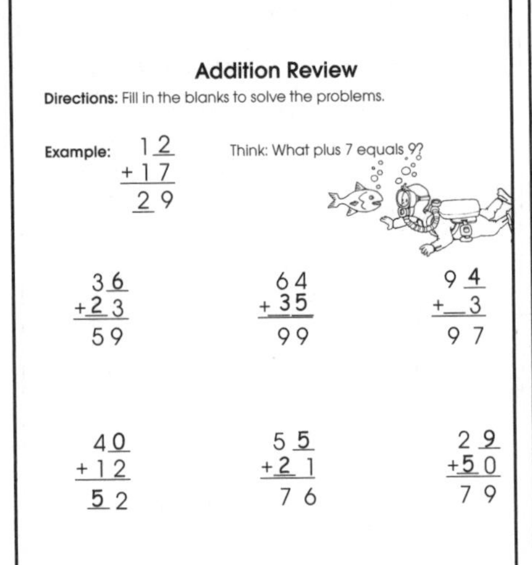

Addition Review

Directions: Fill in the blanks to solve the problems.

Example: 12 + 17 = 29   Think: What plus 7 equals 9?

36 +23 59	64 +35 99	94 + 3 97
40 +12 52	55 +21 76	29 +50 79

173

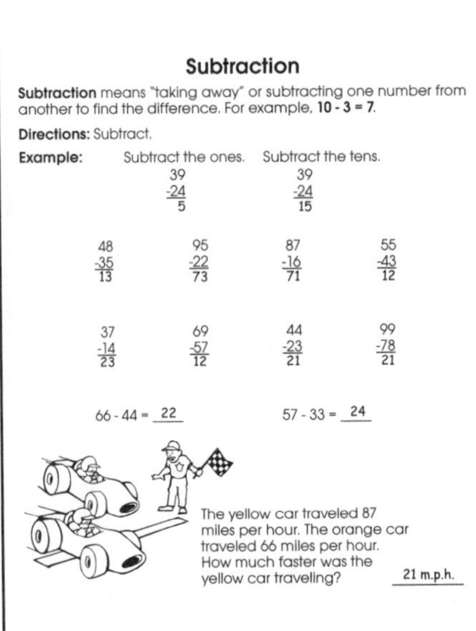

Subtraction

Subtraction means "taking away" or subtracting one number from another to find the difference. For example, **10 - 3 = 7**.

Directions: Subtract.

Example: Subtract the ones. 39 - 24 = 5   Subtract the tens. 39 - 24 = 15

48 -35 13	95 -22 73	87 -16 71	55 -43 12
37 -14 23	69 -57 12	44 -23 21	99 -78 21

66 - 44 = 22   57 - 33 = 24

The yellow car traveled 87 miles per hour. The orange car traveled 66 miles per hour. How much faster was the yellow car traveling? 21 m.p.h.

174

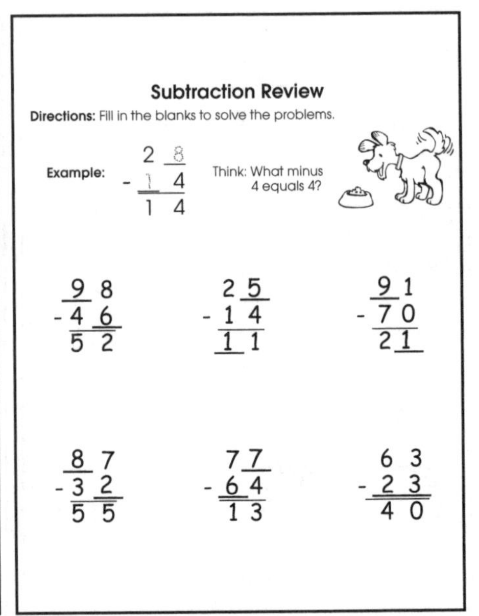

Subtraction Review

Directions: Fill in the blanks to solve the problems.

Example: 28 - 14 = 14   Think: What minus 4 equals 4?

98 - 46 52	25 - 14 11	91 - 70 21
87 - 32 55	77 - 64 13	63 - 23 40

175

Subtraction: Mental Math

Directions: Try to do these subtraction problems in your head without using paper and pencil.

9 -3 6	12 - 6 6	7 -6 1	5 -1 4	15 - 5 10	2 -0 2
40 -20 [illegible]	90 -80 10	100 - 50 50	20 -20 0	60 -10 50	70 -40 30
450 -250 200	500 -300 200	250 - 20 230	690 -100 590	320 - 20 300	900 -600 300
1,000 - 400 600	8,000 - 500 7,500	7,000 - 900 6,100	4,000 -2,000 2,000	9,500 -4,000 5,500	5,000 -2,000 3,000

176

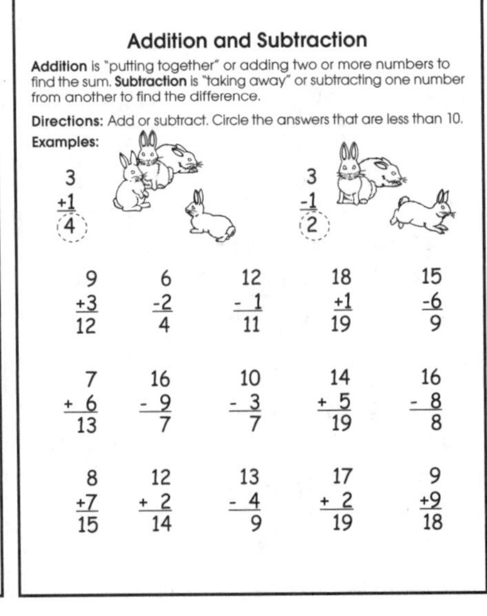

Addition and Subtraction

Addition is "putting together" or adding two or more numbers to find the sum. **Subtraction** is "taking away" or subtracting one number from another to find the difference.

Directions: Add or subtract. Circle the answers that are less than 10.

Examples: 3 + 1 = 4   3 - 1 = 2

9 +3 12	6 -2 4	12 - 1 11	18 +1 19	15 -6 9
7 + 6 13	16 - 9 7	10 - 3 7	14 + 5 19	16 - 8 8
8 +7 15	12 + 2 14	13 - 4 9	17 + 2 19	9 +9 18

177

Review

Directions: Fill in the missing numbers by counting by 10's.

10, 20, 30, 40, 50, 60, 70, 80

Directions: Draw a line to the correct numbers.

6 tens + 3 ones	45
4 tens + 5 ones	77
7 tens + 7 ones	63
9 tens + 3 ones	27
2 tens + 7 ones	93

Directions: Fill in the correct symbol, + or –.

12 5 17	7 3 4	15 5 10	14 4 18

Directions: Add or subtract.

3 +1 4	8 -6 2	12 + 7 19	10 + 1 11

178

Answer Key

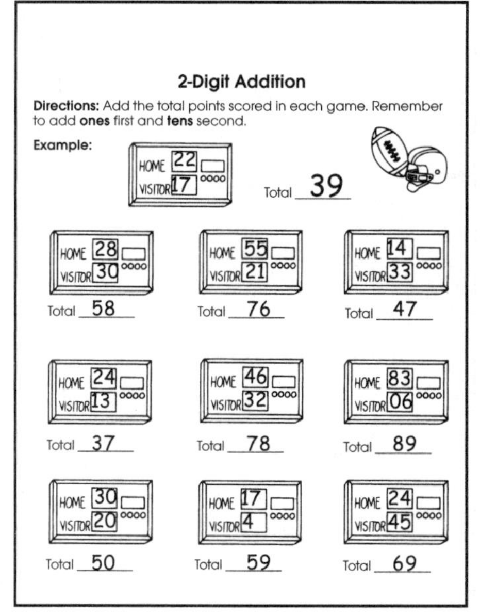

2-Digit Addition

Directions: Add the total points scored in each game. Remember to add **ones** first and **tens** second.

Example: HOME 22, VISITOR 17 — Total 39

HOME 28, VISITOR 30 — Total 58
HOME 55, VISITOR 21 — Total 76
HOME 14, VISITOR 33 — Total 47
HOME 24, VISITOR 13 — Total 37
HOME 46, VISITOR 32 — Total 78
HOME 83, VISITOR 06 — Total 89
HOME 30, VISITOR 20 — Total 50
HOME 17, VISITOR 4 — Total 59
HOME 24, VISITOR 45 — Total 69

179

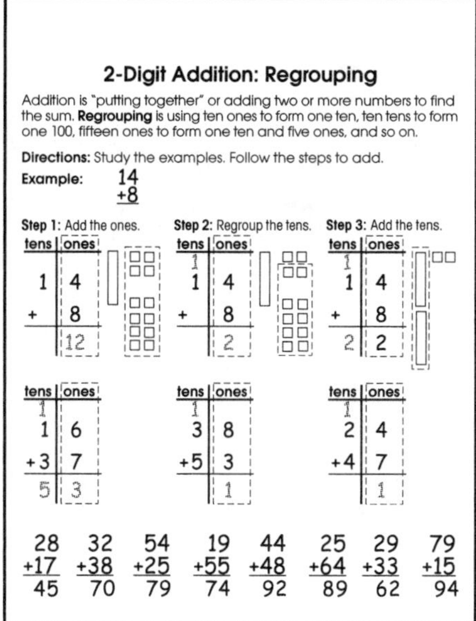

2-Digit Addition: Regrouping

Addition is "putting together" or adding two or more numbers to find the sum. **Regrouping** is using ten ones to form one ten, ten tens to form one 100, fifteen ones to form one ten and five ones, and so on.

Directions: Study the examples. Follow the steps to add.

Example: 14 + 8

Step 1: Add the ones. **Step 2:** Regroup the tens. **Step 3:** Add the tens.

14 + 8 = 22

16 + 37 = 53; 38 + 53 = 91; 24 + 47 = 71

28 + 17 = 45; 32 + 38 = 70; 54 + 25 = 79; 19 + 55 = 74; 44 + 48 = 92; 25 + 64 = 89; 29 + 33 = 62; 79 + 15 = 94

180

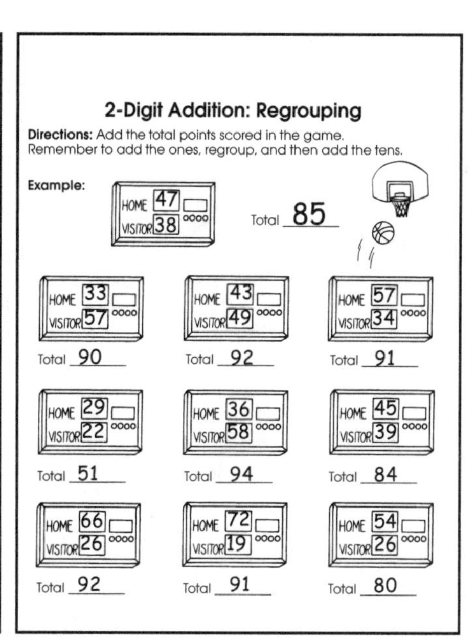

2-Digit Addition: Regrouping

Directions: Add the total points scored in the game. Remember to add the ones, regroup, and then add the tens.

Example: HOME 47, VISITOR 38 — Total 85

HOME 33, VISITOR 57 — Total 90
HOME 43, VISITOR 49 — Total 92
HOME 57, VISITOR 34 — Total 91
HOME 29, VISITOR 22 — Total 51
HOME 36, VISITOR 58 — Total 94
HOME 45, VISITOR 39 — Total 84
HOME 66, VISITOR 26 — Total 92
HOME 72, VISITOR 19 — Total 91
HOME 54, VISITOR 26 — Total 80

181

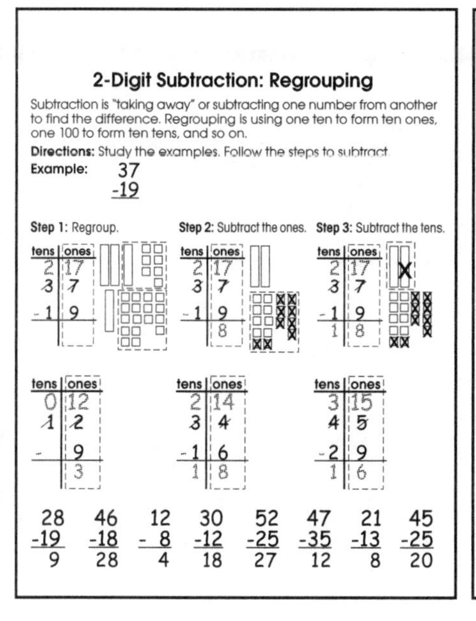

2-Digit Subtraction: Regrouping

Subtraction is "taking away" or subtracting one number from another to find the difference. Regrouping is using one ten to form ten ones, one 100 to form ten tens, and so on.

Directions: Study the examples. Follow the steps to subtract.

Example: 37 − 19

Step 1: Regroup. **Step 2:** Subtract the ones. **Step 3:** Subtract the tens.

37 − 19 = 18

12 − 9 = 3; 34 − 16 = 18; 45 − 29 = 16

28 − 19 = 9; 46 − 18 = 28; 12 − 8 = 4; 30 − 12 = 18; 52 − 25 = 27; 47 − 35 = 12; 21 − 13 = 8; 45 − 25 = 20

182

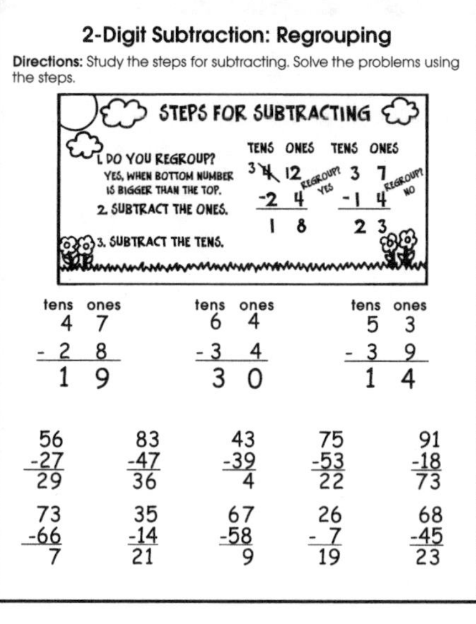

2-Digit Subtraction: Regrouping

Directions: Study the steps for subtracting. Solve the problems using the steps.

STEPS FOR SUBTRACTING
1. DO YOU REGROUP?
YES, WHEN BOTTOM NUMBER IS BIGGER THAN THE TOP.
2. SUBTRACT THE ONES.
3. SUBTRACT THE TENS.
TENS ONES
REGROUP? YES
REGROUP? NO

34 − 24 = 18 (regroup: yes); 37 − 14 = 23 (regroup: no)

47 − 28 = 19; 64 − 34 = 30; 53 − 39 = 14

56 − 27 = 29; 83 − 47 = 36; 43 − 39 = 4; 75 − 53 = 22; 91 − 18 = 73

73 − 66 = 7; 35 − 14 = 21; 67 − 58 = 9; 26 − 7 = 19; 68 − 45 = 23

183

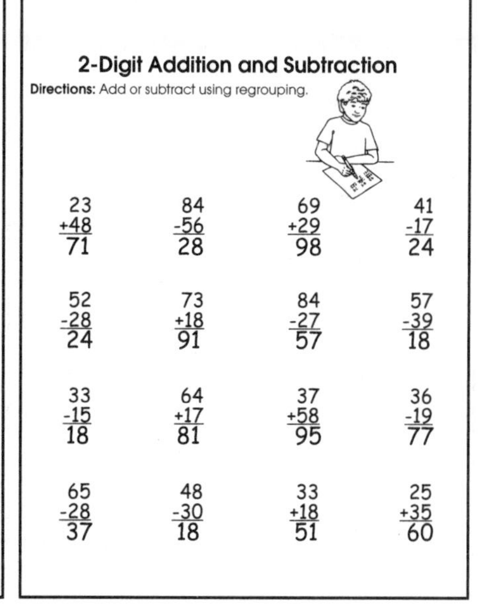

2-Digit Addition and Subtraction

Directions: Add or subtract using regrouping.

23 + 48 = 71; 84 − 56 = 28; 69 + 29 = 98; 41 − 17 = 24

52 − 28 = 24; 73 + 18 = 91; 84 − 27 = 57; 57 − 39 = 18

33 − 15 = 18; 64 + 17 = 81; 37 + 58 = 95; 36 − 19 = 77

65 − 28 = 37; 48 − 30 = 18; 33 + 18 = 51; 25 + 35 = 60

184

Answer Key

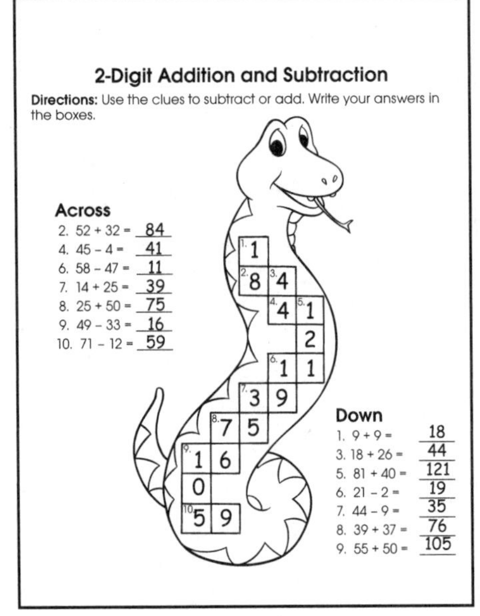

2-Digit Addition and Subtraction

Directions: Use the clues to subtract or add. Write your answers in the boxes.

Across
2. 52 + 32 = 84
4. 45 − 4 = 41
6. 58 − 47 = 11
7. 14 + 25 = 39
8. 25 + 50 = 75
9. 49 − 33 = 16
10. 71 − 12 = 59

Down
1. 9 + 9 = 18
3. 18 + 26 = 44
5. 81 + 40 = 121
6. 21 − 2 = 19
7. 44 − 9 = 35
8. 39 + 37 = 76
9. 55 + 50 = 105

185

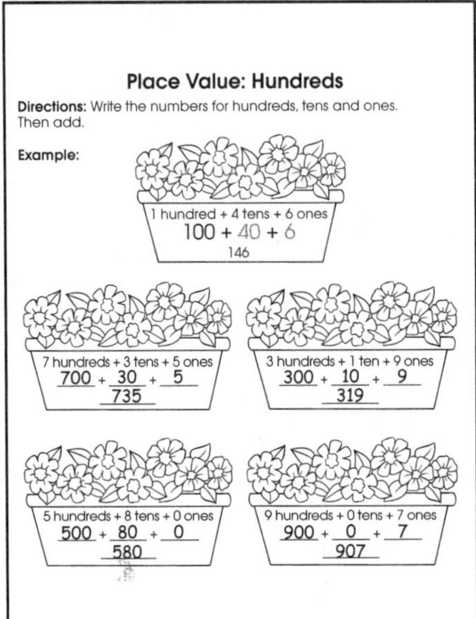

Place Value: Hundreds

Directions: Write the numbers for hundreds, tens and ones. Then add.

Example:
1 hundred + 4 tens + 6 ones
100 + 40 + 6
146

7 hundreds + 3 tens + 5 ones
700 + 30 + 5
735

3 hundreds + 1 ten + 9 ones
300 + 10 + 9
319

5 hundreds + 8 tens + 0 ones
500 + 80 + 0
580

9 hundreds + 0 tens + 7 ones
900 + 0 + 7
907

186

Rounding: The Nearest Ten

If the ones number is 5 or greater, "round up" to the nearest 10. If the ones number is 4 or less, the tens number stays the same and the ones number becomes a zero.

Examples: 15 round up to 20 23 round down to 20 47 round up to 50

7 10 58 60
12 10 81 80
33 30 94 90
27 30 44 40
73 70 88 90
25 30 66 70
39 40 70 70

187

Rounding: The Nearest Hundred

If the tens number is 5 or greater, "round up" to the nearest hundred. If the tens number is 4 or less, the hundreds number remains the same.

REMEMBER . . . Look at the number directly to the right of the place you are rounding to.

Example:
230 round down to 200 470 round up to 500
150 round up to 200 732 round down to 700

456 500 120 100
340 300 923 900
867 900 550 600
686 700 231 200
770 800 492 500

188

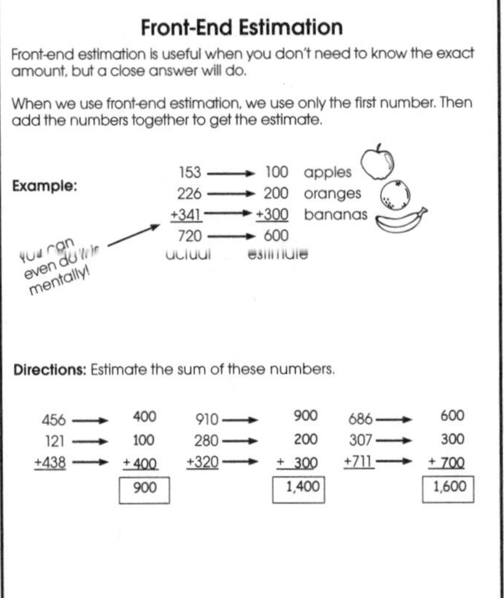

Front-End Estimation

Front-end estimation is useful when you don't need to know the exact amount, but a close answer will do.

When we use front-end estimation, we use only the first number. Then add the numbers together to get the estimate.

Example:
153 → 100 apples
226 → 200 oranges
+341 → +300 bananas
720 → 600
actual estimate

You can even do this mentally!

Directions: Estimate the sum of these numbers.

456 → 400
121 → 100
+438 → + 400
900

910 → 900
280 → 200
+320 → + 300
1,400

686 → 600
307 → 300
+711 → + 700
1,600

189

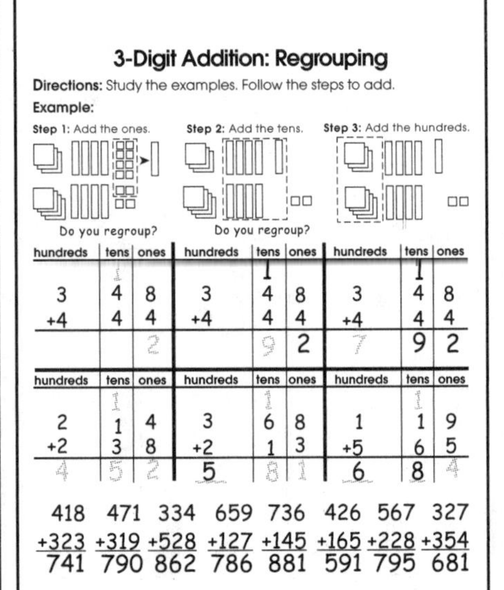

3-Digit Addition: Regrouping

Directions: Study the examples. Follow the steps to add.

Example:
Step 1: Add the ones. **Step 2:** Add the tens. **Step 3:** Add the hundreds.

Do you regroup? Do you regroup?

hundreds	tens	ones	hundreds	tens	ones	hundreds	tens	ones
	1			1			1	
3	4	8	3	4	8	3	4	8
+4	4	4	+4	4	4	+4	4	4
		2		9	2	7	9	2

hundreds	tens	ones	hundreds	tens	ones	hundreds	tens	ones
	1			1			1	
2	1	4	3	6	8	1	1	9
+2	3	8	+2	1	3	+5	6	5
4	5	2	5	8	1	6	8	4

418	471	334	659	736	426	567	327
+323	+319	+528	+127	+145	+165	+228	+354
741	790	862	786	881	591	795	681

190

Answer Key

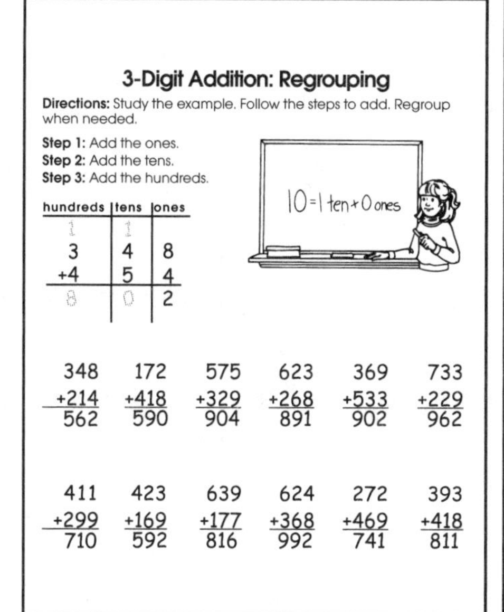

3-Digit Addition: Regrouping

Directions: Study the example. Follow the steps to add. Regroup when needed.

Step 1: Add the ones.
Step 2: Add the tens.
Step 3: Add the hundreds.

hundreds	tens	ones
1	1	
3	4	8
+4	5	4
8	0	2

348 + 214 = 562; 172 + 418 = 590; 575 + 329 = 904; 623 + 268 = 891; 369 + 533 = 902; 733 + 229 = 962

411 + 299 = 710; 423 + 169 = 592; 639 + 177 = 816; 624 + 368 = 992; 272 + 469 = 741; 393 + 418 = 811

191

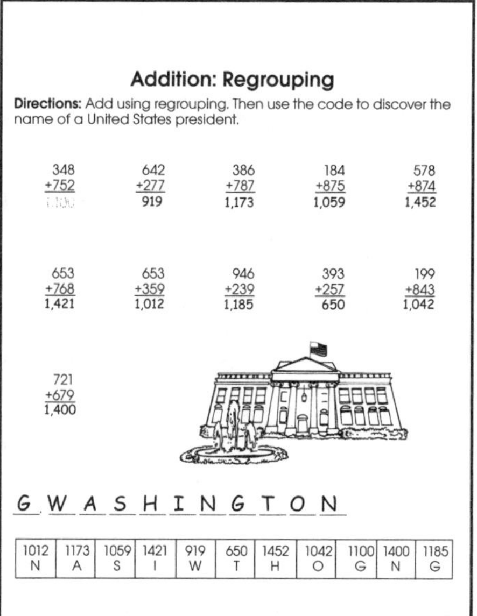

Addition: Regrouping

Directions: Add using regrouping. Then use the code to discover the name of a United States president.

348 + 752 = 1,100; 642 + 277 = 919; 386 + 787 = 1,173; 184 + 875 = 1,059; 578 + 874 = 1,452

653 + 768 = 1,421; 653 + 359 = 1,012; 946 + 239 = 1,185; 393 + 257 = 650; 199 + 843 = 1,042

721 + 679 = 1,400

G W A S H I N G T O N

1012	1173	1059	1421	919	650	1452	1042	1100	1400	1185
N	A	S	I	W	T	H	O	G	N	G

192

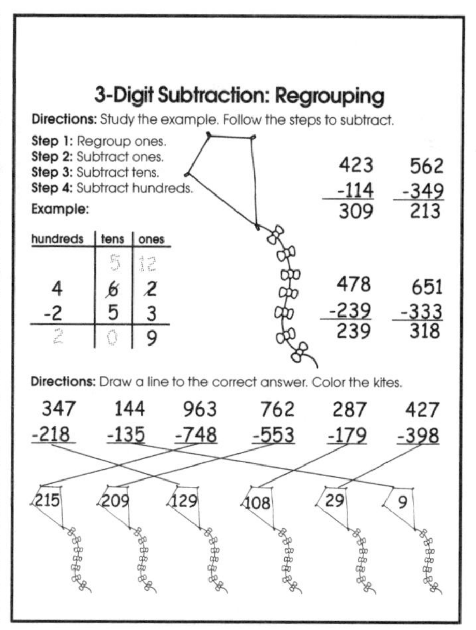

3-Digit Subtraction: Regrouping

Directions: Study the example. Follow the steps to subtract.

Step 1: Regroup ones.
Step 2: Subtract ones.
Step 3: Subtract tens.
Step 4: Subtract hundreds.
Example:

hundreds	tens	ones
	5	12
4	6	2
-2	5	3
2	0	9

423 − 114 = 309; 562 − 349 = 213; 478 − 239 = 239; 651 − 333 = 318

Directions: Draw a line to the correct answer. Color the kites.

347 − 218; 144 − 135; 963 − 748; 762 − 553; 287 − 179; 427 − 398

193

Subtraction: Regrouping

Directions: Study the example. Follow the steps. Subtract using regrouping. If you have to regroup to subtract ones and there are no tens, you must regroup twice.

Example:

300 − 182 = 118

Steps:
1. Subtract ones. You cannot subtract 2 ones from 0 ones.
2. Regroup. No tens. Regroup hundreds (2 hundreds + 10 tens).
3. Regroup tens (9 tens + 10 ones).
4. Subtract 2 ones from ten ones.
5. Subtract 8 tens from 9 tens.
6. Subtract 1 hundred from 2 hundreds.

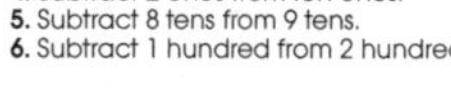

602 − 423 = 179; 306 − 128 = 178; 600 − 263 = 337; 807 − 499 = 308; 703 − 328 = 375

800 − 557 = 243; 206 − 137 = 69; 400 − 224 = 176; 508 − 379 = 129; 909 − 769 = 140

207 − 138 = 69; 604 − 397 = 207; 308 − 199 = 109; 700 − 531 = 169; 900 − 278 = 622

194

Review

Directions: Add or subtract. Use the code to color the rocket.

If the answer has:
9 hundreds, color it gray.
7 tens, color it blue.
5 ones, color it orange.
4 ones, color it red.

338 + 267 = 605 (orange)
933 − 189 = 744 (red)
479 + 398 = 877 (blue)
379 − 208 = 171 (blue)
162 + 582 = 744 (red)
281 − 146 = 135 (orange)
526 + 318 = 844 (red)
493 − 248 = 245 (orange)
682 + 298 = 980 (gray)

195

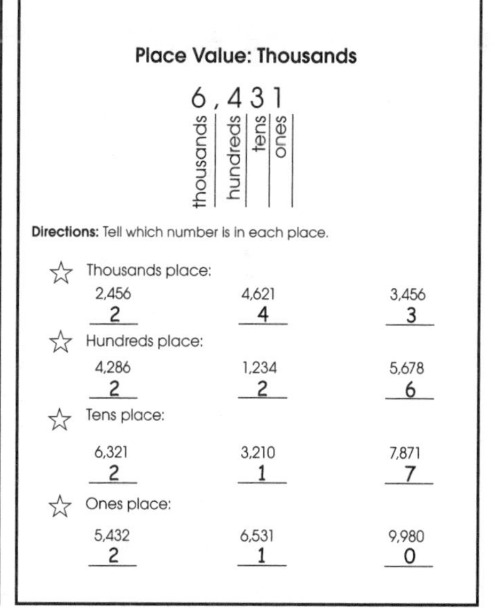

Place Value: Thousands

6,431
thousands | hundreds | tens | ones

Directions: Tell which number is in each place.

Thousands place: 2,456 → 2; 4,621 → 4; 3,456 → 3

Hundreds place: 4,286 → 2; 1,234 → 2; 5,678 → 6

Tens place: 6,321 → 2; 3,210 → 1; 7,871 → 7

Ones place: 5,432 → 2; 6,531 → 1; 9,980 → 0

196

Answer Key

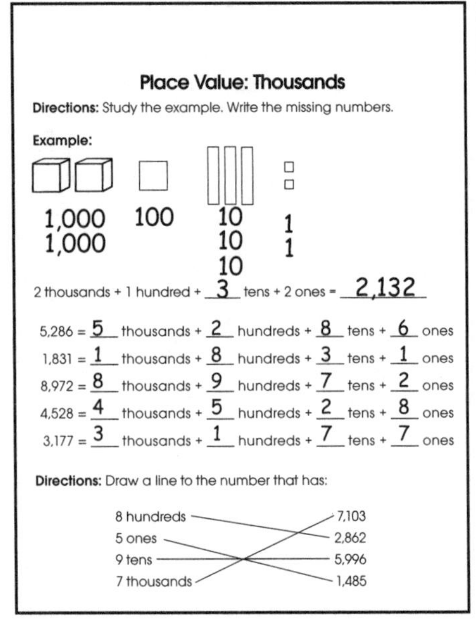

Place Value: Thousands

Directions: Study the example. Write the missing numbers.

Example:

1,000 1,000 100 10 10 10 1 1

2 thousands + 1 hundred + 3 tens + 2 ones = 2,132

5,286 = 5 thousands + 2 hundreds + 8 tens + 6 ones

1,831 = 1 thousands + 8 hundreds + 3 tens + 1 ones

8,972 = 8 thousands + 9 hundreds + 7 tens + 2 ones

4,528 = 4 thousands + 5 hundreds + 2 tens + 8 ones

3,177 = 3 thousands + 1 hundreds + 7 tens + 7 ones

Directions: Draw a line to the number that has:

8 hundreds — 7,103

5 ones — 2,862

9 tens — 5,996

7 thousands — 1,485

197

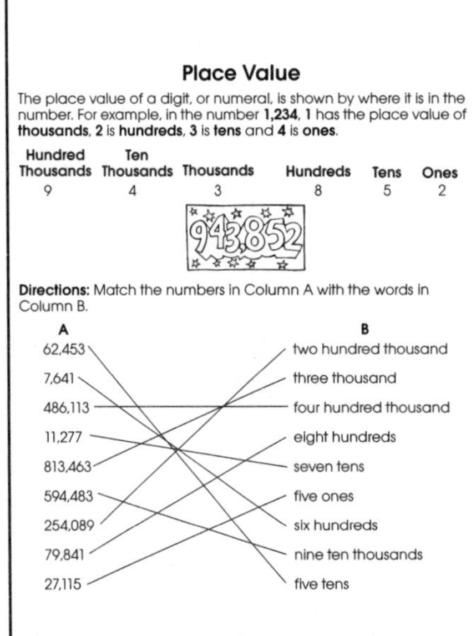

Place Value

The place value of a digit, or numeral, is shown by where it is in the number. For example, in the number **1,234**, **1** has the place value of **thousands**, **2** is **hundreds**, **3** is **tens** and **4** is **ones**.

Hundred Thousands	Ten Thousands	Thousands	Hundreds	Tens	Ones
9	4	3	8	5	2

943,852

Directions: Match the numbers in Column A with the words in Column B.

A	B
62,453	two hundred thousand
7,641	three thousand
486,113	four hundred thousand
11,277	eight hundreds
813,463	seven tens
594,483	five ones
254,089	six hundreds
79,841	nine ten thousands
27,115	five tens

198

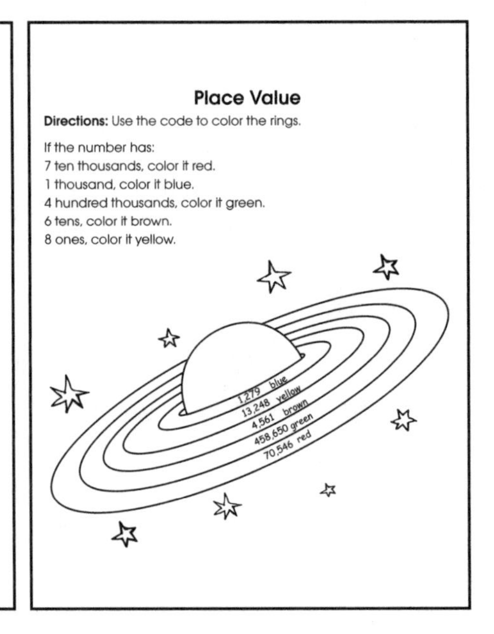

Place Value

Directions: Use the code to color the rings.

If the number has:

7 ten thousands, color it red.

1 thousand, color it blue.

4 hundred thousands, color it green.

6 tens, color it brown.

8 ones, color it yellow.

199

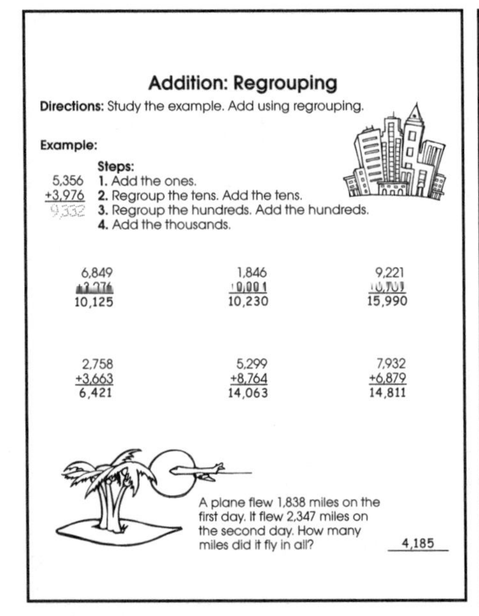

Addition: Regrouping

Directions: Study the example. Add using regrouping.

Example:

5,356 +3,976 = 9,332

Steps:
1. Add the ones.
2. Regroup the tens. Add the tens.
3. Regroup the hundreds. Add the hundreds.
4. Add the thousands.

6,849 + [illegible] = 10,125

1,846 + [illegible] = 10,230

9,221 + [illegible] = 15,990

2,758 + 3,663 = 6,421

5,299 + 8,764 = 14,063

7,932 + 6,879 = 14,811

A plane flew 1,838 miles on the first day. It flew 2,347 miles on the second day. How many miles did it fly in all? 4,185

200

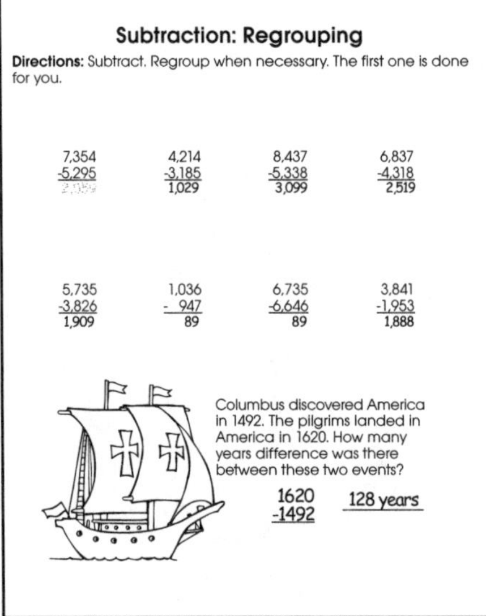

Subtraction: Regrouping

Directions: Subtract. Regroup when necessary. The first one is done for you.

7,354 − 5,295 = 2,059

4,214 − 3,185 = 1,029

8,437 − 5,338 = 3,099

6,837 − 4,318 = 2,519

5,735 − 3,826 = 1,909

1,036 − 947 = 89

6,735 − 6,646 = 89

3,841 − 1,953 = 1,888

Columbus discovered America in 1492. The pilgrims landed in America in 1620. How many years difference was there between these two events?

1620 − 1492 = 128 years

201

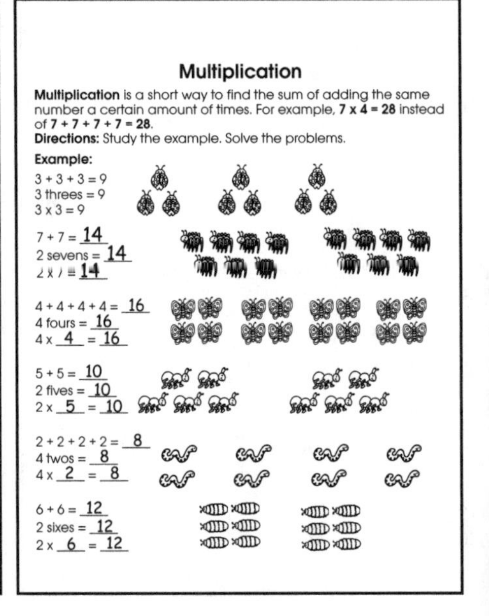

Multiplication

Multiplication is a short way to find the sum of adding the same number a certain amount of times. For example, **7 x 4 = 28** instead of **7 + 7 + 7 + 7 = 28**.

Directions: Study the example. Solve the problems.

Example:

3 + 3 + 3 = 9
3 threes = 9
3 x 3 = 9

7 + 7 = 14
2 sevens = 14
2 x 7 = 14

4 + 4 + 4 + 4 = 16
4 fours = 16
4 x 4 = 16

5 + 5 = 10
2 fives = 10
2 x 5 = 10

2 + 2 + 2 + 2 = 8
4 twos = 8
4 x 2 = 8

6 + 6 = 12
2 sixes = 12
2 x 6 = 12

202

Answer Key

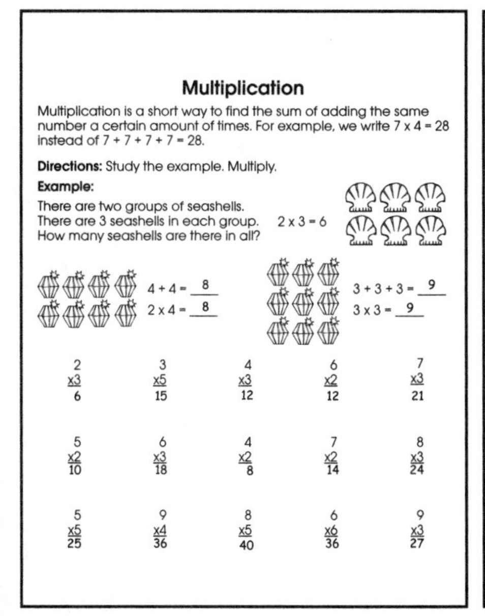

Multiplication

Multiplication is a short way to find the sum of adding the same number a certain amount of times. For example, we write 7 x 4 = 28 instead of 7 + 7 + 7 + 7 = 28.

Directions: Study the example. Multiply.

Example:

There are two groups of seashells. There are 3 seashells in each group. How many seashells are there in all? 2 x 3 = 6

4 + 4 = 8
2 x 4 = 8

3 + 3 + 3 = 9
3 x 3 = 9

2 x3 = 6	3 x5 = 15	4 x3 = 12	6 x2 = 12	7 x3 = 21
5 x2 = 10	6 x3 = 18	4 x2 = 8	7 x2 = 14	8 x3 = 24
5 x5 = 25	9 x4 = 36	8 x5 = 40	6 x6 = 36	9 x3 = 27

203

Multiplication

Directions: Multiply.

3 x5 = 15	4 x6 = 24	3 x8 = 24		
5 x5 = 25	4 x8 = 32	5 x4 = 20		
6 x7 = 42	3 x9 = 27	2 x8 = 16	7 x6 = 42	9 x4 = 36
6 x8 = 48	5 x6 = 30	7 x7 = 49	5 x3 = 15	8 x9 = 72

A river boat makes 3 trips a day every day. How many trips does it make in a week? 21

204

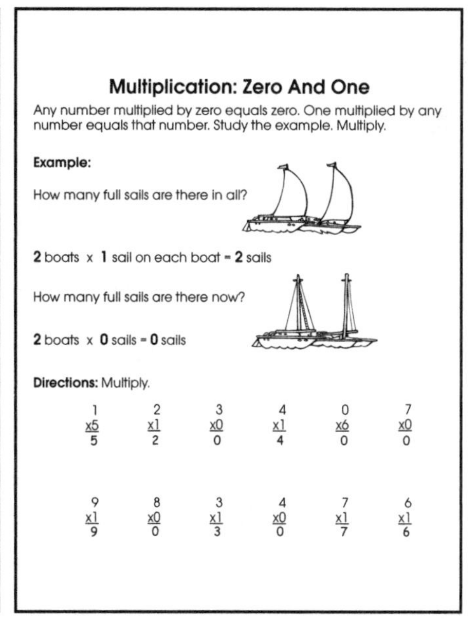

Multiplication: Zero And One

Any number multiplied by zero equals zero. One multiplied by any number equals that number. Study the example. Multiply.

Example:

How many full sails are there in all?

2 boats x **1** sail on each boat = **2** sails

How many full sails are there now?

2 boats x **0** sails = **0** sails

Directions: Multiply.

1 x5 = 5	2 x1 = 2	3 x0 = 0	4 x1 = 4	0 x6 = 0	7 x0 = 0
9 x1 = 9	8 x0 = 0	3 x1 = 3	4 x0 = 0	7 x1 = 7	6 x1 = 6

205

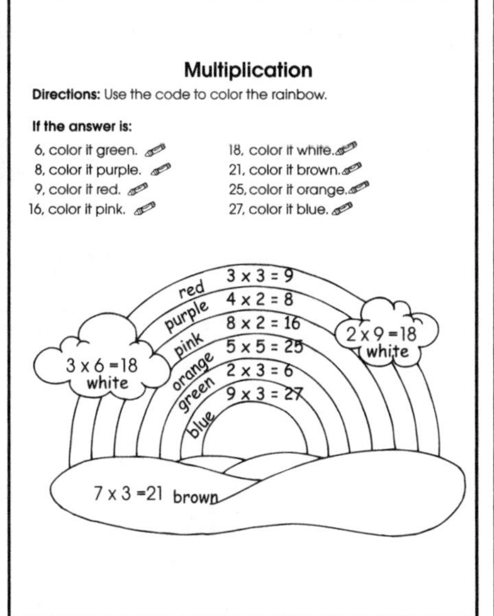

Multiplication

Directions: Use the code to color the rainbow.

If the answer is:

6, color it green.
8, color it purple.
9, color it red.
16, color it pink.
18, color it white.
21, color it brown.
25, color it orange.
27, color it blue.

206

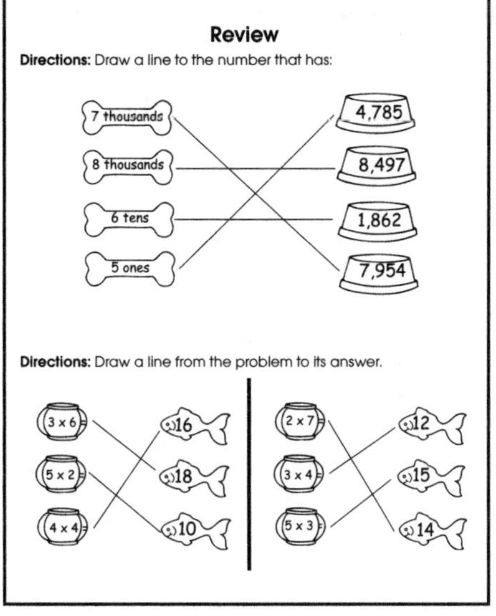

Review

Directions: Draw a line to the number that has:

7 thousands
8 thousands
6 tens
5 ones

4,785
8,497
1,862
7,954

Directions: Draw a line from the problem to its answer.

3 x 6, 5 x 2, 4 x 4 — 16, 18, 10

2 x 7, 3 x 4, 5 x 3 — 12, 15, 14

207

Multiplication

Directions: Time yourself as you multiply. How quickly can you complete this page?

3 x2 = 6	8 x7 = 56	1 x0 = 0	1 x6 = 6	3 x4 = 12	0 x4 = 0
4 x1 = 4	4 x4 = 16	2 x5 = 10	9 x3 = 27	9 x9 = 81	5 x3 = 15
0 x8 = 0	2 x6 = 12	9 x6 = 54	8 x5 = 40	7 x3 = 21	4 x2 = 8
3 x5 = 15	2 x0 = 0	4 x6 = 24	1 x3 = 3	0 x0 = 0	3 x3 = 9

208

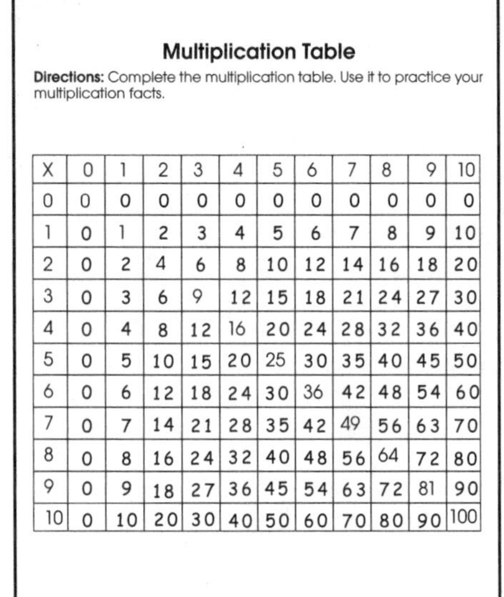

Multiplication Table

Directions: Complete the multiplication table. Use it to practice your multiplication facts.

X	0	1	2	3	4	5	6	7	8	9	10
0	0	0	0	0	0	0	0	0	0	0	0
1	0	1	2	3	4	5	6	7	8	9	10
2	0	2	4	6	8	10	12	14	16	18	20
3	0	3	6	9	12	15	18	21	24	27	30
4	0	4	8	12	16	20	24	28	32	36	40
5	0	5	10	15	20	25	30	35	40	45	50
6	0	6	12	18	24	30	36	42	48	54	60
7	0	7	14	21	28	35	42	49	56	63	70
8	0	8	16	24	32	40	48	56	64	72	80
9	0	9	18	27	36	45	54	63	72	81	90
10	0	10	20	30	40	50	60	70	80	90	100

209

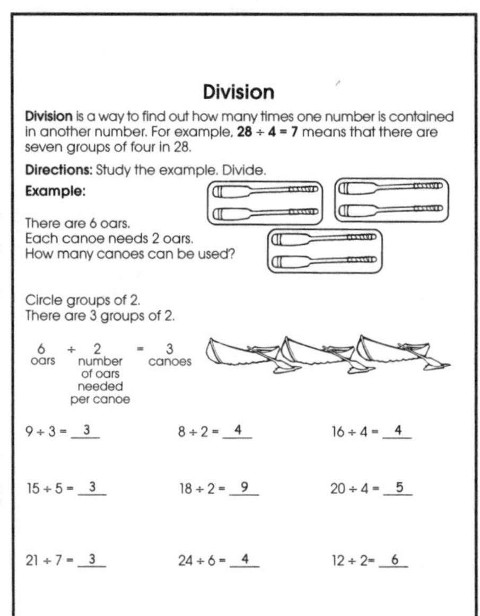

Division

Division is a way to find out how many times one number is contained in another number. For example, **28 ÷ 4 = 7** means that there are seven groups of four in 28.

Directions: Study the example. Divide.

Example:

There are 6 oars.
Each canoe needs 2 oars.
How many canoes can be used?

Circle groups of 2.
There are 3 groups of 2.

6 oars ÷ 2 number of oars needed per canoe = 3 canoes

9 ÷ 3 = 3 | 8 ÷ 2 = 4 | 16 ÷ 4 = 4

15 ÷ 5 = 3 | 18 ÷ 2 = 9 | 20 ÷ 4 = 5

21 ÷ 7 = 3 | 24 ÷ 6 = 4 | 12 ÷ 2 = 6

210

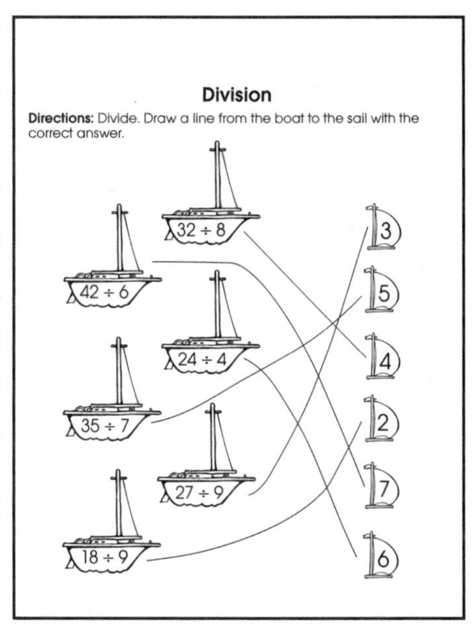

Division

Directions: Divide. Draw a line from the boat to the sail with the correct answer.

211

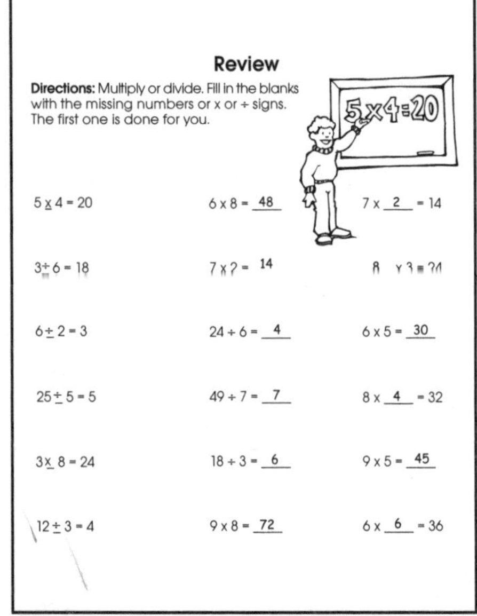

Review

Directions: Multiply or divide. Fill in the blanks with the missing numbers or x or ÷ signs. The first one is done for you.

5 x 4 = 20 | 6 x 8 = 48 | 7 x 2 = 14

3 ÷ 6 = 18 | 7 x 2 = 14 | 8 x 3 = 24

6 ÷ 2 = 3 | 24 ÷ 6 = 4 | 6 x 5 = 30

25 ÷ 5 = 5 | 49 ÷ 7 = 7 | 8 x 4 = 32

3 x 8 = 24 | 18 ÷ 3 = 6 | 9 x 5 = 45

12 ÷ 3 = 4 | 9 x 8 = 72 | 6 x 6 = 36

212

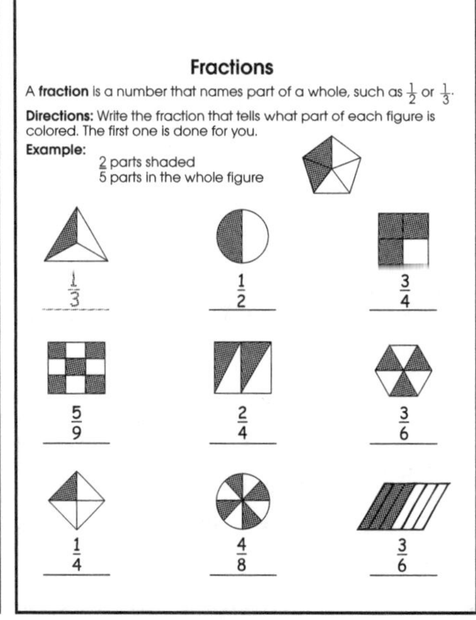

Fractions

A **fraction** is a number that names part of a whole, such as $\frac{1}{2}$ or $\frac{1}{3}$.

Directions: Write the fraction that tells what part of each figure is colored. The first one is done for you.

Example:
2 parts shaded
5 parts in the whole figure

$\frac{1}{3}$ | $\frac{1}{2}$ | $\frac{3}{4}$

$\frac{5}{9}$ | $\frac{2}{4}$ | $\frac{3}{6}$

$\frac{1}{4}$ | $\frac{4}{8}$ | $\frac{3}{6}$

213

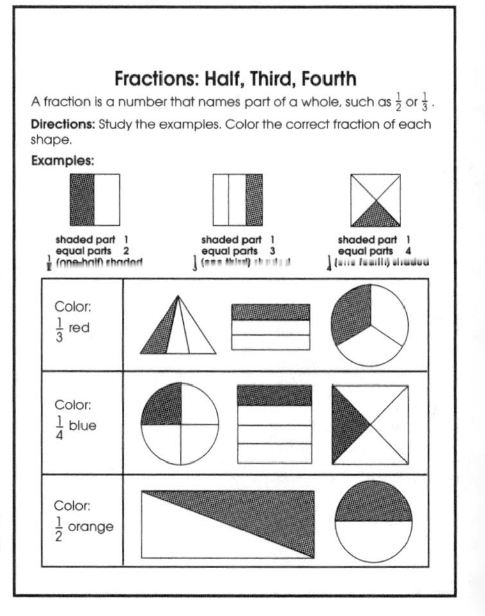

Fractions: Half, Third, Fourth

A fraction is a number that names part of a whole, such as $\frac{1}{2}$ or $\frac{1}{3}$.

Directions: Study the examples. Color the correct fraction of each shape.

Examples:

shaded part 1, equal parts 2, $\frac{1}{2}$ (one-half) shaded

shaded part 1, equal parts 3, $\frac{1}{3}$ (one-third) shaded

shaded part 1, equal parts 4, $\frac{1}{4}$ (one-fourth) shaded

Color: $\frac{1}{3}$ red

Color: $\frac{1}{4}$ blue

Color: $\frac{1}{2}$ orange

214

Answer Key

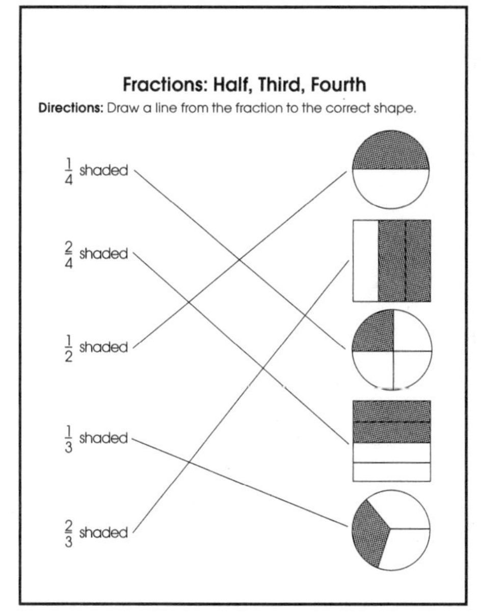

Fractions: Half, Third, Fourth

Directions: Draw a line from the fraction to the correct shape.

$\frac{1}{4}$ shaded

$\frac{2}{4}$ shaded

$\frac{1}{2}$ shaded

$\frac{1}{3}$ shaded

$\frac{2}{3}$ shaded

215

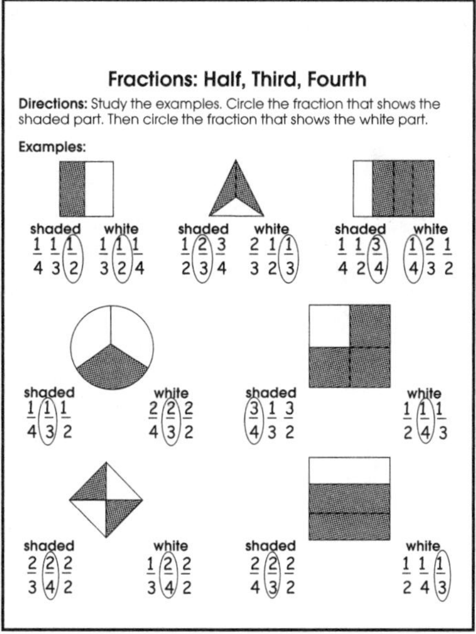

Fractions: Half, Third, Fourth

Directions: Study the examples. Circle the fraction that shows the shaded part. Then circle the fraction that shows the white part.

Examples:

shaded white

shaded white

shaded white

216

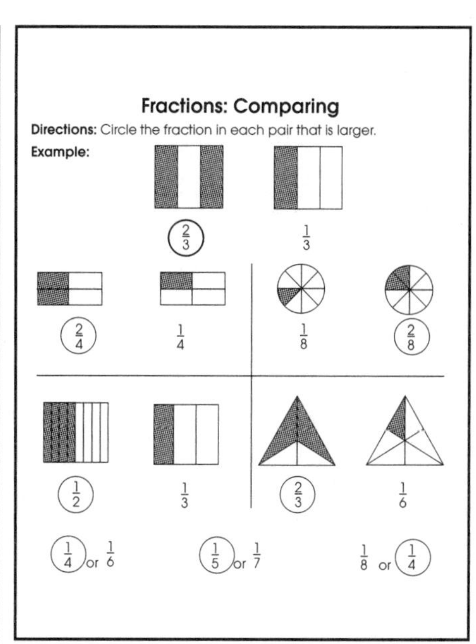

Fractions: Comparing

Directions: Circle the fraction in each pair that is larger.

Example:

$\frac{1}{4}$ or $\frac{1}{6}$

$\frac{1}{5}$ or $\frac{1}{7}$

$\frac{1}{8}$ or $\frac{1}{4}$

217

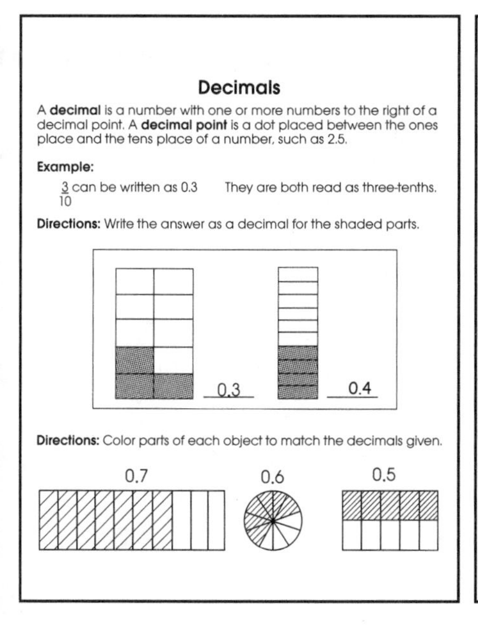

Decimals

A **decimal** is a number with one or more numbers to the right of a decimal point. A **decimal point** is a dot placed between the ones place and the tens place of a number, such as 2.5.

Example:

$\frac{3}{10}$ can be written as 0.3 They are both read as three-tenths.

Directions: Write the answer as a decimal for the shaded parts.

0.3 0.4

Directions: Color parts of each object to match the decimals given.

0.7 0.6 0.5

218

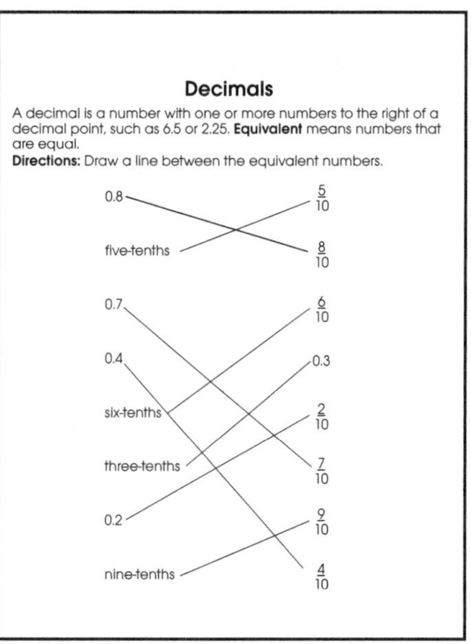

Decimals

A decimal is a number with one or more numbers to the right of a decimal point, such as 6.5 or 2.25. **Equivalent** means numbers that are equal.

Directions: Draw a line between the equivalent numbers.

0.8 — $\frac{5}{10}$

five-tenths — $\frac{8}{10}$

0.7 — $\frac{6}{10}$

0.4 — 0.3

six-tenths — $\frac{2}{10}$

three-tenths — $\frac{7}{10}$

0.2 — $\frac{9}{10}$

nine-tenths — $\frac{4}{10}$

219

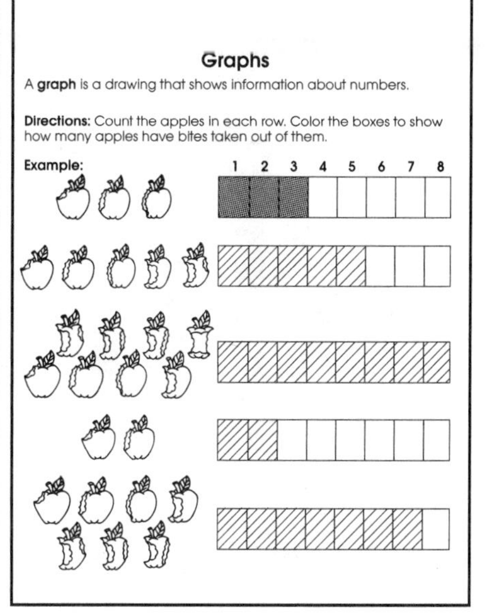

Graphs

A **graph** is a drawing that shows information about numbers.

Directions: Count the apples in each row. Color the boxes to show how many apples have bites taken out of them.

Example: 1 2 3 4 5 6 7 8

220

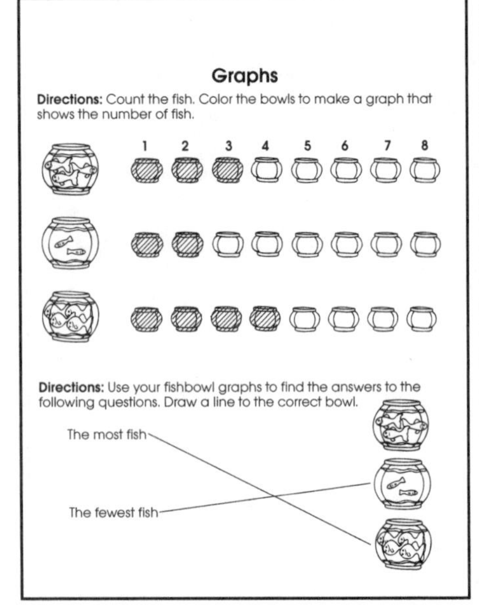

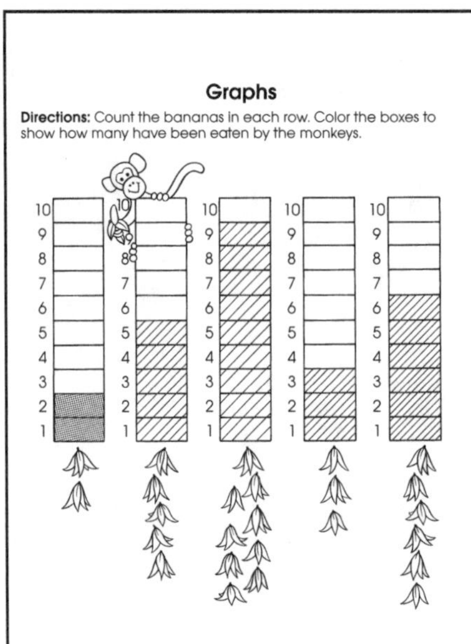

Graphs
Directions: Count the bananas in each row. Color the boxes to show how many have been eaten by the monkeys.

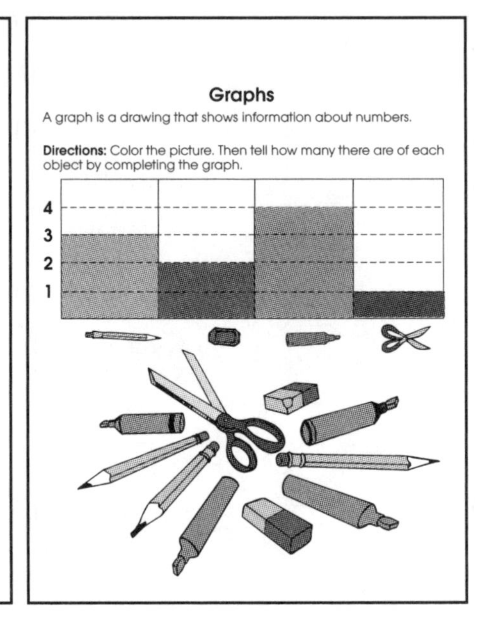

221

222

223

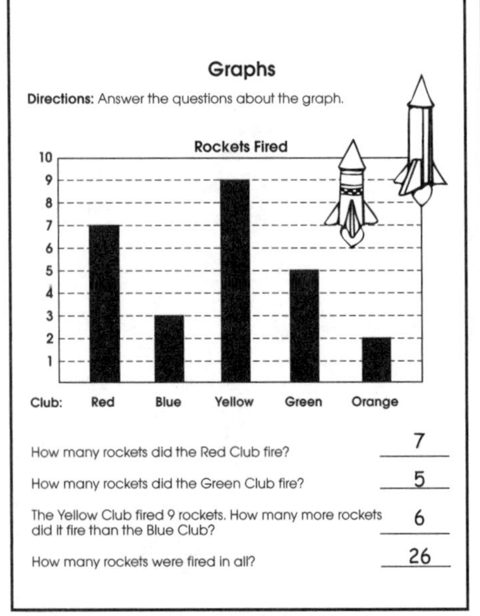

Graphs
Directions: Answer the questions about the graph.
Rockets Fired
Club: Red Blue Yellow Green Orange
How many rockets did the Red Club fire? 7
How many rockets did the Green Club fire? 5
The Yellow Club fired 9 rockets. How many more rockets did it fire than the Blue Club? 6
How many rockets were fired in all? 26

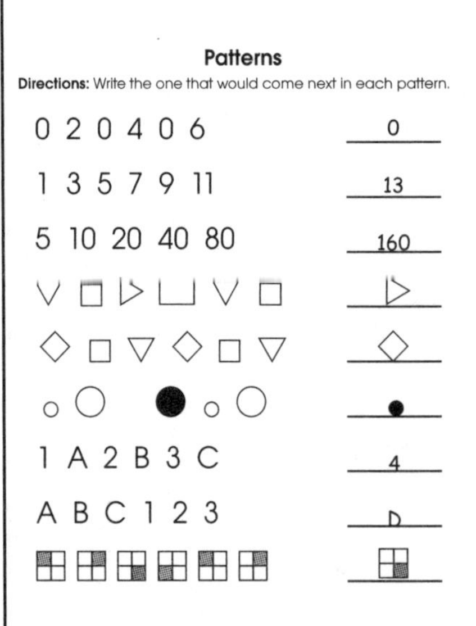

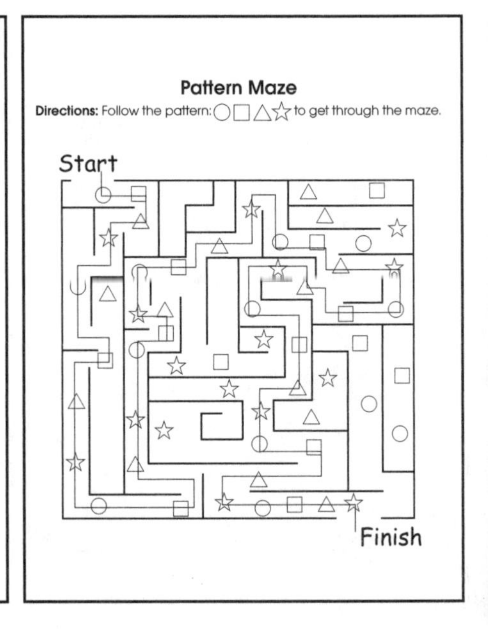

224

225

226

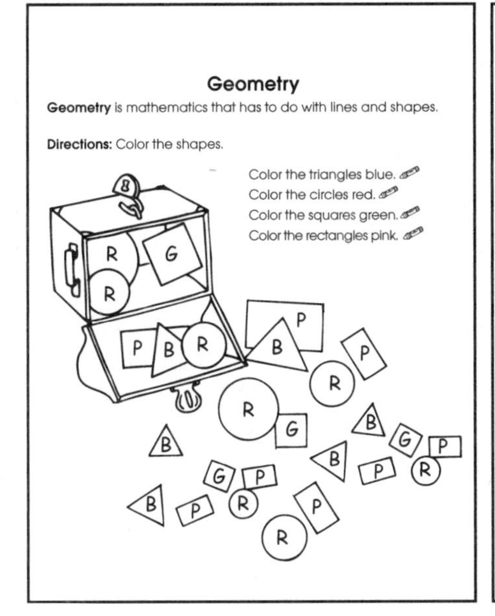
Geometry

Geometry is mathematics that has to do with lines and shapes.

Directions: Color the shapes.

Color the triangles blue.
Color the circles red.
Color the squares green.
Color the rectangles pink.

227

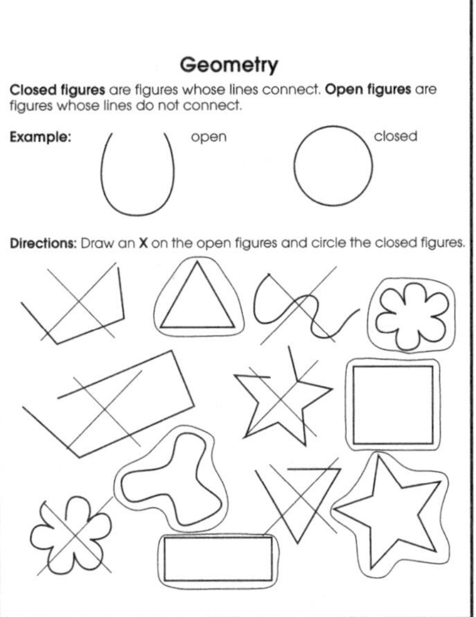
Geometry

Closed figures are figures whose lines connect. **Open figures** are figures whose lines do not connect.

Example: open closed

Directions: Draw an **X** on the open figures and circle the closed figures.

228

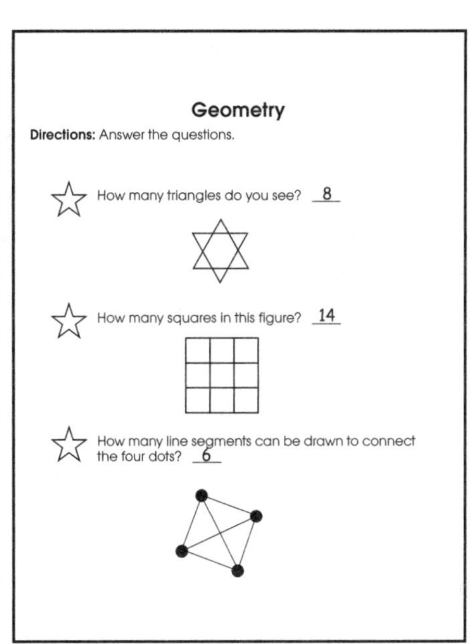
Geometry

Directions: Answer the questions.

How many triangles do you see? 8

How many squares in this figure? 14

How many line segments can be drawn to connect the four dots? 6

229

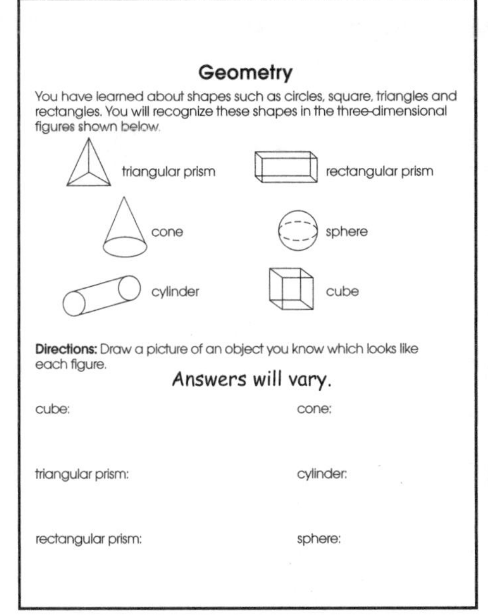
Geometry

You have learned about shapes such as circles, square, triangles and rectangles. You will recognize these shapes in the three-dimensional figures shown below.

triangular prism
rectangular prism
cone
sphere
cylinder
cube

Directions: Draw a picture of an object you know which looks like each figure.

Answers will vary.

cube:
cone:
triangular prism:
cylinder:
rectangular prism:
sphere:

230

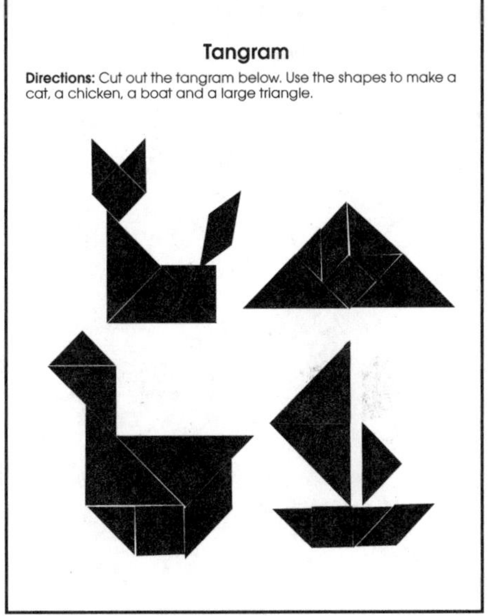
Tangram

Directions: Cut out the tangram below. Use the shapes to make a cat, a chicken, a boat and a large triangle.

231

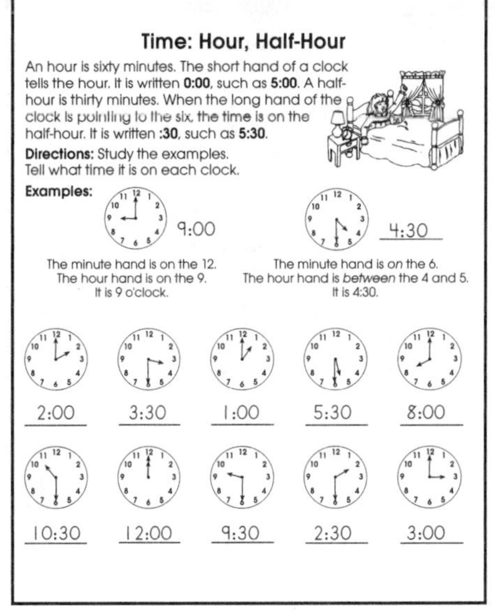
Time: Hour, Half-Hour

An hour is sixty minutes. The short hand of a clock tells the hour. It is written **0:00**, such as **5:00**. A half-hour is thirty minutes. When the long hand of the clock is pointing to the six, the time is on the half-hour. It is written **:30**, such as **5:30**.

Directions: Study the examples.
Tell what time it is on each clock.

Examples:

9:00
The minute hand is on the 12.
The hour hand is on the 9.
It is 9 o'clock.

4:30
The minute hand is on the 6.
The hour hand is *between* the 4 and 5.
It is 4:30.

2:00 3:30 1:00 5:30 8:00

10:30 12:00 9:30 2:30 3:00

233

Answer Key

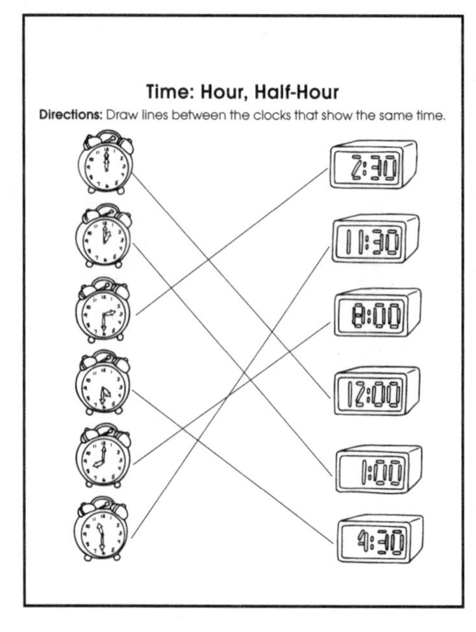

Time: Hour, Half-Hour

Directions: Draw lines between the clocks that show the same time.

2:30
11:30
8:00
12:00
1:00
4:30

234

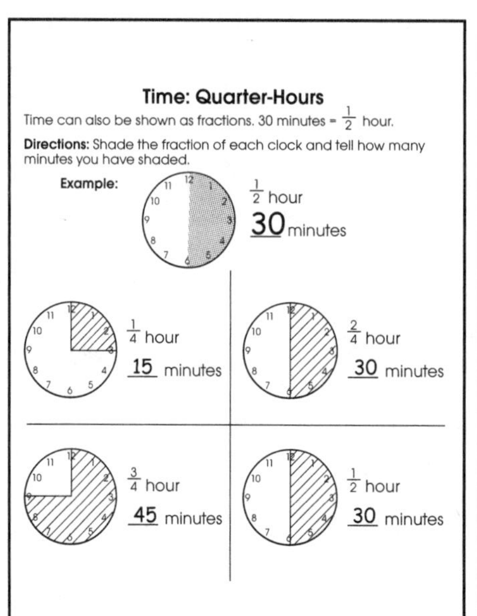

Time: Quarter-Hours

Time can also be shown as fractions. 30 minutes = $\frac{1}{2}$ hour.

Directions: Shade the fraction of each clock and tell how many minutes you have shaded.

Example: $\frac{1}{2}$ hour 30 minutes

$\frac{1}{4}$ hour 15 minutes

$\frac{2}{4}$ hour 30 minutes

$\frac{3}{4}$ hour 45 minutes

$\frac{1}{2}$ hour 30 minutes

235

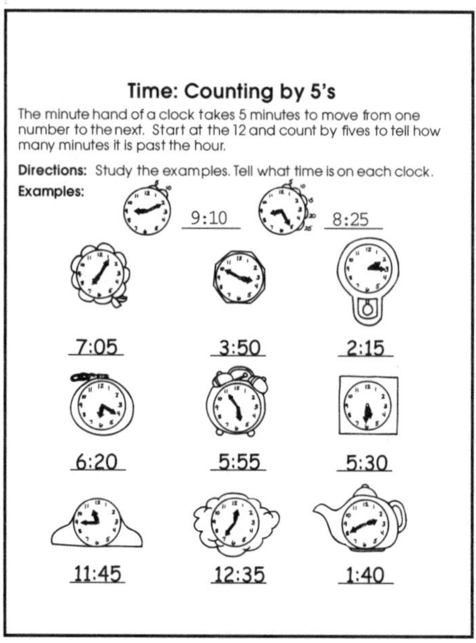

Time: Counting by 5's

The minute hand of a clock takes 5 minutes to move from one number to the next. Start at the 12 and count by fives to tell how many minutes it is past the hour.

Directions: Study the examples. Tell what time is on each clock.

Examples: 9:10 8:25

7:05 3:50 2:15

6:20 5:55 5:30

11:45 12:35 1:40

236

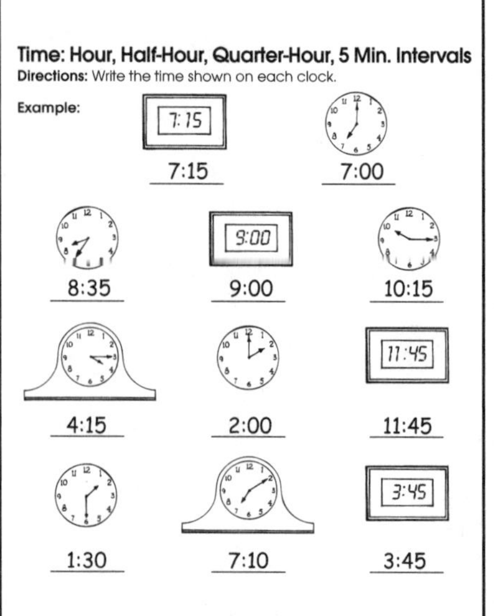

Time: Hour, Half-Hour, Quarter-Hour, 5 Min. Intervals

Directions: Write the time shown on each clock.

Example: 7:15 7:15 7:00

9:00
8:35 9:00 10:15

11:45
4:15 2:00 11:45

3:45
1:30 7:10 3:45

237

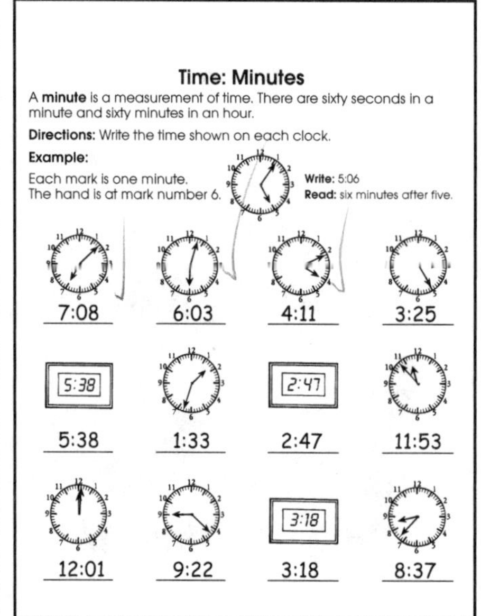

Time: Minutes

A **minute** is a measurement of time. There are sixty seconds in a minute and sixty minutes in an hour.

Directions: Write the time shown on each clock.

Example:
Each mark is one minute.
The hand is at mark number 6.
Write: 5:06
Read: six minutes after five.

7:08 6:03 4:11 3:25

5:38 1:33 2:47 11:53

12:01 9:22 3:18 8:37

238

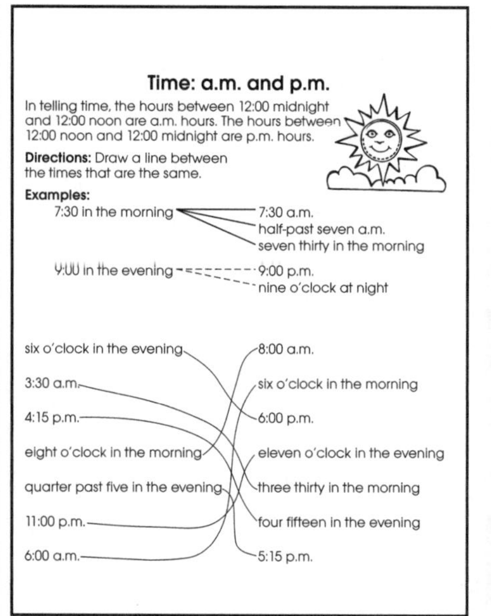

Time: a.m. and p.m.

In telling time, the hours between 12:00 midnight and 12:00 noon are a.m. hours. The hours between 12:00 noon and 12:00 midnight are p.m. hours.

Directions: Draw a line between the times that are the same.

Examples:

7:30 in the morning — 7:30 a.m.; half-past seven a.m.; seven thirty in the morning

9:00 in the evening — 9:00 p.m.; nine o'clock at night

six o'clock in the evening — 8:00 a.m.
3:30 a.m. — six o'clock in the morning
4:15 p.m. — 6:00 p.m.
eight o'clock in the morning — eleven o'clock in the evening
quarter past five in the evening — three thirty in the morning
11:00 p.m. — four fifteen in the evening
6:00 a.m. — 5:15 p.m.

239

Answer Key

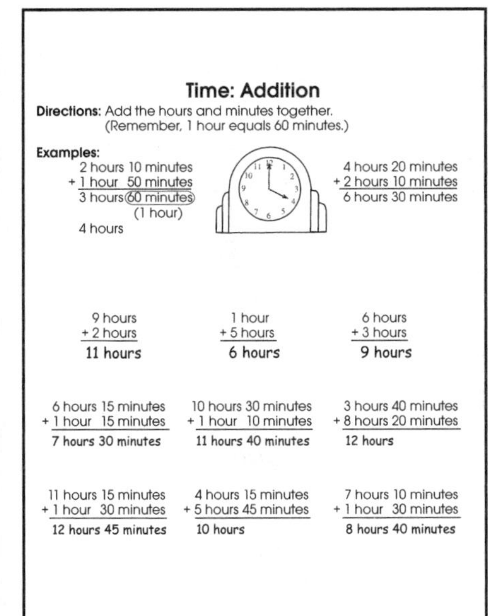

Time: Addition

Directions: Add the hours and minutes together.
(Remember, 1 hour equals 60 minutes.)

Examples:

2 hours 10 minutes
+ 1 hour 50 minutes
3 hours (60 minutes)
(1 hour)
4 hours

4 hours 20 minutes
+ 2 hours 10 minutes
6 hours 30 minutes

9 hours + 2 hours = 11 hours
1 hour + 5 hours = 6 hours
6 hours + 3 hours = 9 hours

6 hours 15 minutes + 1 hour 15 minutes = 7 hours 30 minutes
10 hours 30 minutes + 1 hour 10 minutes = 11 hours 40 minutes
3 hours 40 minutes + 8 hours 20 minutes = 12 hours

11 hours 15 minutes + 1 hour 30 minutes = 12 hours 45 minutes
4 hours 15 minutes + 5 hours 45 minutes = 10 hours
7 hours 10 minutes + 1 hour 30 minutes = 8 hours 40 minutes

240

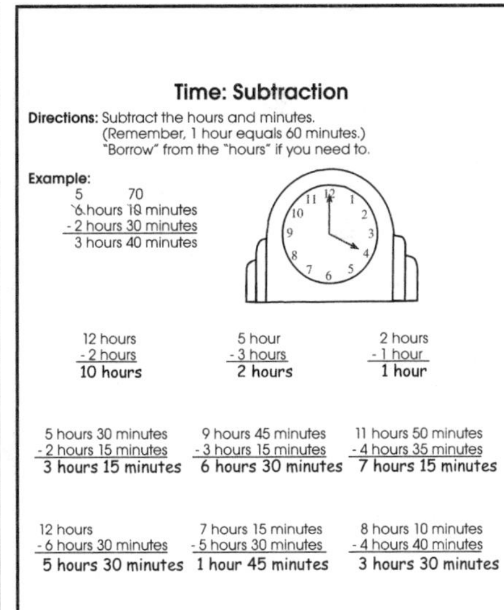

Time: Subtraction

Directions: Subtract the hours and minutes.
(Remember, 1 hour equals 60 minutes.)
"Borrow" from the "hours" if you need to.

Example:

5 70
6 hours 10 minutes
- 2 hours 30 minutes
3 hours 40 minutes

12 hours - 2 hours = 10 hours
5 hour - 3 hours = 2 hours
2 hours - 1 hour = 1 hour

5 hours 30 minutes - 2 hours 15 minutes = 3 hours 15 minutes
9 hours 45 minutes - 3 hours 15 minutes = 6 hours 30 minutes
11 hours 50 minutes - 4 hours 35 minutes = 7 hours 15 minutes

12 hours - 6 hours 30 minutes = 5 hours 30 minutes
7 hours 15 minutes - 5 hours 30 minutes = 1 hour 45 minutes
8 hours 10 minutes - 4 hours 40 minutes = 3 hours 30 minutes

241

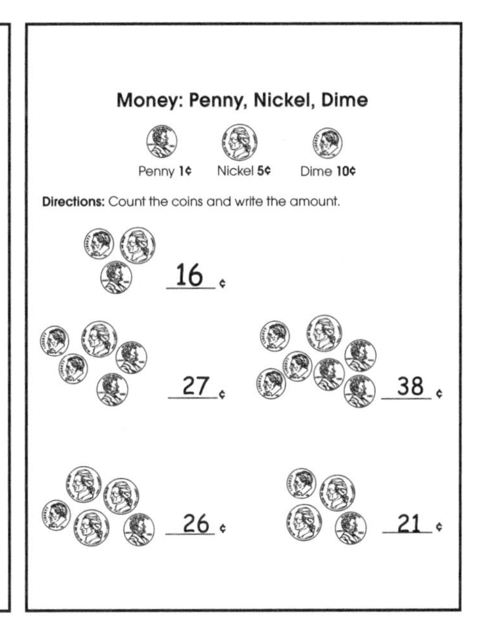

Money: Penny, Nickel, Dime

Penny 1¢ Nickel 5¢ Dime 10¢

Directions: Count the coins and write the amount.

16 ¢

27 ¢

38 ¢

26 ¢

21 ¢

242

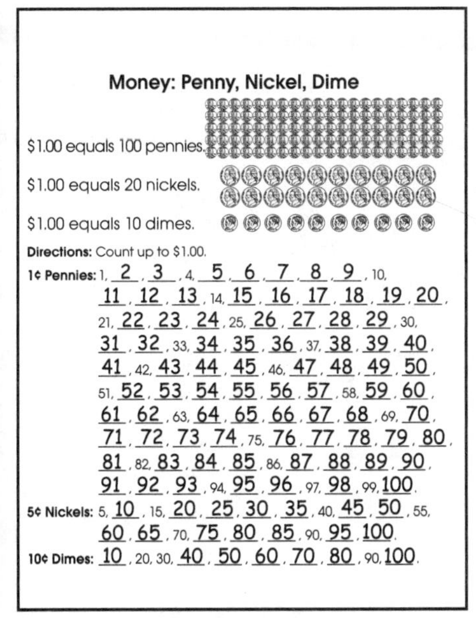

Money: Penny, Nickel, Dime

$1.00 equals 100 pennies.

$1.00 equals 20 nickels.

$1.00 equals 10 dimes.

Directions: Count up to $1.00.

1¢ Pennies: 1, 2, 3, 4, 5, 6, 7, 8, 9, 10, 11, 12, 13, 14, 15, 16, 17, 18, 19, 20, 21, 22, 23, 24, 25, 26, 27, 28, 29, 30, 31, 32, 33, 34, 35, 36, 37, 38, 39, 40, 41, 42, 43, 44, 45, 46, 47, 48, 49, 50, 51, 52, 53, 54, 55, 56, 57, 58, 59, 60, 61, 62, 63, 64, 65, 66, 67, 68, 69, 70, 71, 72, 73, 74, 75, 76, 77, 78, 79, 80, 81, 82, 83, 84, 85, 86, 87, 88, 89, 90, 91, 92, 93, 94, 95, 96, 97, 98, 99, 100.

5¢ Nickels: 5, 10, 15, 20, 25, 30, 35, 40, 45, 50, 55, 60, 65, 70, 75, 80, 85, 90, 95, 100.

10¢ Dimes: 10, 20, 30, 40, 50, 60, 70, 80, 90, 100.

243

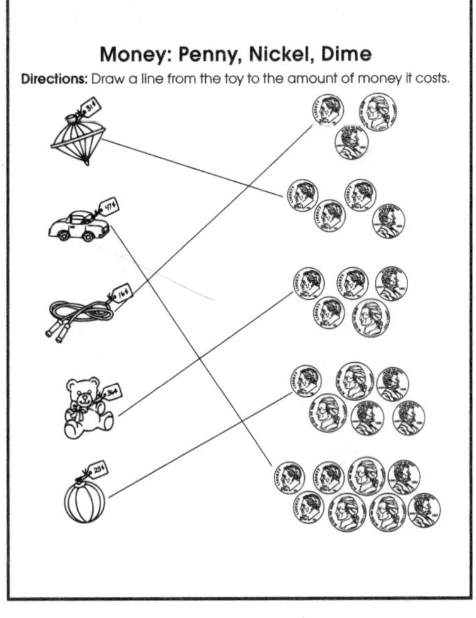

Money: Penny, Nickel, Dime

Directions: Draw a line from the toy to the amount of money it costs.

244

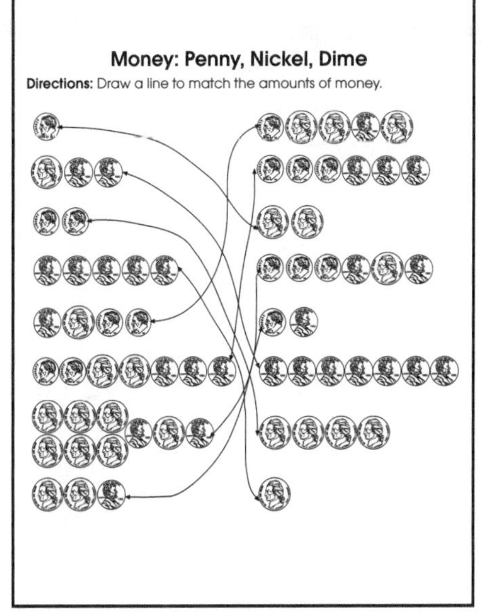

Money: Penny, Nickel, Dime

Directions: Draw a line to match the amounts of money.

245

Answer Key

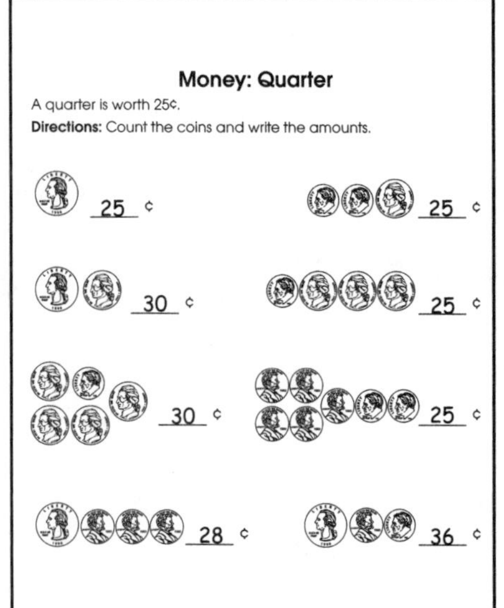

Money: Quarter

A quarter is worth 25¢.

Directions: Count the coins and write the amounts.

25 ¢ 25 ¢

30 ¢ 25 ¢

30 ¢ 25 ¢

28 ¢ 36 ¢

246

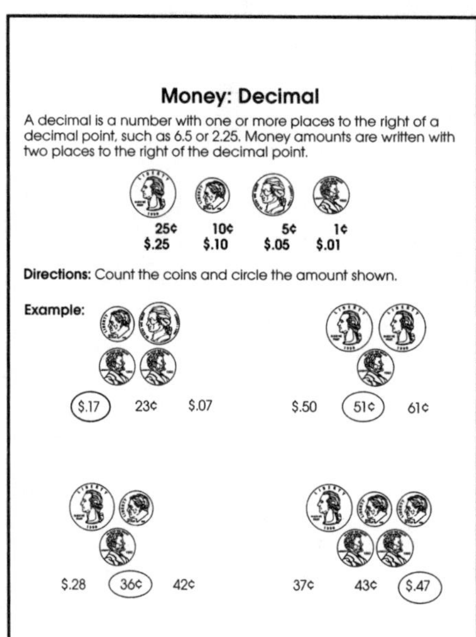

Money: Decimal

A decimal is a number with one or more places to the right of a decimal point, such as 6.5 or 2.25. Money amounts are written with two places to the right of the decimal point.

25¢ $.25 10¢ $.10 5¢ $.05 1¢ $.01

Directions: Count the coins and circle the amount shown.

Example:

($.17) 23¢ $.07 $.50 (51¢) 61¢

$.28 (36¢) 42¢ 37¢ 43¢ ($.47)

247

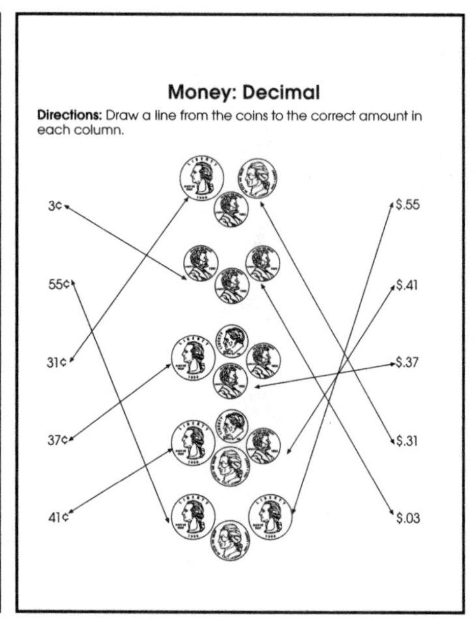

Money: Decimal

Directions: Draw a line from the coins to the correct amount in each column.

3¢ 55¢ 31¢ 37¢ 41¢

$.55 $.41 $.37 $.31 $.03

248

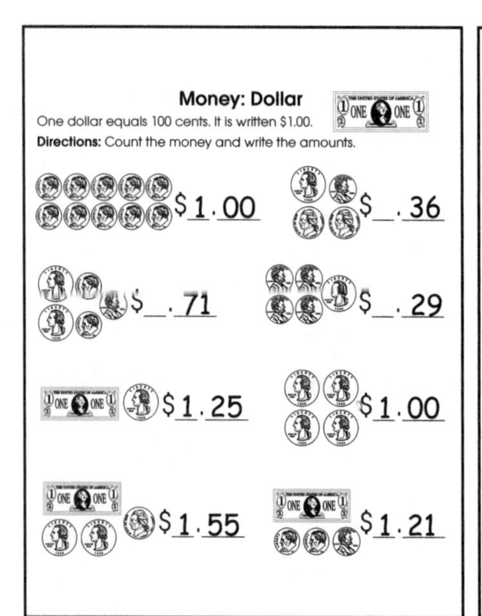

Money: Dollar

One dollar equals 100 cents. It is written $1.00.

Directions: Count the money and write the amounts.

$1.00 $.36

$.71 $.29

$1.25 $1.00

$1.55 $1.21

249

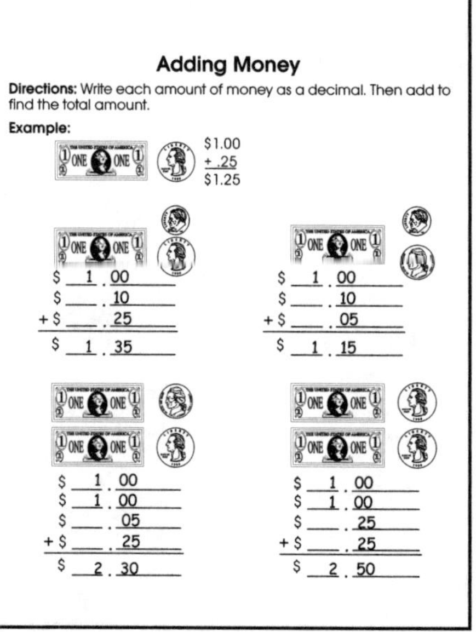

Adding Money

Directions: Write each amount of money as a decimal. Then add to find the total amount.

Example:

$1.00
+ .25
$1.25

$ 1 . 00
$. 10
+ $. 25
$ 1 . 35

$ 1 . 00
$. 10
+ $. 05
$ 1 . 15

$ 1 . 00
$ 1 . 00
$. 05
+ $. 25
$ 2 . 30

$ 1 . 00
$ 1 . 00
$. 25
+ $. 25
$ 2 . 50

250

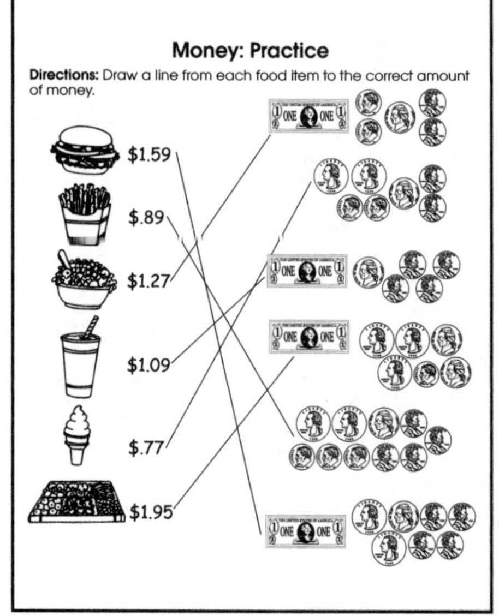

Money: Practice

Directions: Draw a line from each food item to the correct amount of money.

$1.59
$.89
$1.27
$1.09
$.77
$1.95

251

Answer Key

Money: Five-Dollar Bill and Ten-Dollar Bill

Directions: Write the amount for each group of money shown. Use a dollar sign and decimal point. The first one is done for you.

Five-dollar bill = 5 one-dollar bills

Ten-dollar bill = 2 five-dollar bills or 10 one-dollar bills

$15.00

$6.00

$6.35

$16.31

7 one-dollar bills, 2 quarters $7.50

2 five-dollar bills, 3 one-dollar bills, half-dollar $13.50

3 ten-dollar bills, 1 five-dollar bill, 3 quarters $35.75

252

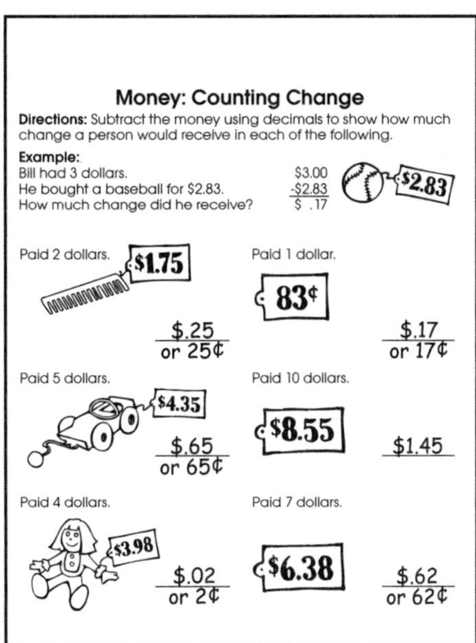

Money: Counting Change

Directions: Subtract the money using decimals to show how much change a person would receive in each of the following.

Example:
Bill had 3 dollars.
He bought a baseball for $2.83.
How much change did he receive?

$3.00
-$2.83
$ .17

Paid 2 dollars. $1.75 — $.25 or 25¢

Paid 1 dollar. 83¢ — $.17 or 17¢

Paid 5 dollars. $4.35 — $.65 or 65¢

Paid 10 dollars. $8.55 — $1.45

Paid 4 dollars. $3.98 — $.02 or 2¢

Paid 7 dollars. $6.38 — $.62 or 62¢

253

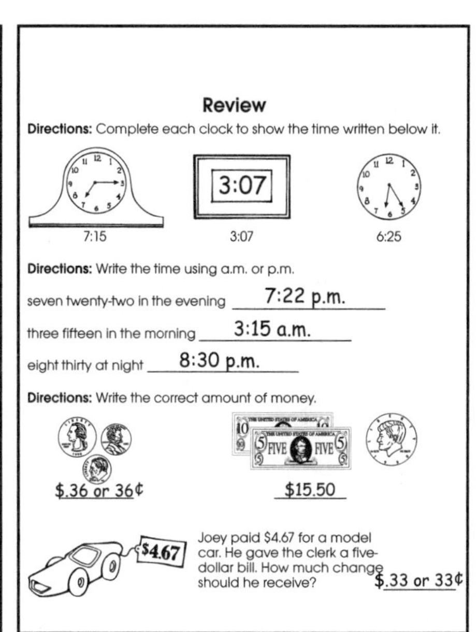

Review

Directions: Complete each clock to show the time written below it.

7:15 3:07 6:25

Directions: Write the time using a.m. or p.m.

seven twenty-two in the evening 7:22 p.m.

three fifteen in the morning 3:15 a.m.

eight thirty at night 8:30 p.m.

Directions: Write the correct amount of money.

$.36 or 36¢

$15.50

Joey paid $4.67 for a model car. He gave the clerk a five-dollar bill. How much change should he receive? $.33 or 33¢

254

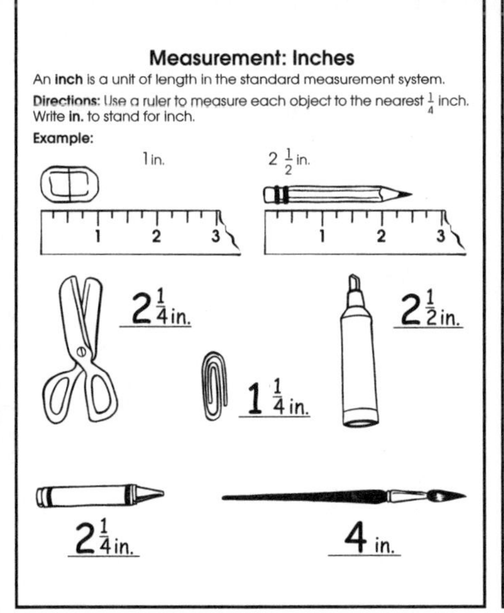

Measurement: Inches

An **inch** is a unit of length in the standard measurement system.

Directions: Use a ruler to measure each object to the nearest $\frac{1}{4}$ inch. Write **in.** to stand for inch.

Example:

1 in.

$2\frac{1}{2}$ in.

$2\frac{1}{4}$ in.

$2\frac{1}{2}$ in.

$1\frac{1}{4}$ in.

$2\frac{1}{4}$ in.

4 in.

255

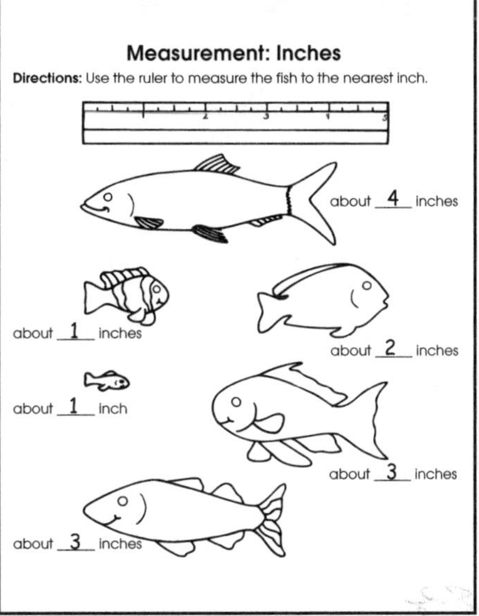

Measurement: Inches

Directions: Use the ruler to measure the fish to the nearest inch.

about 4 inches

about 1 inches

about 2 inches

about 1 inch

about 3 inches

about 3 inches

256

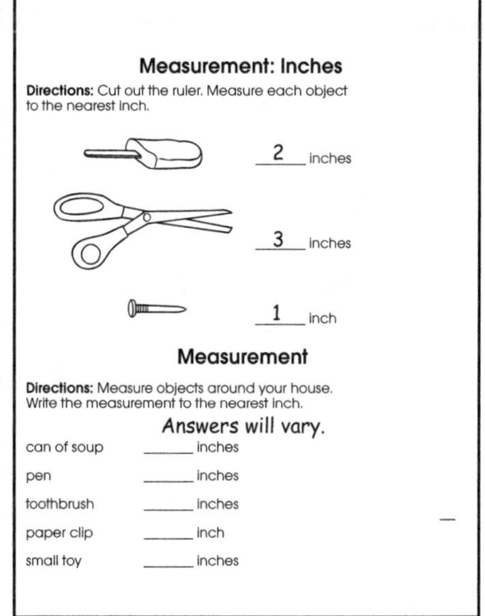

Measurement: Inches

Directions: Cut out the ruler. Measure each object to the nearest inch.

2 inches

3 inches

1 inch

Measurement

Directions: Measure objects around your house. Write the measurement to the nearest inch.

Answers will vary.

can of soup ______ inches

pen ______ inches

toothbrush ______ inches

paper clip ______ inch

small toy ______ inches

257

Answer Key

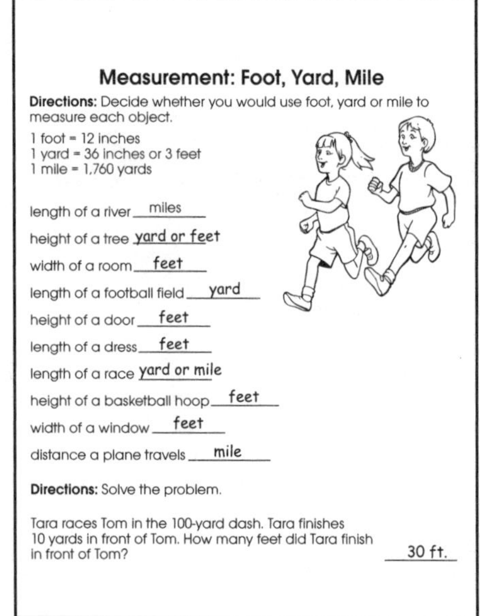

Measurement: Foot, Yard, Mile

Directions: Decide whether you would use foot, yard or mile to measure each object.

1 foot = 12 inches
1 yard = 36 inches or 3 feet
1 mile = 1,760 yards

length of a river miles
height of a tree yard or feet
width of a room feet
length of a football field yard
height of a door feet
length of a dress feet
length of a race yard or mile
height of a basketball hoop feet
width of a window feet
distance a plane travels mile

Directions: Solve the problem.

Tara races Tom in the 100-yard dash. Tara finishes 10 yards in front of Tom. How many feet did Tara finish in front of Tom? 30 ft.

259

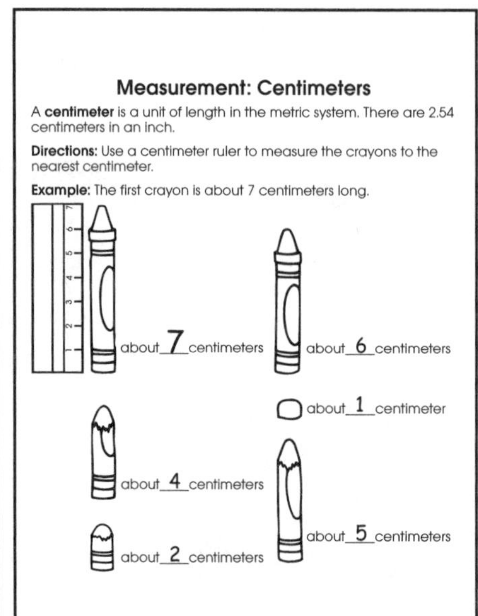

Measurement: Centimeters

A **centimeter** is a unit of length in the metric system. There are 2.54 centimeters in an inch.

Directions: Use a centimeter ruler to measure the crayons to the nearest centimeter.

Example: The first crayon is about 7 centimeters long.

about 7 centimeters
about 6 centimeters
about 1 centimeter
about 4 centimeters
about 5 centimeters
about 2 centimeters

260

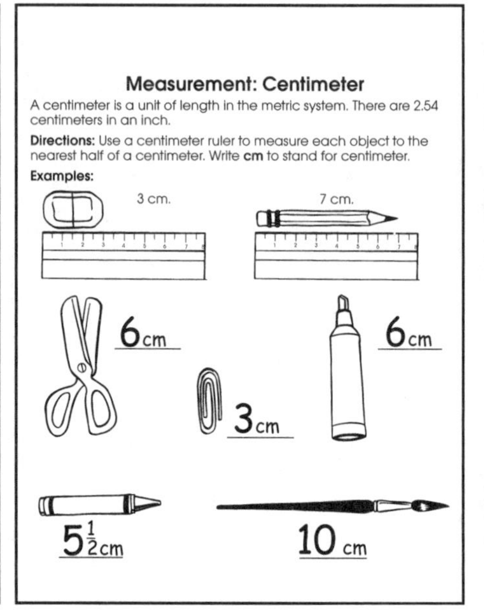

Measurement: Centimeter

A centimeter is a unit of length in the metric system. There are 2.54 centimeters in an inch.

Directions: Use a centimeter ruler to measure each object to the nearest half of a centimeter. Write **cm** to stand for centimeter.

Examples:

3 cm. 7 cm.

6cm 6cm 3cm

$5\frac{1}{2}$cm 10 cm

261

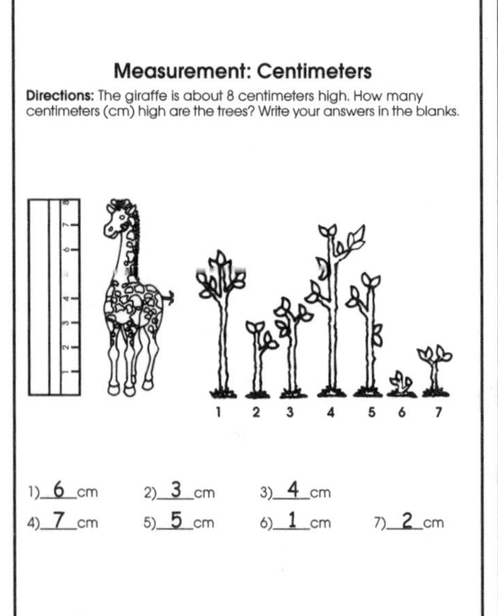

Measurement: Centimeters

Directions: The giraffe is about 8 centimeters high. How many centimeters (cm) high are the trees? Write your answers in the blanks.

1 2 3 4 5 6 7

1) 6 cm 2) 3 cm 3) 4 cm
4) 7 cm 5) 5 cm 6) 1 cm 7) 2 cm

262

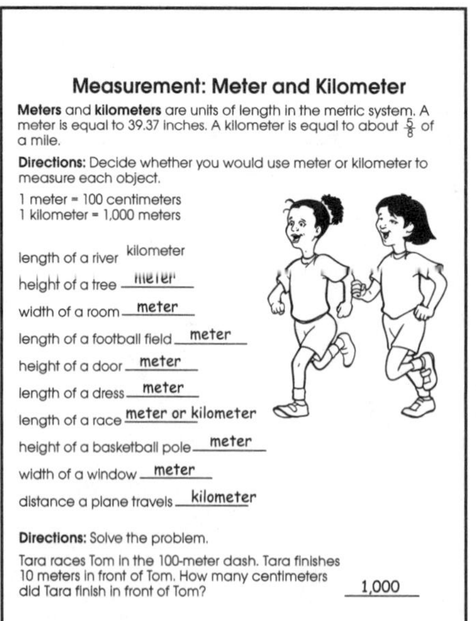

Measurement: Meter and Kilometer

Meters and **kilometers** are units of length in the metric system. A meter is equal to 39.37 inches. A kilometer is equal to about $\frac{5}{8}$ of a mile.

Directions: Decide whether you would use meter or kilometer to measure each object.

1 meter = 100 centimeters
1 kilometer = 1,000 meters

length of a river kilometer
height of a tree meter
width of a room meter
length of a football field meter
height of a door meter
length of a dress meter
length of a race meter or kilometer
height of a basketball pole meter
width of a window meter
distance a plane travels kilometer

Directions: Solve the problem.

Tara races Tom in the 100-meter dash. Tara finishes 10 meters in front of Tom. How many centimeters did Tara finish in front of Tom? 1,000

263

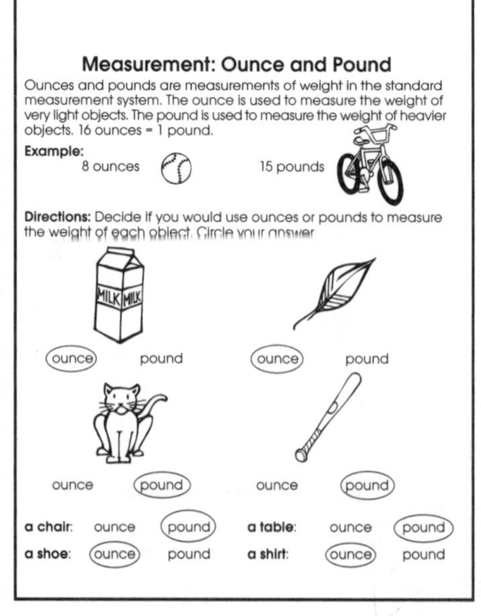

Measurement: Ounce and Pound

Ounces and pounds are measurements of weight in the standard measurement system. The ounce is used to measure the weight of very light objects. The pound is used to measure the weight of heavier objects. 16 ounces = 1 pound.

Example:

8 ounces 15 pounds

Directions: Decide if you would use ounces or pounds to measure the weight of each object. Circle your answer.

(ounce) pound (ounce) pound

ounce (pound) ounce (pound)

a chair: ounce (pound) **a table:** ounce (pound)
a shoe: (ounce) pound **a shirt:** (ounce) pound

264

Answer Key

Problem Solving

Directions: Tell whether you should add or subtract. "In all" is a clue to add. "Left" is a clue to subtract. Draw pictures to help you.

Example:
Jane's dog has 5 bones. He ate 3 bones. How many bones are left?

subtract   5 − 3 = 2 bones

Lucky the cat had 5 mice. She got 4 more for her birthday. How many mice did she have in all?

add   5 + 4 = 9 mice

Sam bought 6 fish. She gave 2 fish to a friend. How many fish does she have left?

subtract   6 − 2 = 4 fish

265

Problem Solving: Addition, Subtraction, Multiplication

Directions: Tell if you add, subtract or multiply. Then write the answer. **Hints**: "In all" means to add. "Left" means to subtract. "In each" means to multiply.

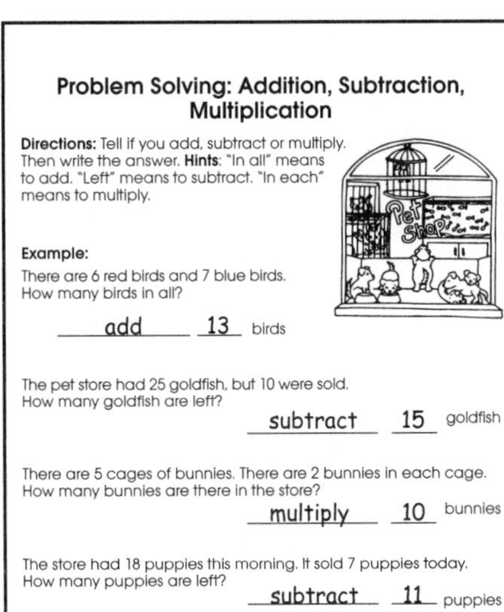

Example:
There are 6 red birds and 7 blue birds. How many birds in all?

add   13 birds

The pet store had 25 goldfish, but 10 were sold. How many goldfish are left?

subtract   15 goldfish

There are 5 cages of bunnies. There are 2 bunnies in each cage. How many bunnies are there in the store?

multiply   10 bunnies

The store had 18 puppies this morning. It sold 7 puppies today. How many puppies are left?

subtract   11 puppies

266

Problem Solving: Addition, Subtraction, Multiplication

Directions: Tell if you add, subtract or multiply. Then write the answer.

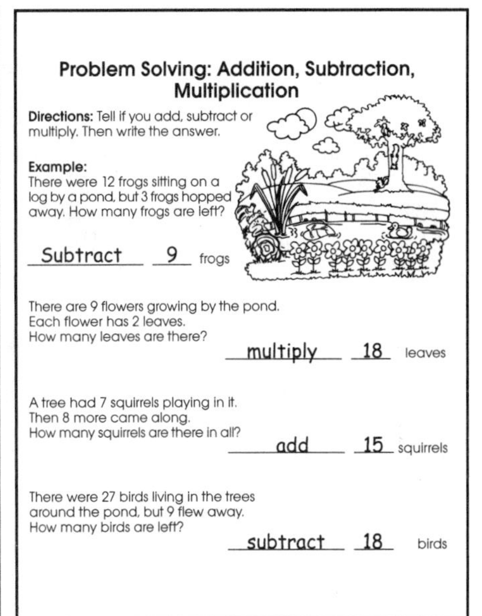

Example:
There were 12 frogs sitting on a log by a pond, but 3 frogs hopped away. How many frogs are left?

Subtract   9 frogs

There are 9 flowers growing by the pond. Each flower has 2 leaves. How many leaves are there?

multiply   18 leaves

A tree had 7 squirrels playing in it. Then 8 more came along. How many squirrels are there in all?

add   15 squirrels

There were 27 birds living in the trees around the pond, but 9 flew away. How many birds are left?

subtract   18 birds

267

Problem Solving: Fractions

A **fraction** is a number that names part of a whole, such as $\frac{1}{2}$ or $\frac{1}{3}$.
Directions: Read each problem. Use the pictures to help you solve the problem. Write the fraction that answers the question.

Simon and Jessie shared a pizza. Together they ate $\frac{3}{4}$ of the pizza. How much of the pizza is left? $\frac{1}{4}$

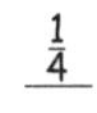

Sylvia baked a cherry pie. She gave $\frac{1}{3}$ to her grandmother and $\frac{1}{3}$ to a friend. How much of the pie did she keep? $\frac{1}{3}$

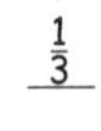

Timmy erased $\frac{1}{2}$ of the blackboard before the bell rang for recess. How much of the blackboard does he have left to erase? $\frac{1}{2}$

Directions: Read the problem. Draw your own picture to help you solve the problem. Write the fraction that answers the question.

Sarah mowed $\frac{1}{4}$ of the yard before lunch. How much does she have left to mow? $\frac{3}{4}$

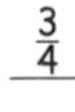
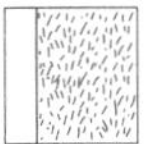

268

Problem Solving: Time

Directions: Solve each problem.

Tracy wakes up at 7:00. She has 30 minutes before her bus comes. What time does her bus come?   7 : 30

Vera walks her dog for 15 minutes after supper. She finishes supper at 6:30. When does she get home from walking her dog?   6 : 45

Chip practices the piano for 30 minutes when he gets home from school. He gets home at 3:30. When does he stop practicing?   4 : 00

Tanya starts mowing the grass at 4:30. She finishes at 5:00. For how many minutes does she mow the lawn?   30 minutes

Don does his homework for 45 minutes. He starts his work at 7:15. When does he stop working?   8 : 00

269

Problem Solving: Measurement

Directions: Read and solve each problem.

This year, hundreds of people ran in the Capital City Marathon. The race is 4.2 kilometers long. When the first person crossed the finish line, the last person was at the 3.7 kilometer point. How far ahead was the winner?   .5

Dennis crossed the finish line 10 meters ahead of Lucy. Lucy was 5 meters ahead of Sam. How far ahead of Sam was Dennis?   15

Tony ran 320 yards from school to his home. Then he ran 290 yards to Jay's house. Together Tony and Jay ran 545 yards to the store. How many yards in all did Tony run?   1,155

The teacher measured the heights of three children in her class. Marsha was 51 inches tall, Jimmy was 48 inches tall and Ted was $52\frac{1}{2}$ inches tall. How much taller is Ted than Marsha? $1\frac{1}{2}$ in.

How much taller is he than Jimmy? $4\frac{1}{2}$ in.

270

Answer Key

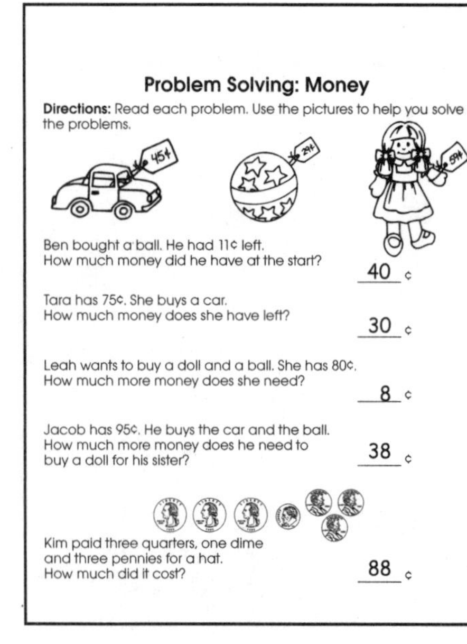
Problem Solving: Money

Directions: Read each problem. Use the pictures to help you solve the problems.

Ben bought a ball. He had 11¢ left.
How much money did he have at the start? 40 ¢

Tara has 75¢. She buys a car.
How much money does she have left? 30 ¢

Leah wants to buy a doll and a ball. She has 80¢.
How much more money does she need? 8 ¢

Jacob has 95¢. He buys the car and the ball.
How much more money does he need to buy a doll for his sister? 38 ¢

Kim paid three quarters, one dime and three pennies for a hat.
How much did it cost? 88 ¢

271

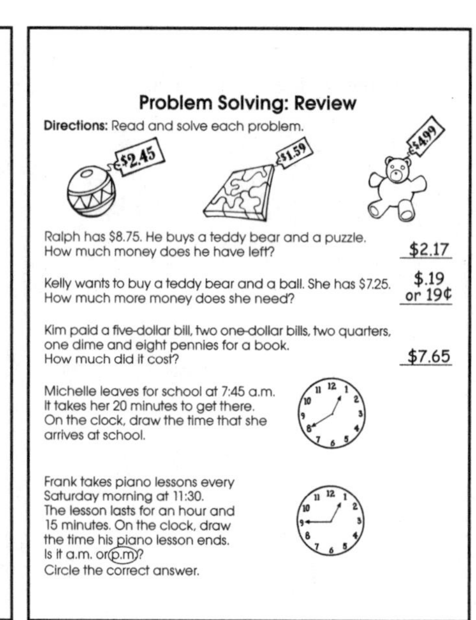
Problem Solving: Review

Directions: Read and solve each problem.

Ralph has $8.75. He buys a teddy bear and a puzzle.
How much money does he have left? $2.17

Kelly wants to buy a teddy bear and a ball. She has $7.25.
How much more money does she need? $.19 or 19¢

Kim paid a five-dollar bill, two one-dollar bills, two quarters, one dime and eight pennies for a book.
How much did it cost? $7.65

Michelle leaves for school at 7:45 a.m.
It takes her 20 minutes to get there.
On the clock, draw the time that she arrives at school.

Frank takes piano lessons every Saturday morning at 11:30.
The lesson lasts for an hour and 15 minutes. On the clock, draw the time his piano lesson ends.
Is it a.m. or p.m.?
Circle the correct answer.

272

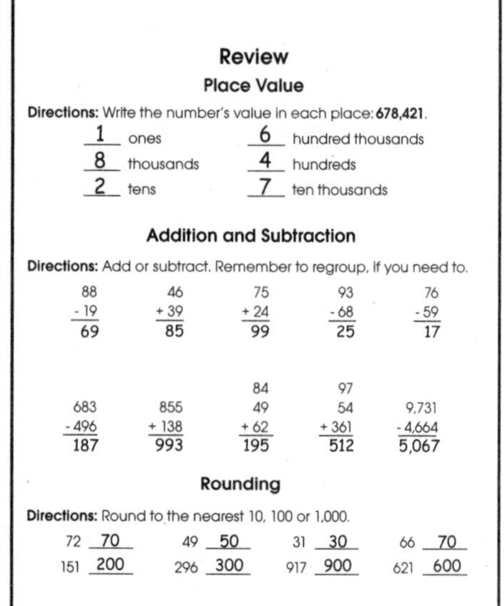
Review

Place Value

Directions: Write the number's value in each place: 678,421.

1 ones — 6 hundred thousands
8 thousands — 4 hundreds
2 tens — 7 ten thousands

Addition and Subtraction

Directions: Add or subtract. Remember to regroup, if you need to.

88 − 19 = 69; 46 + 39 = 85; 75 + 24 = 99; 93 − 68 = 25; 76 − 59 = 17

683 − 496 = 187; 855 + 138 = 993; 84 + 49 + 62 = 195; 97 + 54 + 361 = 512; 9,731 − 4,664 = 5,067

Rounding

Directions: Round to the nearest 10, 100 or 1,000.

72 70; 49 50; 31 30; 66 70
151 200; 296 300; 917 900; 621 600

273

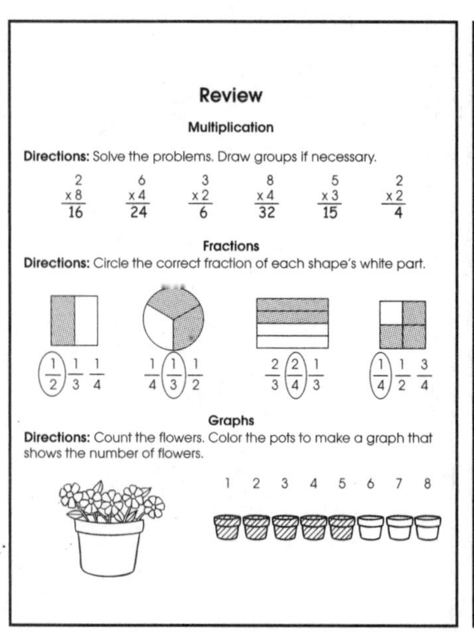
Review

Multiplication

Directions: Solve the problems. Draw groups if necessary.

2 x 8 = 16; 6 x 4 = 24; 3 x 2 = 6; 8 x 4 = 32; 5 x 3 = 15; 2 x 2 = 4

Fractions

Directions: Circle the correct fraction of each shape's white part.

1/2 1/3 1/4; 1/4 1/3 1/2; 2/3 2/4 1/3; 1/4 1/2 3/4

Graphs

Directions: Count the flowers. Color the pots to make a graph that shows the number of flowers.

1 2 3 4 5 6 7 8

274

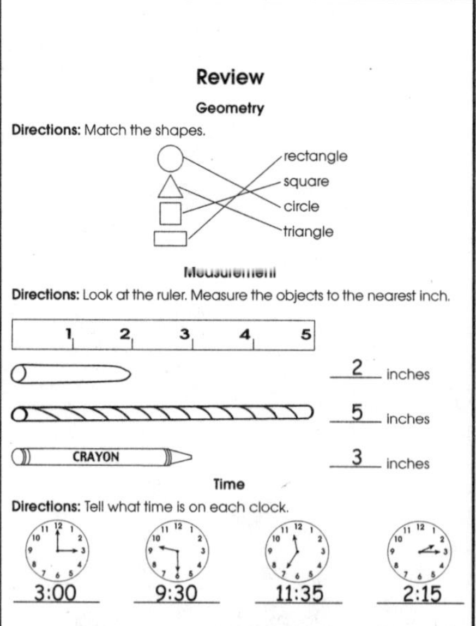
Review

Geometry

Directions: Match the shapes.

rectangle
square
circle
triangle

Measurement

Directions: Look at the ruler. Measure the objects to the nearest inch.

1 2 3 4 5

2 inches

5 inches

CRAYON 3 inches

Time

Directions: Tell what time is on each clock.

3:00 9:30 11:35 2:15

275

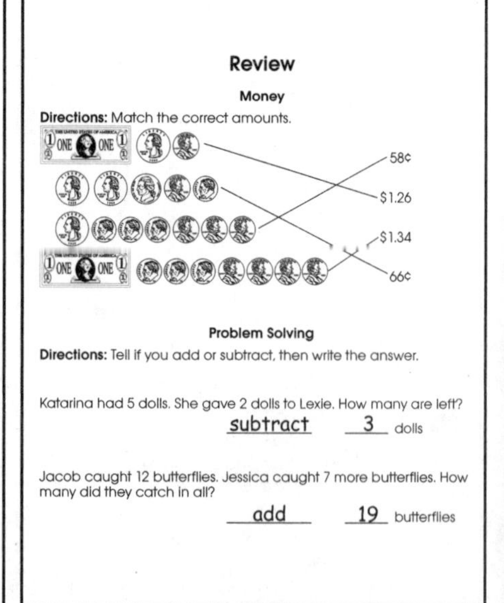
Review

Money

Directions: Match the correct amounts.

58¢
$1.26
$1.34
66¢

Problem Solving

Directions: Tell if you add or subtract, then write the answer.

Katarina had 5 dolls. She gave 2 dolls to Lexie. How many are left?
subtract 3 dolls

Jacob caught 12 butterflies. Jessica caught 7 more butterflies. How many did they catch in all?
add 19 butterflies

276